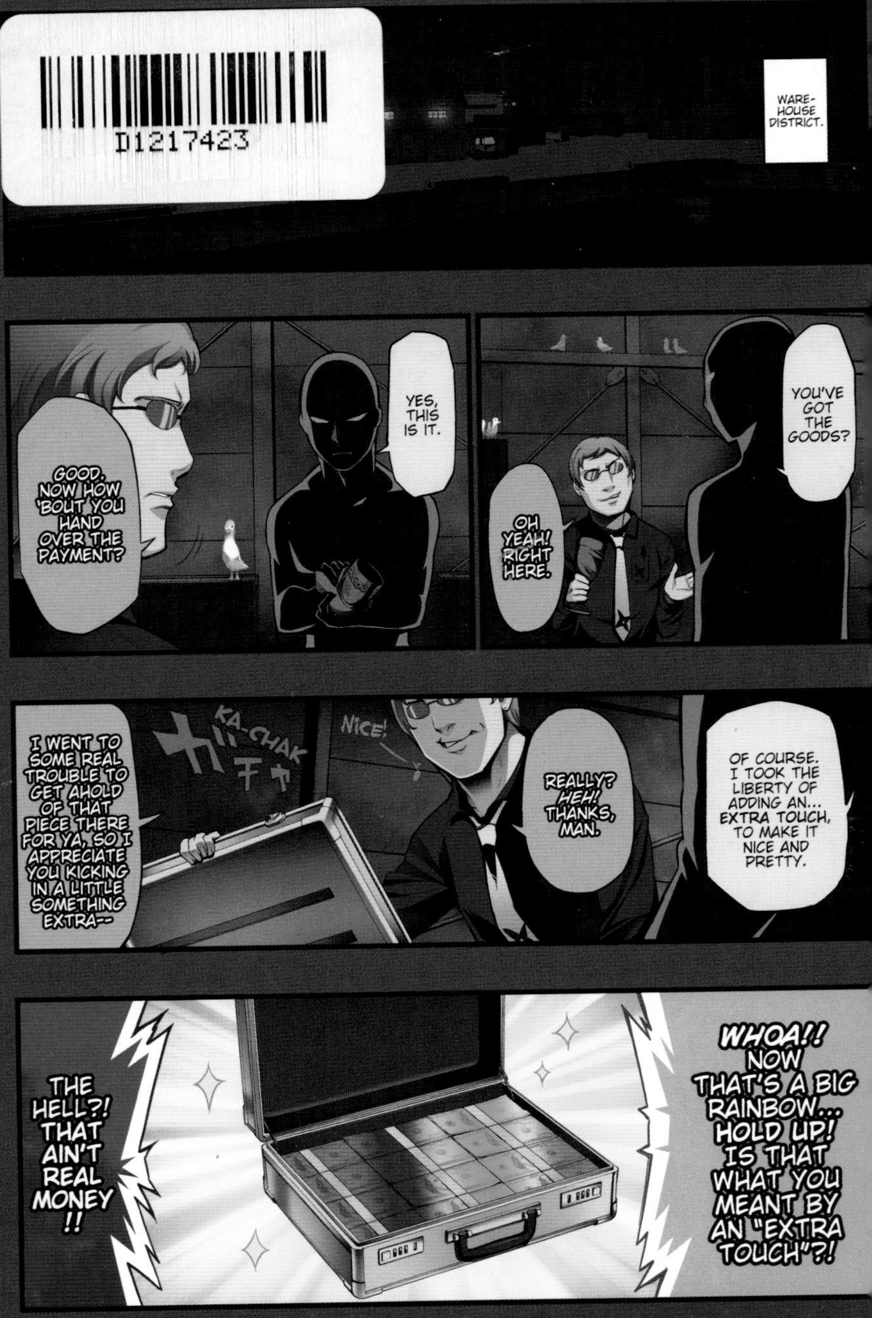
WARE-HOUSE DISTRICT.
YOU'VE GOT THE GOODS?
OH YEAH! RIGHT HERE.
YES, THIS IS IT.
GOOD. NOW HOW 'BOUT YOU HAND OVER THE PAYMENT?
OF COURSE. I TOOK THE LIBERTY OF ADDING AN... EXTRA TOUCH, TO MAKE IT NICE AND PRETTY.
REALLY? HEH! THANKS, MAN.
NICE!
KA-CHAK
I WENT TO SOME REAL TROUBLE TO GET AHOLD OF THAT PIECE THERE FOR YA, SO I APPRECIATE YOU KICKING IN A LITTLE SOMETHING EXTRA--
WHOA!! NOW THAT'S A BIG RAINBOW... HOLD UP! IS THAT WHAT YOU MEANT BY AN "EXTRA TOUCH"?!
THE HELL?! THAT AIN'T REAL MONEY!!

Chapter 37
Damn You, Sean Connery!!

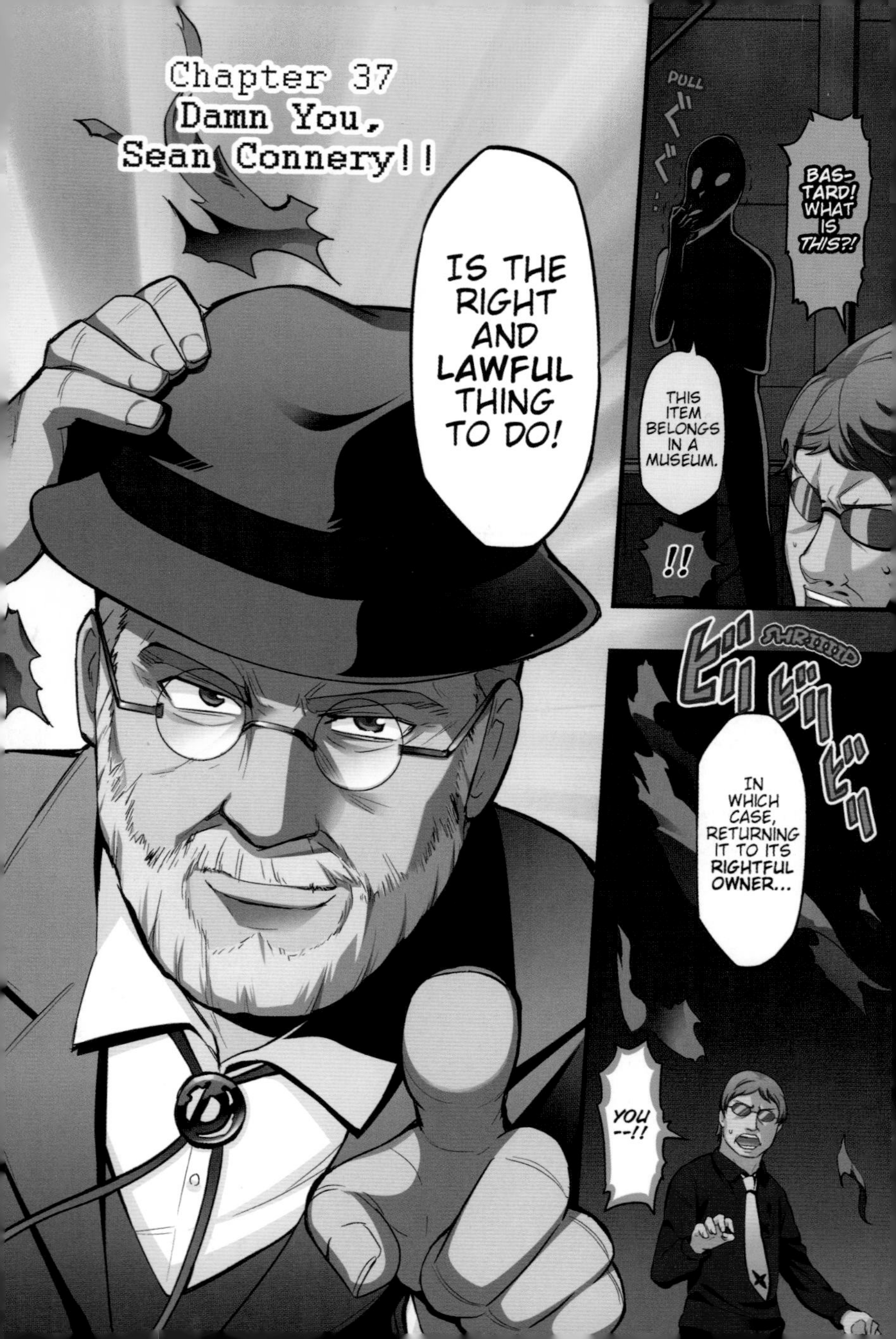
PULL
BASTARD! WHAT IS THIS?!
THIS ITEM BELONGS IN A MUSEUM.
!!
SHRRRRIP
IN WHICH CASE, RETURNING IT TO ITS RIGHTFUL OWNER...
YOU --!!
IS THE RIGHT AND LAWFUL THING TO DO!

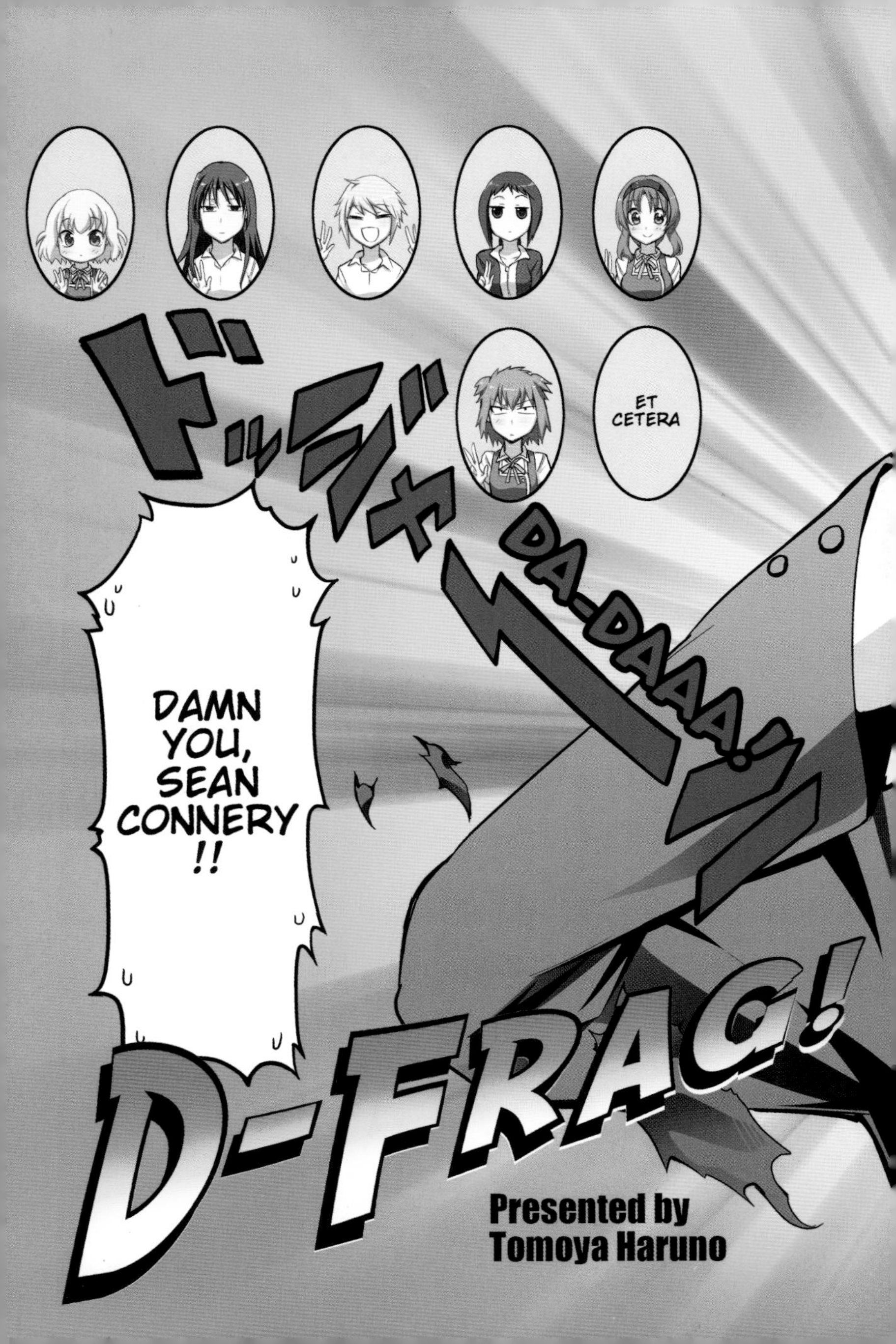
ET CETERA
DA-DAAA!!
DAMN YOU, SEAN CONNERY!!
D-FRAG!
Presented by Tomoya Haruno

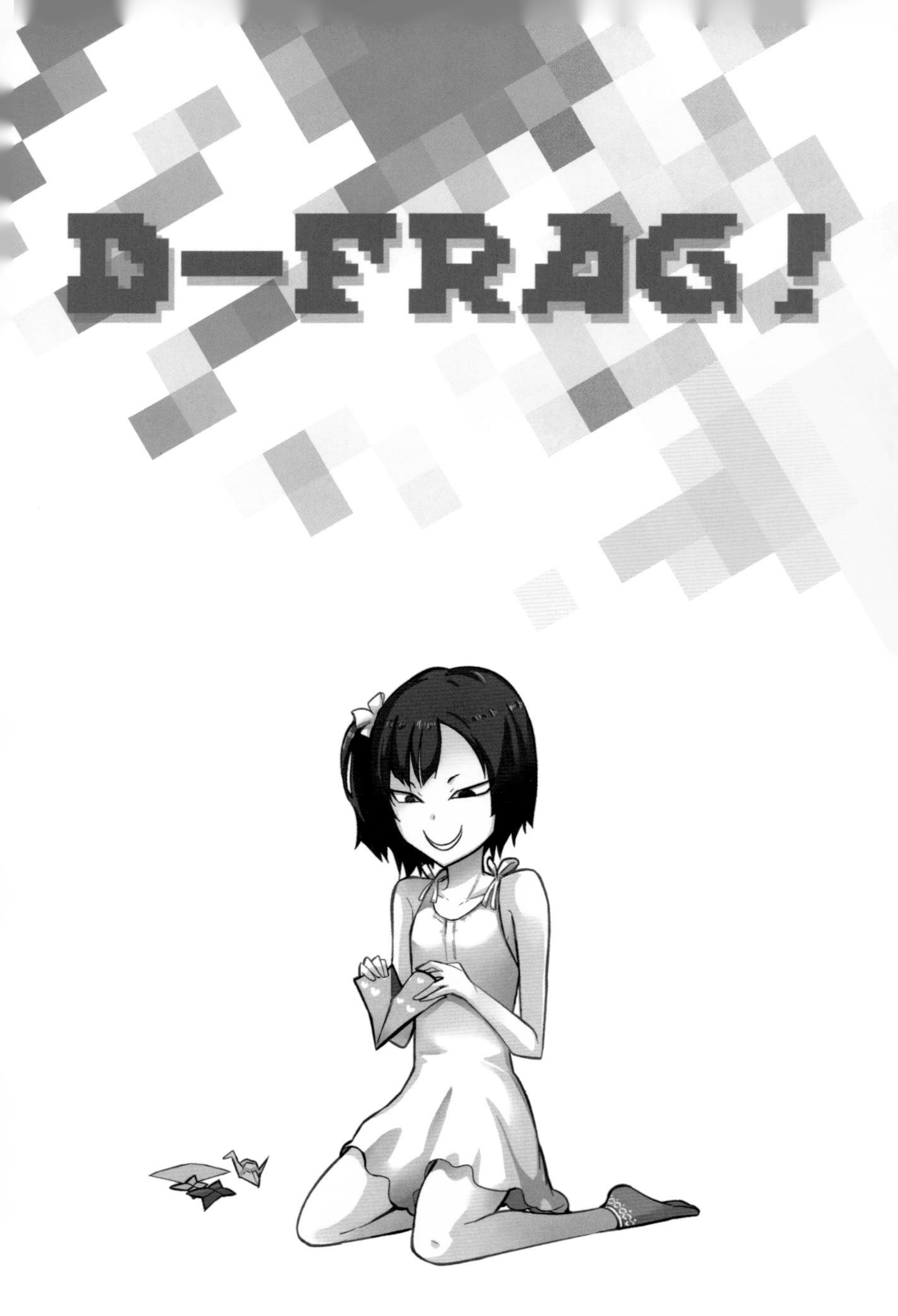
D-FRAG!

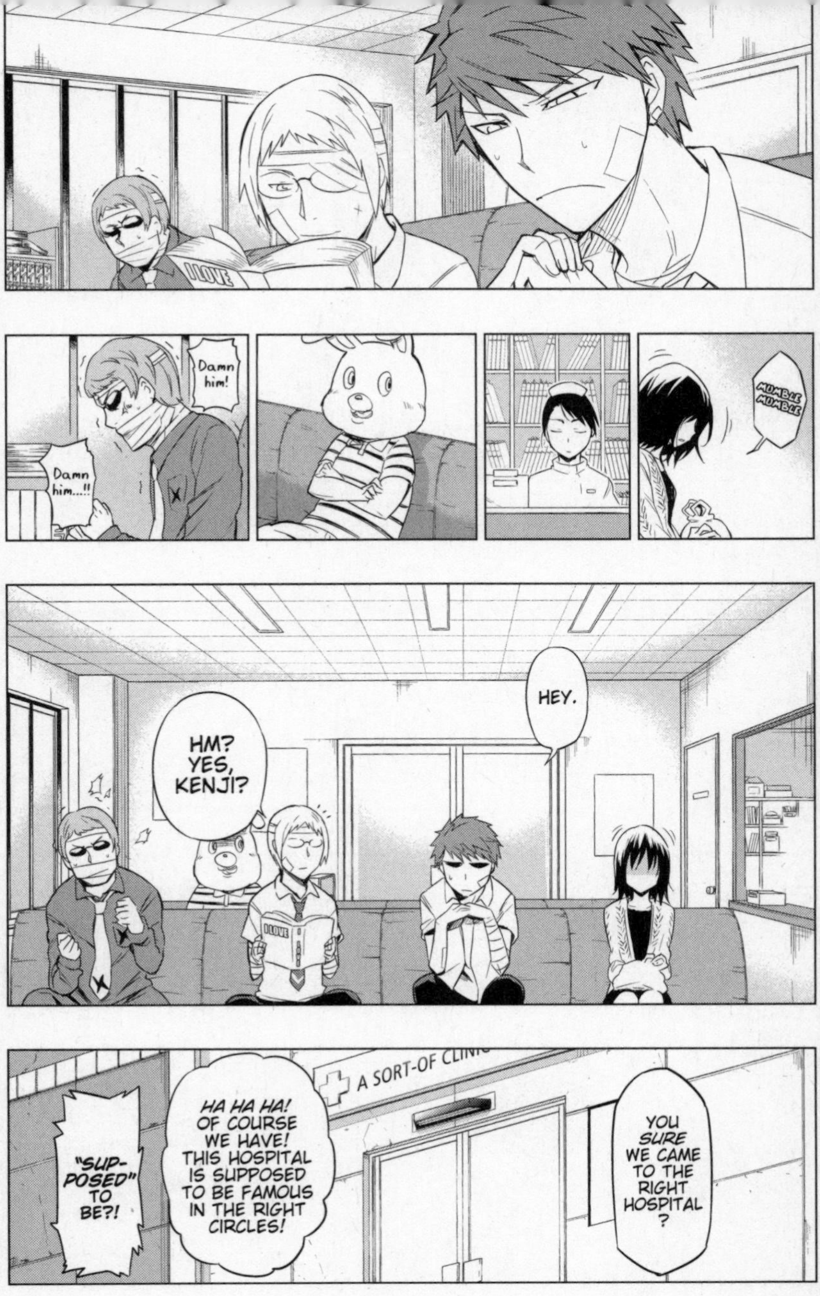
I LOVE
MUMBLE MUMBLE
Damn him!
Damn him...!!
HEY.
HM? YES, KENJI?
I LOVE
A SORT-OF CLINI
YOU SURE WE CAME TO THE RIGHT HOSPITAL?
HA HA HA! OF COURSE WE HAVE! THIS HOSPITAL IS SUPPOSED TO BE FAMOUS IN THE RIGHT CIRCLES!
"SUP-POSED" TO BE?!

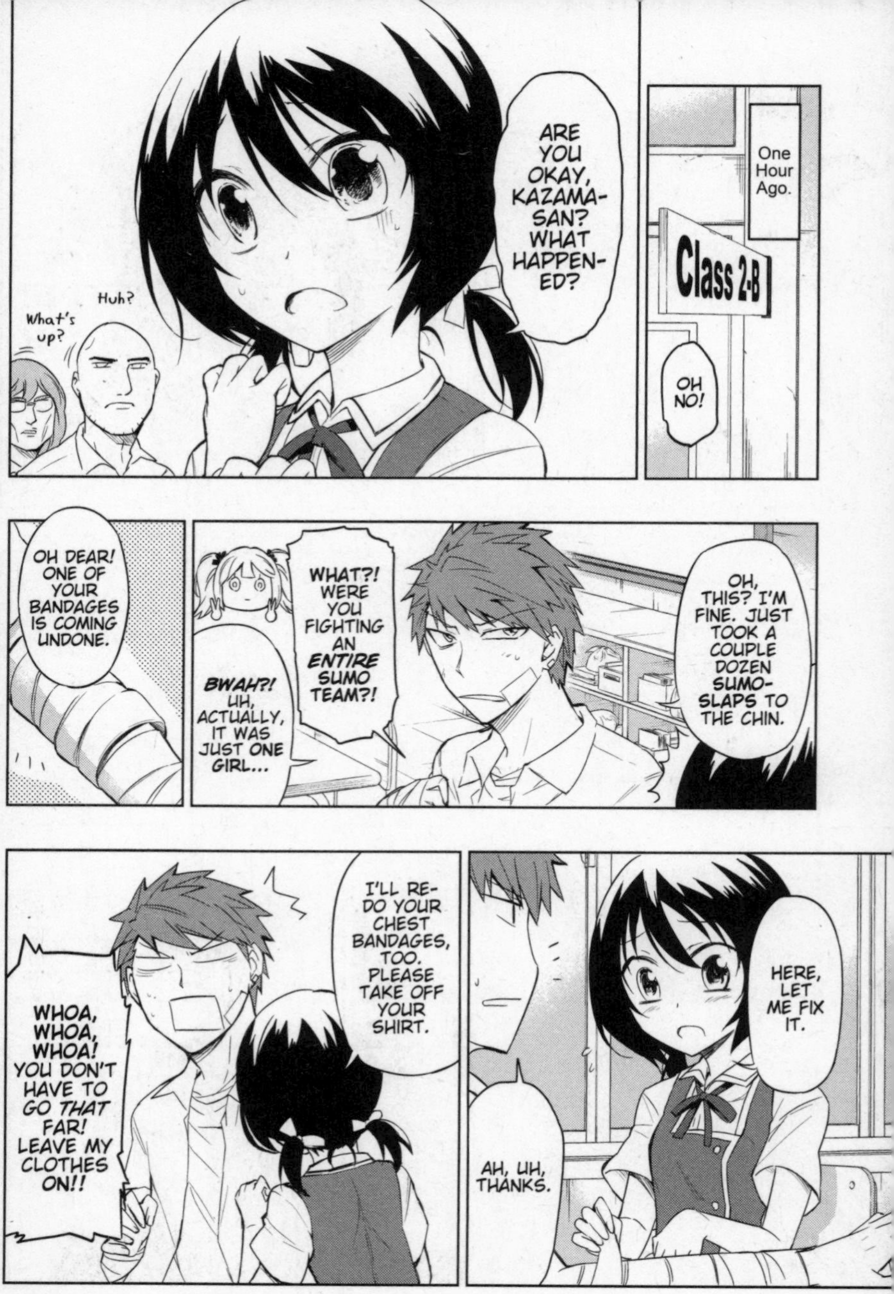
One Hour Ago.
Class 2-B
OH NO!
ARE YOU OKAY, KAZAMA-SAN? WHAT HAPPENED?
Huh?
What's up?
OH, THIS? I'M FINE. JUST TOOK A COUPLE DOZEN SUMO-SLAPS TO THE CHIN.
WHAT?! WERE YOU FIGHTING AN *ENTIRE* SUMO TEAM?!
BWAH?! UH, ACTUALLY, IT WAS JUST ONE GIRL...
OH DEAR! ONE OF YOUR BANDAGES IS COMING UNDONE.
HERE, LET ME FIX IT.
AH, UH, THANKS.
I'LL RE-DO YOUR CHEST BANDAGES, TOO. PLEASE TAKE OFF YOUR SHIRT.
WHOA, WHOA, WHOA! YOU DON'T HAVE TO GO *THAT* FAR! LEAVE MY CLOTHES *ON!!*

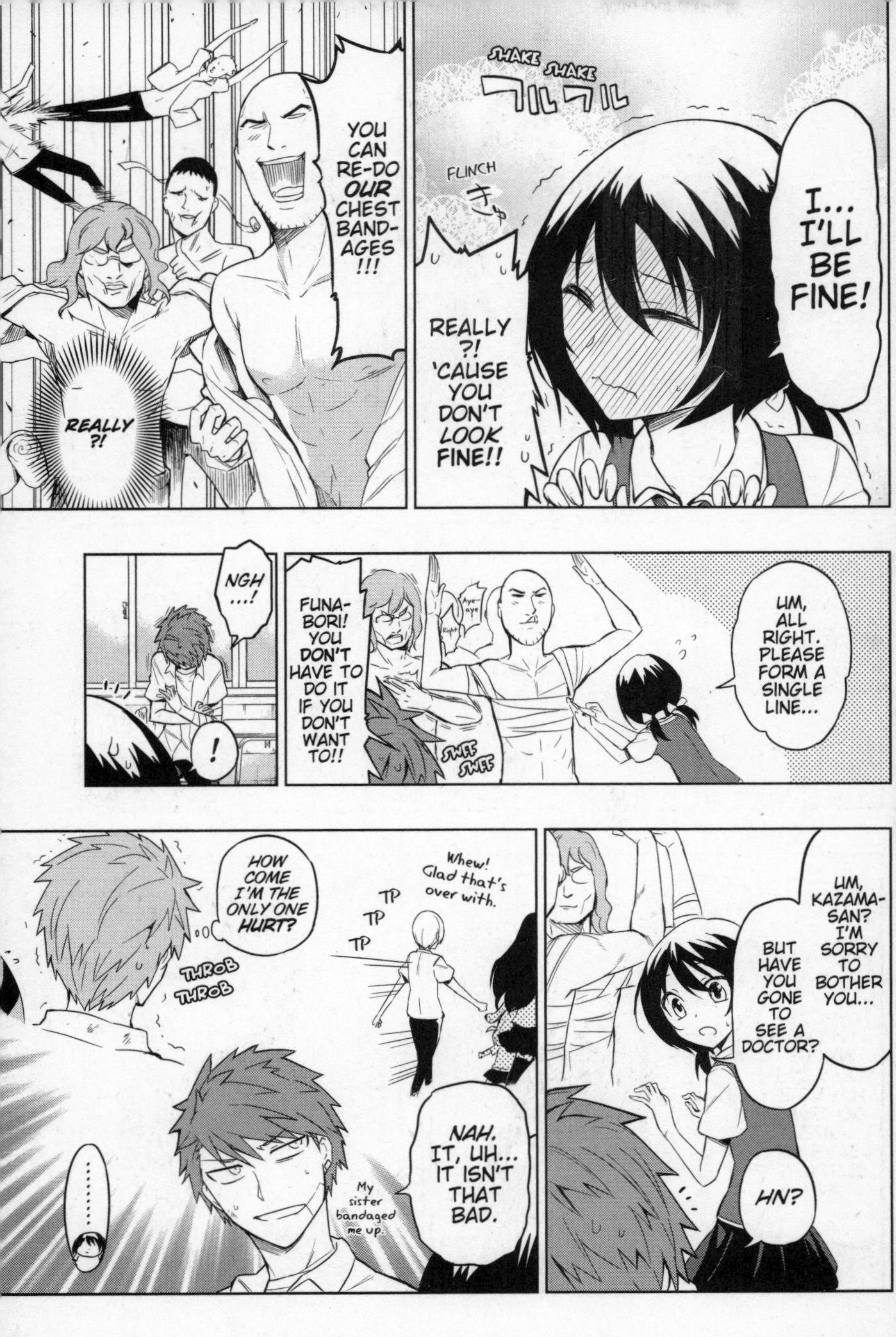
SHAKE SHAKE
フルフル
I... I'LL BE FINE!
FLINCH
きゅ
REALLY?! 'CAUSE YOU DON'T LOOK FINE!!
YOU CAN RE-DO OUR CHEST BANDAGES!!!
REALLY?!
UM, ALL RIGHT. PLEASE FORM A SINGLE LINE...
Aye-aye
Right
FUNA-BORI! YOU DON'T HAVE TO DO IT IF YOU DON'T WANT TO!!
SWFF SWFF
NGH...!
!
UM, KAZAMA-SAN? I'M SORRY TO BOTHER YOU...
BUT HAVE YOU GONE TO SEE A DOCTOR?
HN?
HOW COME I'M THE ONLY ONE HURT?
THROB THROB
Whew! Glad that's over with.
TP TP TP
NAH. IT, UH... IT ISN'T THAT BAD.
My sister bandaged me up.
......

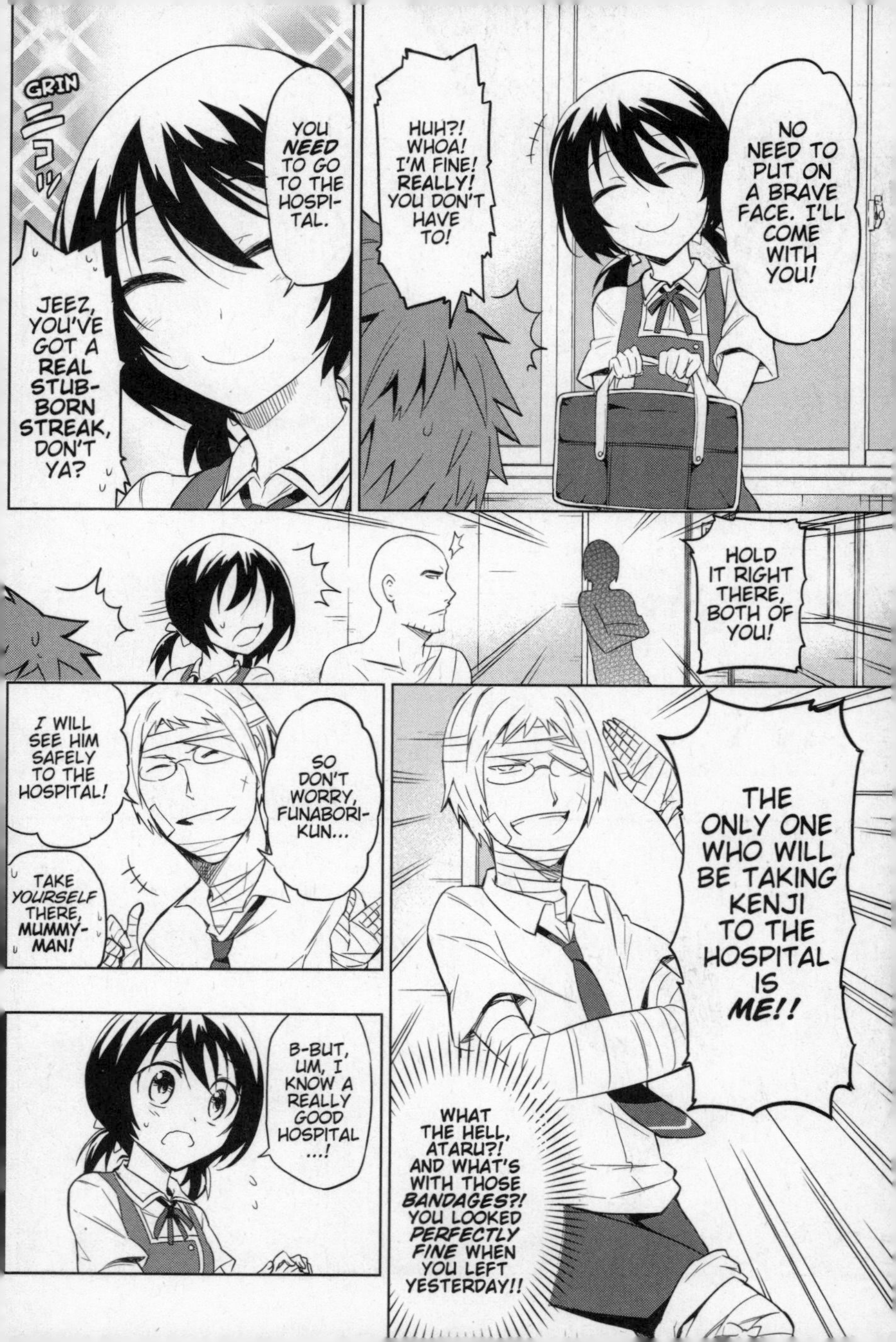
NO NEED TO PUT ON A BRAVE FACE. I'LL COME WITH YOU!
HUH?! WHOA! I'M FINE! REALLY! YOU DON'T HAVE TO!
YOU NEED TO GO TO THE HOSPITAL.
GRIN
ニコッ
JEEZ, YOU'VE GOT A REAL STUBBORN STREAK, DON'T YA?
HOLD IT RIGHT THERE, BOTH OF YOU!
THE ONLY ONE WHO WILL BE TAKING KENJI TO THE HOSPITAL IS ME!!
WHAT THE HELL, ATARU?! AND WHAT'S WITH THOSE BANDAGES?! YOU LOOKED PERFECTLY FINE WHEN YOU LEFT YESTERDAY!!
I WILL SEE HIM SAFELY TO THE HOSPITAL!
SO DON'T WORRY, FUNABORI-KUN...
TAKE YOURSELF THERE, MUMMY-MAN!
B-BUT, UM, I KNOW A REALLY GOOD HOSPITAL ...!

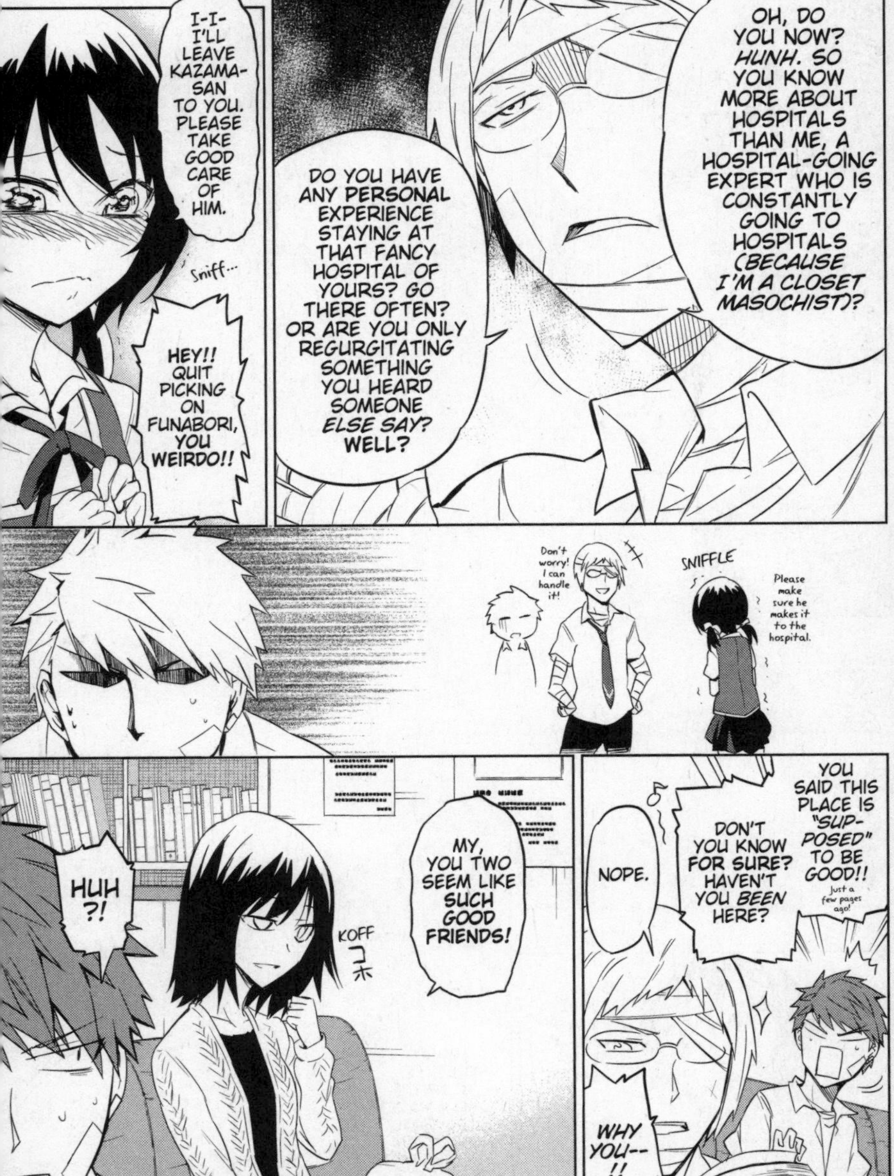
OH, DO YOU NOW? *HUNH.* SO YOU KNOW MORE ABOUT HOSPITALS THAN ME, A HOSPITAL-GOING EXPERT WHO IS CONSTANTLY GOING TO HOSPITALS (*BECAUSE I'M A CLOSET MASOCHIST*)?
DO YOU HAVE ANY PERSONAL EXPERIENCE STAYING AT THAT FANCY HOSPITAL OF YOURS? GO THERE OFTEN? OR ARE YOU ONLY REGURGITATING SOMETHING YOU HEARD SOMEONE *ELSE SAY?* WELL?
I-I-I'LL LEAVE KAZAMA-SAN TO YOU. PLEASE TAKE GOOD CARE OF HIM.
Sniff...
HEY!! QUIT PICKING ON FUNABORI, YOU WEIRDO!!
SNIFFLE
Please make sure he makes it to the hospital.
Don't worry! I can handle it!
YOU SAID THIS PLACE IS "SUP-POSED" TO BE GOOD!!
Just a few pages ago!
DON'T YOU KNOW FOR SURE? HAVEN'T YOU *BEEN* HERE?
NOPE.
WHY YOU--!!
MY, YOU TWO SEEM LIKE SUCH GOOD FRIENDS!
KOFF
HUH ?!

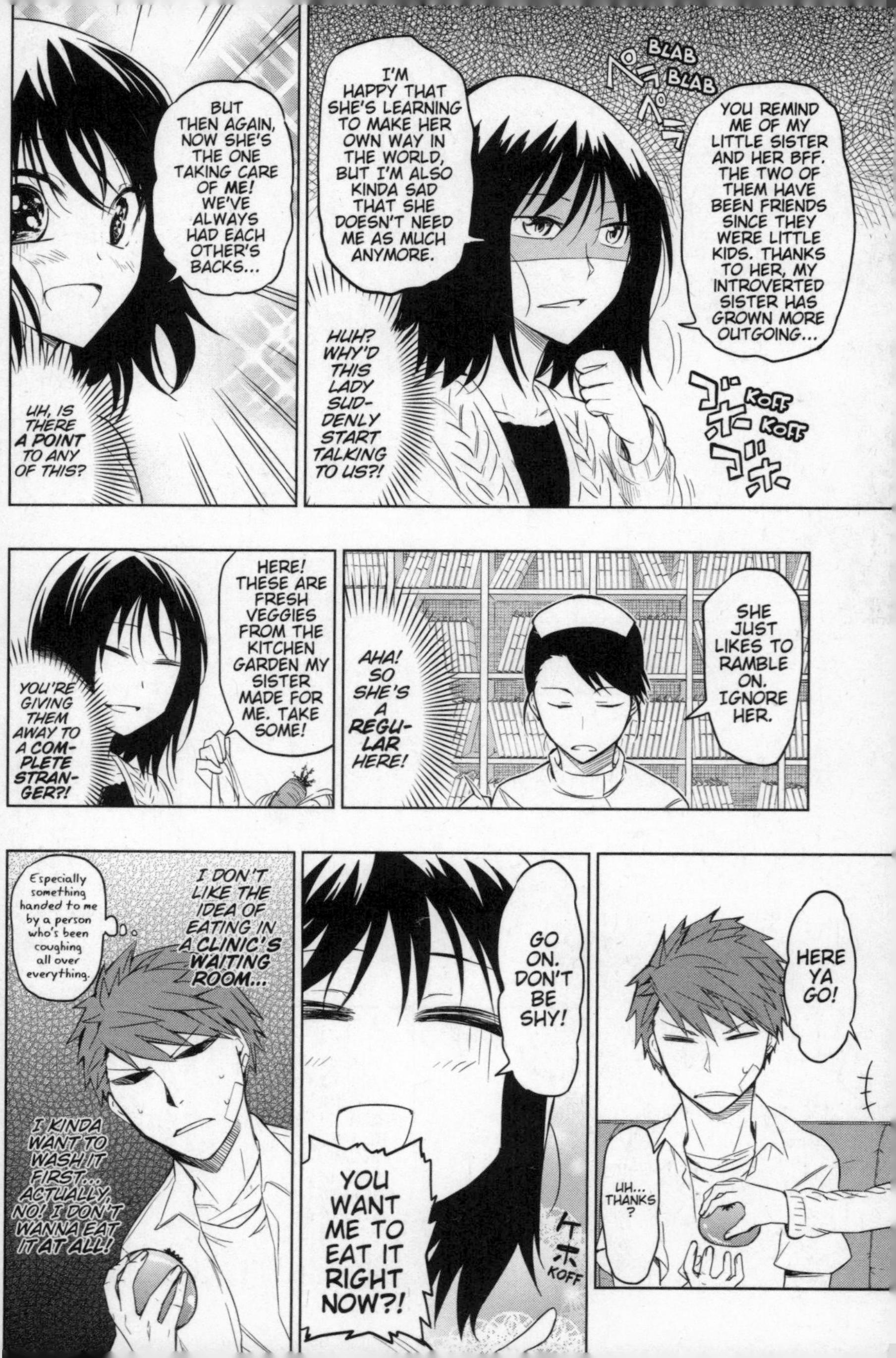
BLAB BLAB
YOU REMIND ME OF MY LITTLE SISTER AND HER BFF. THE TWO OF THEM HAVE BEEN FRIENDS SINCE THEY WERE LITTLE KIDS. THANKS TO HER, MY INTROVERTED SISTER HAS GROWN MORE OUTGOING...
I'M HAPPY THAT SHE'S LEARNING TO MAKE HER OWN WAY IN THE WORLD, BUT I'M ALSO KINDA SAD THAT SHE DOESN'T NEED ME AS MUCH ANYMORE.
KOFF KOFF
HUH? WHY'D THIS LADY SUDDENLY START TALKING TO US?!
BUT THEN AGAIN, NOW SHE'S THE ONE TAKING CARE OF ME! WE'VE ALWAYS HAD EACH OTHER'S BACKS...
UH, IS THERE A POINT TO ANY OF THIS?
SHE JUST LIKES TO RAMBLE ON. IGNORE HER.
AHA! SO SHE'S A REGULAR HERE!
HERE! THESE ARE FRESH VEGGIES FROM THE KITCHEN GARDEN MY SISTER MADE FOR ME. TAKE SOME!
YOU'RE GIVING THEM AWAY TO A COMPLETE STRANGER?!
HERE YA GO!
UH... THANKS?
GO ON. DON'T BE SHY!
KOFF
YOU WANT ME TO EAT IT RIGHT NOW?!
I DON'T LIKE THE IDEA OF EATING IN A CLINIC'S WAITING ROOM...
Especially something handed to me by a person who's been coughing all over everything.
I KINDA WANT TO WASH IT FIRST... ACTUALLY, NO! I DON'T WANNA EAT IT AT ALL!

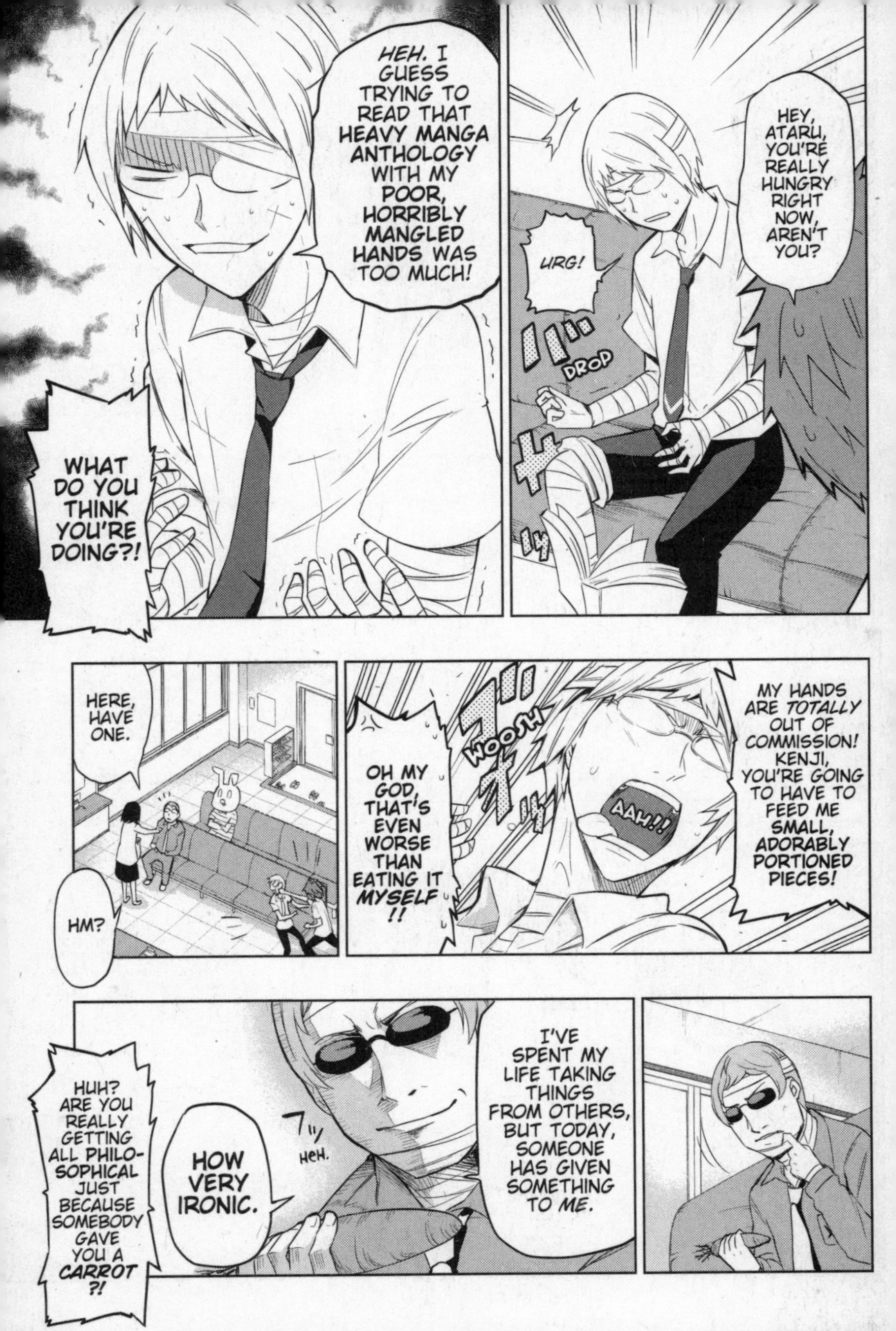

HEY, ATARU, YOU'RE REALLY HUNGRY RIGHT NOW, AREN'T YOU?
URG!
DROP
HEH. I GUESS TRYING TO READ THAT HEAVY MANGA ANTHOLOGY WITH MY POOR, HORRIBLY MANGLED HANDS WAS TOO MUCH!
WHAT DO YOU THINK YOU'RE DOING?!
MY HANDS ARE TOTALLY OUT OF COMMISSION! KENJI, YOU'RE GOING TO HAVE TO FEED ME SMALL, ADORABLY PORTIONED PIECES!
WOOSH
AAH!!
OH MY GOD, THAT'S EVEN WORSE THAN EATING IT MYSELF!!
HERE, HAVE ONE.
HM?
I'VE SPENT MY LIFE TAKING THINGS FROM OTHERS, BUT TODAY, SOMEONE HAS GIVEN SOMETHING TO ME.
HEH.
HOW VERY IRONIC.
HUH? ARE YOU REALLY GETTING ALL PHILOSOPHICAL JUST BECAUSE SOMEBODY GAVE YOU A CARROT?!

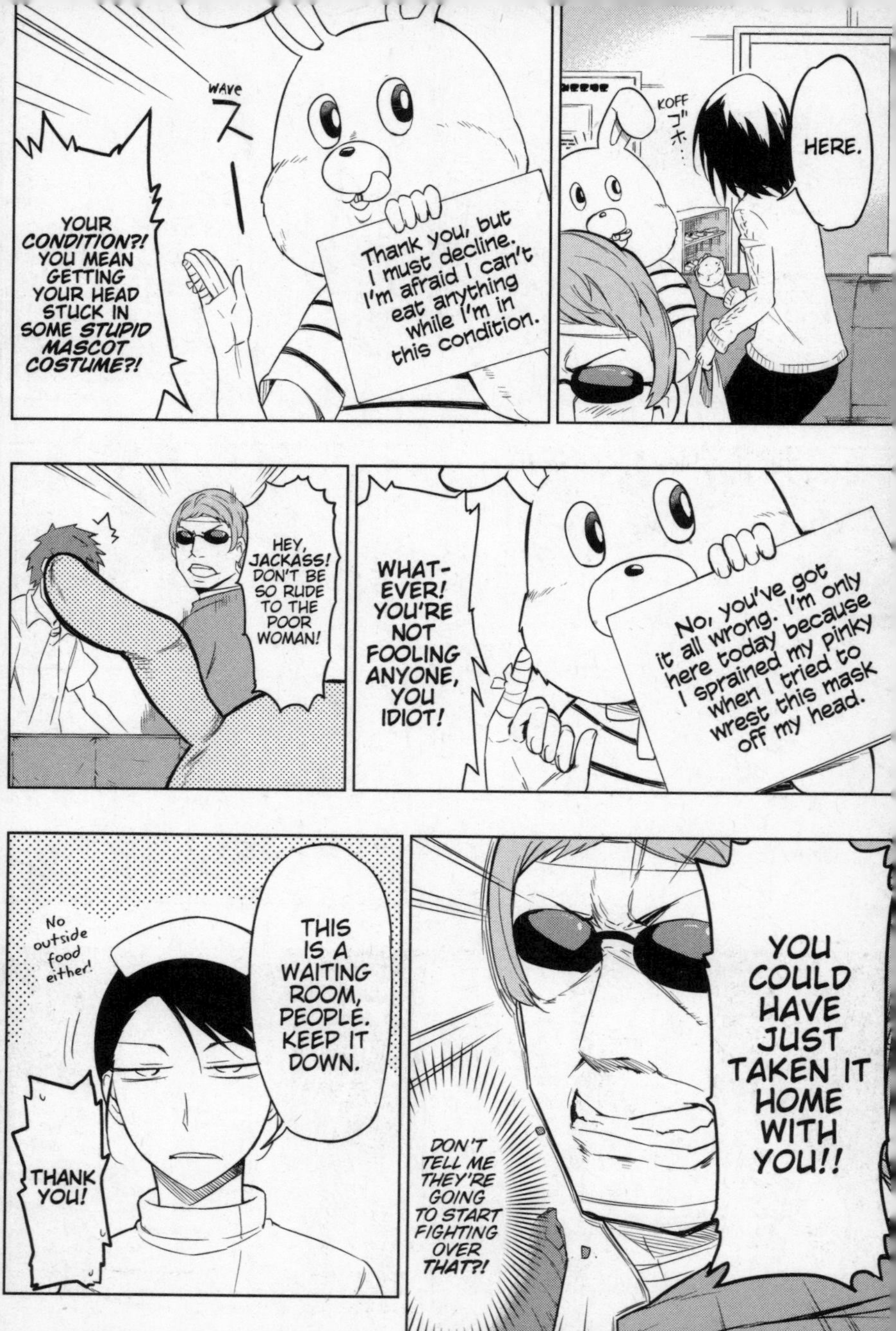
HERE.
KOFF
ゴホ…
Thank you, but I must decline. I'm afraid I can't eat anything while I'm in this condition.
wave
ス
YOUR CONDITION?! YOU MEAN GETTING YOUR HEAD STUCK IN SOME STUPID MASCOT COSTUME?!
No, you've got it all wrong. I'm only here today because I sprained my pinky when I tried to wrest this mask off my head.
WHAT-EVER! YOU'RE NOT FOOLING ANYONE, YOU IDIOT!
HEY, JACKASS! DON'T BE SO RUDE TO THE POOR WOMAN!
YOU COULD HAVE JUST TAKEN IT HOME WITH YOU!!
DON'T TELL ME THEY'RE GOING TO START FIGHTING OVER THAT?!
THIS IS A WAITING ROOM, PEOPLE. KEEP IT DOWN.
No outside food either!
THANK YOU!

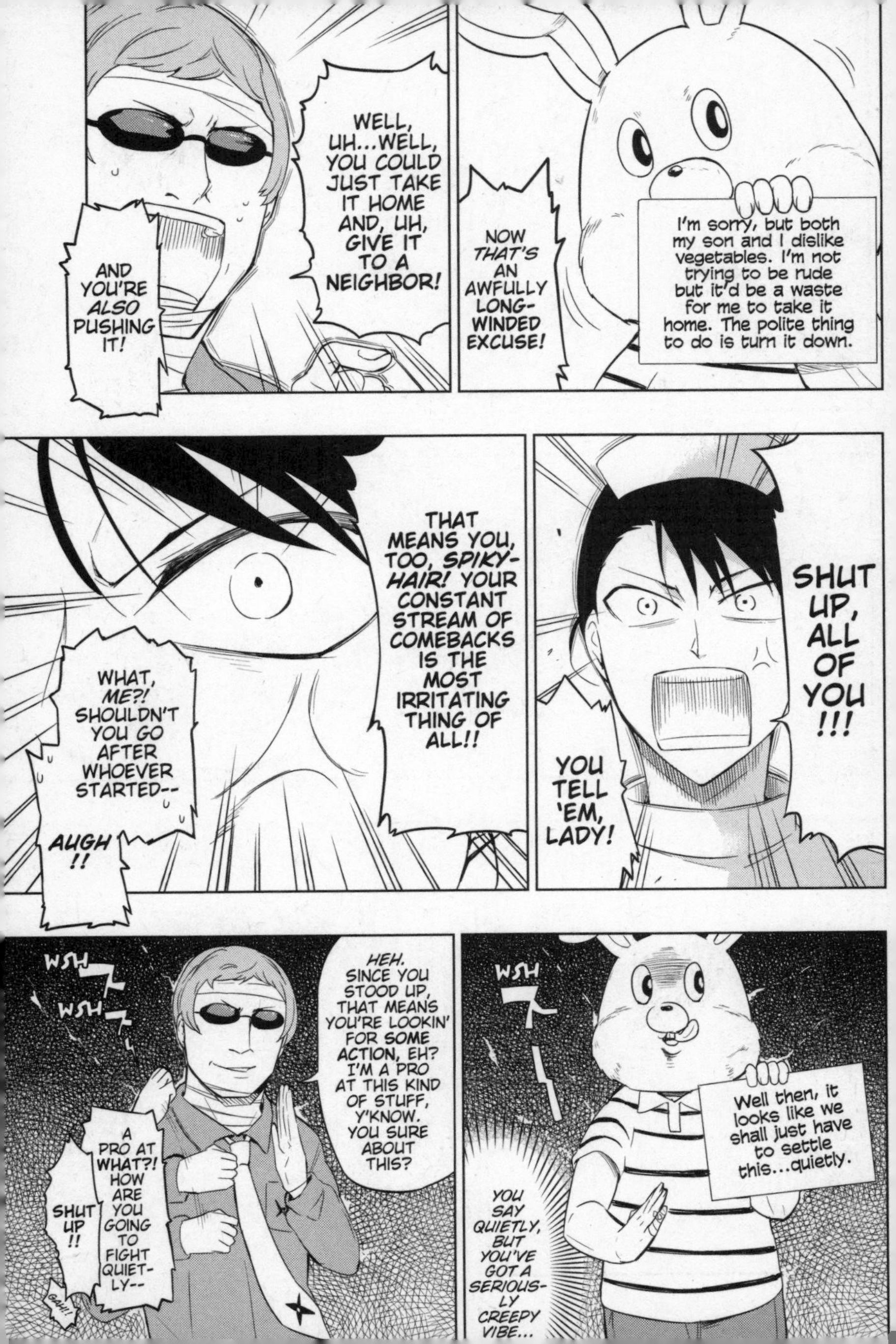
I'm sorry, but both my son and I dislike vegetables. I'm not trying to be rude but it'd be a waste for me to take it home. The polite thing to do is turn it down.
NOW *THAT'S* AN AWFULLY LONG-WINDED EXCUSE!
WELL, UH...WELL, YOU COULD JUST TAKE IT HOME AND, UH, GIVE IT TO A NEIGHBOR!
AND YOU'RE *ALSO* PUSHING IT!
SHUT UP, ALL OF YOU!!!
YOU TELL 'EM, LADY!
THAT MEANS YOU, TOO, *SPIKY-HAIR!* YOUR CONSTANT STREAM OF COMEBACKS IS THE MOST IRRITATING THING OF ALL!!
WHAT, *ME?!* SHOULDN'T YOU GO AFTER WHOEVER STARTED--
AUGH!!
WSH
Well then, it looks like we shall just have to settle this...quietly.
YOU SAY QUIETLY, BUT YOU'VE GOT A SERIOUSLY CREEPY VIBE...
WSH
WSH
HEH. SINCE YOU STOOD UP, THAT MEANS YOU'RE LOOKIN' FOR SOME ACTION, EH? I'M A PRO AT THIS KIND OF STUFF, Y'KNOW. YOU SURE ABOUT THIS?
A PRO AT WHAT?! HOW ARE YOU GOING TO FIGHT QUIET-LY--
SHUT UP!!
GAH!!

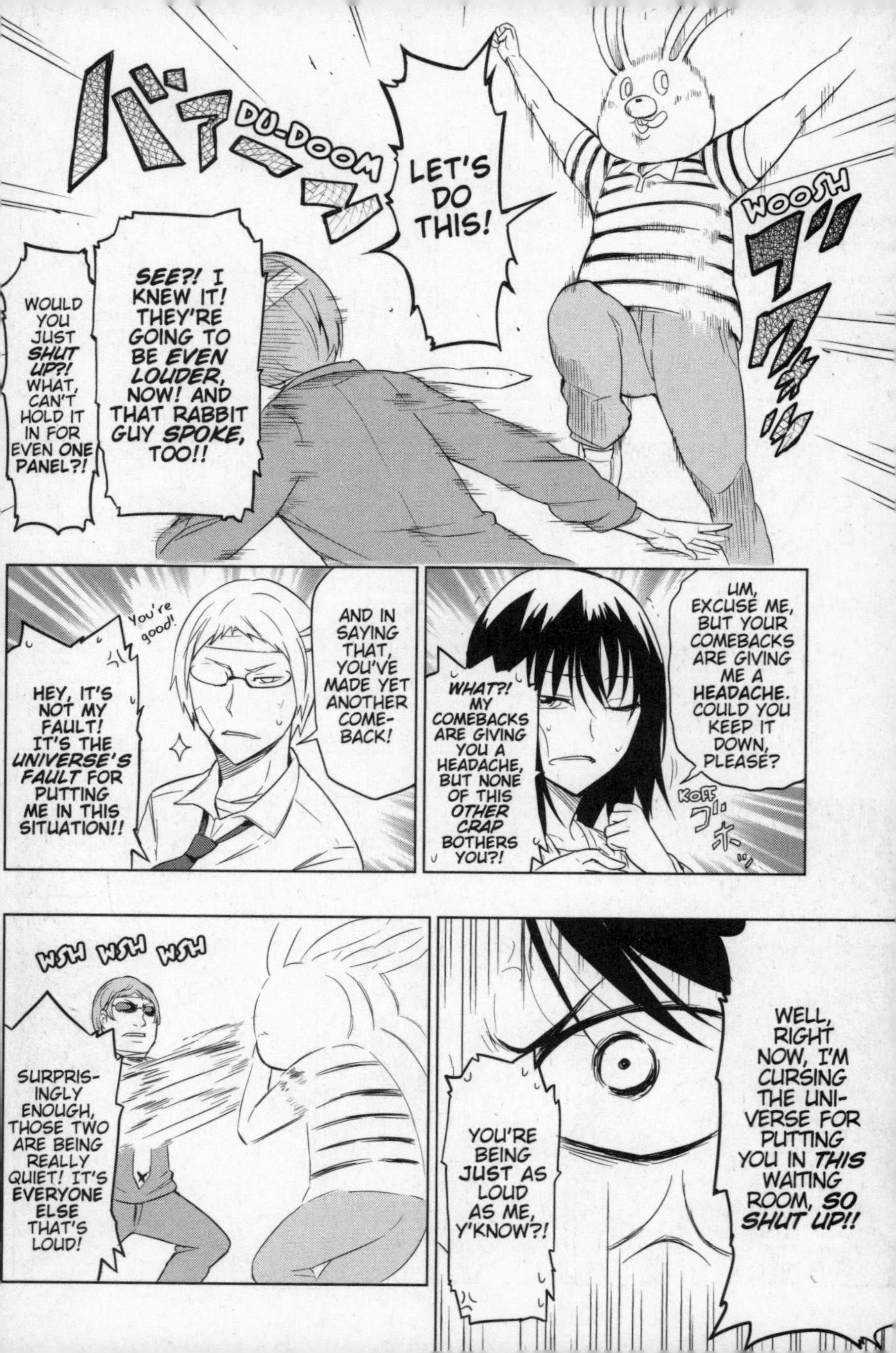
WOOSH
LET'S DO THIS!
DU-DOOM
SEE?! I KNEW IT! THEY'RE GOING TO BE EVEN LOUDER, NOW! AND THAT RABBIT GUY SPOKE, TOO!!
WOULD YOU JUST SHUT UP?! WHAT, CAN'T HOLD IT IN FOR EVEN ONE PANEL?!
UM, EXCUSE ME, BUT YOUR COMEBACKS ARE GIVING ME A HEADACHE. COULD YOU KEEP IT DOWN, PLEASE?
KOFF
WHAT?! MY COMEBACKS ARE GIVING YOU A HEADACHE, BUT NONE OF THIS OTHER CRAP BOTHERS YOU?!
AND IN SAYING THAT, YOU'VE MADE YET ANOTHER COME-BACK!
You're good!
HEY, IT'S NOT MY FAULT! IT'S THE UNIVERSE'S FAULT FOR PUTTING ME IN THIS SITUATION!!
WELL, RIGHT NOW, I'M CURSING THE UNI-VERSE FOR PUTTING YOU IN THIS WAITING ROOM, SO SHUT UP!!
YOU'RE BEING JUST AS LOUD AS ME, Y'KNOW?!
WSH WSH WSH
SURPRIS-INGLY ENOUGH, THOSE TWO ARE BEING REALLY QUIET! IT'S EVERYONE ELSE THAT'S LOUD!

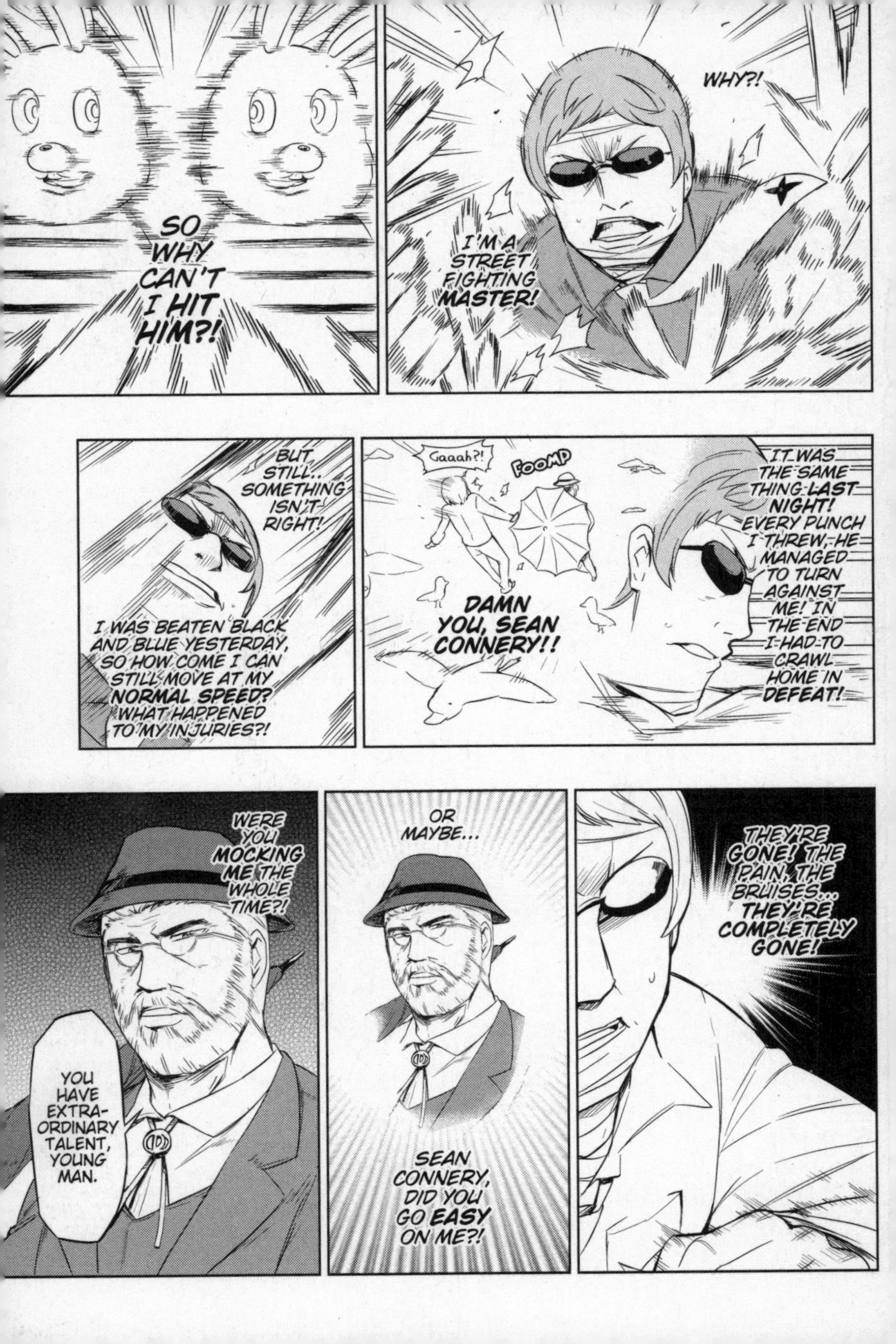
WHY?!
I'M A STREET FIGHTING MASTER!
SO WHY CAN'T I HIT HIM?!
IT WAS THE SAME THING LAST NIGHT! EVERY PUNCH I THREW, HE MANAGED TO TURN AGAINST ME! IN THE END I HAD TO CRAWL HOME IN DEFEAT!
FOOMP
Gaaah?!
DAMN YOU, SEAN CONNERY!!
BUT STILL.. SOMETHING ISN'T RIGHT!
I WAS BEATEN BLACK AND BLUE YESTERDAY, SO HOW COME I CAN STILL MOVE AT MY NORMAL SPEED? WHAT HAPPENED TO MY INJURIES?!
THEY'RE GONE! THE PAIN, THE BRUISES... THEY'RE COMPLETELY GONE!
OR MAYBE...
SEAN CONNERY, DID YOU GO EASY ON ME?!
WERE YOU MOCKING ME THE WHOLE TIME?!
YOU HAVE EXTRA-ORDINARY TALENT, YOUNG MAN.

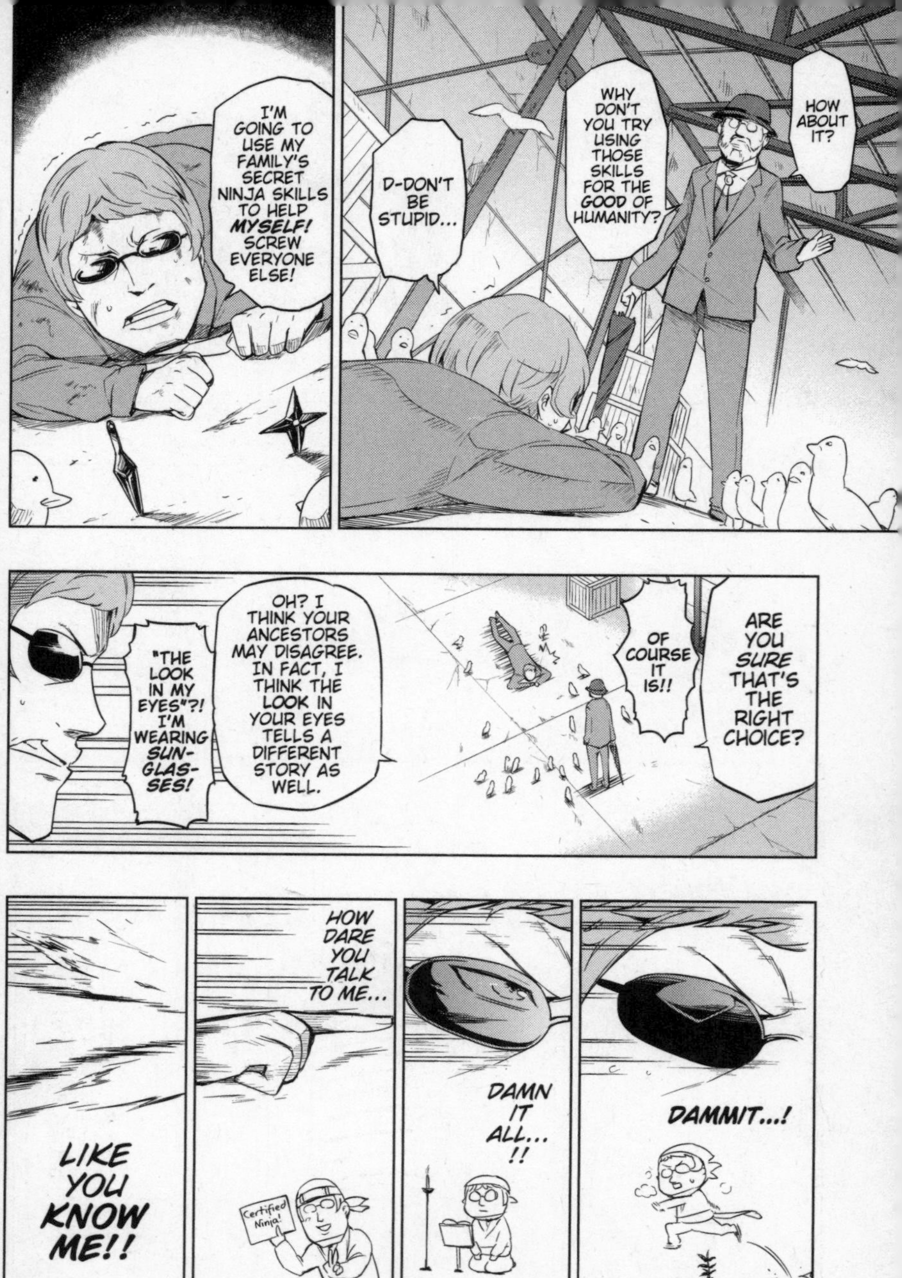
HOW ABOUT IT?
WHY DON'T YOU TRY USING THOSE SKILLS FOR THE GOOD OF HUMANITY?
D-DON'T BE STUPID...
I'M GOING TO USE MY FAMILY'S SECRET NINJA SKILLS TO HELP MYSELF! SCREW EVERYONE ELSE!
ARE YOU SURE THAT'S THE RIGHT CHOICE?
OF COURSE IT IS!!
OH? I THINK YOUR ANCESTORS MAY DISAGREE. IN FACT, I THINK THE LOOK IN YOUR EYES TELLS A DIFFERENT STORY AS WELL.
"THE LOOK IN MY EYES"?! I'M WEARING SUN-GLAS-SES!
DAMMIT...!
DAMN IT ALL... !!
HOW DARE YOU TALK TO ME...
Certified Ninja!
LIKE YOU KNOW ME!!

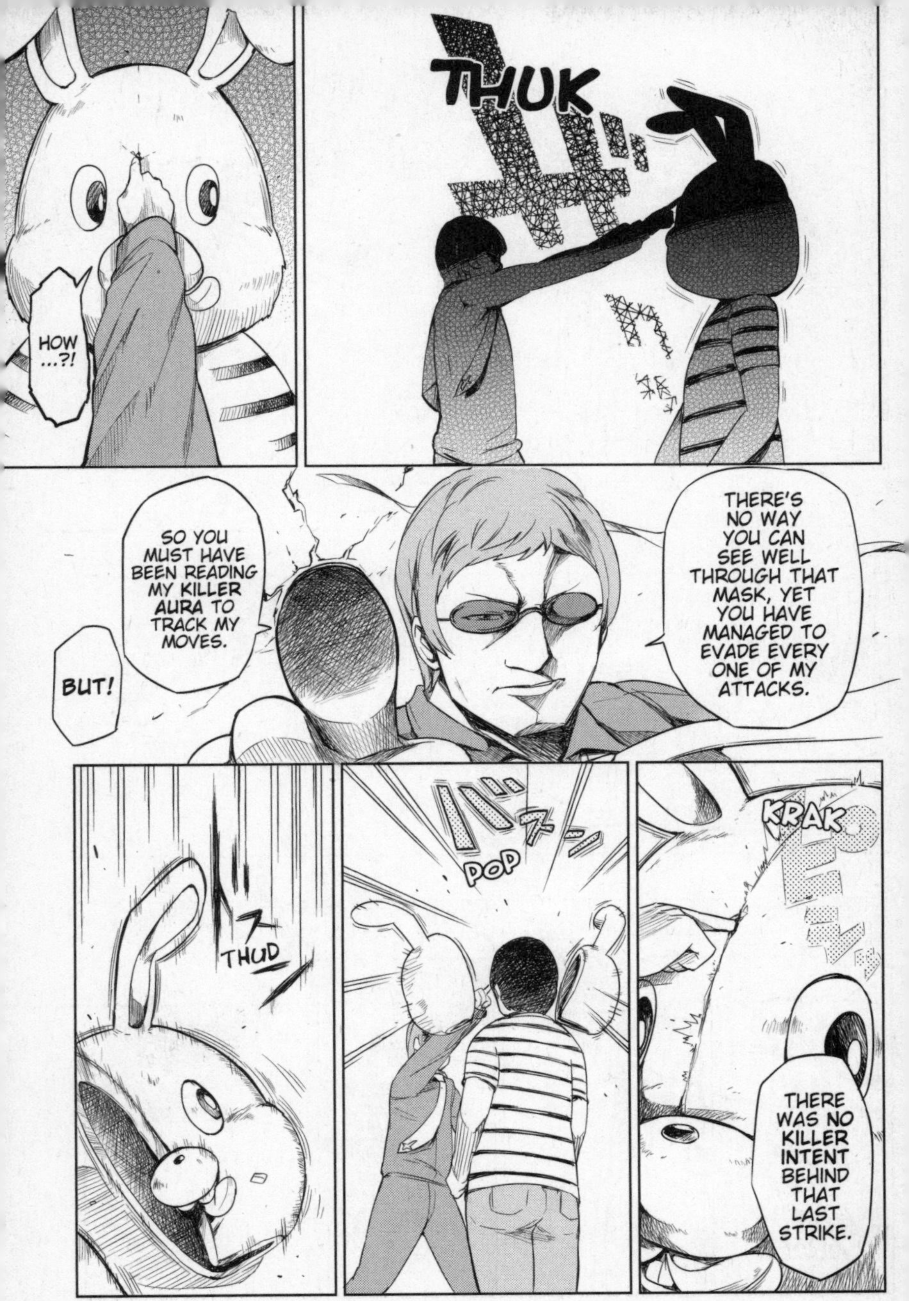
THUK
HOW ...?!
THERE'S NO WAY YOU CAN SEE WELL THROUGH THAT MASK, YET YOU HAVE MANAGED TO EVADE EVERY ONE OF MY ATTACKS.
SO YOU MUST HAVE BEEN READING MY KILLER AURA TO TRACK MY MOVES.
BUT!
KRAK
THERE WAS NO KILLER INTENT BEHIND THAT LAST STRIKE.
POP
THUD

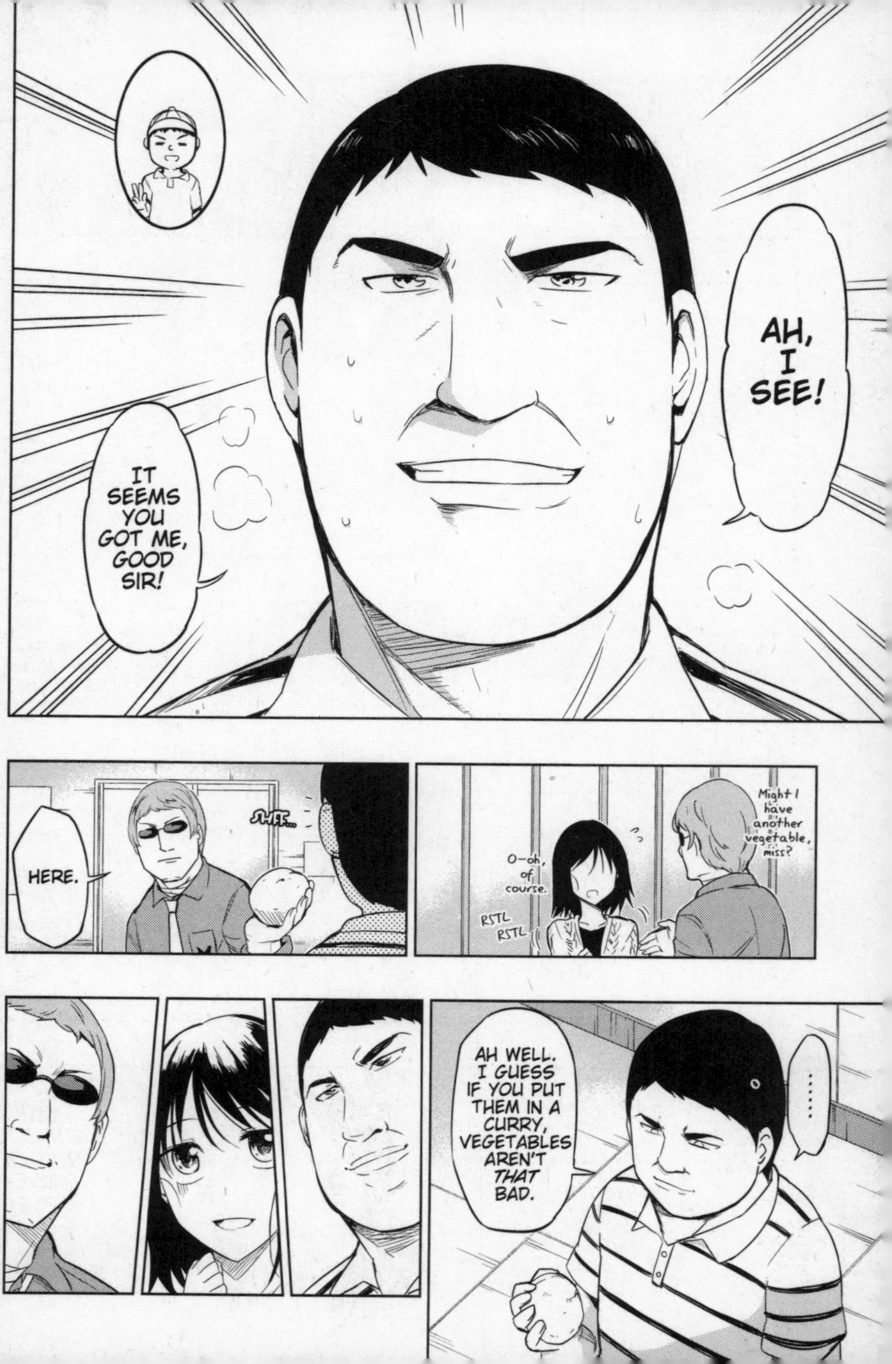
AH, I SEE!
IT SEEMS YOU GOT ME, GOOD SIR!
Might I have another vegetable, miss?
O-oh, of course.
RSTL RSTL
SHFF...
HERE.
......
AH WELL. I GUESS IF YOU PUT THEM IN A CURRY, VEGETABLES AREN'T *THAT* BAD.

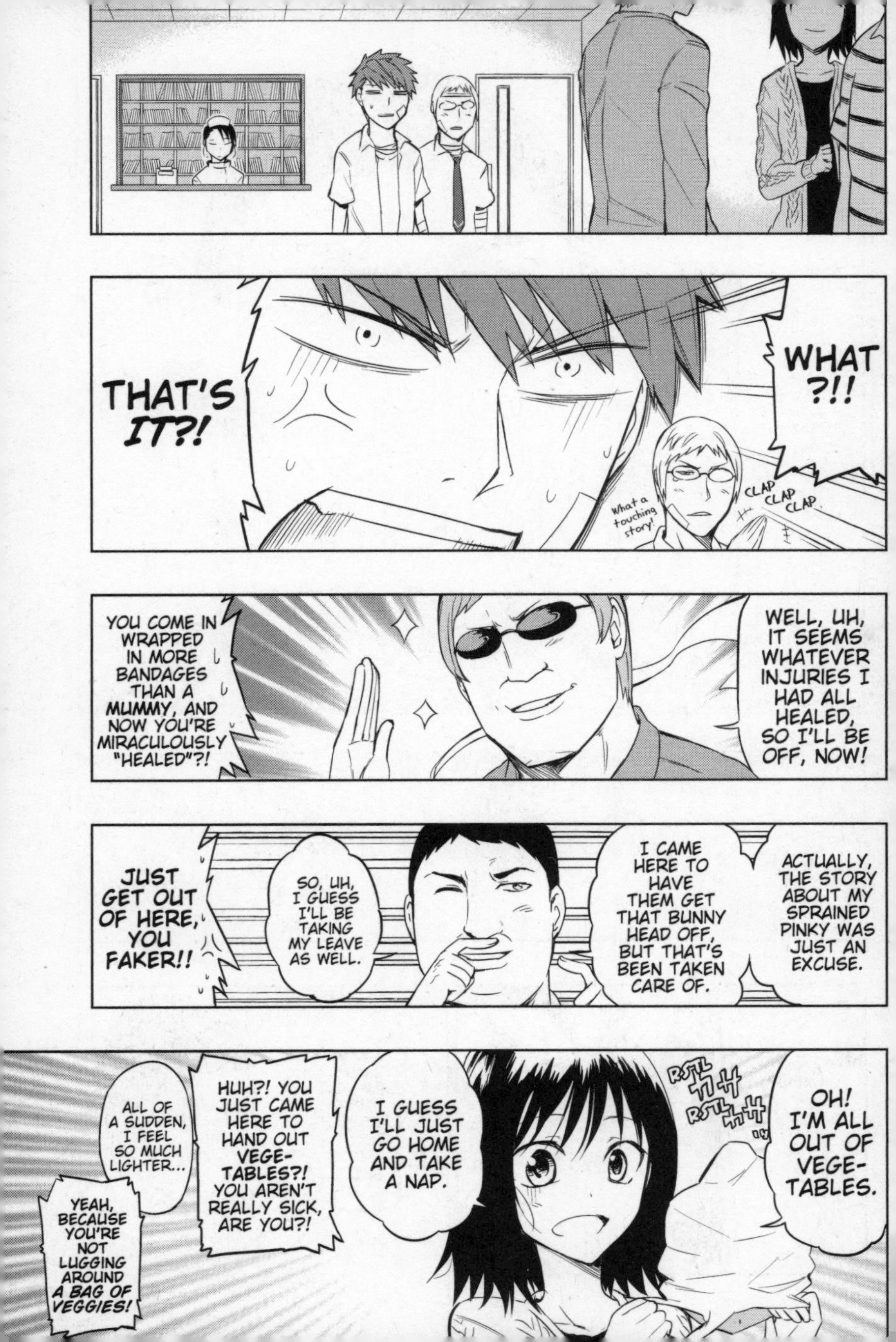
WHAT ?!!
THAT'S IT?!
CLAP CLAP CLAP
What a touching story!
WELL, UH, IT SEEMS WHATEVER INJURIES I HAD ALL HEALED, SO I'LL BE OFF, NOW!
YOU COME IN WRAPPED IN MORE BANDAGES THAN A MUMMY, AND NOW YOU'RE MIRACULOUSLY "HEALED"?!
ACTUALLY, THE STORY ABOUT MY SPRAINED PINKY WAS JUST AN EXCUSE.
I CAME HERE TO HAVE THEM GET THAT BUNNY HEAD OFF, BUT THAT'S BEEN TAKEN CARE OF.
SO, UH, I GUESS I'LL BE TAKING MY LEAVE AS WELL.
JUST GET OUT OF HERE, YOU FAKER!!
OH! I'M ALL OUT OF VEGE-TABLES.
RSTL
RSTL
I GUESS I'LL JUST GO HOME AND TAKE A NAP.
HUH?! YOU JUST CAME HERE TO HAND OUT VEGE-TABLES?! YOU AREN'T REALLY SICK, ARE YOU?!
ALL OF A SUDDEN, I FEEL SO MUCH LIGHTER...
YEAH, BECAUSE YOU'RE NOT LUGGING AROUND A BAG OF VEGGIES!

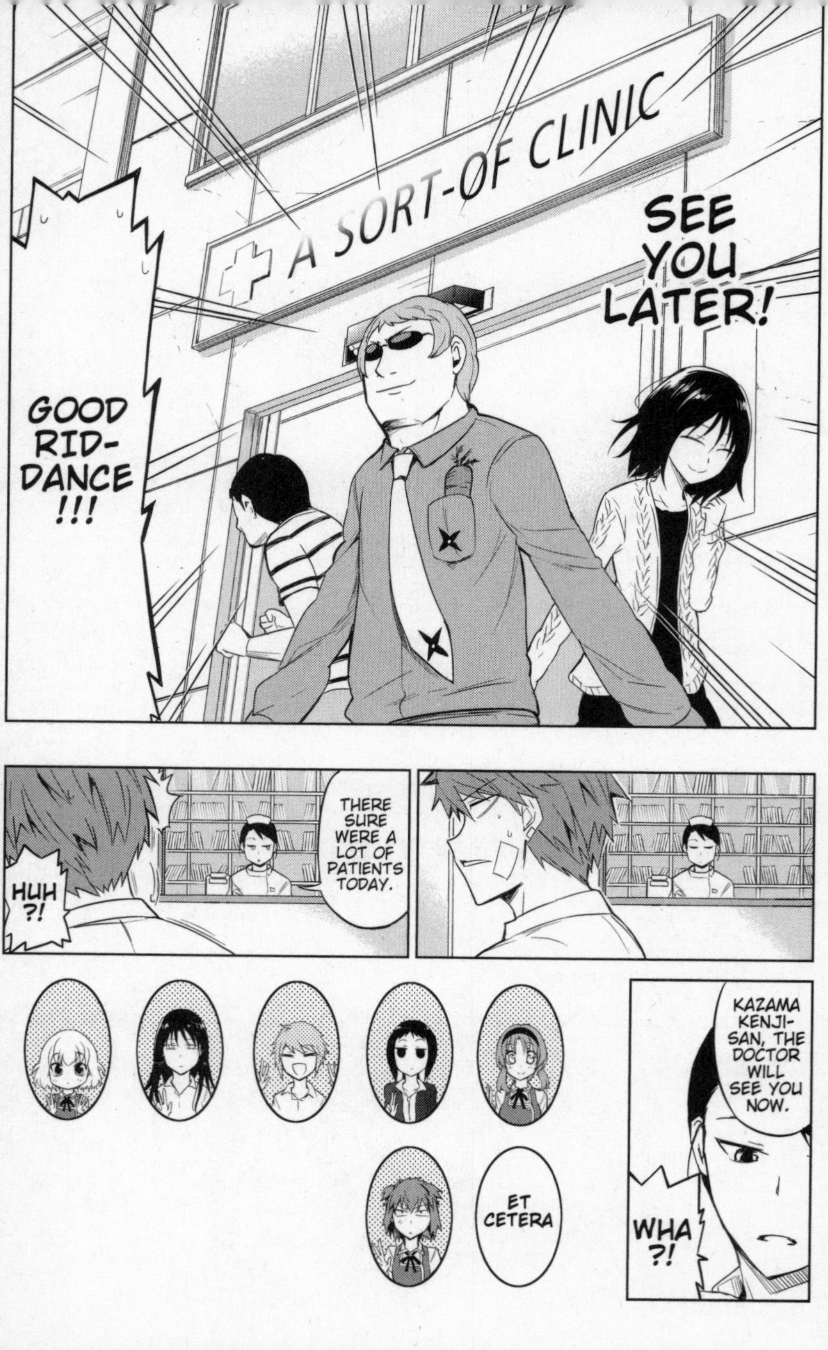
A SORT-OF CLINIC
SEE YOU LATER!
GOOD RID-DANCE!!!
THERE SURE WERE A LOT OF PATIENTS TODAY.
HUH?!
KAZAMA KENJI-SAN, THE DOCTOR WILL SEE YOU NOW.
WHA?!
ET CETERA

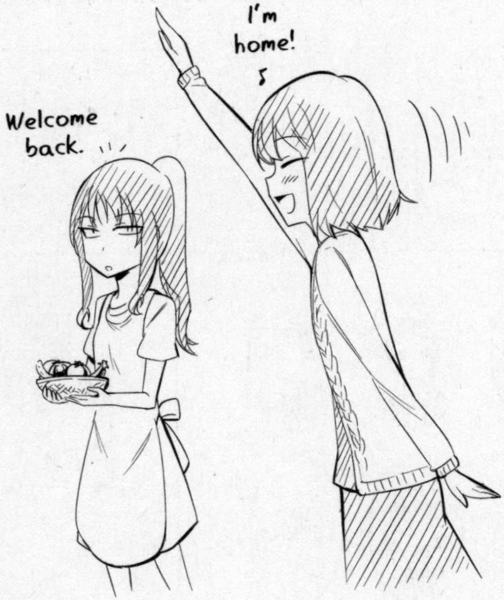
I'm home!
Welcome back.

D-FRAGMENTS

ディーふらぐ!

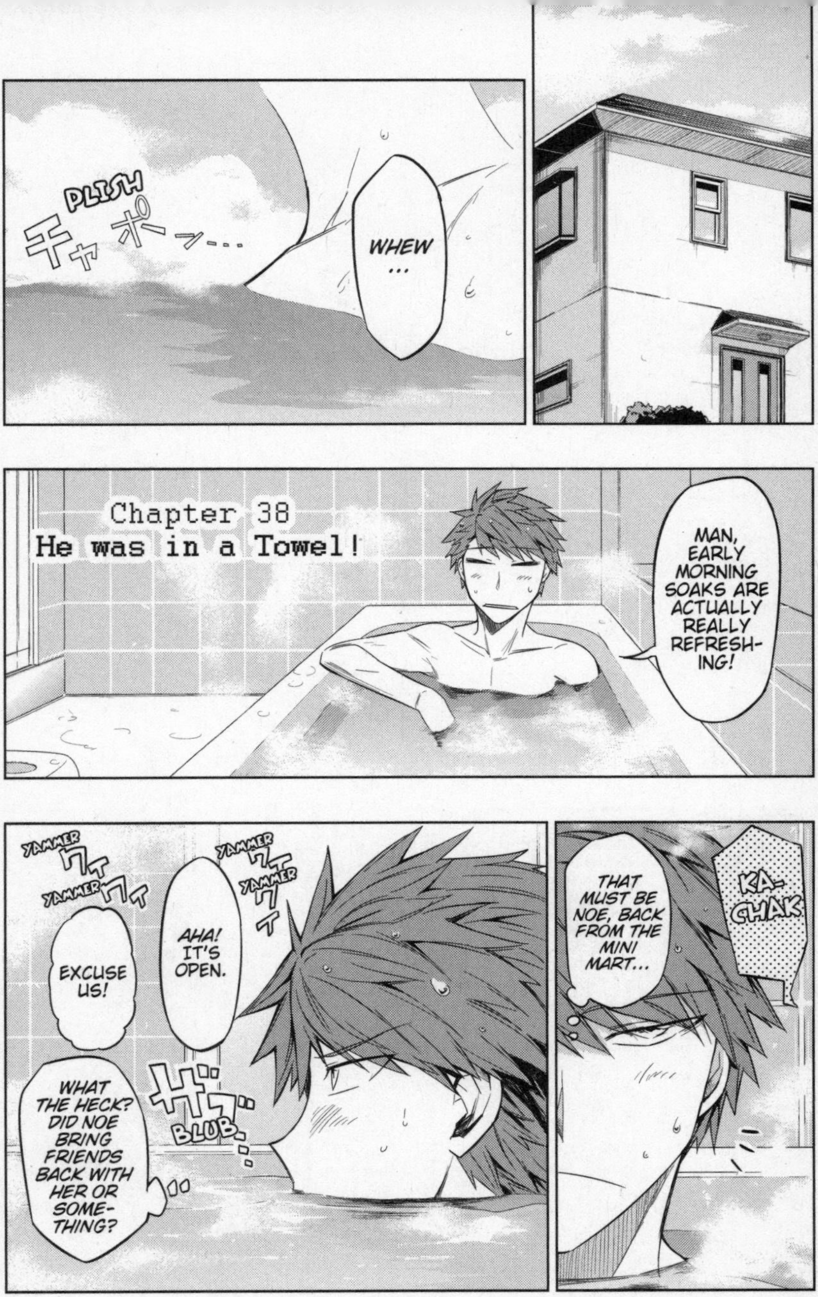
WHEW...
PLISH
チャポーン...
Chapter 38
He was in a Towel!
MAN, EARLY MORNING SOAKS ARE ACTUALLY REALLY REFRESHING!
KA-CHAK
THAT MUST BE NOE, BACK FROM THE MINI MART...
YAMMER
ワイ
YAMMER
ワイ
AHA! IT'S OPEN.
YAMMER
ワィ
YAMMER
ワィ
EXCUSE US!
ガブ
BLUB
WHAT THE HECK? DID NOE BRING FRIENDS BACK WITH HER OR SOMETHING?

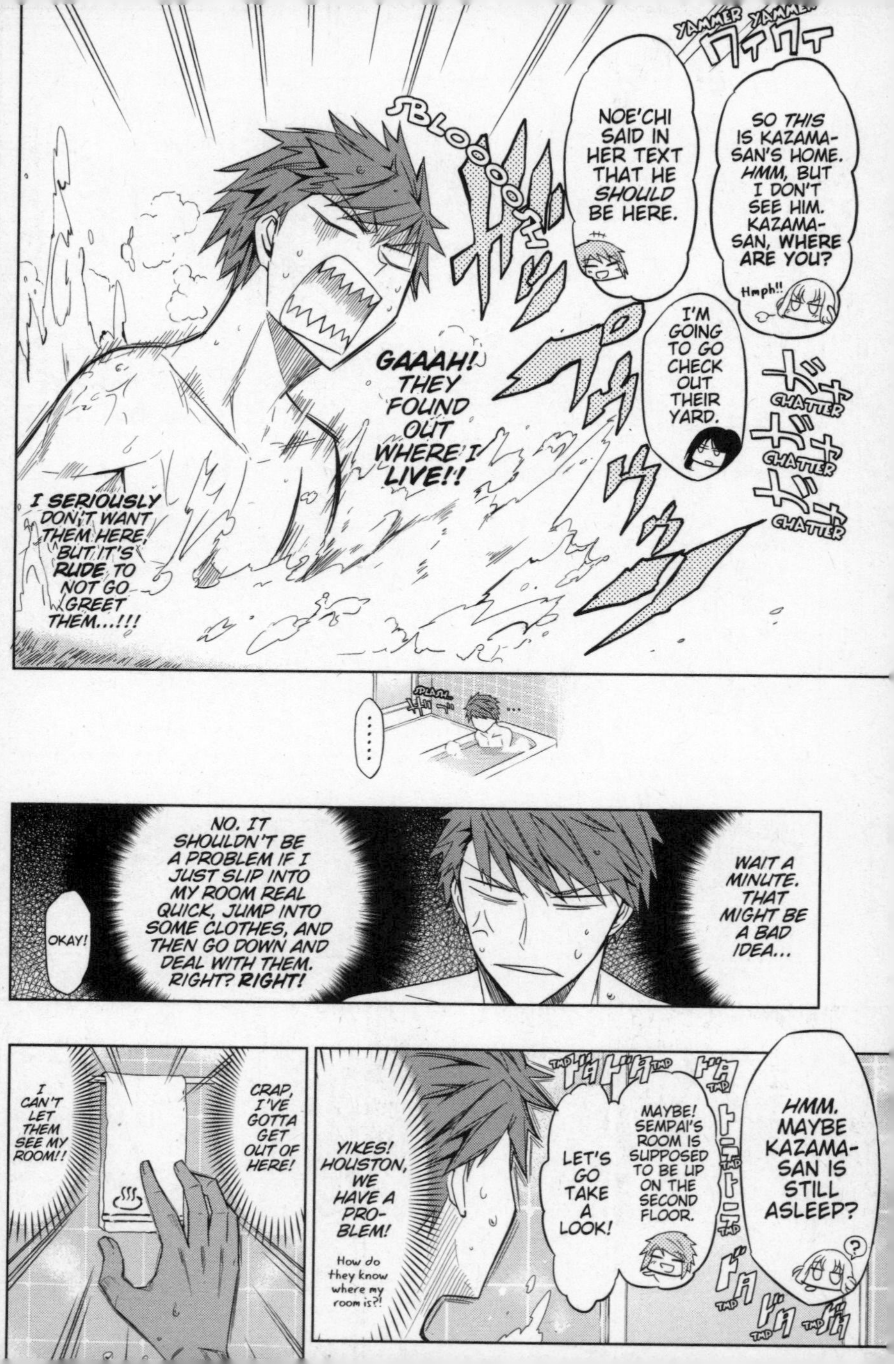
YAMMER YAMMER
SO THIS IS KAZAMA-SAN'S HOME. HMM, BUT I DON'T SEE HIM. KAZAMA-SAN, WHERE ARE YOU?
Hmph!!
NOE'CHI SAID IN HER TEXT THAT HE SHOULD BE HERE.
I'M GOING TO GO CHECK OUT THEIR YARD.
CHATTER
CHATTER
CHATTER
SBLOOOOOSH
GAAAH! THEY FOUND OUT WHERE I LIVE!!
I SERIOUSLY DON'T WANT THEM HERE, BUT IT'S RUDE TO NOT GO GREET THEM...!!!
SPLASH
...
......
WAIT A MINUTE. THAT MIGHT BE A BAD IDEA...
NO. IT SHOULDN'T BE A PROBLEM IF I JUST SLIP INTO MY ROOM REAL QUICK, JUMP INTO SOME CLOTHES, AND THEN GO DOWN AND DEAL WITH THEM. RIGHT? RIGHT!
OKAY!
HMM. MAYBE KAZAMA-SAN IS STILL ASLEEP?
MAYBE! SEMPAI'S ROOM IS SUPPOSED TO BE UP ON THE SECOND FLOOR.
LET'S GO TAKE A LOOK!
TMD TMD TMD TMD TMD TMD TMD TMD
YIKES! HOUSTON, WE HAVE A PROBLEM!
How do they know where my room is?!
CRAP, I'VE GOTTA GET OUT OF HERE!
I CAN'T LET THEM SEE MY ROOM!!

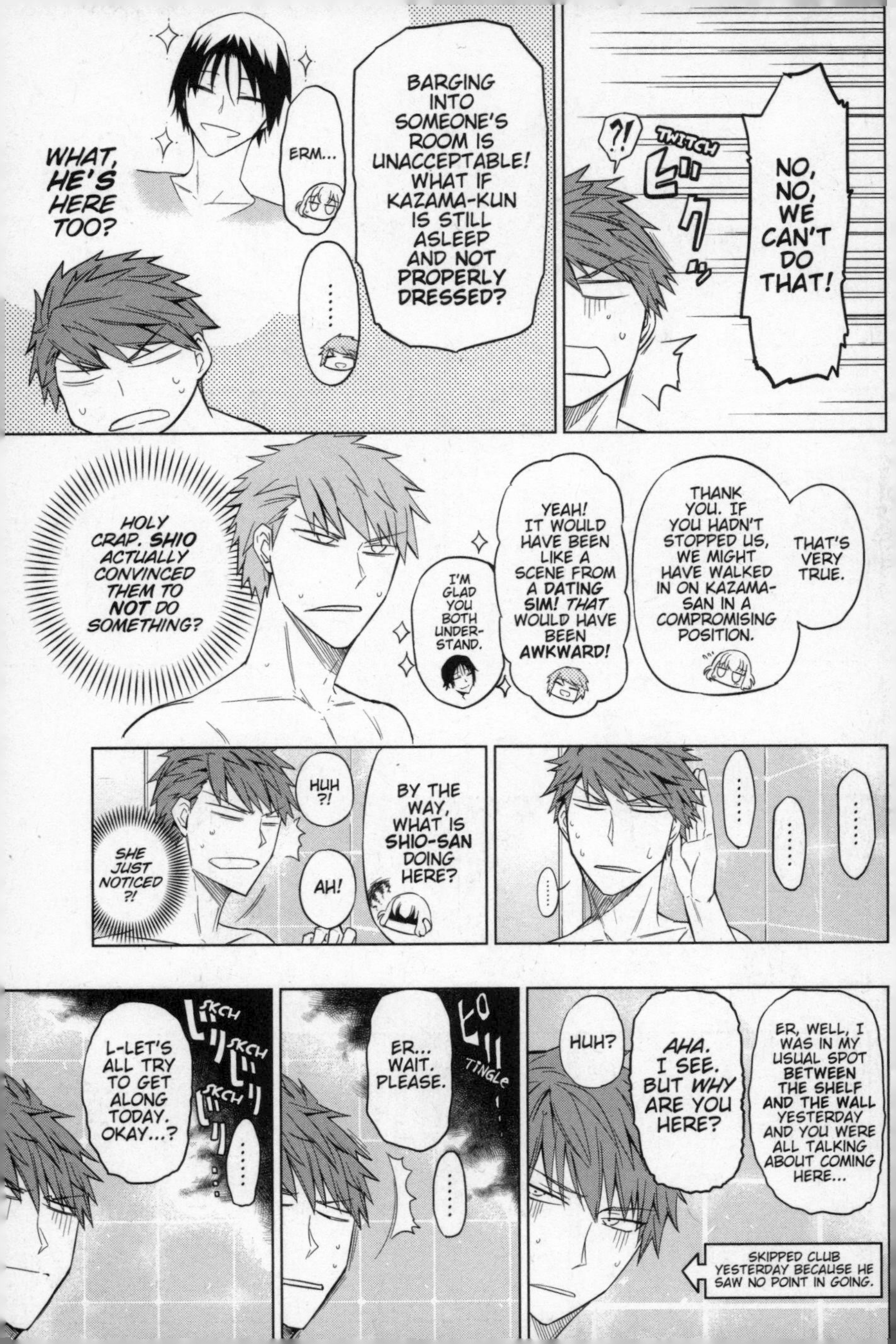

?!
TWITCH
NO, NO, WE CAN'T DO THAT!
BARGING INTO SOMEONE'S ROOM IS UNACCEPTABLE! WHAT IF KAZAMA-KUN IS STILL ASLEEP AND NOT PROPERLY DRESSED?
ERM...
......
WHAT, HE'S HERE TOO?
THAT'S VERY TRUE.
THANK YOU. IF YOU HADN'T STOPPED US, WE MIGHT HAVE WALKED IN ON KAZAMA-SAN IN A COMPROMISING POSITION.
YEAH! IT WOULD HAVE BEEN LIKE A SCENE FROM A DATING SIM! THAT WOULD HAVE BEEN AWKWARD!
I'M GLAD YOU BOTH UNDER-STAND.
HOLY CRAP. SHIO ACTUALLY CONVINCED THEM TO NOT DO SOMETHING?
......
......
......
......
BY THE WAY, WHAT IS SHIO-SAN DOING HERE?
HUH ?!
AH!
SHE JUST NOTICED ?!
ER, WELL, I WAS IN MY USUAL SPOT BETWEEN THE SHELF AND THE WALL YESTERDAY AND YOU WERE ALL TALKING ABOUT COMING HERE...
AHA. I SEE. BUT WHY ARE YOU HERE?
HUH?
SKIPPED CLUB YESTERDAY BECAUSE HE SAW NO POINT IN GOING.
TINGLE
ER... WAIT. PLEASE.
......
SKCH
SKCH
SKCH
L-LET'S ALL TRY TO GET ALONG TODAY. OKAY...?
......

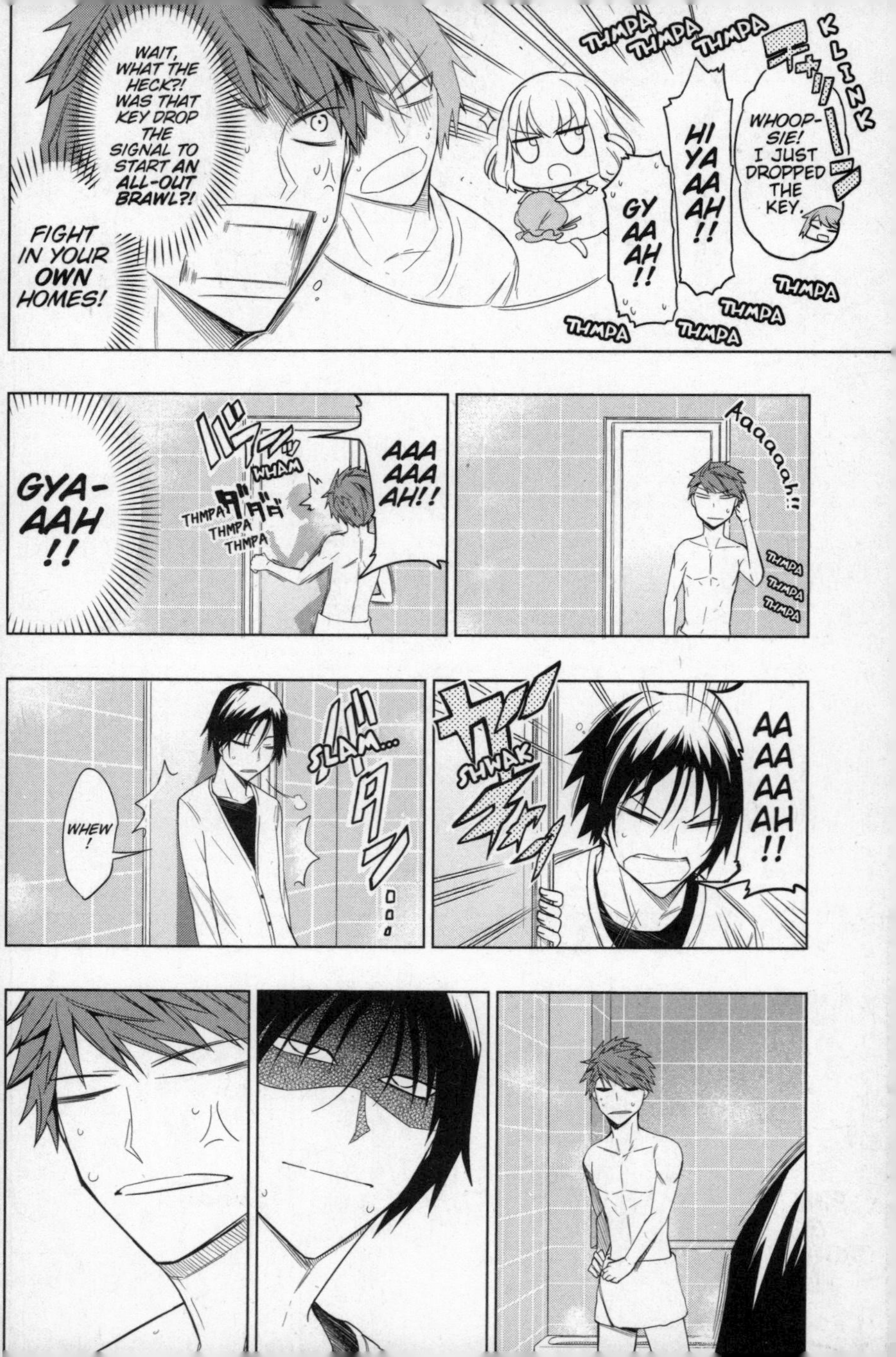
KLINK
WHOOPSIE! I JUST DROPPED THE KEY.
THMPA THMPA THMPA
HIYAAAAAH!!
GYAAAH!!
WAIT, WHAT THE HECK?! WAS THAT KEY DROP THE SIGNAL TO START AN ALL-OUT BRAWL?!
FIGHT IN YOUR OWN HOMES!
THMPA THMPA THMPA THMPA
Aaaaaah!!
THMPA THMPA THMPA
AAAAAAAH!!
WHAM
THMPA THMPA THMPA
GYA-AAH!!
AAAAAAAAH!!
SHWAK
SLAM...
WHEW!

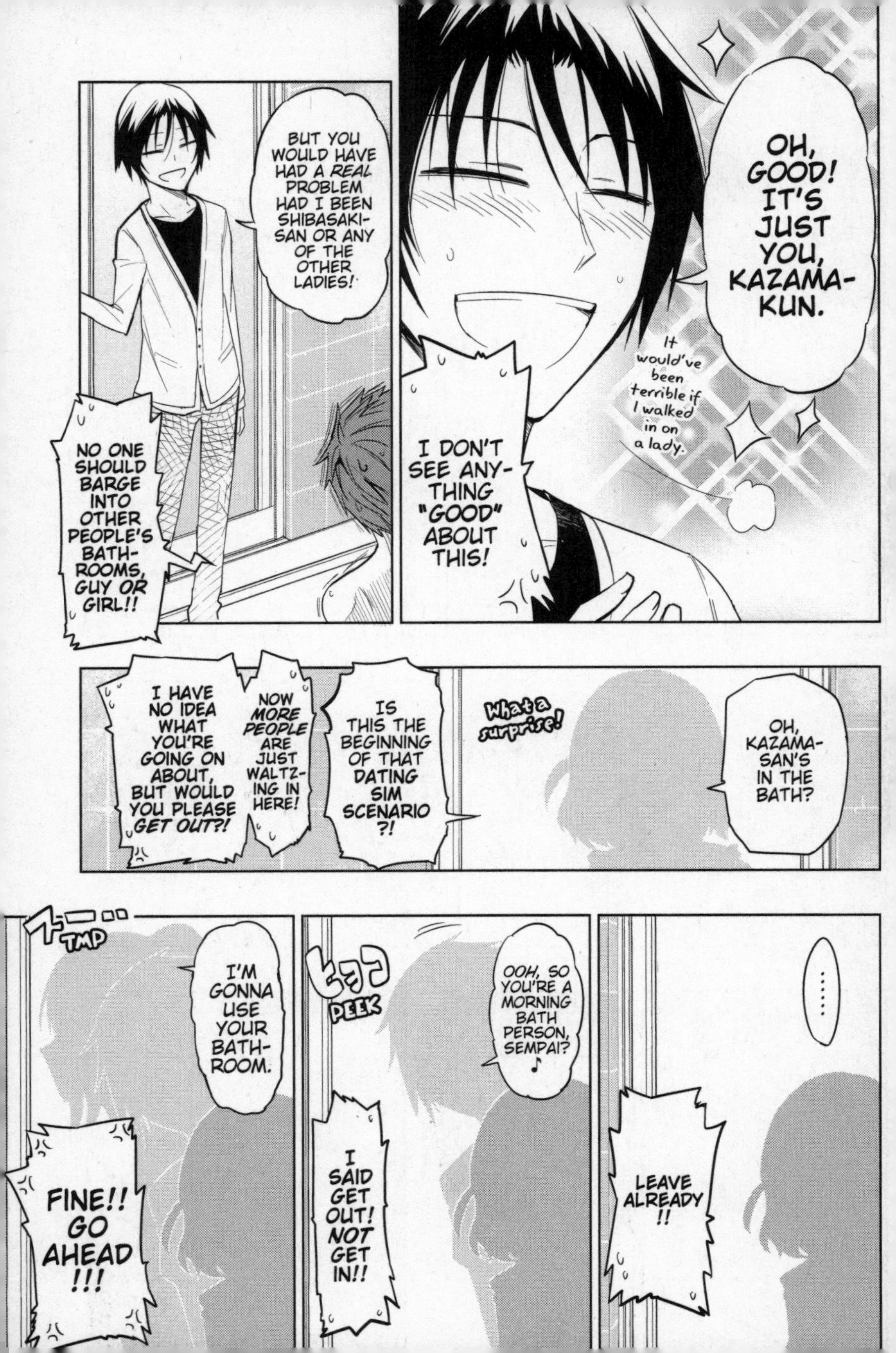
OH, GOOD! IT'S JUST YOU, KAZAMA-KUN.
It would've been terrible if I walked in on a lady.
I DON'T SEE ANYTHING "GOOD" ABOUT THIS!
BUT YOU WOULD HAVE HAD A *REAL* PROBLEM HAD I BEEN SHIBASAKI-SAN OR ANY OF THE OTHER LADIES!
NO ONE SHOULD BARGE INTO OTHER PEOPLE'S BATHROOMS, GUY *OR* GIRL!!
OH, KAZAMA-SAN'S IN THE BATH?
What a surprise!
IS THIS THE BEGINNING OF THAT DATING SIM SCENARIO?!
NOW *MORE PEOPLE* ARE JUST WALTZING IN HERE!
I HAVE NO IDEA WHAT YOU'RE GOING ON ABOUT, BUT WOULD YOU PLEASE *GET OUT?!*
......
LEAVE ALREADY!!
PEEK
OOH, SO YOU'RE A MORNING BATH PERSON, SEMPAI? ♪
I SAID GET OUT! *NOT* GET IN!!
TMP
I'M GONNA USE YOUR BATHROOM.
FINE!! GO AHEAD!!!

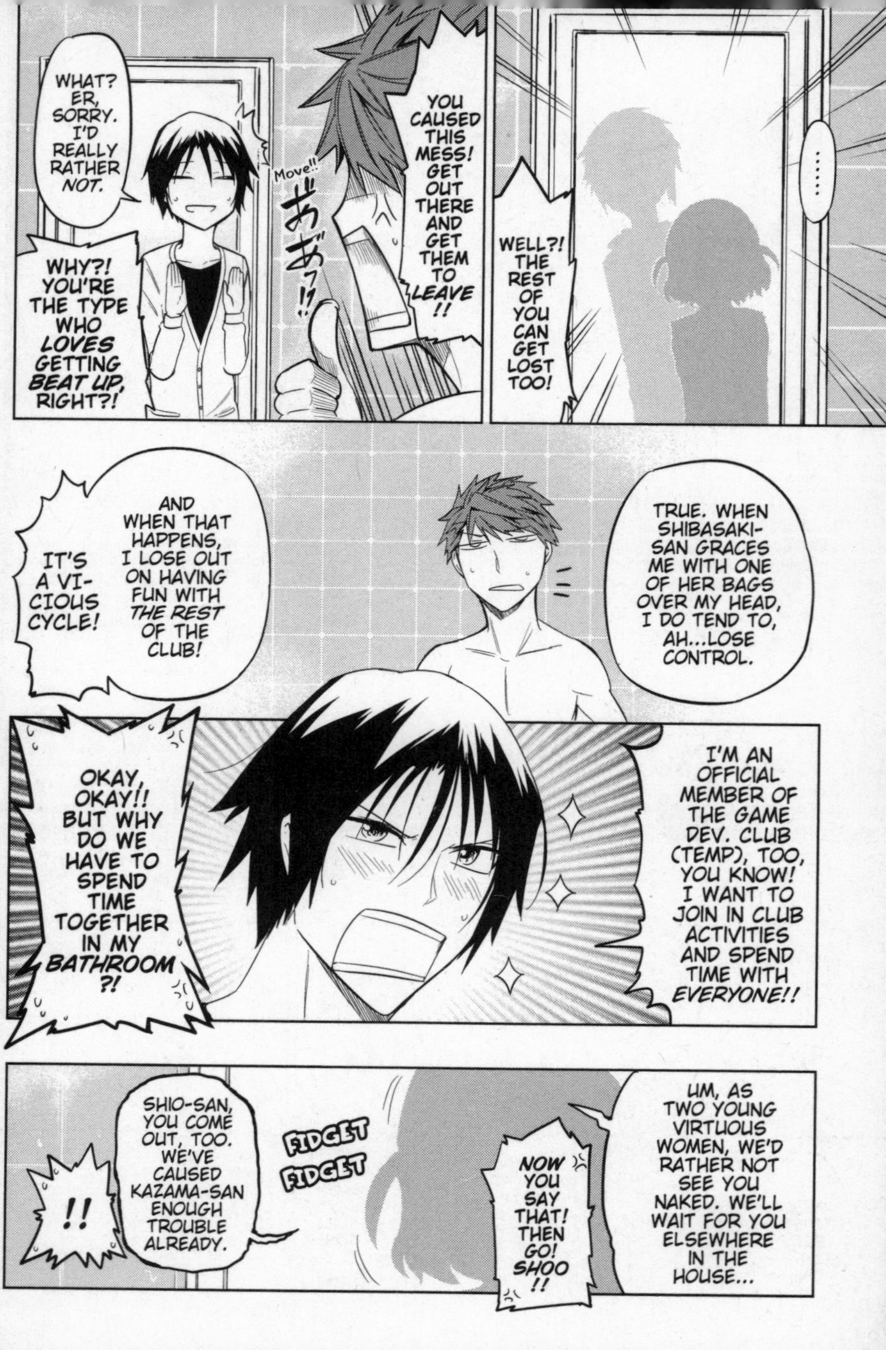
......
WELL?! THE REST OF YOU CAN GET LOST TOO!
YOU CAUSED THIS MESS! GET OUT THERE AND GET THEM TO LEAVE!!
Move!!
ああっ!!
WHAT? ER, SORRY. I'D REALLY RATHER NOT.
WHY?! YOU'RE THE TYPE WHO LOVES GETTING BEAT UP, RIGHT?!
TRUE. WHEN SHIBASAKI-SAN GRACES ME WITH ONE OF HER BAGS OVER MY HEAD, I DO TEND TO, AH...LOSE CONTROL.
AND WHEN THAT HAPPENS, I LOSE OUT ON HAVING FUN WITH THE REST OF THE CLUB!
IT'S A VI-CIOUS CYCLE!
I'M AN OFFICIAL MEMBER OF THE GAME DEV. CLUB (TEMP), TOO, YOU KNOW! I WANT TO JOIN IN CLUB ACTIVITIES AND SPEND TIME WITH EVERYONE!!
OKAY, OKAY!! BUT WHY DO WE HAVE TO SPEND TIME TOGETHER IN MY BATHROOM?!
UM, AS TWO YOUNG VIRTUOUS WOMEN, WE'D RATHER NOT SEE YOU NAKED. WE'LL WAIT FOR YOU ELSEWHERE IN THE HOUSE...
NOW YOU SAY THAT! THEN GO! SHOO!!
FIDGET FIDGET
SHIO-SAN, YOU COME OUT, TOO. WE'VE CAUSED KAZAMA-SAN ENOUGH TROUBLE ALREADY.
!!

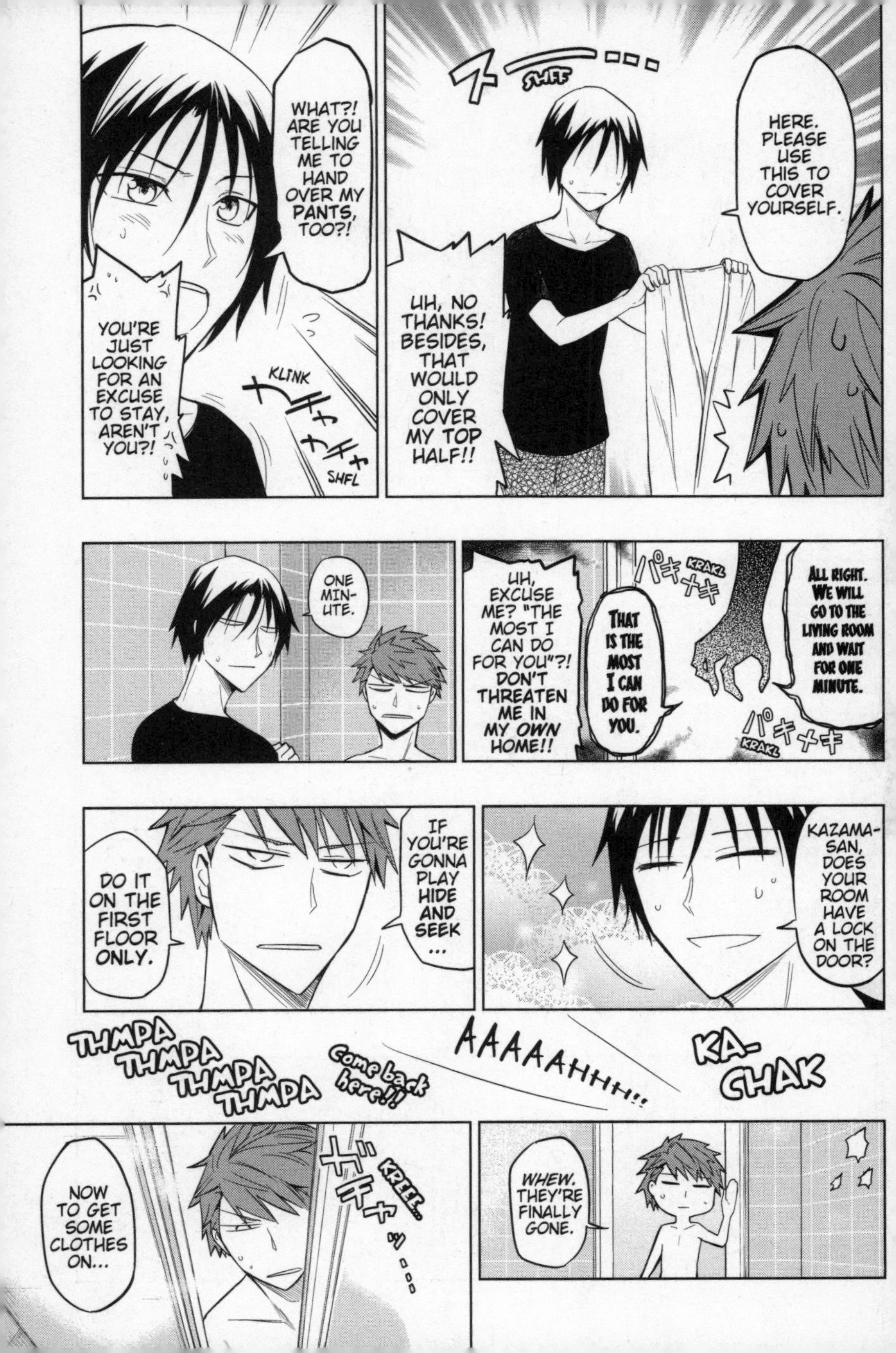
SHFF
HERE. PLEASE USE THIS TO COVER YOURSELF.
UH, NO THANKS! BESIDES, THAT WOULD ONLY COVER MY TOP HALF!!
WHAT?! ARE YOU TELLING ME TO HAND OVER MY PANTS, TOO?!
YOU'RE JUST LOOKING FOR AN EXCUSE TO STAY, AREN'T YOU?!
KLINK
SHFL
KRAKL
ALL RIGHT. WE WILL GO TO THE LIVING ROOM AND WAIT FOR ONE MINUTE.
THAT IS THE MOST I CAN DO FOR YOU.
UH, EXCUSE ME? "THE MOST I CAN DO FOR YOU"?! DON'T THREATEN ME IN MY OWN HOME!!
KRAKL
ONE MIN-UTE.
KAZAMA-SAN, DOES YOUR ROOM HAVE A LOCK ON THE DOOR?
IF YOU'RE GONNA PLAY HIDE AND SEEK ...
DO IT ON THE FIRST FLOOR ONLY.
KA-CHAK
AAAAAHHHH!!
Come back here!!
THMPA THMPA THMPA THMPA
WHEW. THEY'RE FINALLY GONE.
KREEE...
NOW TO GET SOME CLOTHES ON...

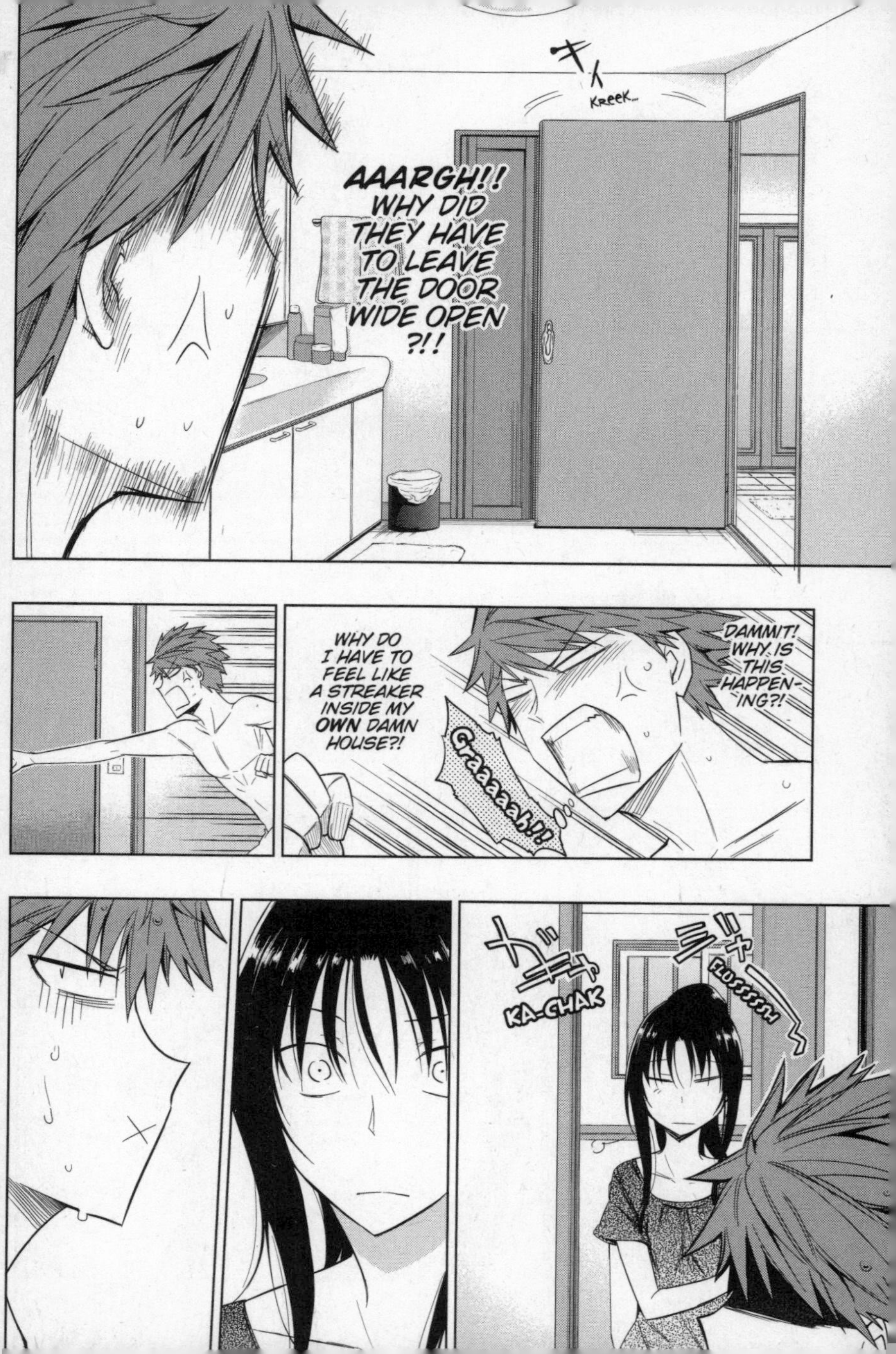
キィ
KREEK...
AAARGH!! WHY DID THEY HAVE TO LEAVE THE DOOR WIDE OPEN?!!
DAMMIT! WHY IS THIS HAPPEN-ING?!
WHY DO I HAVE TO FEEL LIKE A STREAKER INSIDE MY OWN DAMN HOUSE?!
Graaaaaah!!
ジャー
FLUSSSSH
ガチャ
KA-CHAK

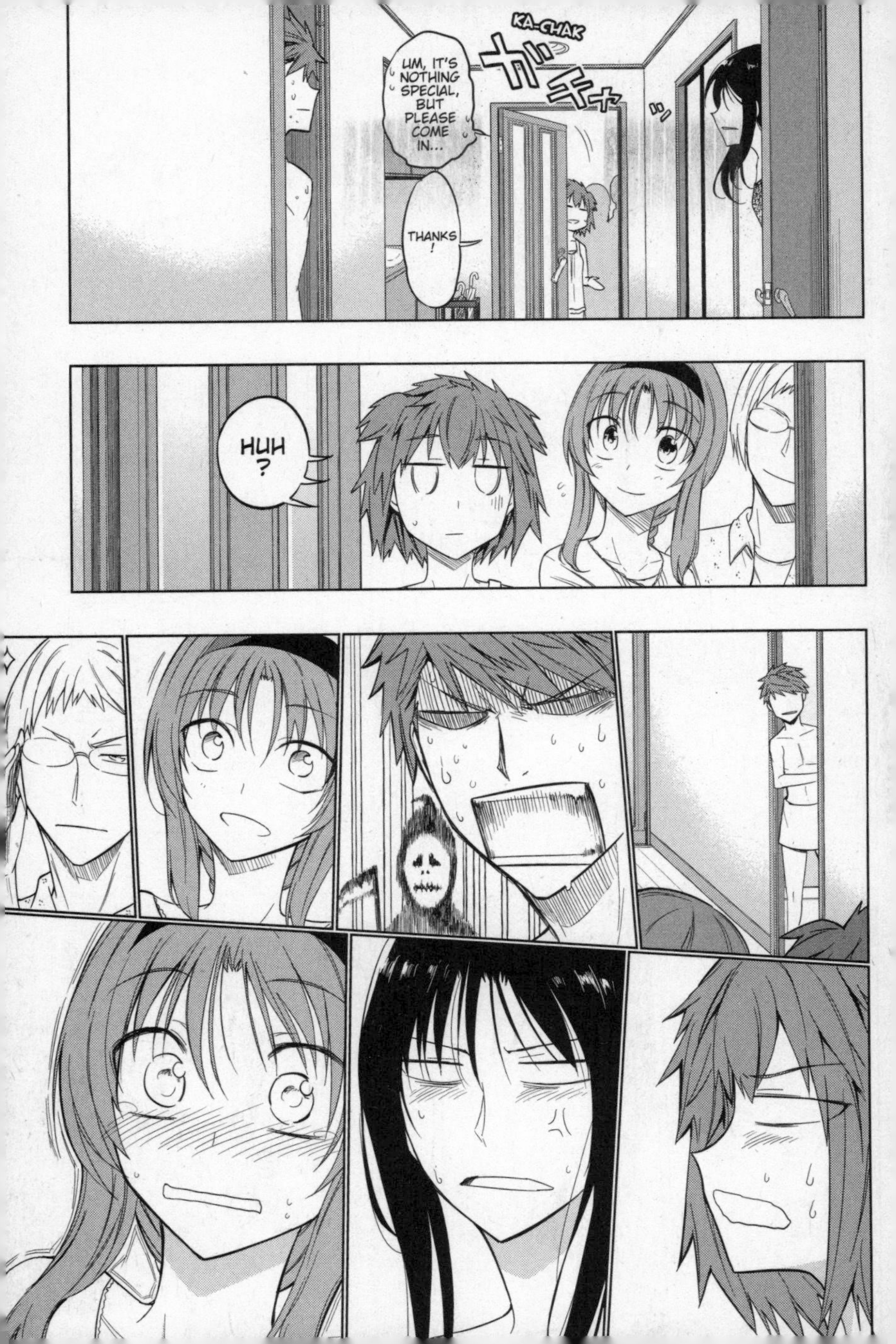
KA-CHAK
ガチャッ
UM, IT'S NOTHING SPECIAL, BUT PLEASE COME IN...
THANKS!
HUH?

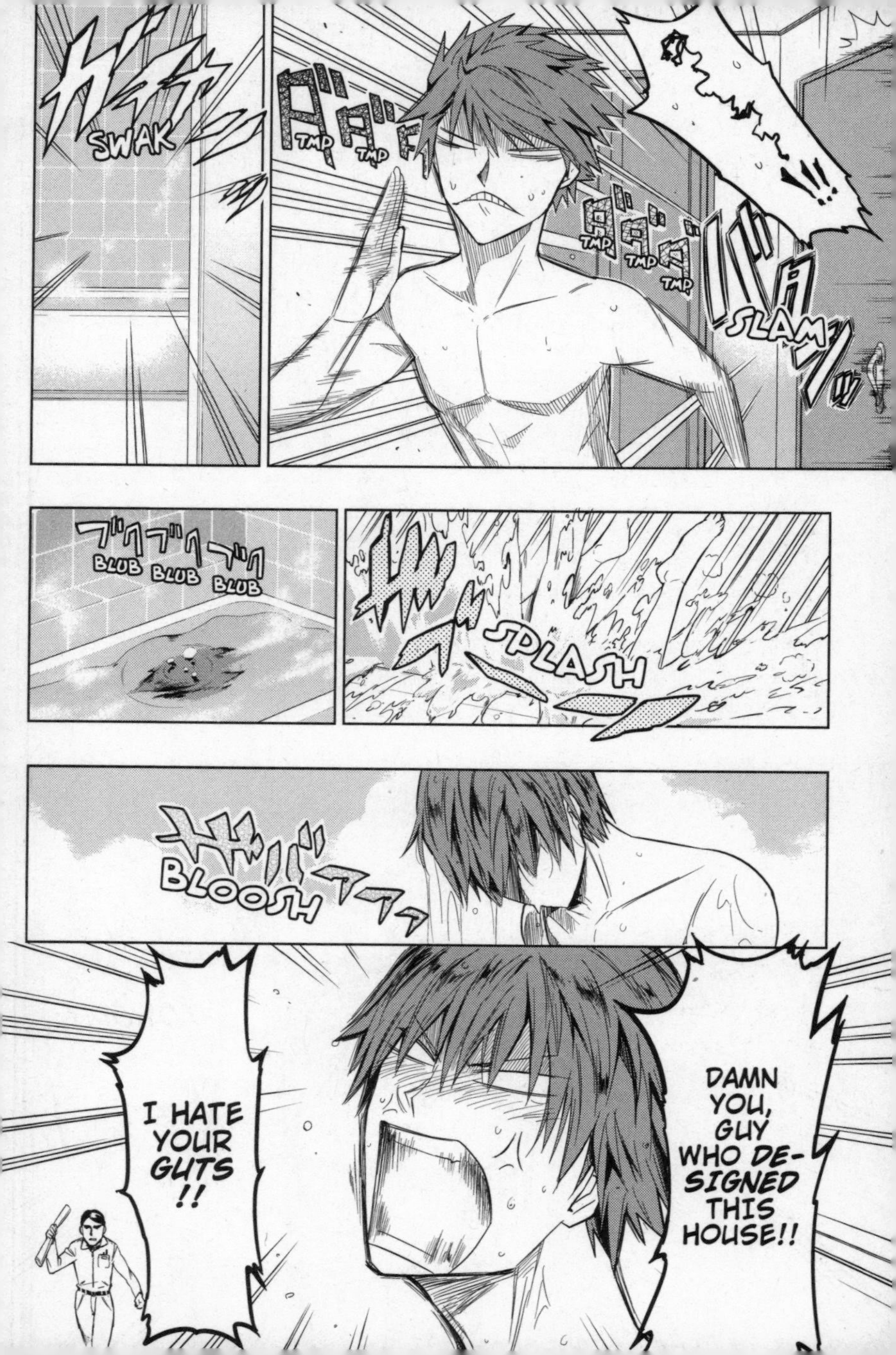

TMP TMP
TMP TMP TMP
SLAM
SWAK
SPLASH
BLUB BLUB BLUB
BLOOSH
DAMN YOU, GUY WHO DE-SIGNED THIS HOUSE!!
I HATE YOUR GUTS!!

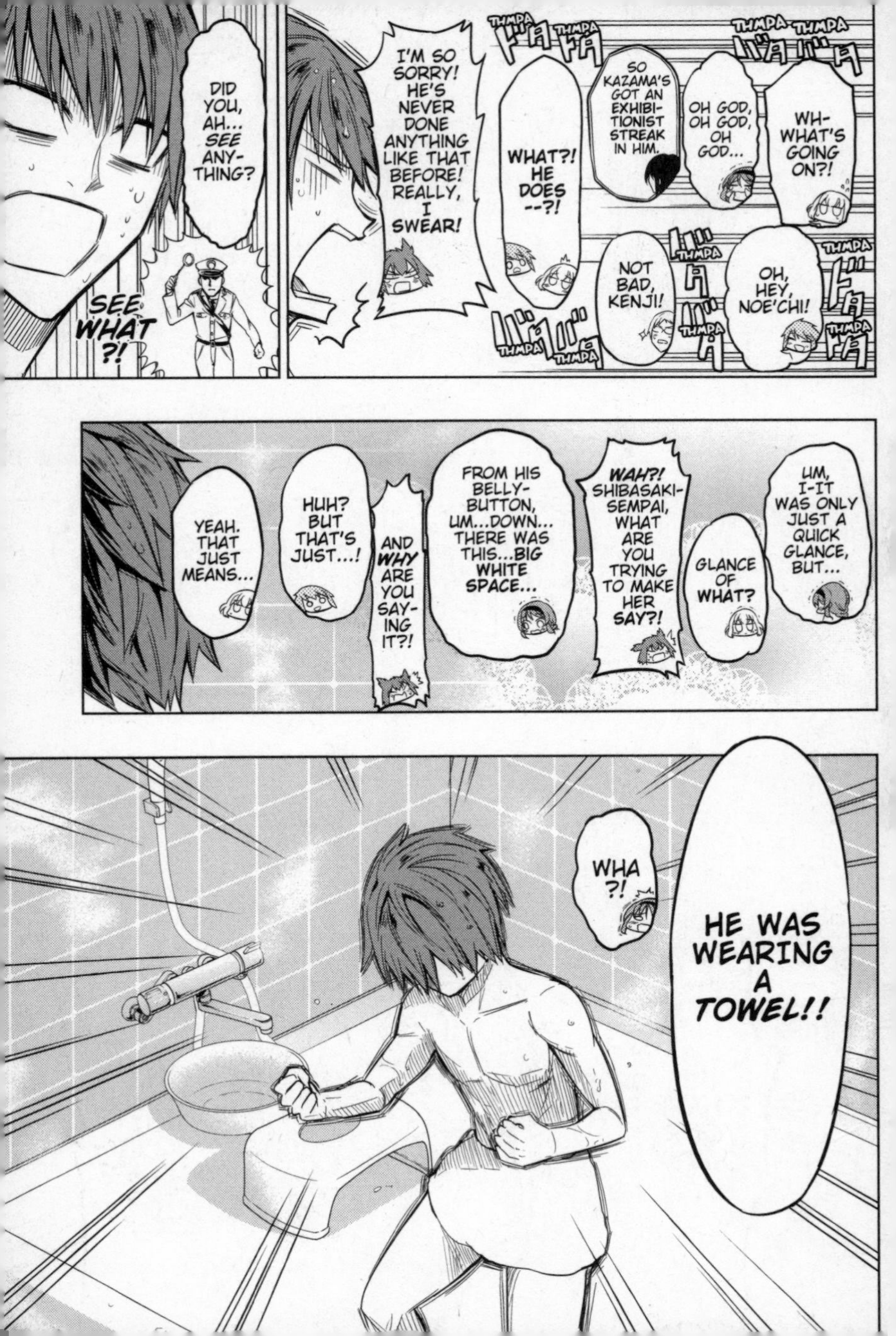
THMPA THMPA
ドタ ドタ
THMPA THMPA
バタ バタ
WH-WHAT'S GOING ON?!
OH GOD, OH GOD, OH GOD...
SO KAZAMA'S GOT AN EXHIBITIONIST STREAK IN HIM.
WHAT?! HE DOES--?!
OH, HEY, NOE'CHI!
NOT BAD, KENJI!
THMPA THMPA THMPA THMPA
I'M SO SORRY! HE'S NEVER DONE ANYTHING LIKE THAT BEFORE! REALLY, I SWEAR!
DID YOU, AH... SEE ANYTHING?
SEE WHAT?!
UM, I-IT WAS ONLY JUST A QUICK GLANCE, BUT...
GLANCE OF WHAT?
WAH?! SHIBASAKI-SEMPAI, WHAT ARE YOU TRYING TO MAKE HER SAY?!
FROM HIS BELLY-BUTTON, UM...DOWN... THERE WAS THIS...BIG WHITE SPACE...
AND WHY ARE YOU SAYING IT?!
HUH? BUT THAT'S JUST...!
YEAH. THAT JUST MEANS...
HE WAS WEARING A TOWEL!!
WHA?!

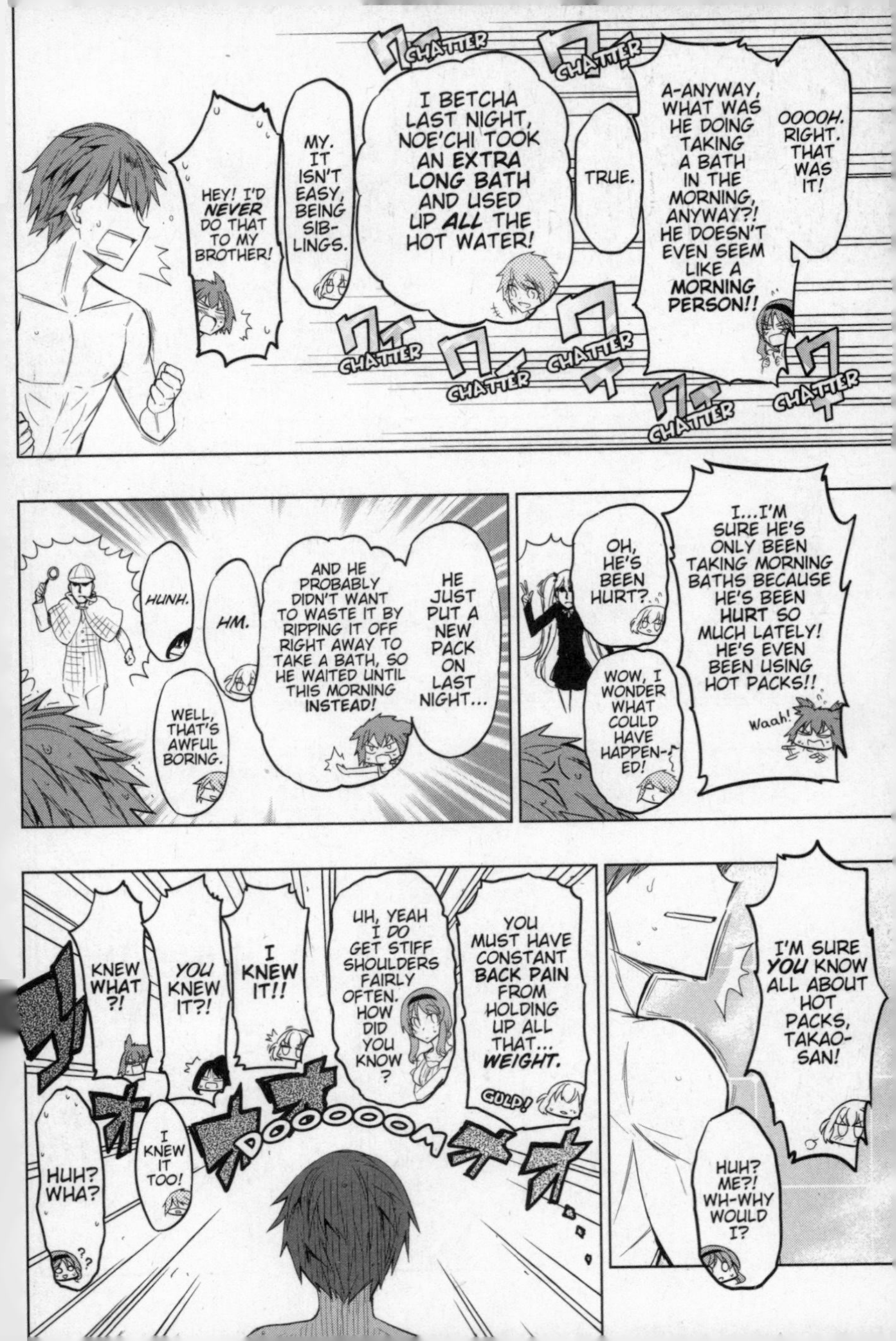
CHATTER
CHATTER
OOOOH. RIGHT. THAT WAS IT!
A-ANYWAY, WHAT WAS HE DOING TAKING A BATH IN THE MORNING, ANYWAY?! HE DOESN'T EVEN SEEM LIKE A MORNING PERSON!!
TRUE.
I BETCHA LAST NIGHT, NOE'CHI TOOK AN EXTRA LONG BATH AND USED UP ALL THE HOT WATER!
MY. IT ISN'T EASY, BEING SIB-LINGS.
HEY! I'D NEVER DO THAT TO MY BROTHER!
CHATTER
CHATTER
CHATTER
CHATTER
CHATTER
I...I'M SURE HE'S ONLY BEEN TAKING MORNING BATHS BECAUSE HE'S BEEN HURT SO MUCH LATELY! HE'S EVEN BEEN USING HOT PACKS!!
Waah!
OH, HE'S BEEN HURT?
WOW, I WONDER WHAT COULD HAVE HAPPEN-ED!
HE JUST PUT A NEW PACK ON LAST NIGHT...
AND HE PROBABLY DIDN'T WANT TO WASTE IT BY RIPPING IT OFF RIGHT AWAY TO TAKE A BATH, SO HE WAITED UNTIL THIS MORNING INSTEAD!
HM.
HUNH.
WELL, THAT'S AWFUL BORING.
I'M SURE YOU KNOW ALL ABOUT HOT PACKS, TAKAO-SAN!
HUH? ME?! WH-WHY WOULD I?
YOU MUST HAVE CONSTANT BACK PAIN FROM HOLDING UP ALL THAT... WEIGHT.
GULP!
UH, YEAH I DO GET STIFF SHOULDERS FAIRLY OFTEN. HOW DID YOU KNOW?
I KNEW IT!!
YOU KNEW IT?!
KNEW WHAT?!
DOOOOOOM
I KNEW IT TOO!
HUH? WHA?

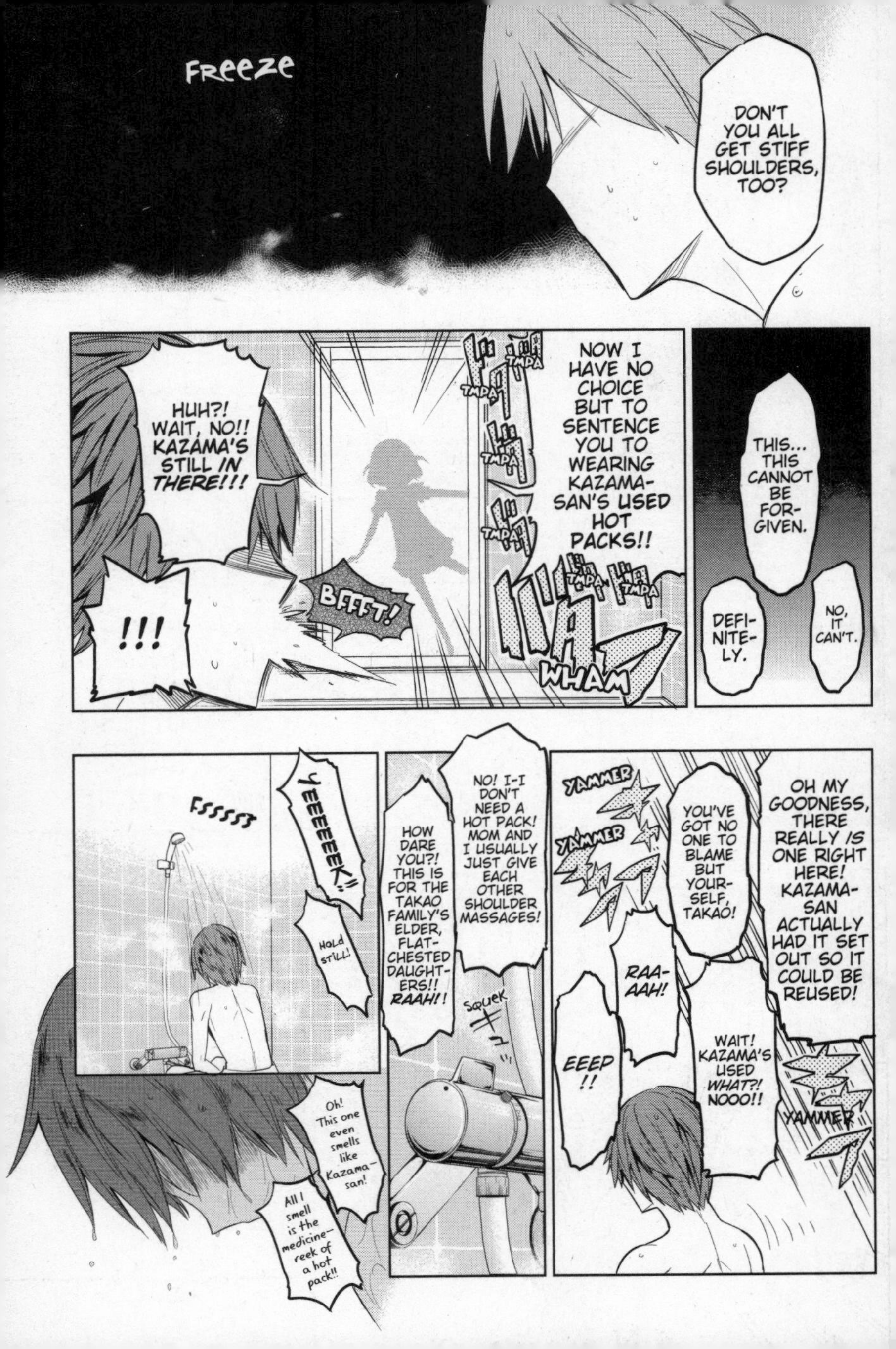
DON'T YOU ALL GET STIFF SHOULDERS, TOO?
Freeze
THIS... THIS CANNOT BE FOR-GIVEN.
NO, IT CAN'T.
DEFI-NITE-LY.
NOW I HAVE NO CHOICE BUT TO SENTENCE YOU TO WEARING KAZAMA-SAN'S USED HOT PACKS!!
TMPA TMPA TMPA TMPA
TMPA TMPA
WHAM
BFFFT!
HUH?! WAIT, NO!! KAZAMA'S STILL *IN THERE!!!*
!!!
OH MY GOODNESS, THERE REALLY *IS* ONE RIGHT HERE! KAZAMA-SAN ACTUALLY HAD IT SET OUT SO IT COULD BE REUSED!
YAMMER
YAMMER
YOU'VE GOT NO ONE TO BLAME BUT YOUR-SELF, TAKAO!
RAA-AAH!
WAIT! KAZAMA'S USED *WHAT?!* NOOO!!
EEEP !!
YAMMER
NO! I-I DON'T NEED A HOT PACK! MOM AND I USUALLY JUST GIVE EACH OTHER SHOULDER MASSAGES!
HOW DARE YOU?! THIS IS FOR THE TAKAO FAMILY'S ELDER, FLAT-CHESTED DAUGHT-ERS!! *RAAH!!*
SQUEK
YEEEEEEK!!
FSSSSS
Hold still!
Oh! This one even smells like Kazama-san!
All I smell is the medicine-reek of a hot pack!!

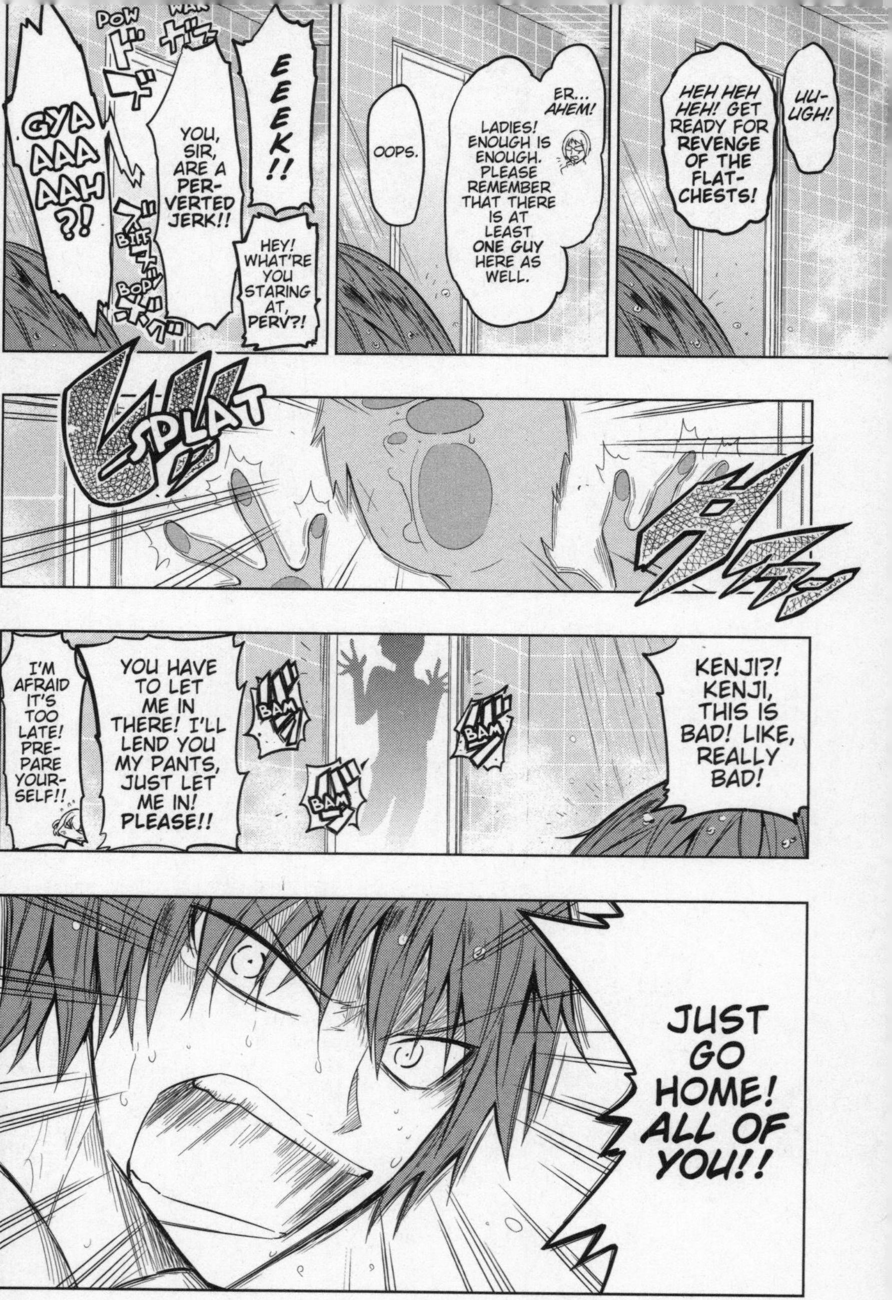
UU-UGH!
HEH HEH HEH! GET READY FOR REVENGE OF THE FLAT-CHESTS!
ER... AHEM!
LADIES! ENOUGH IS ENOUGH. PLEASE REMEMBER THAT THERE IS AT LEAST ONE GUY HERE AS WELL.
OOPS.
EEEEK!!
WAH
HEY! WHAT'RE YOU STARING AT, PERV?!
YOU, SIR, ARE A PERVERTED JERK!!
POW
GYAAAAAAH?!
BIFF
BOP
SPLAT
KENJI?! KENJI, THIS IS BAD! LIKE, REALLY BAD!
BAM
BAM
BAM
YOU HAVE TO LET ME IN THERE! I'LL LEND YOU MY PANTS, JUST LET ME IN! PLEASE!!
I'M AFRAID IT'S TOO LATE! PREPARE YOURSELF!!
JUST GO HOME! ALL OF YOU!!

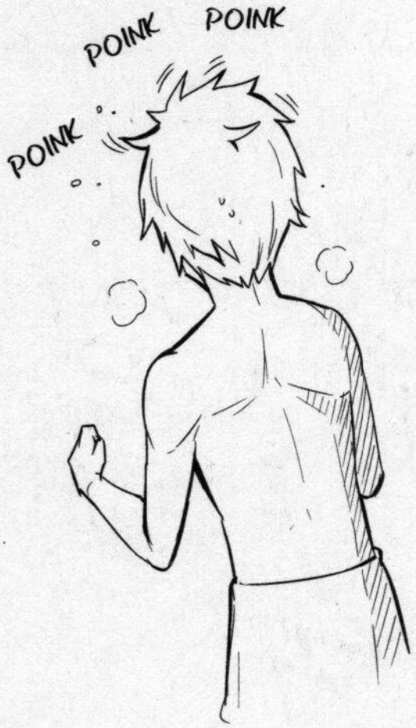
POINK
POINK
POINK

D-FRAGMENTS

ディーふらぐ!

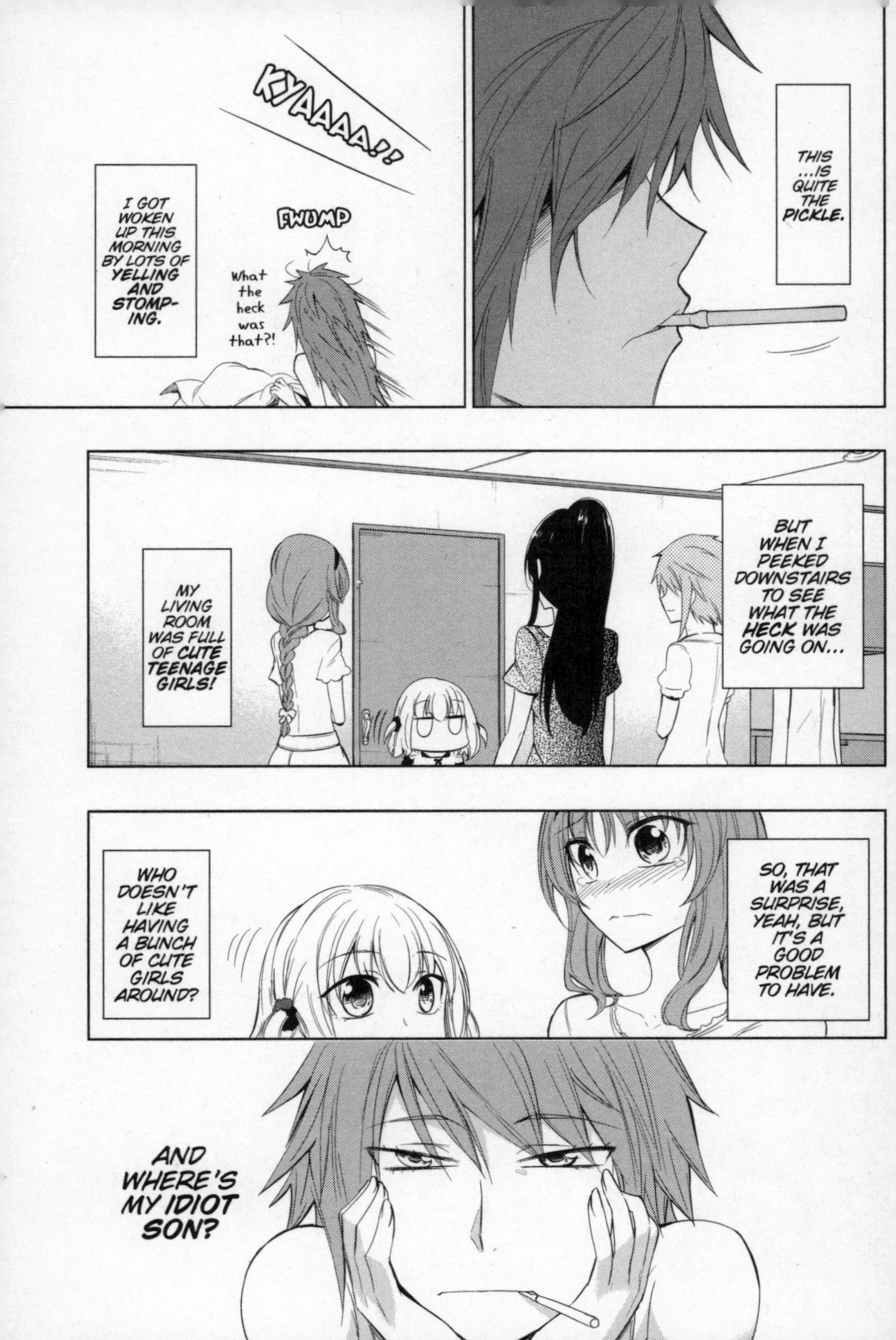
THIS ...IS QUITE THE PICKLE.
KYAAAA!!
I GOT WOKEN UP THIS MORNING BY LOTS OF YELLING AND STOMPING.
FWUMP
What the heck was that?!
BUT WHEN I PEEKED DOWNSTAIRS TO SEE WHAT THE HECK WAS GOING ON...
MY LIVING ROOM WAS FULL OF CUTE TEENAGE GIRLS!
SO, THAT WAS A SURPRISE, YEAH, BUT IT'S A GOOD PROBLEM TO HAVE.
WHO DOESN'T LIKE HAVING A BUNCH OF CUTE GIRLS AROUND?
AND WHERE'S MY IDIOT SON?

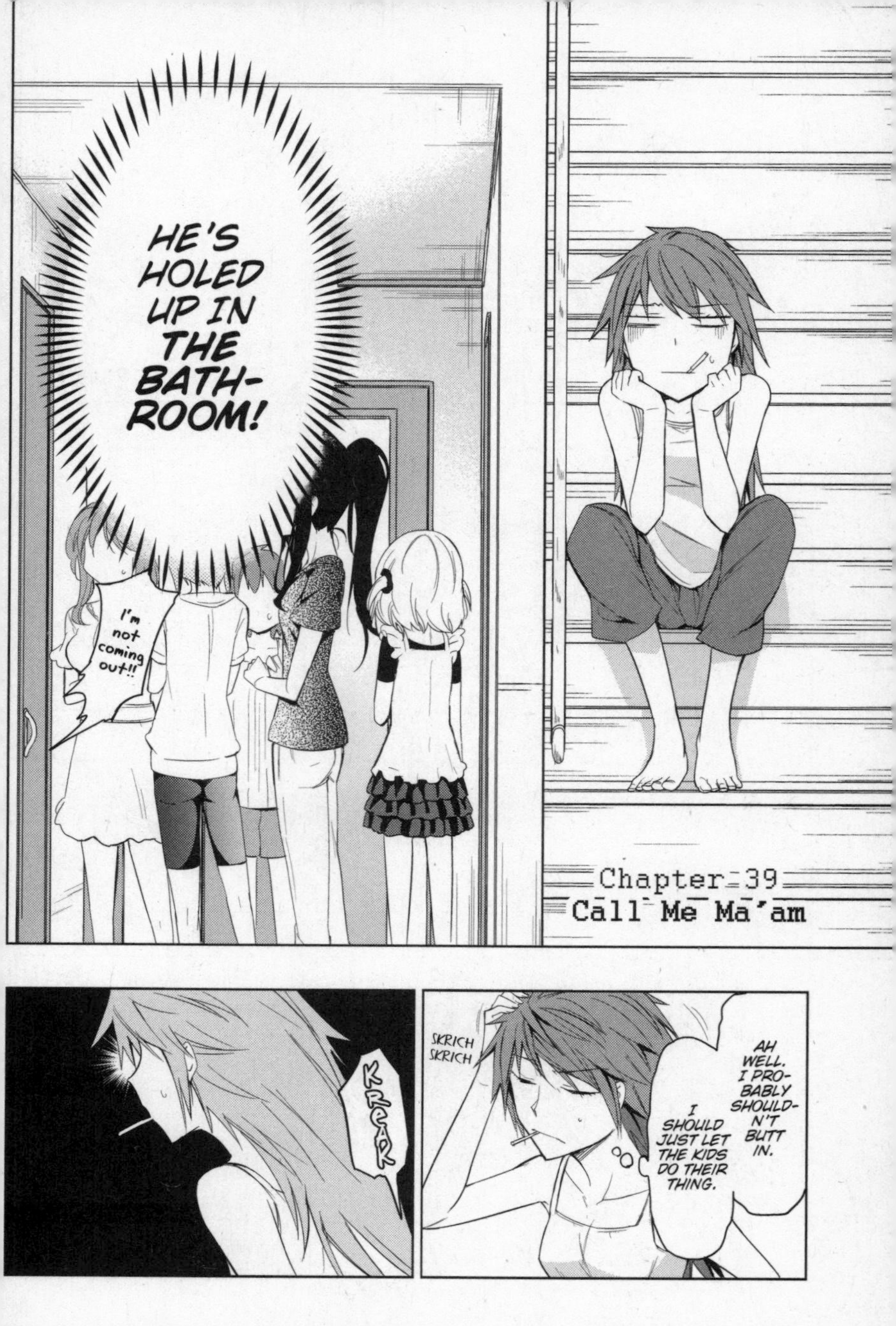
Chapter 39
Call Me Ma'am
HE'S HOLED UP IN THE BATHROOM!
I'm not coming out!!
SKRICH SKRICH
AH WELL. I PROBABLY SHOULDN'T BUTT IN.
I SHOULD JUST LET THE KIDS DO THEIR THING.
KREAK

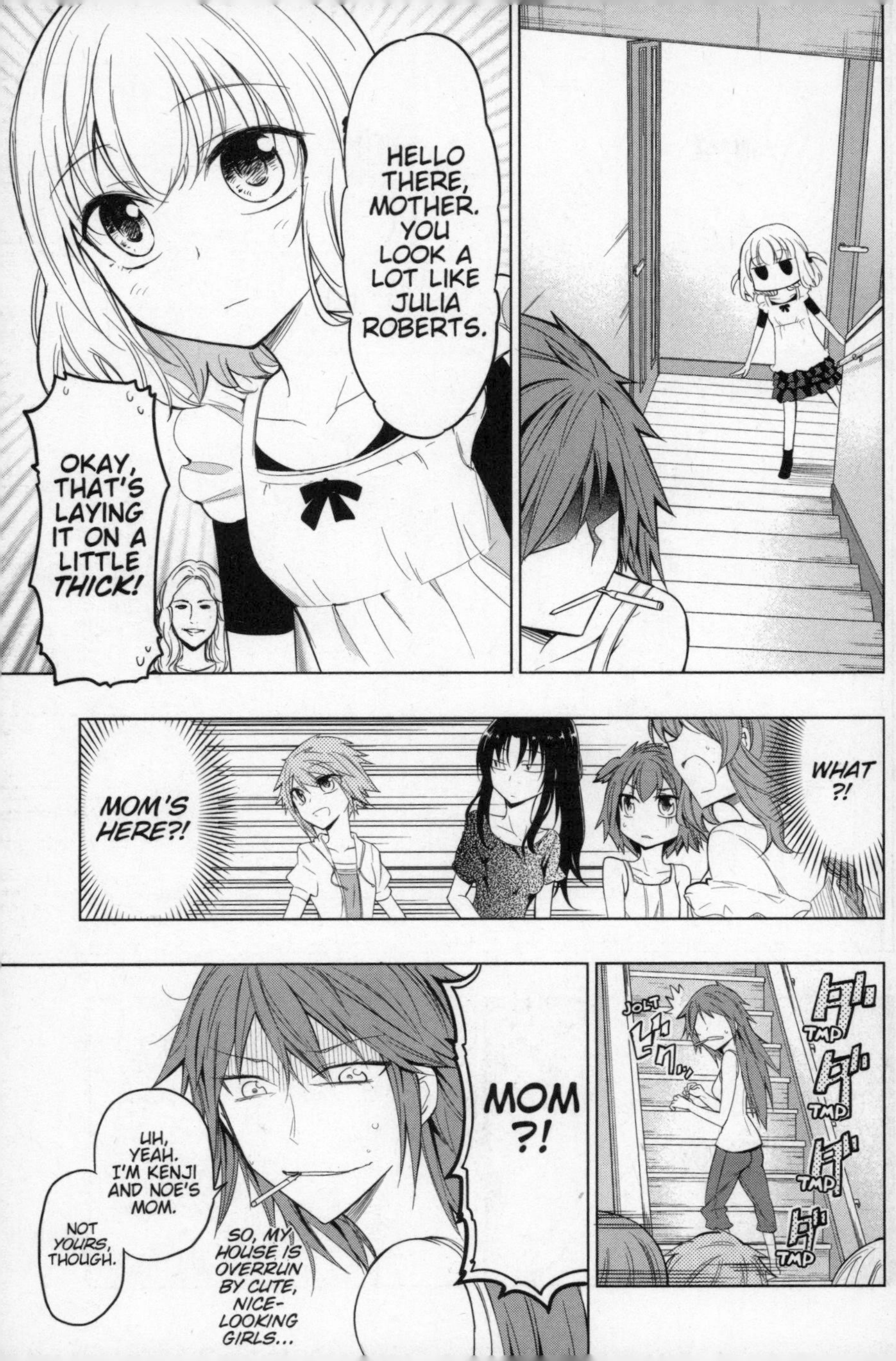
HELLO THERE, MOTHER. YOU LOOK A LOT LIKE JULIA ROBERTS.
OKAY, THAT'S LAYING IT ON A LITTLE *THICK!*
WHAT ?!
MOM'S HERE?!
JOLT
TMP
TMP
TMP
TMP
MOM ?!
UH, YEAH. I'M KENJI AND NOE'S MOM.
NOT YOURS, THOUGH.
SO, MY HOUSE IS OVERRUN BY CUTE, NICE-LOOKING GIRLS...

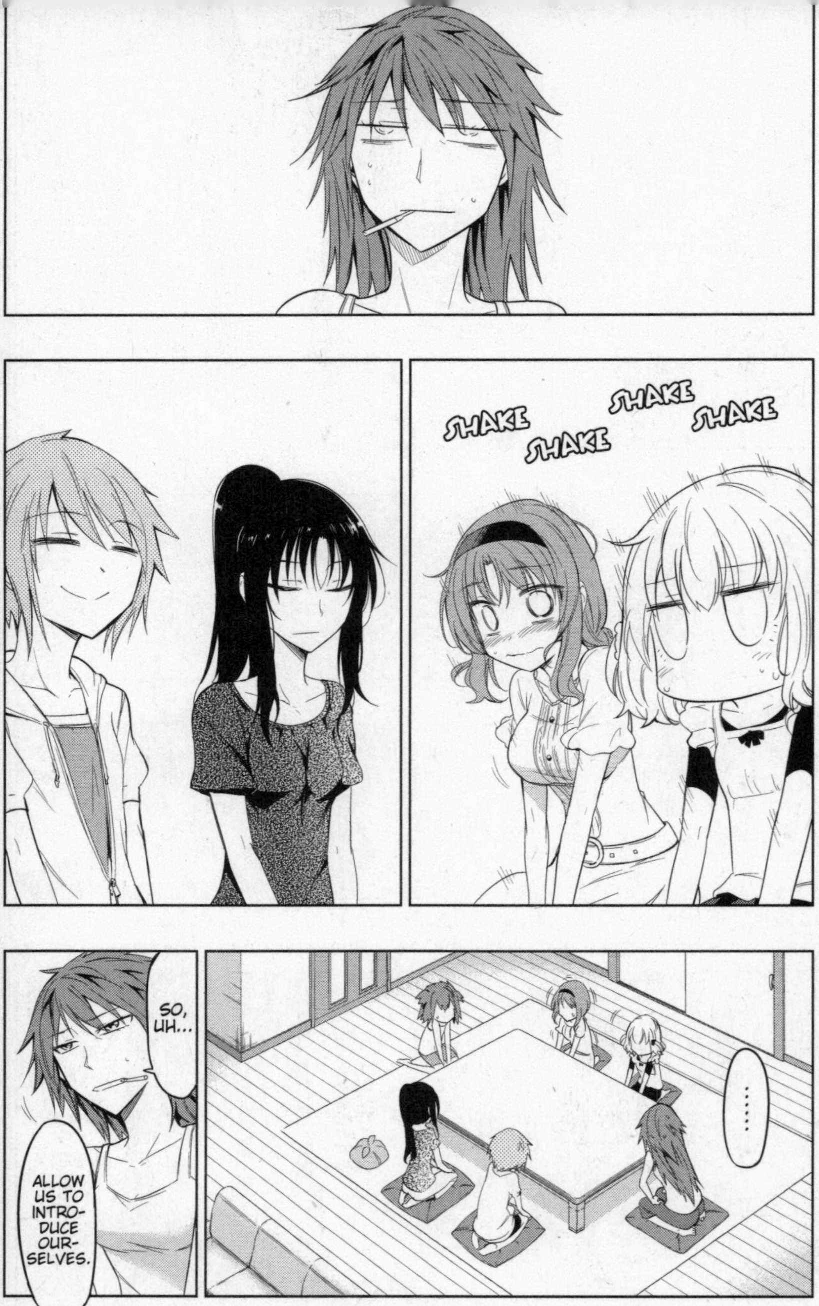
SHAKE
SHAKE
SHAKE
SHAKE
......
SO, UH...
ALLOW US TO INTRO-DUCE OUR-SELVES.

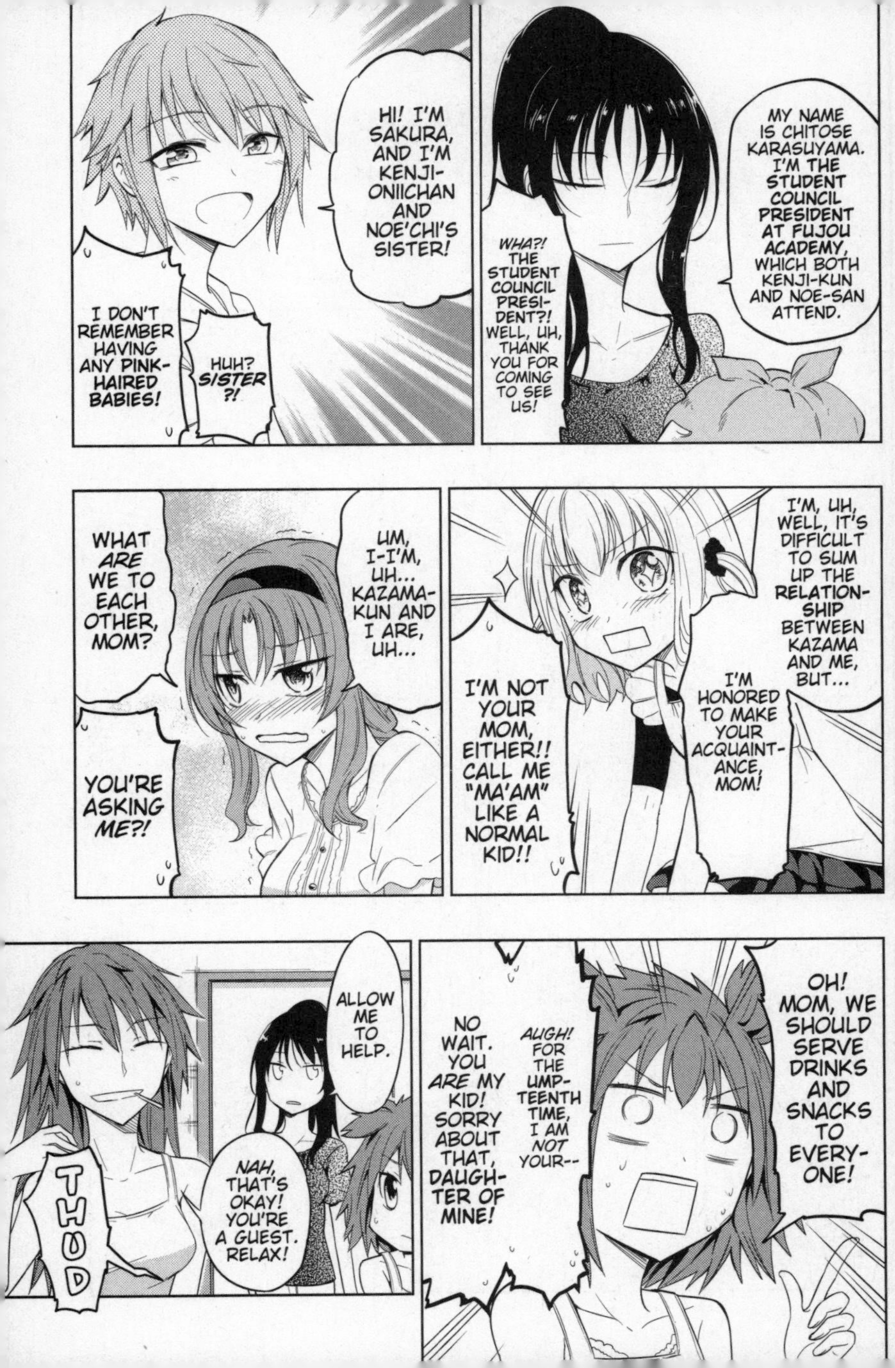
MY NAME IS CHITOSE KARASUYAMA. I'M THE STUDENT COUNCIL PRESIDENT AT FUJOU ACADEMY, WHICH BOTH KENJI-KUN AND NOE-SAN ATTEND.
WHA?! THE STUDENT COUNCIL PRESIDENT?! WELL, UH, THANK YOU FOR COMING TO SEE US!
HI! I'M SAKURA, AND I'M KENJI-ONIICHAN AND NOE'CHI'S SISTER!
HUH? SISTER?!
I DON'T REMEMBER HAVING ANY PINK-HAIRED BABIES!
I'M, UH, WELL, IT'S DIFFICULT TO SUM UP THE RELATIONSHIP BETWEEN KAZAMA AND ME, BUT...
I'M HONORED TO MAKE YOUR ACQUAINTANCE, MOM!
I'M NOT YOUR MOM, EITHER!! CALL ME "MA'AM" LIKE A NORMAL KID!!
UM, I-I'M, UH... KAZAMA-KUN AND I ARE, UH...
WHAT ARE WE TO EACH OTHER, MOM?
YOU'RE ASKING ME?!
OH! MOM, WE SHOULD SERVE DRINKS AND SNACKS TO EVERYONE!
AUGH! FOR THE UMPTEENTH TIME, I AM NOT YOUR--
NO WAIT. YOU ARE MY KID! SORRY ABOUT THAT, DAUGHTER OF MINE!
ALLOW ME TO HELP.
NAH, THAT'S OKAY! YOU'RE A GUEST. RELAX!
THUD

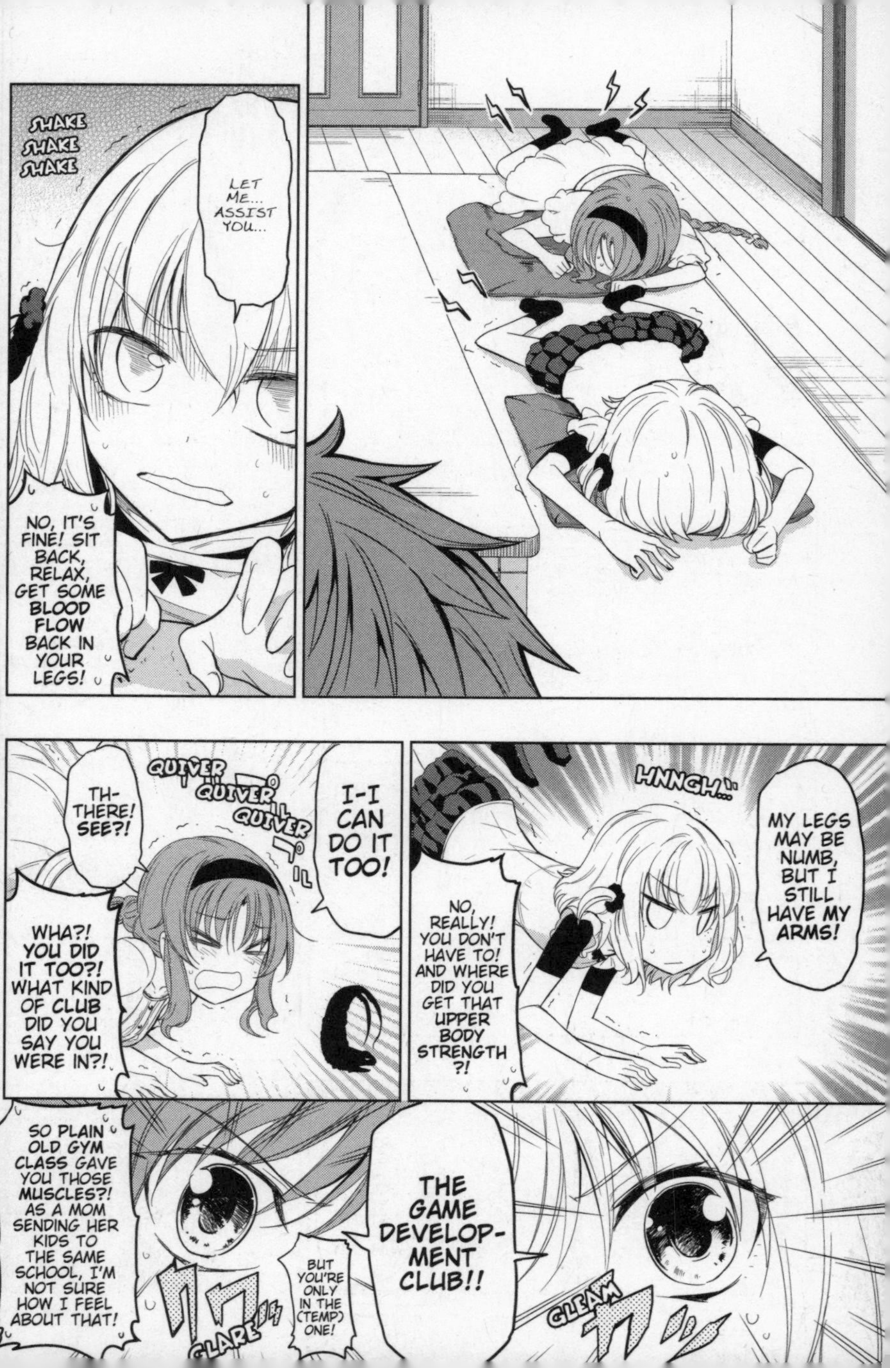
LET ME... ASSIST YOU...
SHAKE SHAKE SHAKE
NO, IT'S FINE! SIT BACK, RELAX, GET SOME BLOOD FLOW BACK IN YOUR LEGS!
HNNGH...
MY LEGS MAY BE NUMB, BUT I STILL HAVE MY ARMS!
NO, REALLY! YOU DON'T HAVE TO! AND WHERE DID YOU GET THAT UPPER BODY STRENGTH?!
I-I CAN DO IT TOO!
QUIVER QUIVER QUIVER
TH-THERE! SEE?!
WHA?! YOU DID IT TOO?! WHAT KIND OF CLUB DID YOU SAY YOU WERE IN?!
GLEAM
THE GAME DEVELOPMENT CLUB!!
BUT YOU'RE ONLY IN THE (TEMP) ONE!
GLARE
SO PLAIN OLD GYM CLASS GAVE YOU THOSE MUSCLES?! AS A MOM SENDING HER KIDS TO THE SAME SCHOOL, I'M NOT SURE HOW I FEEL ABOUT THAT!

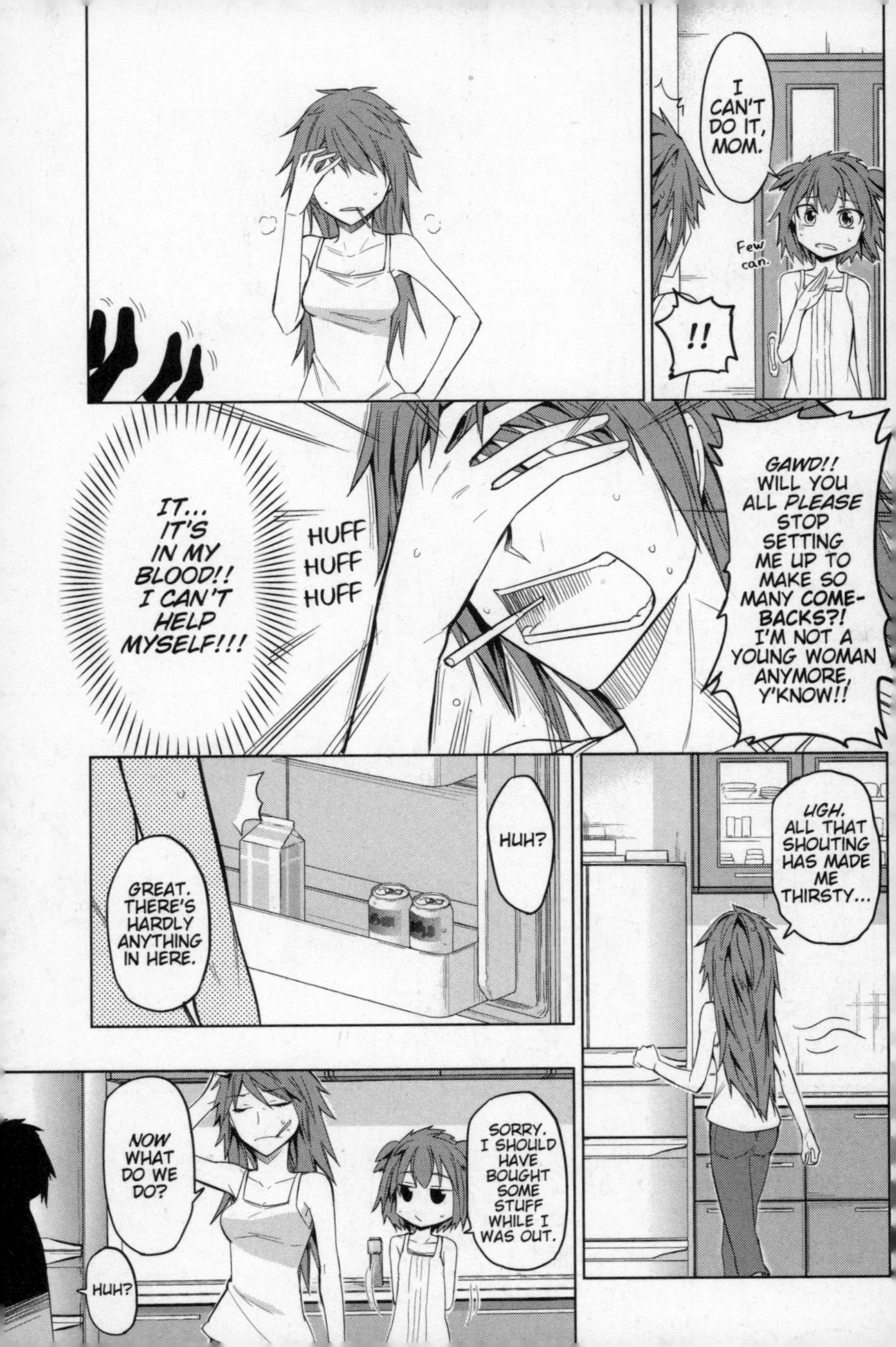
I CAN'T DO IT, MOM.
Few can.
!!
GAWD!! WILL YOU ALL PLEASE STOP SETTING ME UP TO MAKE SO MANY COME-BACKS?! I'M NOT A YOUNG WOMAN ANYMORE, Y'KNOW!!
HUFF HUFF HUFF
IT... IT'S IN MY BLOOD!! I CAN'T HELP MYSELF!!!
UGH. ALL THAT SHOUTING HAS MADE ME THIRSTY...
HUH?
GREAT. THERE'S HARDLY ANYTHING IN HERE.
SORRY. I SHOULD HAVE BOUGHT SOME STUFF WHILE I WAS OUT.
NOW WHAT DO WE DO?
HUH?

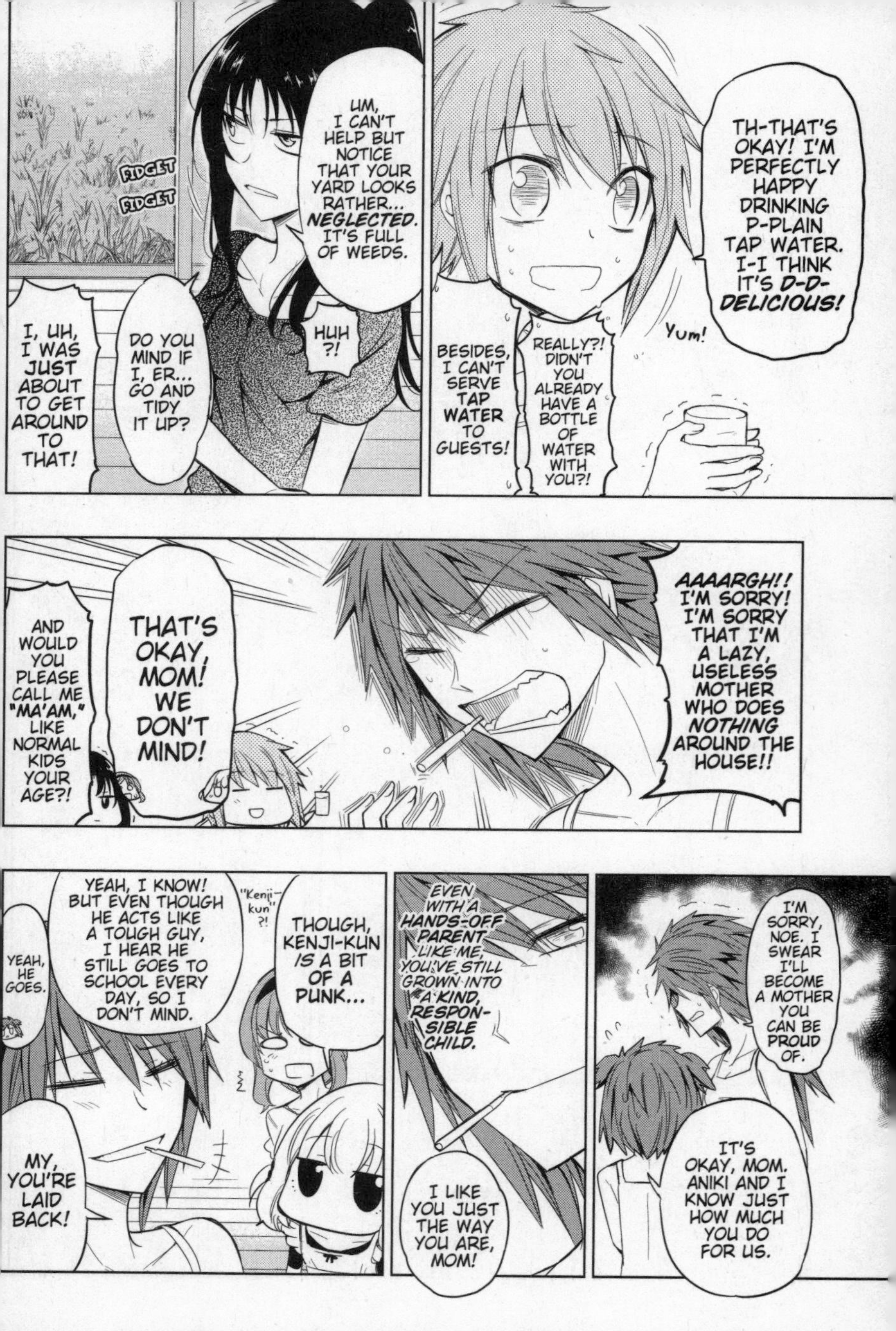
TH-THAT'S OKAY! I'M PERFECTLY HAPPY DRINKING P-PLAIN TAP WATER. I-I THINK IT'S D-D-DELICIOUS!
Yum!
REALLY?! DIDN'T YOU ALREADY HAVE A BOTTLE OF WATER WITH YOU?!
BESIDES, I CAN'T SERVE TAP WATER TO GUESTS!
UM, I CAN'T HELP BUT NOTICE THAT YOUR YARD LOOKS RATHER... NEGLECTED. IT'S FULL OF WEEDS.
FIDGET
FIDGET
HUH?!
DO YOU MIND IF I, ER... GO AND TIDY IT UP?
I, UH, I WAS JUST ABOUT TO GET AROUND TO THAT!
AAAARGH!! I'M SORRY! I'M SORRY THAT I'M A LAZY, USELESS MOTHER WHO DOES NOTHING AROUND THE HOUSE!!
THAT'S OKAY, MOM! WE DON'T MIND!
AND WOULD YOU PLEASE CALL ME "MA'AM," LIKE NORMAL KIDS YOUR AGE?!
I'M SORRY, NOE. I SWEAR I'LL BECOME A MOTHER YOU CAN BE PROUD OF.
IT'S OKAY, MOM. ANIKI AND I KNOW JUST HOW MUCH YOU DO FOR US.
EVEN WITH A HANDS-OFF PARENT LIKE ME, YOU'VE STILL GROWN INTO A KIND, RESPONSIBLE CHILD.
I LIKE YOU JUST THE WAY YOU ARE, MOM!
THOUGH, KENJI-KUN IS A BIT OF A PUNK...
"Kenji-kun"?!
YEAH, I KNOW! BUT EVEN THOUGH HE ACTS LIKE A TOUGH GUY, I HEAR HE STILL GOES TO SCHOOL EVERY DAY, SO I DON'T MIND.
YEAH, HE GOES.
MY, YOU'RE LAID BACK!

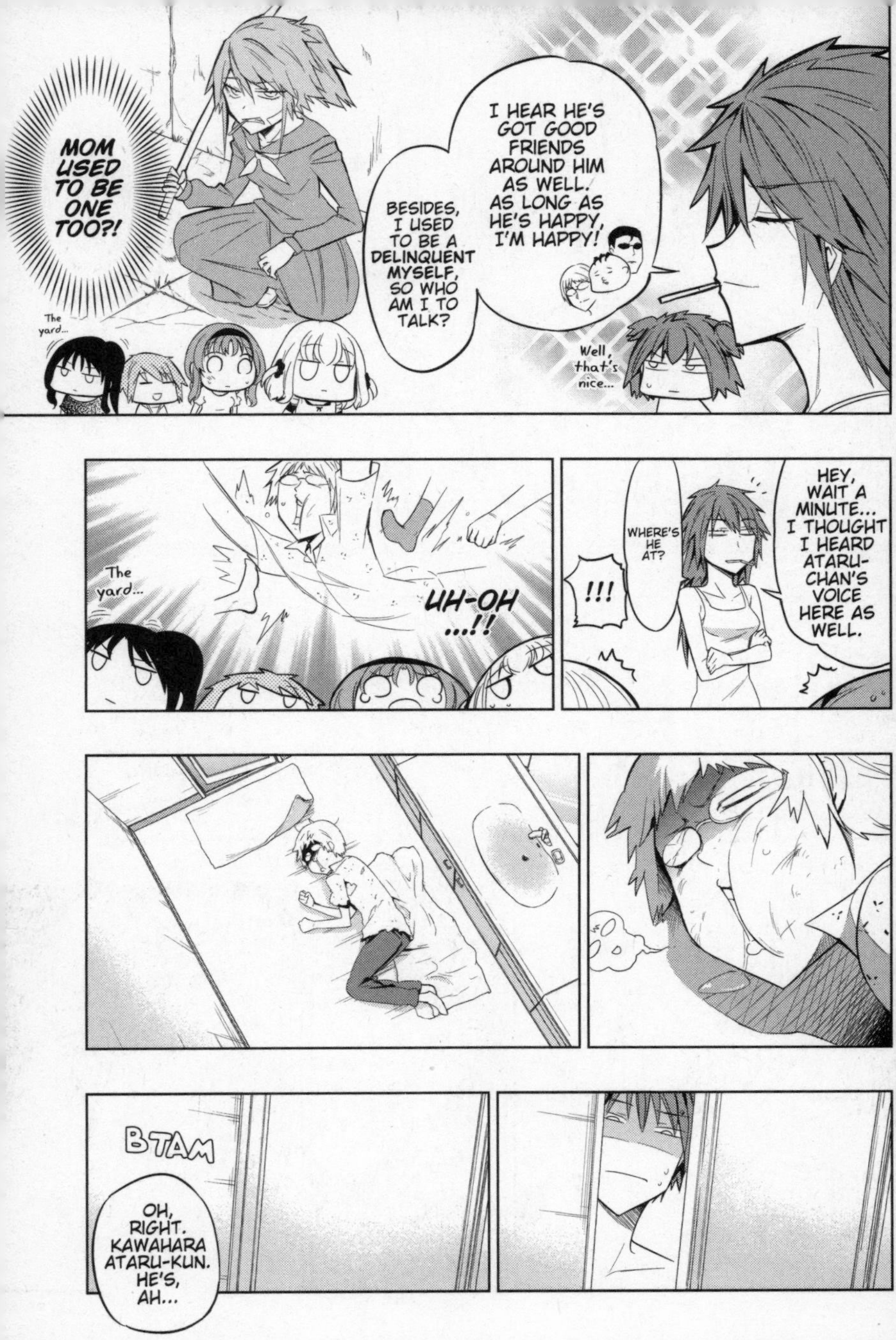
I HEAR HE'S GOT GOOD FRIENDS AROUND HIM AS WELL. AS LONG AS HE'S HAPPY, I'M HAPPY!
Well, that's nice...
BESIDES, I USED TO BE A DELINQUENT MYSELF, SO WHO AM I TO TALK?
MOM USED TO BE ONE TOO?!
The yard...
HEY, WAIT A MINUTE... I THOUGHT I HEARD ATARU-CHAN'S VOICE HERE AS WELL.
WHERE'S HE AT?
!!!
UH-OH ...!!
The yard...
BTAM
OH, RIGHT. KAWAHARA ATARU-KUN. HE'S, AH...

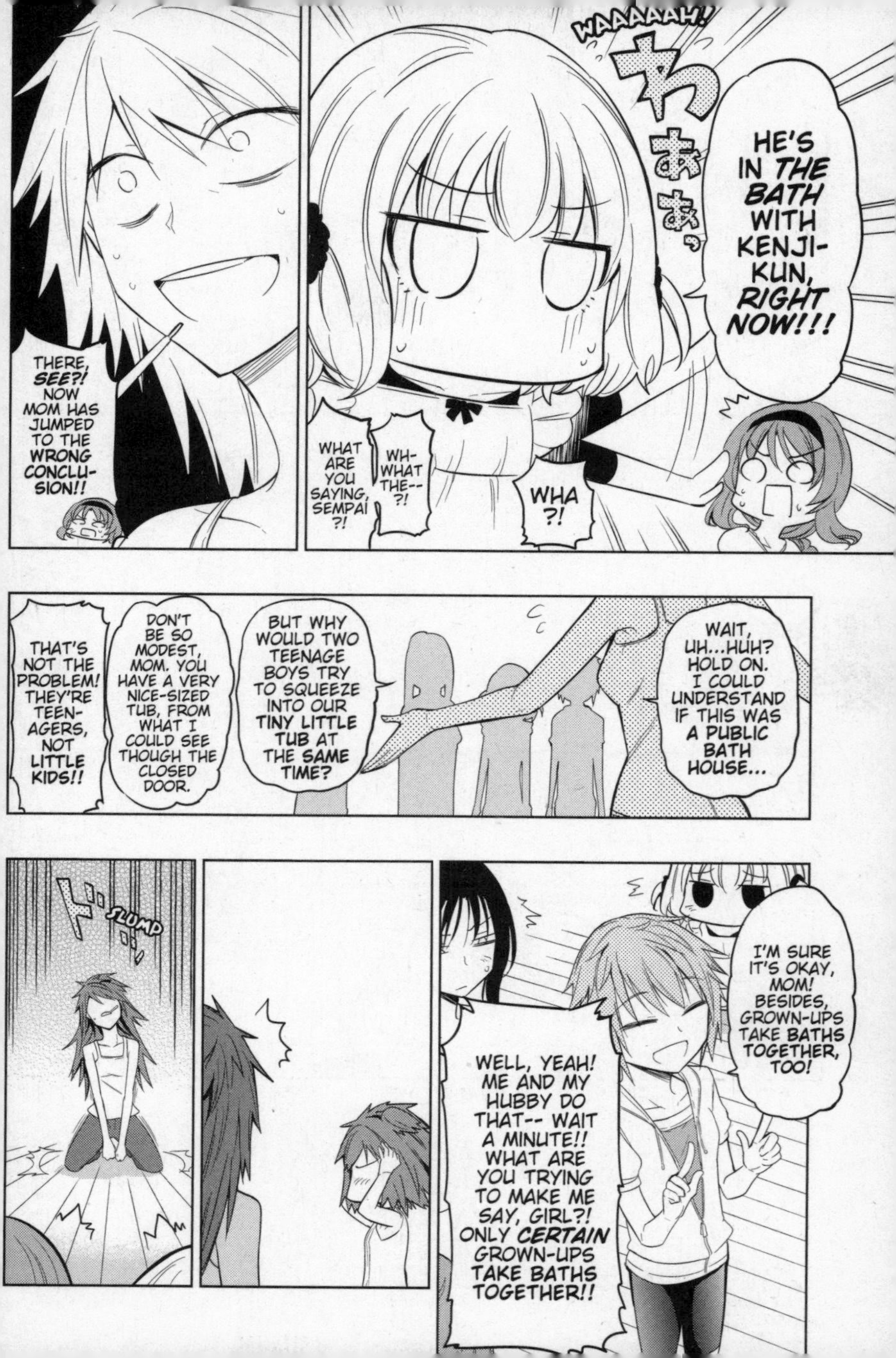
WAAAAAH!
わぁぁっ
HE'S IN THE BATH WITH KENJI-KUN, RIGHT NOW!!!
WHA?!
WH-WHAT THE--?!
WHAT ARE YOU SAYING, SEMPAI?!
THERE, SEE?! NOW MOM HAS JUMPED TO THE WRONG CONCLUSION!!
WAIT, UH...HUH? HOLD ON. I COULD UNDERSTAND IF THIS WAS A PUBLIC BATH HOUSE...
BUT WHY WOULD TWO TEENAGE BOYS TRY TO SQUEEZE INTO OUR TINY LITTLE TUB AT THE SAME TIME?
DON'T BE SO MODEST, MOM. YOU HAVE A VERY NICE-SIZED TUB, FROM WHAT I COULD SEE THOUGH THE CLOSED DOOR.
THAT'S NOT THE PROBLEM! THEY'RE TEEN-AGERS, NOT LITTLE KIDS!!
I'M SURE IT'S OKAY, MOM! BESIDES, GROWN-UPS TAKE BATHS TOGETHER, TOO!
WELL, YEAH! ME AND MY HUBBY DO THAT-- WAIT A MINUTE!! WHAT ARE YOU TRYING TO MAKE ME SAY, GIRL?! ONLY CERTAIN GROWN-UPS TAKE BATHS TOGETHER!!
ド
SLUMP

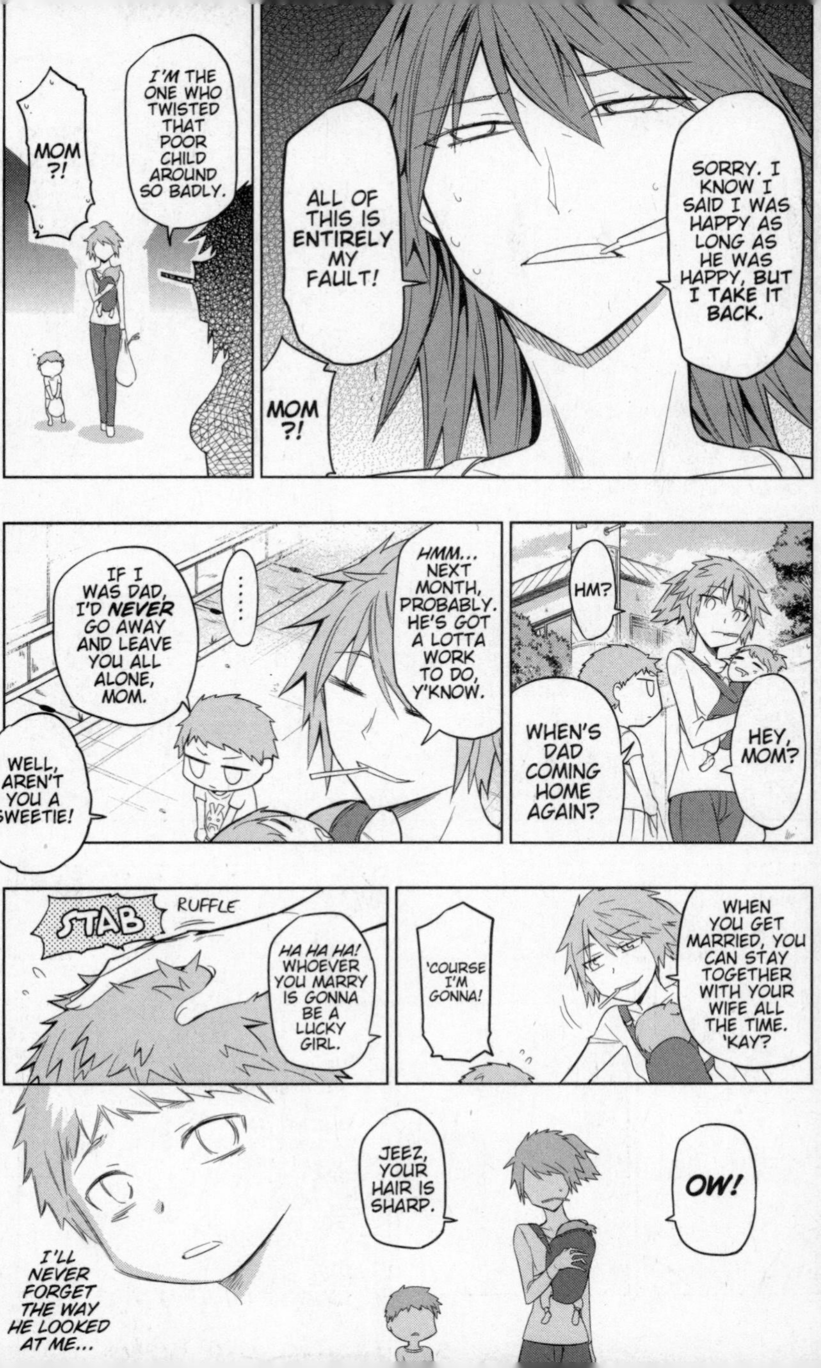
SORRY. I KNOW I SAID I WAS HAPPY AS LONG AS HE WAS HAPPY, BUT I TAKE IT BACK.
ALL OF THIS IS ENTIRELY MY FAULT!
MOM ?!
I'M THE ONE WHO TWISTED THAT POOR CHILD AROUND SO BADLY.
MOM ?!
HEY, MOM?
HM?
WHEN'S DAD COMING HOME AGAIN?
HMM... NEXT MONTH, PROBABLY. HE'S GOT A LOTTA WORK TO DO, Y'KNOW.
......
IF I WAS DAD, I'D NEVER GO AWAY AND LEAVE YOU ALL ALONE, MOM.
WELL, AREN'T YOU A SWEETIE!
WHEN YOU GET MARRIED, YOU CAN STAY TOGETHER WITH YOUR WIFE ALL THE TIME. 'KAY?
'COURSE I'M GONNA!
HA HA HA! WHOEVER YOU MARRY IS GONNA BE A LUCKY GIRL.
RUFFLE
STAB
OW!
JEEZ, YOUR HAIR IS SHARP.
I'LL NEVER FORGET THE WAY HE LOOKED AT ME...

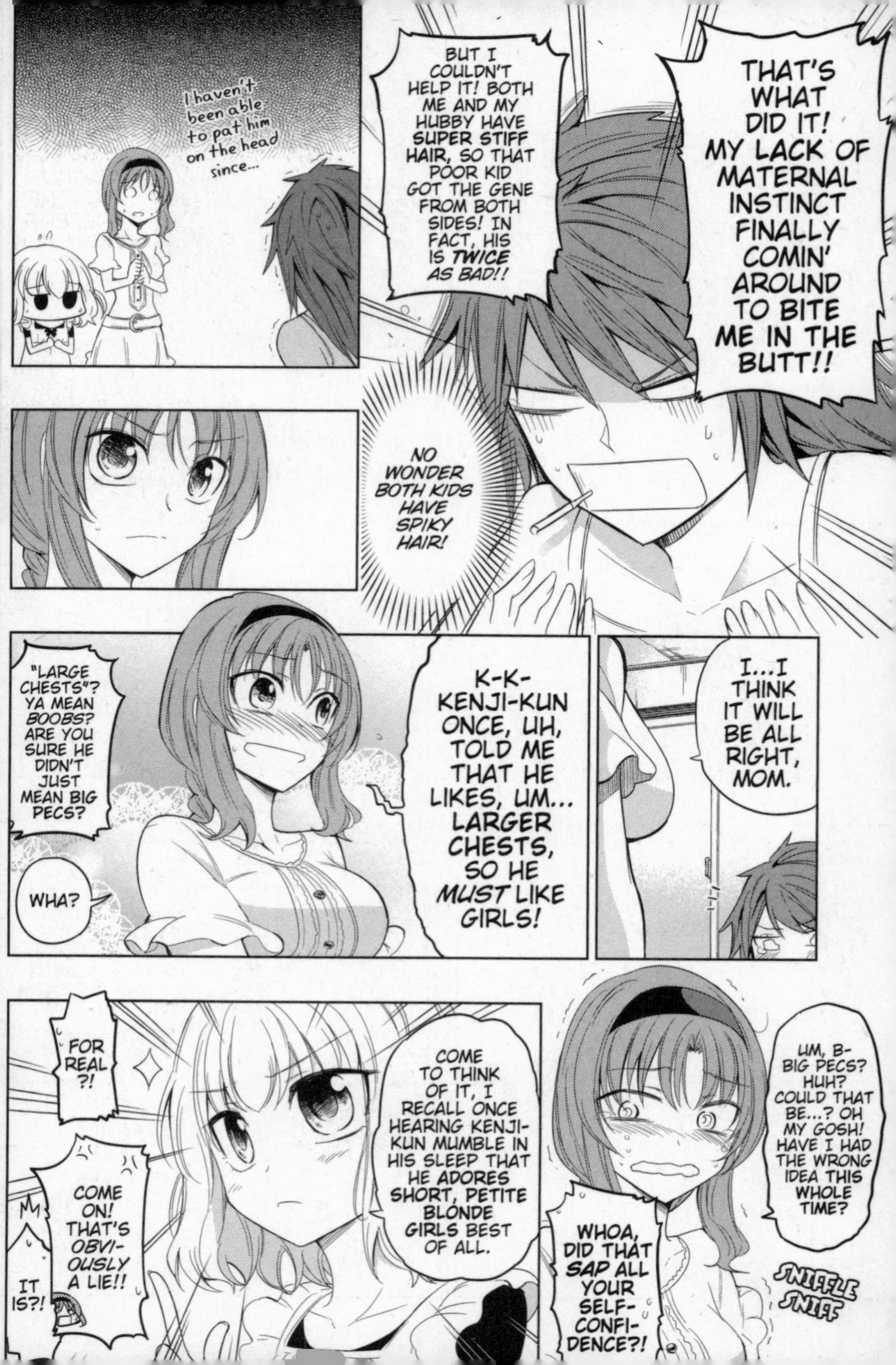
THAT'S WHAT DID IT! MY LACK OF MATERNAL INSTINCT FINALLY COMIN' AROUND TO BITE ME IN THE BUTT!!
BUT I COULDN'T HELP IT! BOTH ME AND MY HUBBY HAVE SUPER STIFF HAIR, SO THAT POOR KID GOT THE GENE FROM BOTH SIDES! IN FACT, HIS IS TWICE AS BAD!!
NO WONDER BOTH KIDS HAVE SPIKY HAIR!
I haven't been able to pat him on the head since...
I...I THINK IT WILL BE ALL RIGHT, MOM.
K-K-KENJI-KUN ONCE, UH, TOLD ME THAT HE LIKES, UM... LARGER CHESTS, SO HE MUST LIKE GIRLS!
"LARGE CHESTS"? YA MEAN BOOBS? ARE YOU SURE HE DIDN'T JUST MEAN BIG PECS?
WHA?
UM, B-BIG PECS? HUH? COULD THAT BE...? OH MY GOSH! HAVE I HAD THE WRONG IDEA THIS WHOLE TIME?
WHOA, DID THAT SAP ALL YOUR SELF-CONFIDENCE?!
SNIFFLE SNIFF
COME TO THINK OF IT, I RECALL ONCE HEARING KENJI-KUN MUMBLE IN HIS SLEEP THAT HE ADORES SHORT, PETITE BLONDE GIRLS BEST OF ALL.
FOR REAL?!
COME ON! THAT'S OBVIOUSLY A LIE!!
IT IS?!

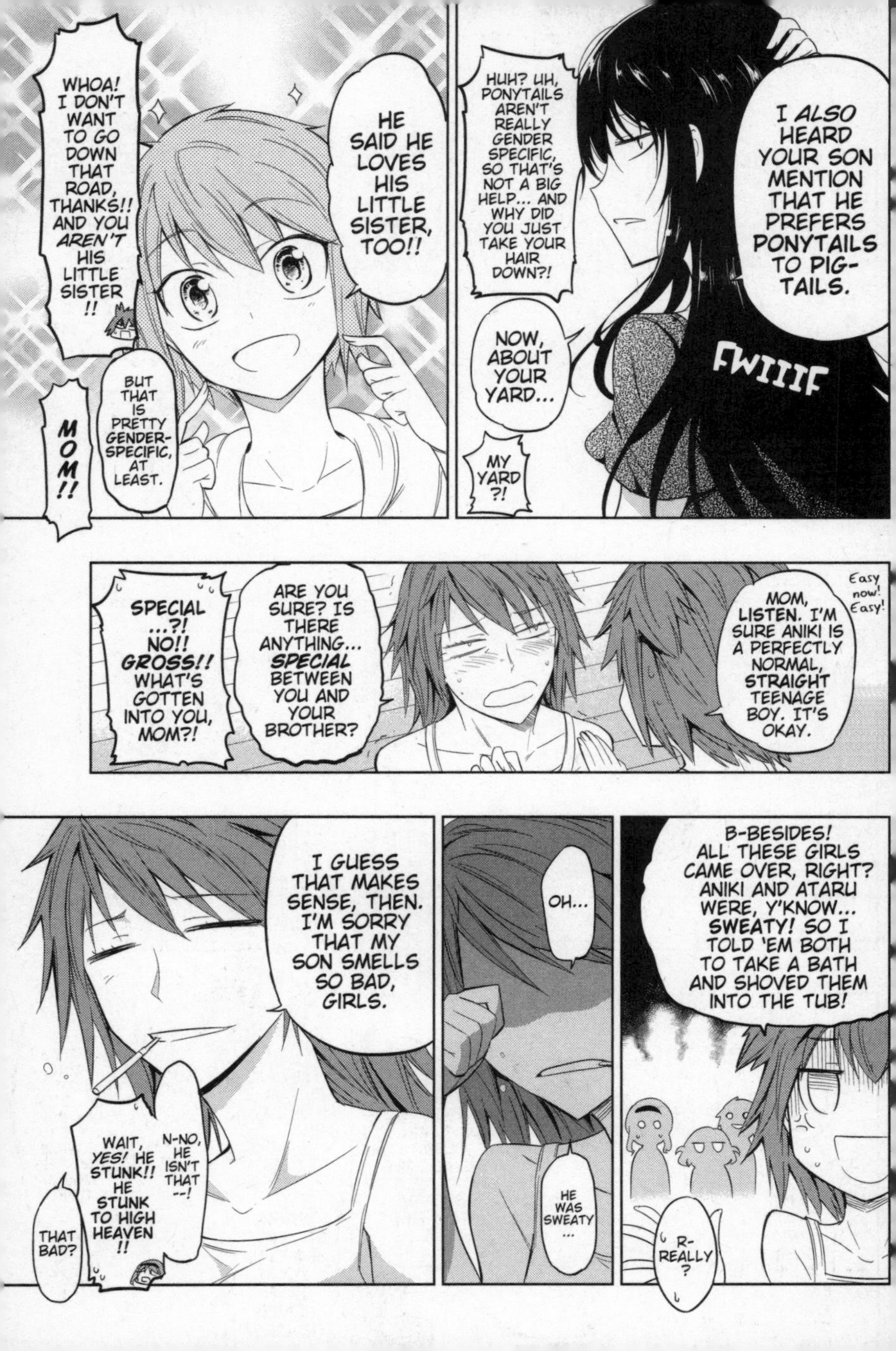

I ALSO HEARD YOUR SON MENTION THAT HE PREFERS PONYTAILS TO PIG-TAILS.
FWIIIF
HUH? UH, PONYTAILS AREN'T REALLY GENDER SPECIFIC, SO THAT'S NOT A BIG HELP... AND WHY DID YOU JUST TAKE YOUR HAIR DOWN?!
NOW, ABOUT YOUR YARD...
MY YARD?!
HE SAID HE LOVES HIS LITTLE SISTER, TOO!!
WHOA! I DON'T WANT TO GO DOWN THAT ROAD, THANKS!! AND YOU AREN'T HIS LITTLE SISTER!!
BUT THAT IS PRETTY GENDER-SPECIFIC, AT LEAST.
MOM!!
Easy now! Easy!
MOM, LISTEN. I'M SURE ANIKI IS A PERFECTLY NORMAL, STRAIGHT TEENAGE BOY. IT'S OKAY.
ARE YOU SURE? IS THERE ANYTHING... SPECIAL BETWEEN YOU AND YOUR BROTHER?
SPECIAL...?! NO!! GROSS!! WHAT'S GOTTEN INTO YOU, MOM?!
B-BESIDES! ALL THESE GIRLS CAME OVER, RIGHT? ANIKI AND ATARU WERE, Y'KNOW... SWEATY! SO I TOLD 'EM BOTH TO TAKE A BATH AND SHOVED THEM INTO THE TUB!
R-REALLY?
OH...
HE WAS SWEATY...
I GUESS THAT MAKES SENSE, THEN. I'M SORRY THAT MY SON SMELLS SO BAD, GIRLS.
N-NO, HE ISN'T THAT--!
WAIT, YES! HE STUNK!! HE STUNK TO HIGH HEAVEN!!
THAT BAD?

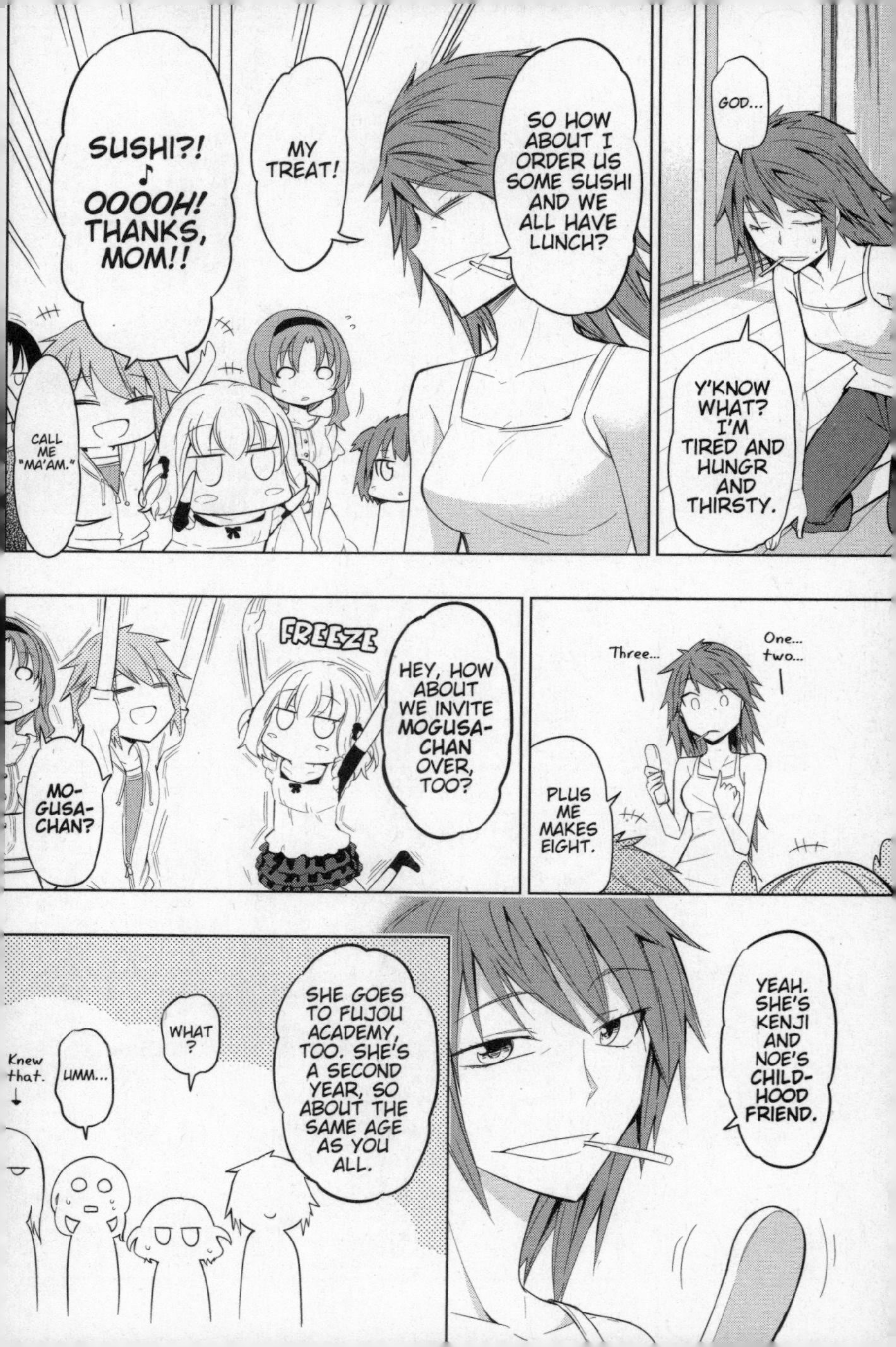
GOD...
Y'KNOW WHAT? I'M TIRED AND HUNGR AND THIRSTY.
SO HOW ABOUT I ORDER US SOME SUSHI AND WE ALL HAVE LUNCH?
MY TREAT!
SUSHI?! ♪ OOOOH! THANKS, MOM!!
CALL ME "MA'AM."
One... two...
Three...
PLUS ME MAKES EIGHT.
FREEZE
HEY, HOW ABOUT WE INVITE MOGUSA-CHAN OVER, TOO?
MO-GUSA-CHAN?
YEAH. SHE'S KENJI AND NOE'S CHILD-HOOD FRIEND.
SHE GOES TO FUJOU ACADEMY, TOO. SHE'S A SECOND YEAR, SO ABOUT THE SAME AGE AS YOU ALL.
WHAT?
UMM...
Knew that.

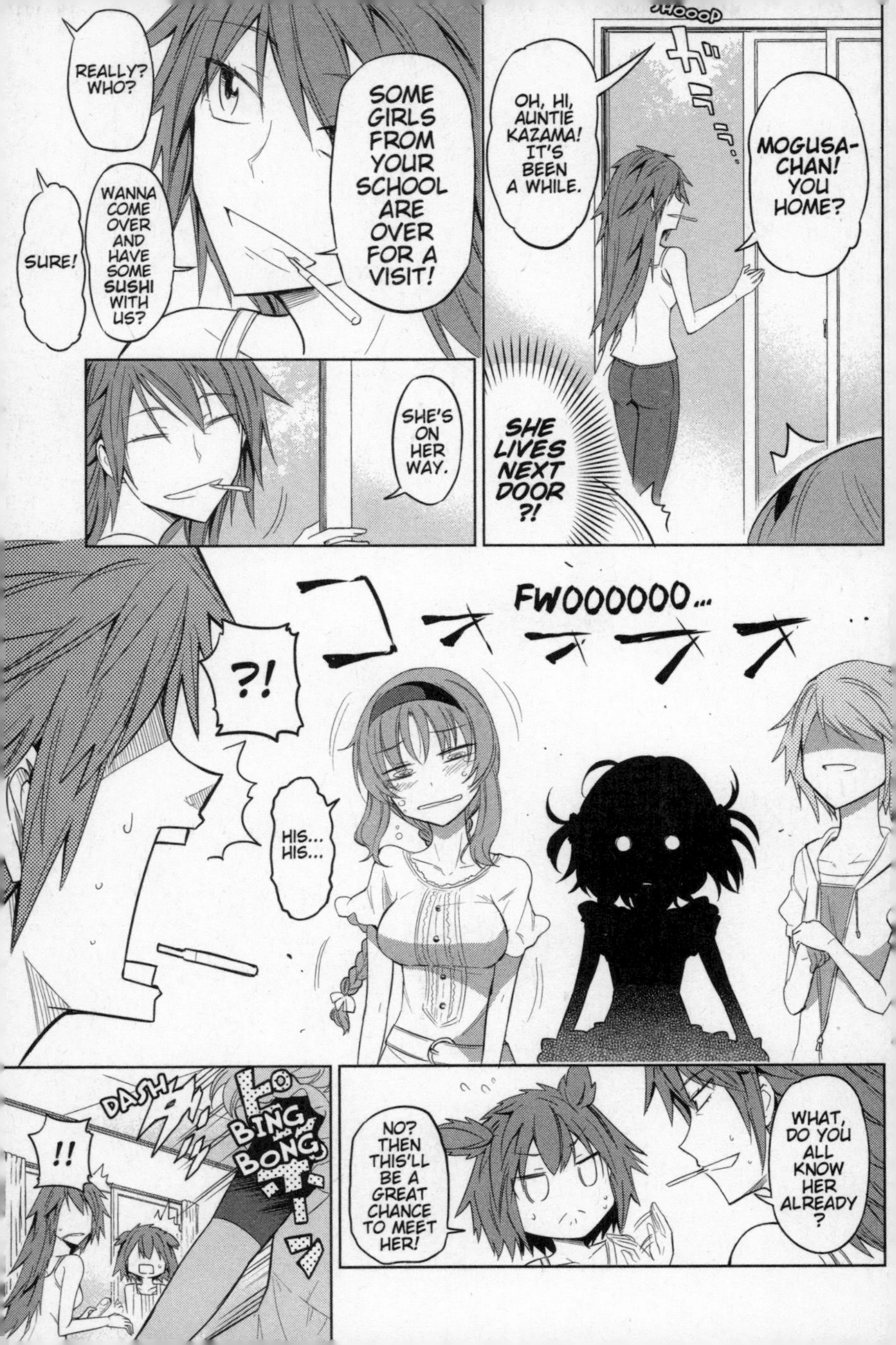
MOGUSA-CHAN! YOU HOME?
OH, HI, AUNTIE KAZAMA! IT'S BEEN A WHILE.
SHE LIVES NEXT DOOR ?!
SOME GIRLS FROM YOUR SCHOOL ARE OVER FOR A VISIT!
REALLY? WHO?
WANNA COME OVER AND HAVE SOME SUSHI WITH US?
SURE!
SHE'S ON HER WAY.
FWOOOOOO...
?!
HIS... HIS...
WHAT, DO YOU ALL KNOW HER ALREADY?
NO? THEN THIS'LL BE A GREAT CHANCE TO MEET HER!
BING BONG
DASH
!!

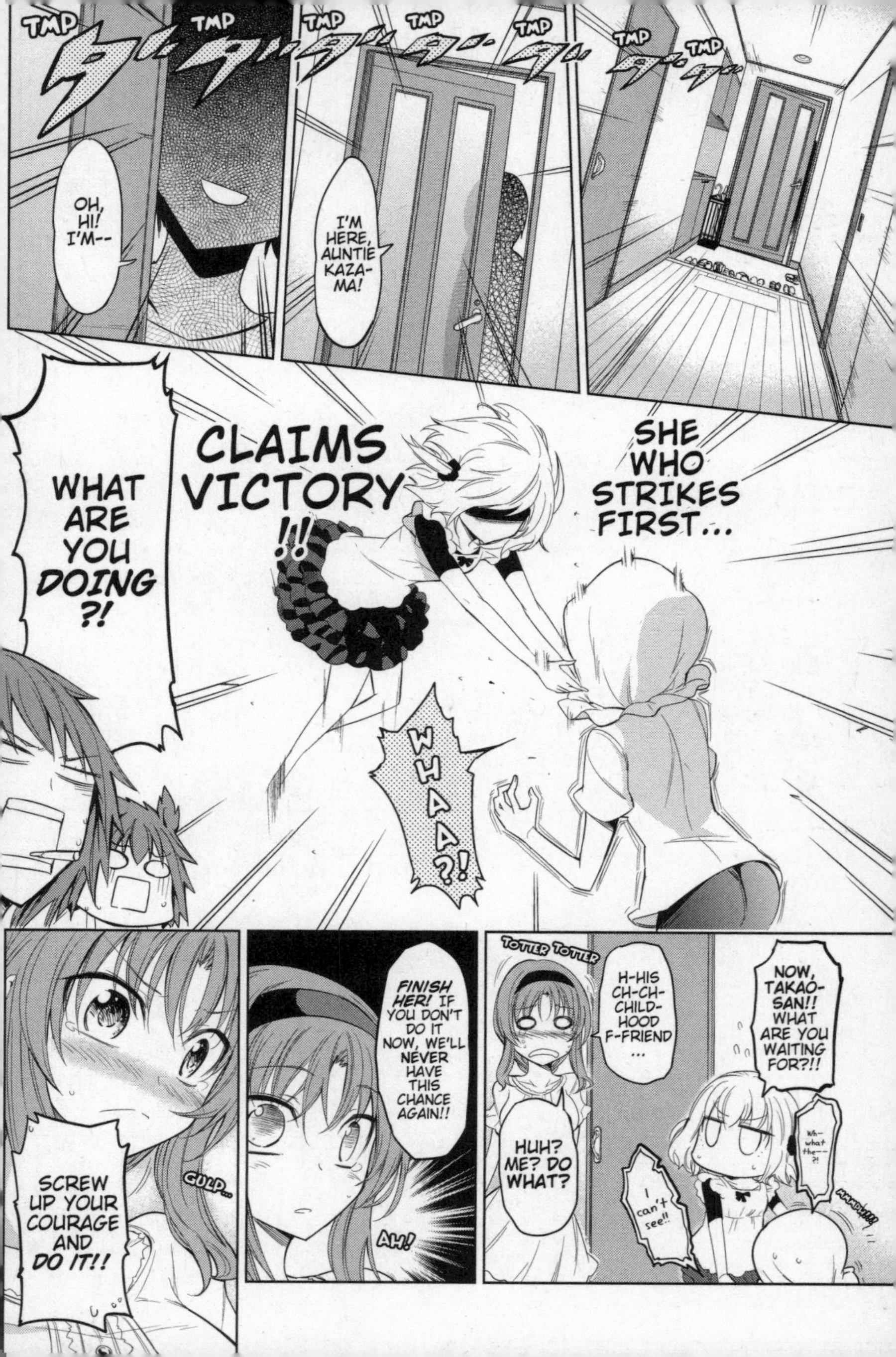
TMP TMP TMP TMP TMP TMP TMP
I'M HERE, AUNTIE KAZAMA!
OH, HI! I'M--
SHE WHO STRIKES FIRST...
CLAIMS VICTORY!!!
WHAT ARE YOU DOING?!
WHAA?!
NOW, TAKAO-SAN!! WHAT ARE YOU WAITING FOR?!!
TOTTER TOTTER
H-HIS CH-CH-CHILDHOOD F-FRIEND...
HUH? ME? DO WHAT?
Wh-what the--?!
I can't see!!
MMMPH!!!
FINISH HER! IF YOU DON'T DO IT NOW, WE'LL NEVER HAVE THIS CHANCE AGAIN!!
AH!
GULP...
SCREW UP YOUR COURAGE AND DO IT!!

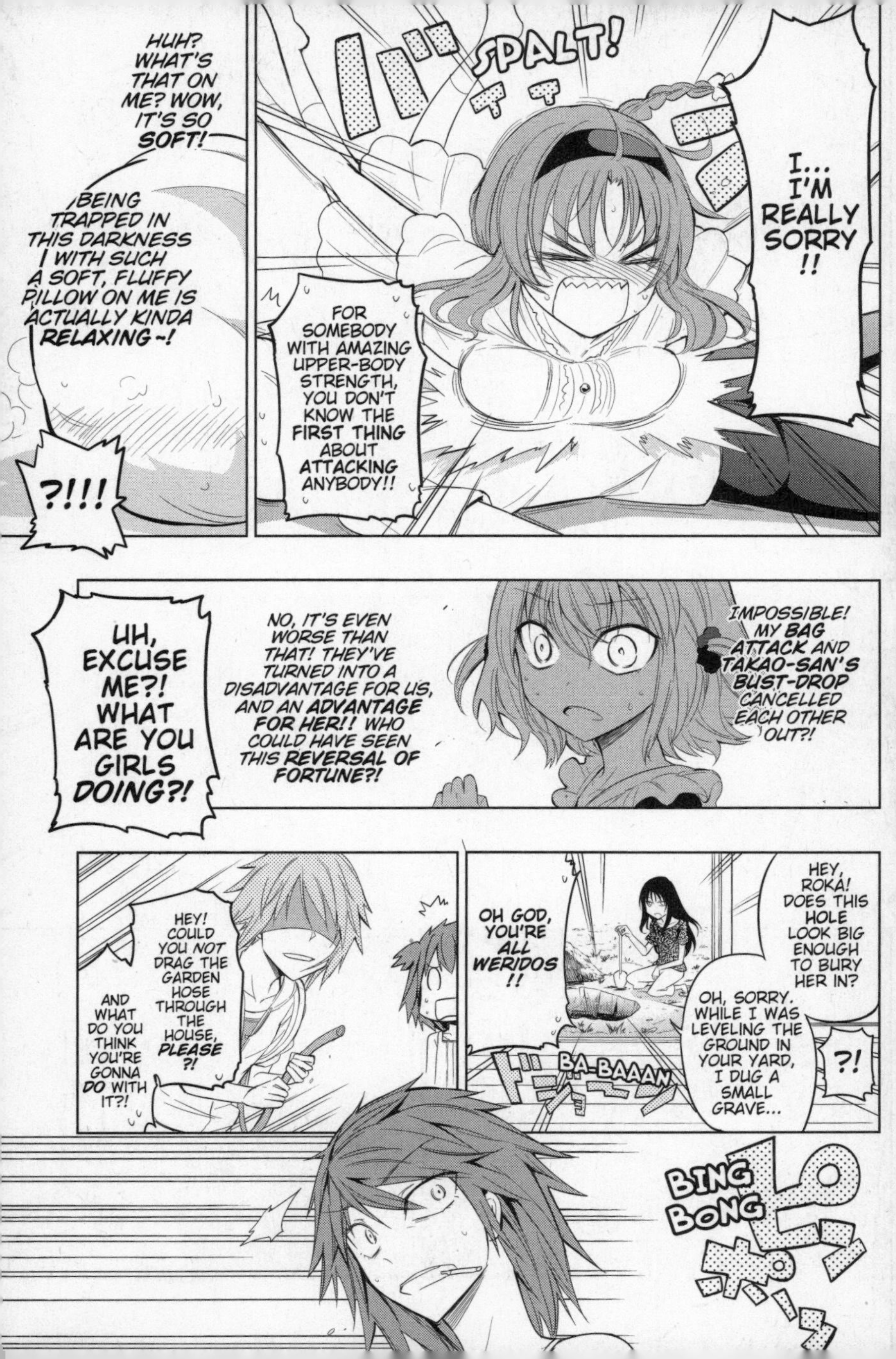
I... I'M REALLY SORRY!!
SPALT!
FOR SOMEBODY WITH AMAZING UPPER-BODY STRENGTH, YOU DON'T KNOW THE FIRST THING ABOUT ATTACKING ANYBODY!!
HUH? WHAT'S THAT ON ME? WOW, IT'S SO SOFT!
BEING TRAPPED IN THIS DARKNESS WITH SUCH A SOFT, FLUFFY PILLOW ON ME IS ACTUALLY KINDA RELAXING~!
?!!!
IMPOSSIBLE! MY BAG ATTACK AND TAKAO-SAN'S BUST-DROP CANCELLED EACH OTHER OUT?!
NO, IT'S EVEN WORSE THAN THAT! THEY'VE TURNED INTO A DISADVANTAGE FOR US, AND AN ADVANTAGE FOR HER!! WHO COULD HAVE SEEN THIS REVERSAL OF FORTUNE?!
UH, EXCUSE ME?! WHAT ARE YOU GIRLS DOING?!
HEY, ROKA! DOES THIS HOLE LOOK BIG ENOUGH TO BURY HER IN?
OH, SORRY. WHILE I WAS LEVELING THE GROUND IN YOUR YARD, I DUG A SMALL GRAVE...
?!
OH GOD, YOU'RE ALL WERIDOS!!
BA-BAAAN
HEY! COULD YOU NOT DRAG THE GARDEN HOSE THROUGH THE HOUSE, PLEASE?!
AND WHAT DO YOU THINK YOU'RE GONNA DO WITH IT?!
BING BONG

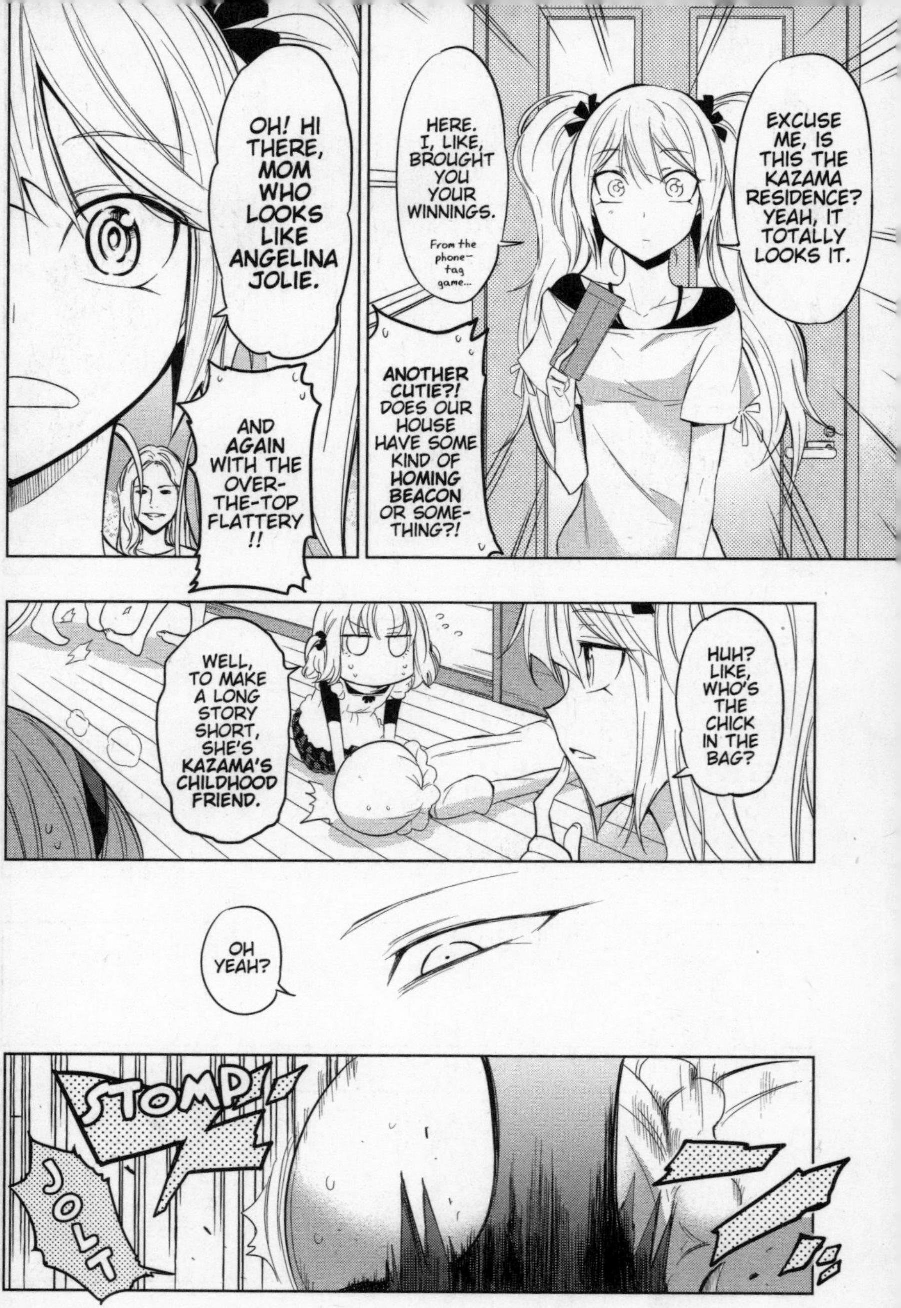
EXCUSE ME, IS THIS THE KAZAMA RESIDENCE? YEAH, IT TOTALLY LOOKS IT.
HERE. I, LIKE, BROUGHT YOU YOUR WINNINGS.
From the phone-tag game...
ANOTHER CUTIE?! DOES OUR HOUSE HAVE SOME KIND OF HOMING BEACON OR SOME-THING?!
OH! HI THERE, MOM WHO LOOKS LIKE ANGELINA JOLIE.
AND AGAIN WITH THE OVER-THE-TOP FLATTERY !!
HUH? LIKE, WHO'S THE CHICK IN THE BAG?
WELL, TO MAKE A LONG STORY SHORT, SHE'S KAZAMA'S CHILDHOOD FRIEND.
OH YEAH?
STOMP!
JOLT

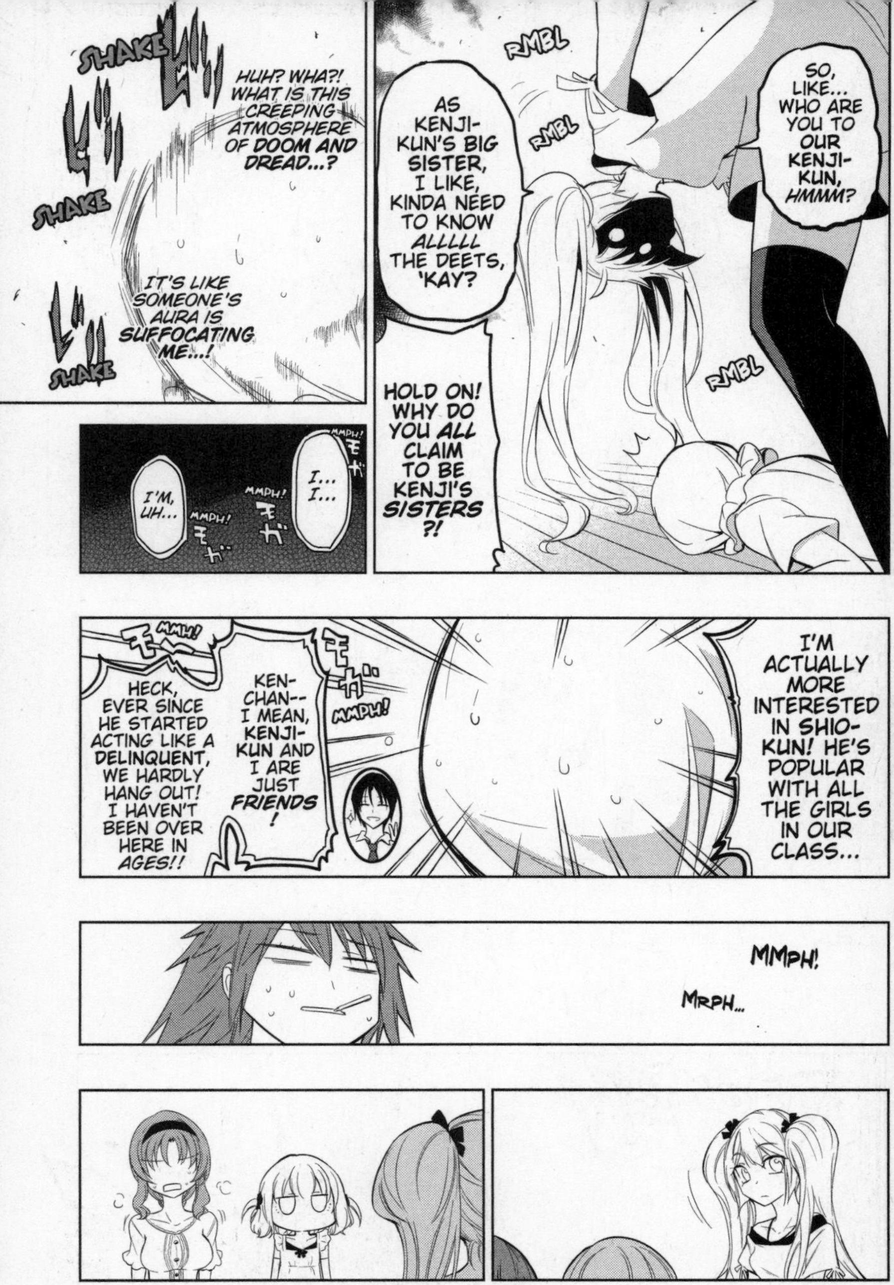
RMBL
SO, LIKE... WHO ARE YOU TO OUR KENJI-KUN, HMMM?
RMBL
AS KENJI-KUN'S BIG SISTER, I LIKE, KINDA NEED TO KNOW ALLLLL THE DEETS, 'KAY?
RMBL
HOLD ON! WHY DO YOU ALL CLAIM TO BE KENJI'S SISTERS?!
SHAKE
HUH? WHA?! WHAT IS THIS CREEPING ATMOSPHERE OF DOOM AND DREAD...?
SHAKE
IT'S LIKE SOMEONE'S AURA IS SUFFOCATING ME...!
SHAKE
MMPH!
I... I...
MMPH!
MMPH!
I'M, UH...
I'M ACTUALLY MORE INTERESTED IN SHIO-KUN! HE'S POPULAR WITH ALL THE GIRLS IN OUR CLASS...
MMPH!
KEN-CHAN-- I MEAN, KENJI-KUN AND I ARE JUST FRIENDS!
MMH!
HECK, EVER SINCE HE STARTED ACTING LIKE A DELINQUENT, WE HARDLY HANG OUT! I HAVEN'T BEEN OVER HERE IN AGES!!
MMPH!
MRPH...

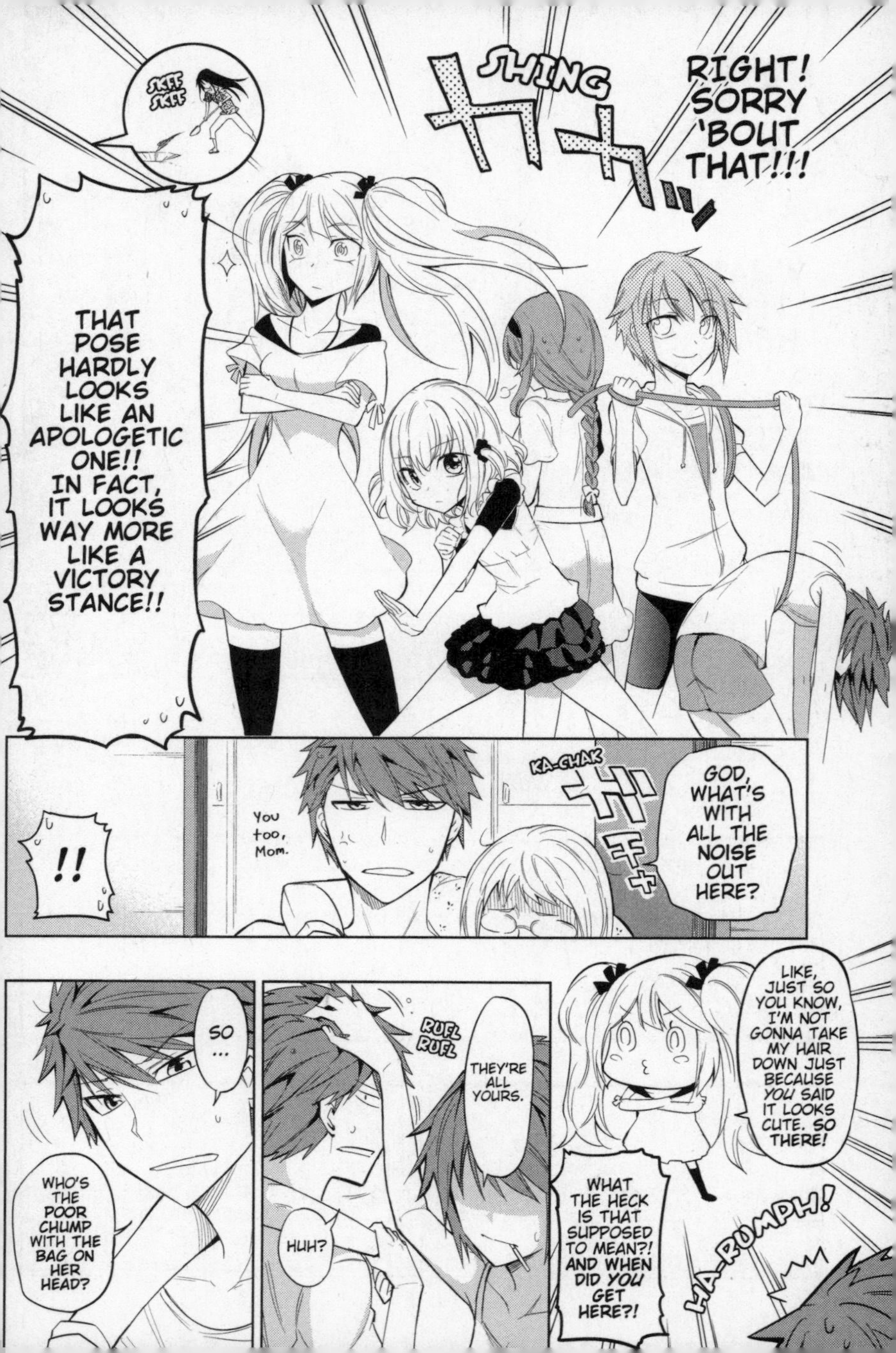
RIGHT! SORRY 'BOUT THAT!!!
SHING
SKFF SKFF
THAT POSE HARDLY LOOKS LIKE AN APOLOGETIC ONE!! IN FACT, IT LOOKS WAY MORE LIKE A VICTORY STANCE!!
GOD, WHAT'S WITH ALL THE NOISE OUT HERE?
KA-CHAK
You too, Mom.
!!
LIKE, JUST SO YOU KNOW, I'M NOT GONNA TAKE MY HAIR DOWN JUST BECAUSE *YOU* SAID IT LOOKS CUTE. SO THERE!
HA-RUMPH!
WHAT THE HECK IS THAT SUPPOSED TO MEAN?! AND WHEN DID *YOU* GET HERE?!
RUFL RUFL
THEY'RE ALL YOURS.
HUH?
SO ...
WHO'S THE POOR CHUMP WITH THE BAG ON HER HEAD?

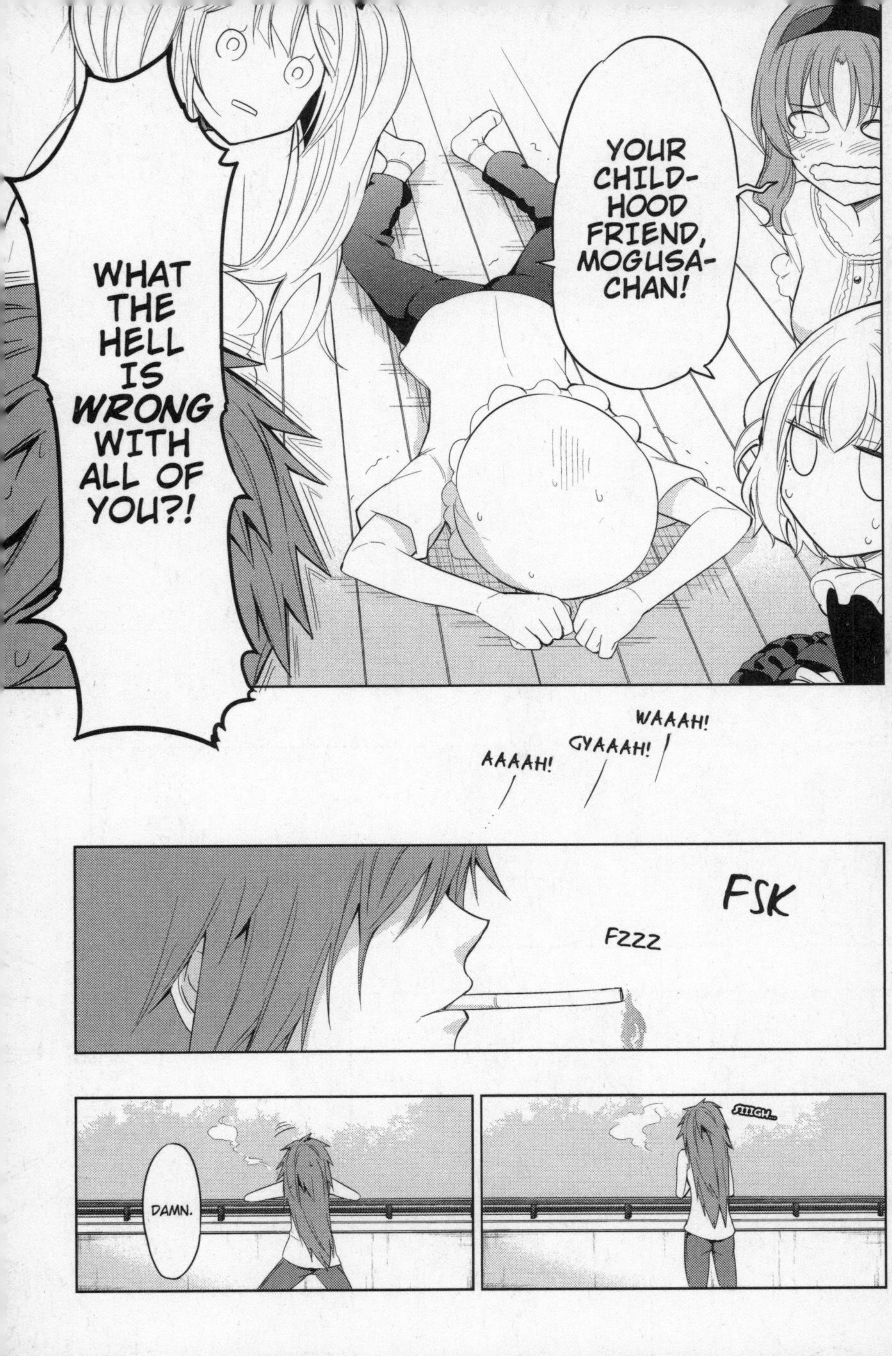
YOUR CHILDHOOD FRIEND, MOGUSA-CHAN!
WHAT THE HELL IS *WRONG* WITH ALL OF YOU?!
WAAAH!
GYAAAH!
AAAAH!
FSK
FZZZ
SIIIGH...
DAMN.

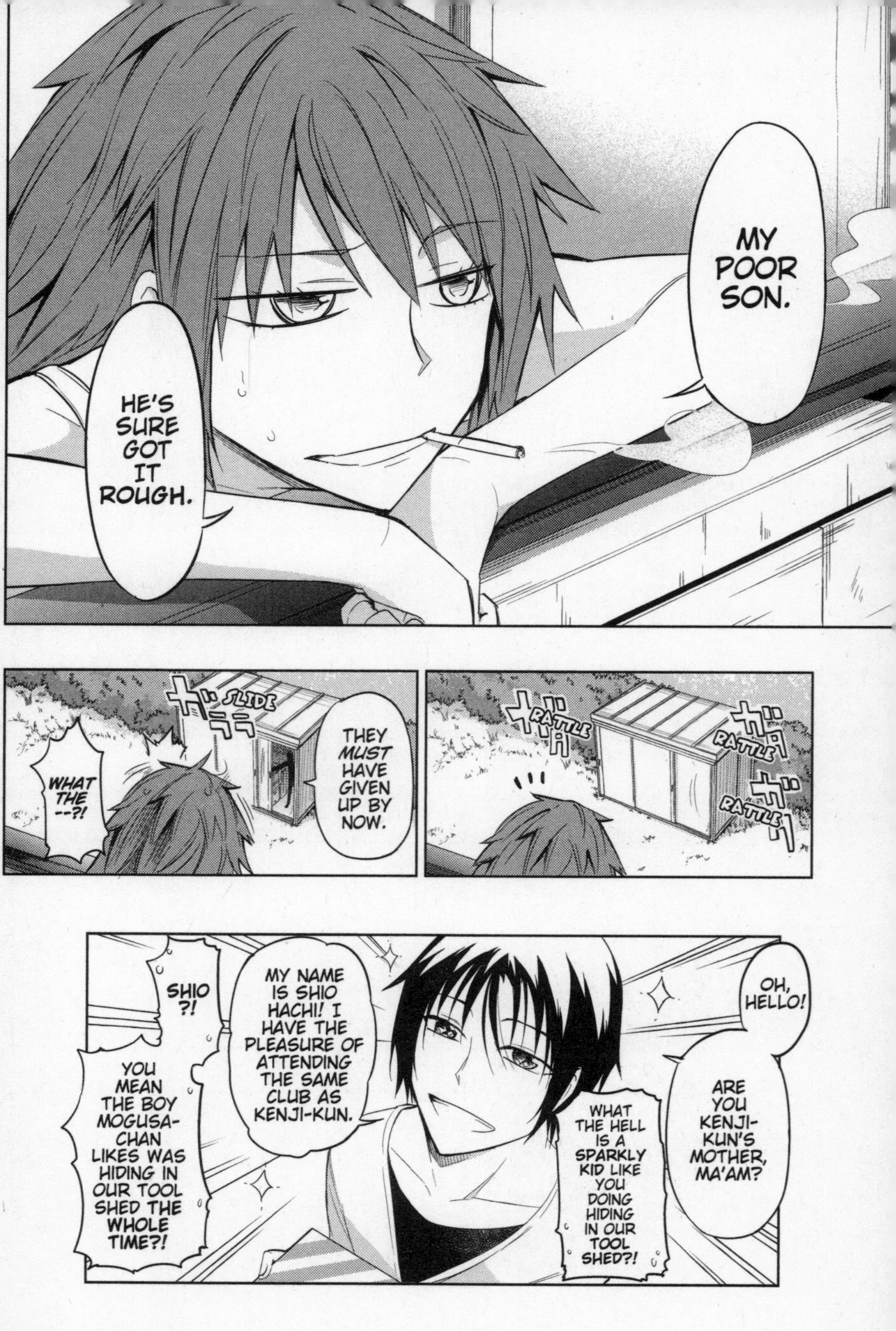
MY POOR SON.
HE'S SURE GOT IT ROUGH.
RATTLE
RATTLE
RATTLE
THEY *MUST* HAVE GIVEN UP BY NOW.
SLIDE
WHAT THE --?!
OH, HELLO!
ARE YOU KENJI-KUN'S MOTHER, MA'AM?
WHAT THE HELL IS A SPARKLY KID LIKE YOU DOING HIDING IN OUR TOOL SHED?!
MY NAME IS SHIO HACHI! I HAVE THE PLEASURE OF ATTENDING THE SAME CLUB AS KENJI-KUN.
SHIO?!
YOU MEAN THE BOY MOGUSA-CHAN LIKES WAS HIDING IN OUR TOOL SHED THE WHOLE TIME?!

Mogusa-chan?!
Huh? Where'd she go?!
SHVR SHVR SHVR SHVR

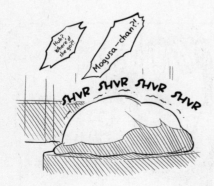

D-FRAGMENTS
ディーふらぐ!

Chapter 40
You Could Say That

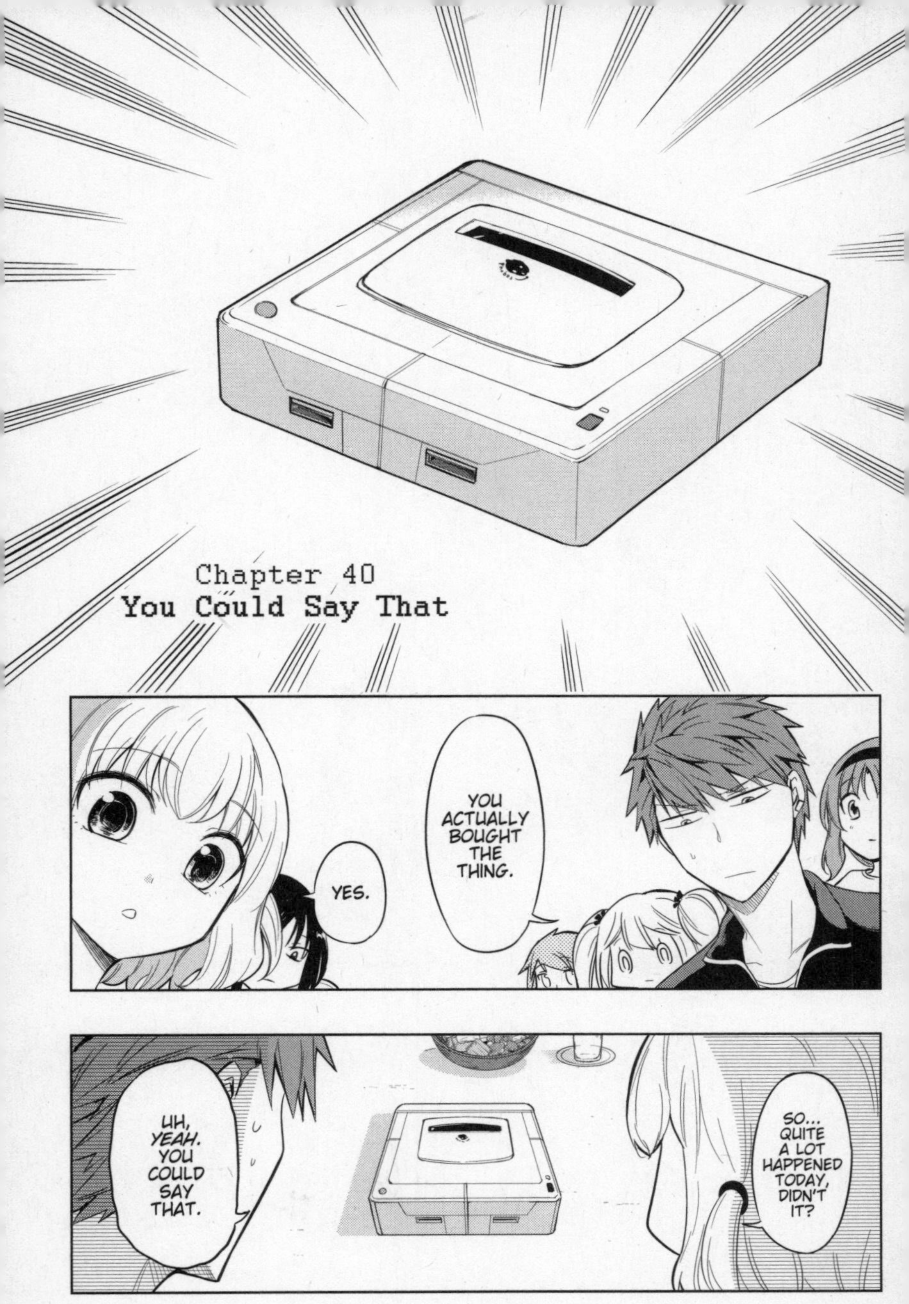
YOU ACTUALLY BOUGHT THE THING.
YES.
SO... QUITE A LOT HAPPENED TODAY, DIDN'T IT?
UH, YEAH. YOU COULD SAY THAT.

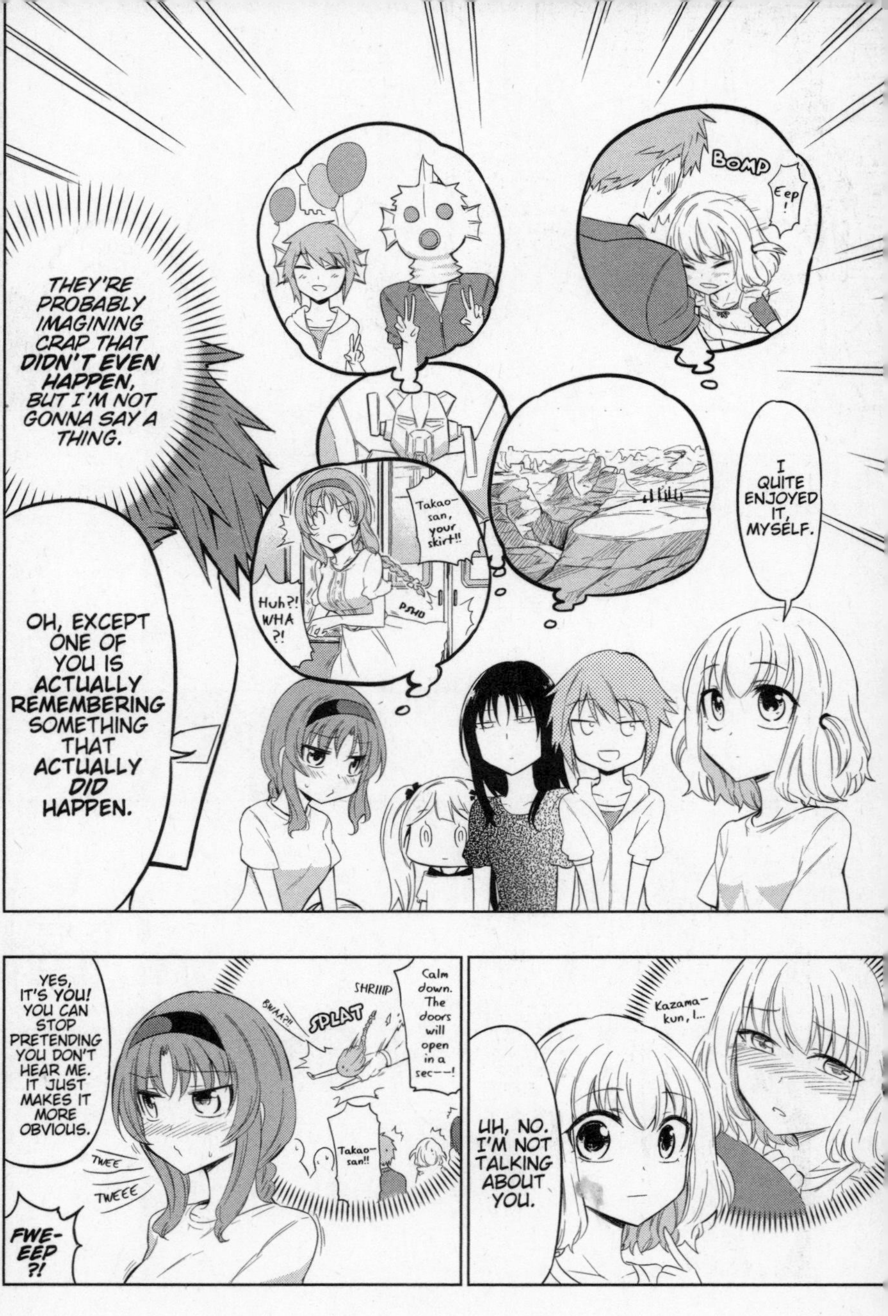
BOMP
Eep!
I QUITE ENJOYED IT, MYSELF.
Takao-san, your skirt!!
Huh?! WHA?!
PSHO
THEY'RE PROBABLY IMAGINING CRAP THAT DIDN'T EVEN HAPPEN, BUT I'M NOT GONNA SAY A THING.
OH, EXCEPT ONE OF YOU IS ACTUALLY REMEMBERING SOMETHING THAT ACTUALLY DID HAPPEN.
Kazama-kun, I...
UH, NO. I'M NOT TALKING ABOUT YOU.
Calm down. The doors will open in a sec--!
SHRIIIP
SPLAT
BWAA?!
Takao-san!!
YES, IT'S YOU! YOU CAN STOP PRETENDING YOU DON'T HEAR ME. IT JUST MAKES IT MORE OBVIOUS.
TWEE
TWEEE
FWEE-EEP?!

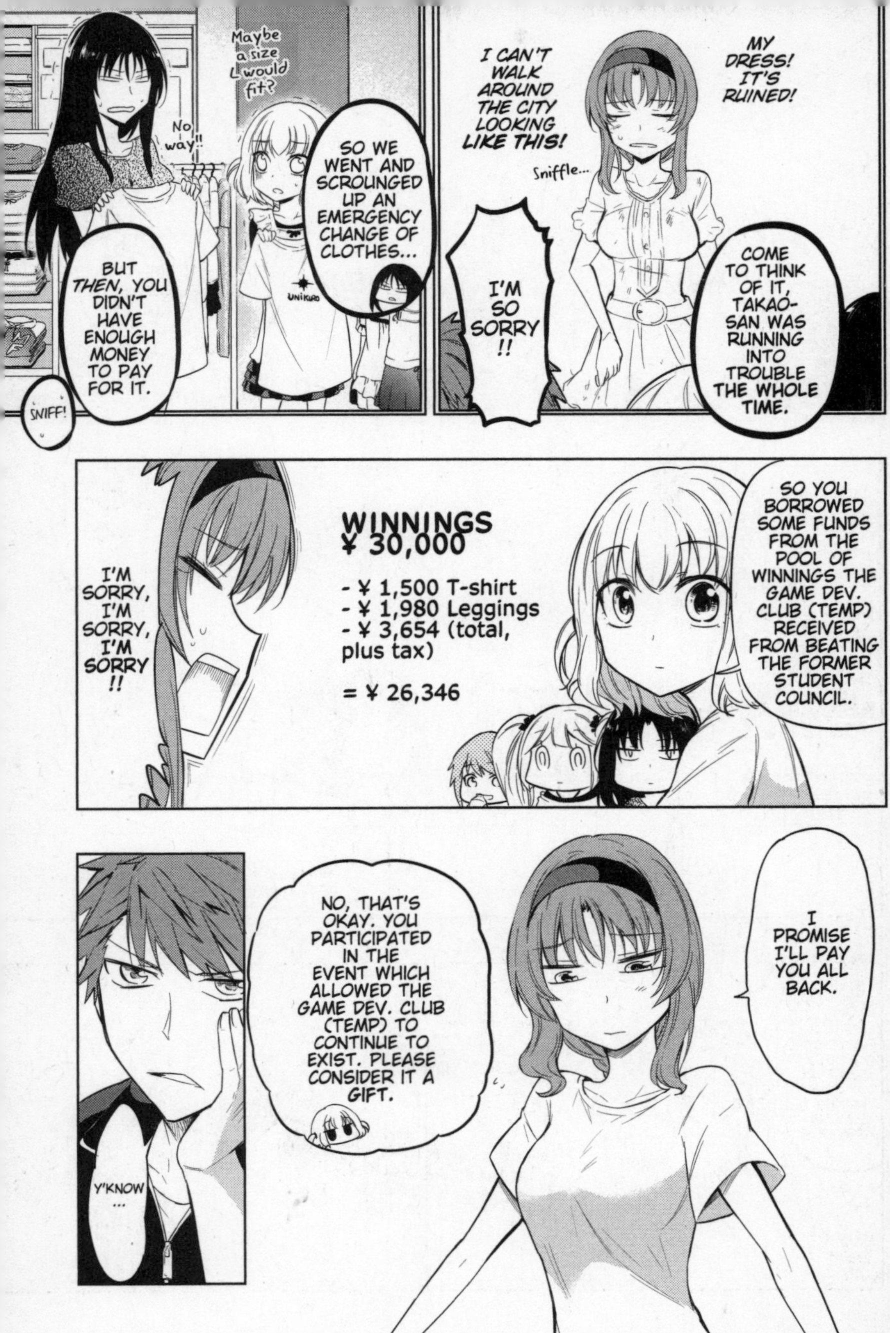
MY DRESS! IT'S RUINED!
I CAN'T WALK AROUND THE CITY LOOKING LIKE THIS!
Sniffle...
COME TO THINK OF IT, TAKAO-SAN WAS RUNNING INTO TROUBLE THE WHOLE TIME.
I'M SO SORRY!!
SO WE WENT AND SCROUNGED UP AN EMERGENCY CHANGE OF CLOTHES...
Maybe a size L would fit?
No way!!
UNIKURO
BUT THEN, YOU DIDN'T HAVE ENOUGH MONEY TO PAY FOR IT.
SNIFF!
SO YOU BORROWED SOME FUNDS FROM THE POOL OF WINNINGS THE GAME DEV. CLUB (TEMP) RECEIVED FROM BEATING THE FORMER STUDENT COUNCIL.
WINNINGS ¥ 30,000
- ¥ 1,500 T-shirt
- ¥ 1,980 Leggings
- ¥ 3,654 (total, plus tax)
= ¥ 26,346
I'M SORRY, I'M SORRY, I'M SORRY!!
I PROMISE I'LL PAY YOU ALL BACK.
NO, THAT'S OKAY. YOU PARTICIPATED IN THE EVENT WHICH ALLOWED THE GAME DEV. CLUB (TEMP) TO CONTINUE TO EXIST. PLEASE CONSIDER IT A GIFT.
Y'KNOW ...

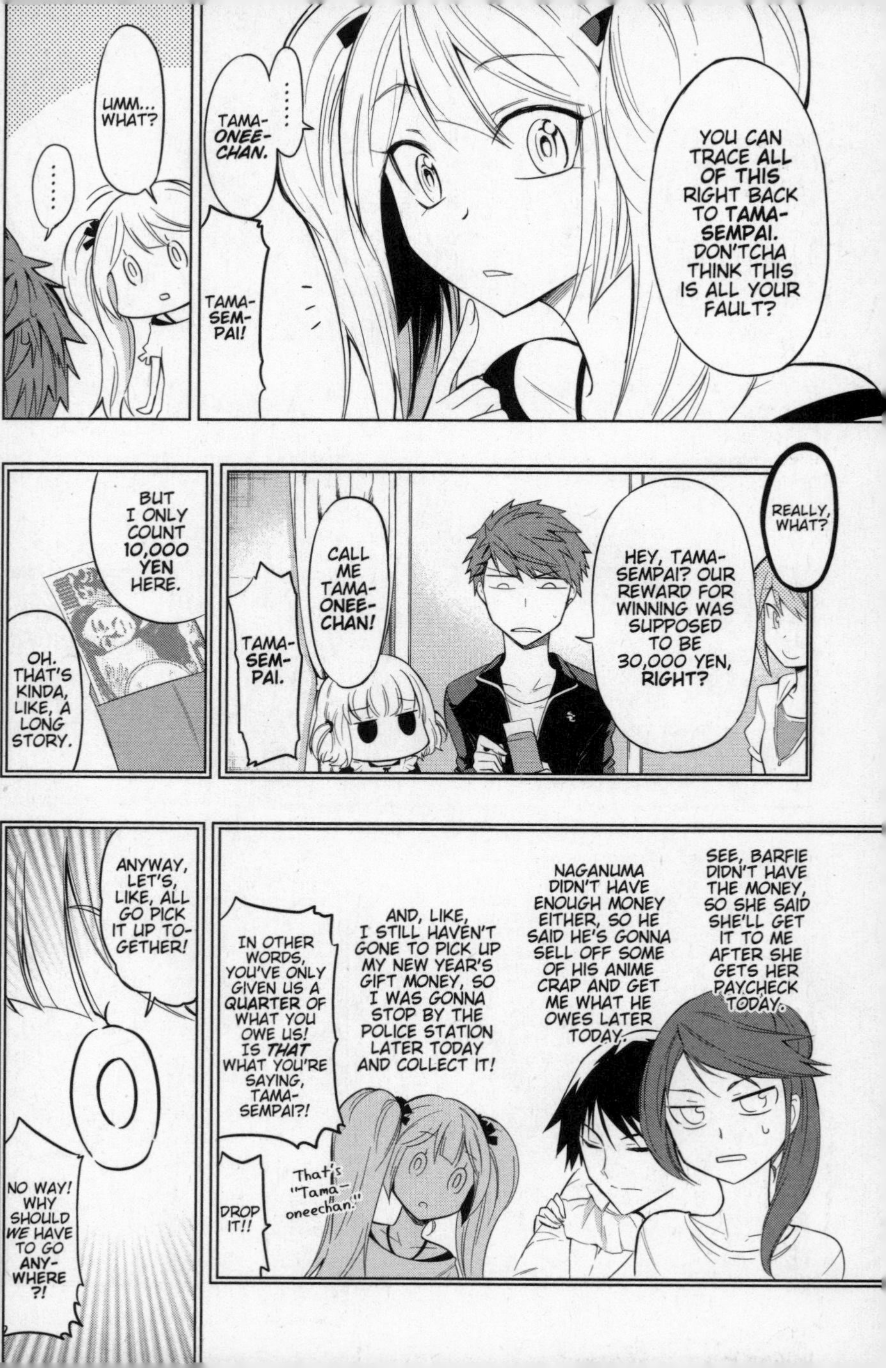
YOU CAN TRACE ALL OF THIS RIGHT BACK TO TAMA-SEMPAI. DON'TCHA THINK THIS IS ALL YOUR FAULT?
......
TAMA-ONEE-CHAN.
TAMA-SEMPAI!
UMM... WHAT?
......
REALLY, WHAT?
HEY, TAMA-SEMPAI? OUR REWARD FOR WINNING WAS SUPPOSED TO BE 30,000 YEN, RIGHT?
CALL ME TAMA-ONEE-CHAN!
TAMA-SEMPAI.
BUT I ONLY COUNT 10,000 YEN HERE.
OH. THAT'S KINDA, LIKE, A LONG STORY.
SEE, BARFIE DIDN'T HAVE THE MONEY, SO SHE SAID SHE'LL GET IT TO ME AFTER SHE GETS HER PAYCHECK TODAY.
NAGANUMA DIDN'T HAVE ENOUGH MONEY EITHER, SO HE SAID HE'S GONNA SELL OFF SOME OF HIS ANIME CRAP AND GET ME WHAT HE OWES LATER TODAY.
AND, LIKE, I STILL HAVEN'T GONE TO PICK UP MY NEW YEAR'S GIFT MONEY, SO I WAS GONNA STOP BY THE POLICE STATION LATER TODAY AND COLLECT IT!
IN OTHER WORDS, YOU'VE ONLY GIVEN US A QUARTER OF WHAT YOU OWE US! IS *THAT* WHAT YOU'RE SAYING, TAMA-SEMPAI?!
That's "Tama-oneechan."
DROP IT!!
ANYWAY, LET'S, LIKE, ALL GO PICK IT UP TO-GETHER!
NO WAY! WHY SHOULD *WE* HAVE TO GO ANY-WHERE?!

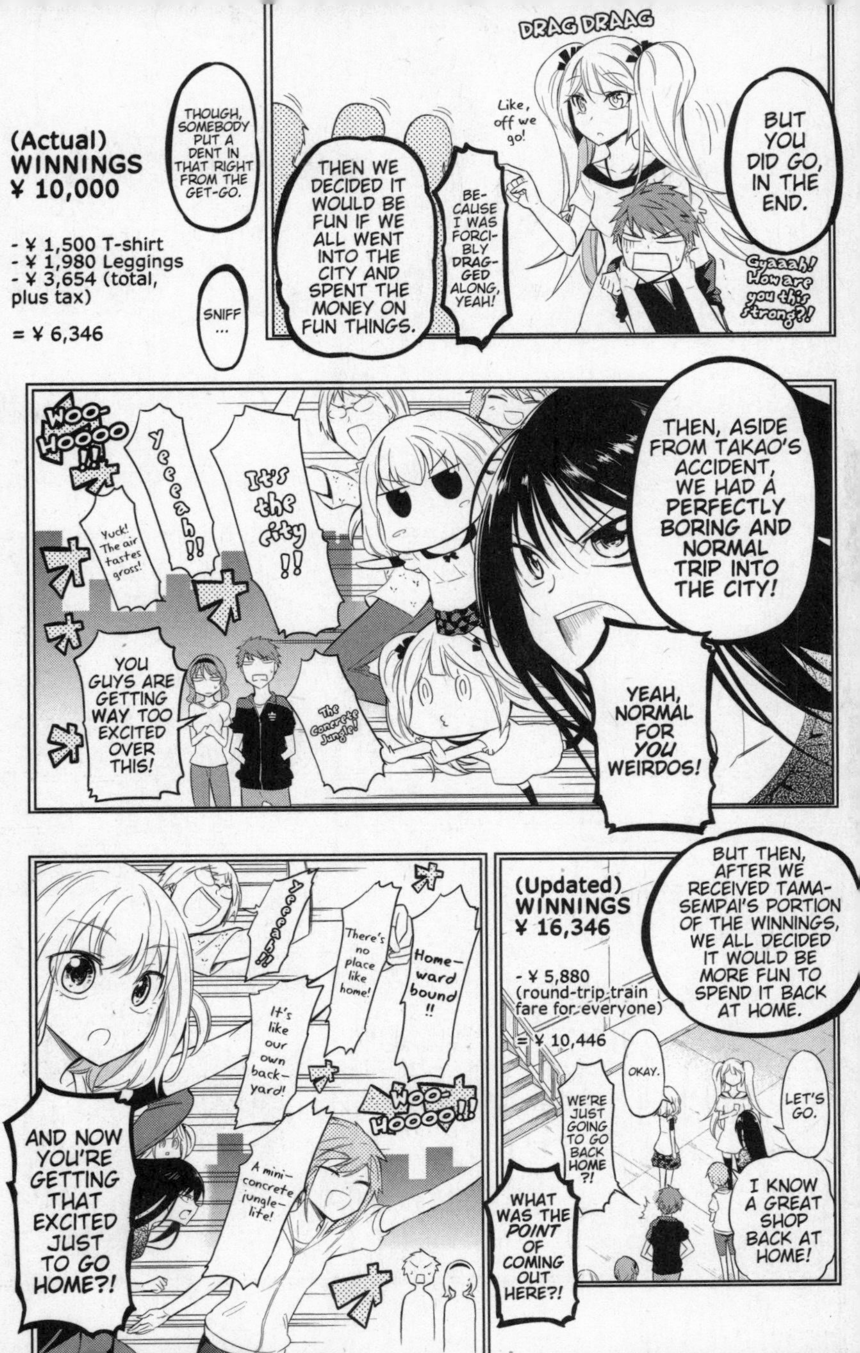
DRAG DRAAG
BUT YOU DID GO, IN THE END.
Gyaaah! How are you this strong?!
Like, off we go!
BECAUSE I WAS FORCIBLY DRAGGED ALONG, YEAH!
THEN WE DECIDED IT WOULD BE FUN IF WE ALL WENT INTO THE CITY AND SPENT THE MONEY ON FUN THINGS.
THOUGH, SOMEBODY PUT A DENT IN THAT RIGHT FROM THE GET-GO.
(Actual) WINNINGS ¥ 10,000
- ¥ 1,500 T-shirt
- ¥ 1,980 Leggings
- ¥ 3,654 (total, plus tax)
= ¥ 6,346
SNIFF ...
THEN, ASIDE FROM TAKAO'S ACCIDENT, WE HAD A PERFECTLY BORING AND NORMAL TRIP INTO THE CITY!
YEAH, NORMAL FOR YOU WEIRDOS!
It's the city!!
Yeeeah!!
WOO-HOOOO!!
Yuck! The air tastes gross!
The Concrete Jungle!
YOU GUYS ARE GETTING WAY TOO EXCITED OVER THIS!
BUT THEN, AFTER WE RECEIVED TAMA-SEMPAI'S PORTION OF THE WINNINGS, WE ALL DECIDED IT WOULD BE MORE FUN TO SPEND IT BACK AT HOME.
(Updated) WINNINGS ¥ 16,346
- ¥ 5,880 (round-trip train fare for everyone)
= ¥ 10,446
LET'S GO.
OKAY.
WE'RE JUST GOING TO GO BACK HOME?!
I KNOW A GREAT SHOP BACK AT HOME!
WHAT WAS THE POINT OF COMING OUT HERE?!
Homeward bound!!
There's no place like home!
Yeeeah!!
It's like our own backyard!
WOO-HOOOO!!
A mini-concrete jungle-life!
AND NOW YOU'RE GETTING THAT EXCITED JUST TO GO HOME?!

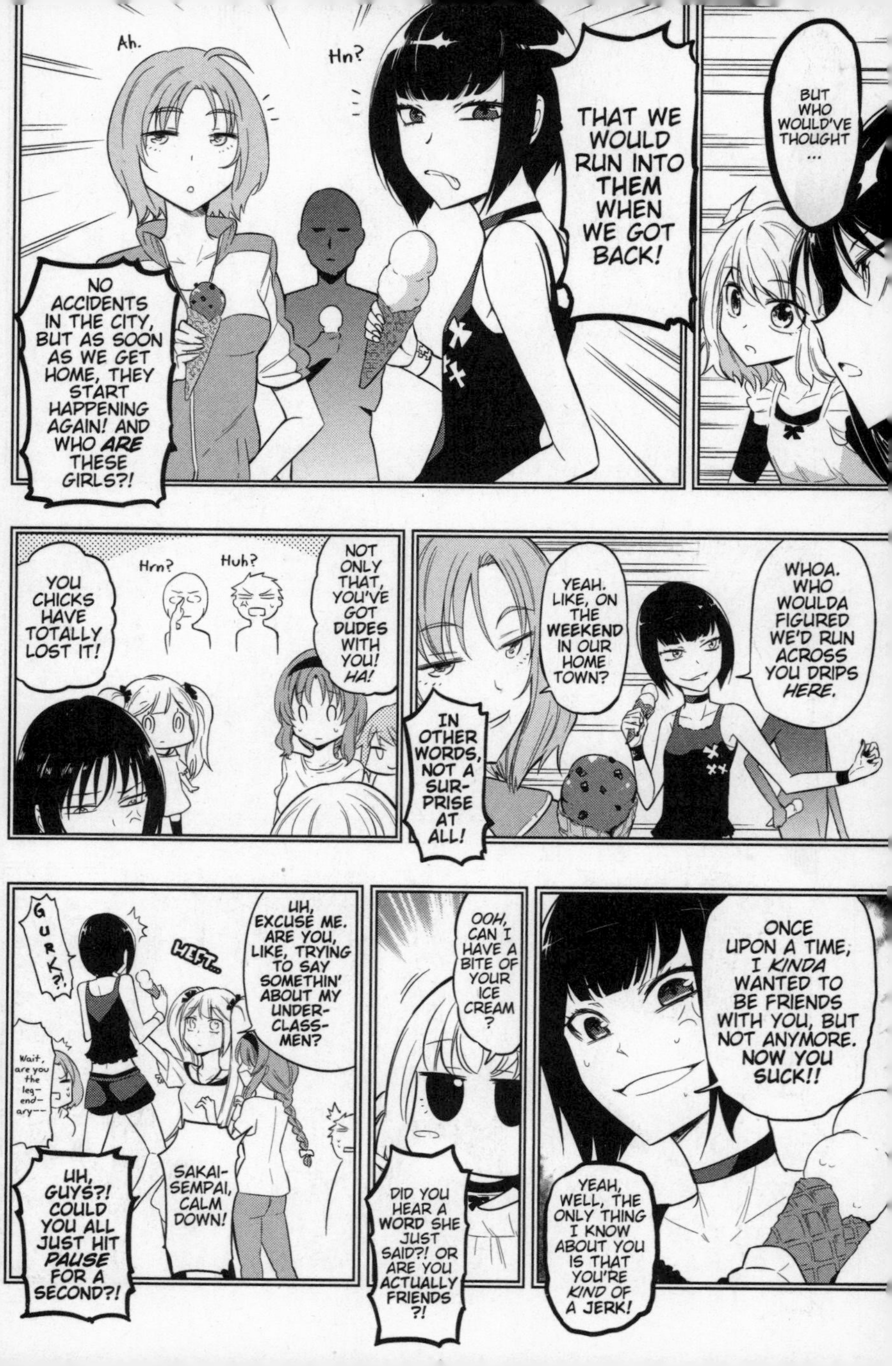
BUT WHO WOULD'VE THOUGHT...
THAT WE WOULD RUN INTO THEM WHEN WE GOT BACK!
Hn?
Ah.
NO ACCIDENTS IN THE CITY, BUT AS SOON AS WE GET HOME, THEY START HAPPENING AGAIN! AND WHO *ARE* THESE GIRLS?!
WHOA. WHO WOULDA FIGURED WE'D RUN ACROSS YOU DRIPS *HERE*.
YEAH. LIKE, ON THE WEEKEND IN OUR HOME TOWN?
IN OTHER WORDS, NOT A SURPRISE AT ALL!
NOT ONLY THAT, YOU'VE GOT DUDES WITH YOU! *HA!*
Huh?
Hrn?
YOU CHICKS HAVE TOTALLY LOST IT!
ONCE UPON A TIME, I *KINDA* WANTED TO BE FRIENDS WITH YOU, BUT NOT ANYMORE. NOW YOU SUCK!!
YEAH, WELL, THE ONLY THING I KNOW ABOUT YOU IS THAT YOU'RE *KIND* OF A JERK!
OOH, CAN I HAVE A BITE OF YOUR ICE CREAM?
DID YOU HEAR A WORD SHE JUST SAID?! OR ARE YOU ACTUALLY FRIENDS?!
UH, EXCUSE ME. ARE YOU, LIKE, TRYING TO SAY SOMETHIN' ABOUT MY UNDER-CLASS-MEN?
HEFT...
GURK?!
Wait, are you the leg-end-ary--
SAKAI-SEMPAI, CALM DOWN!
UH, GUYS?! COULD YOU ALL JUST HIT *PAUSE* FOR A SECOND?!

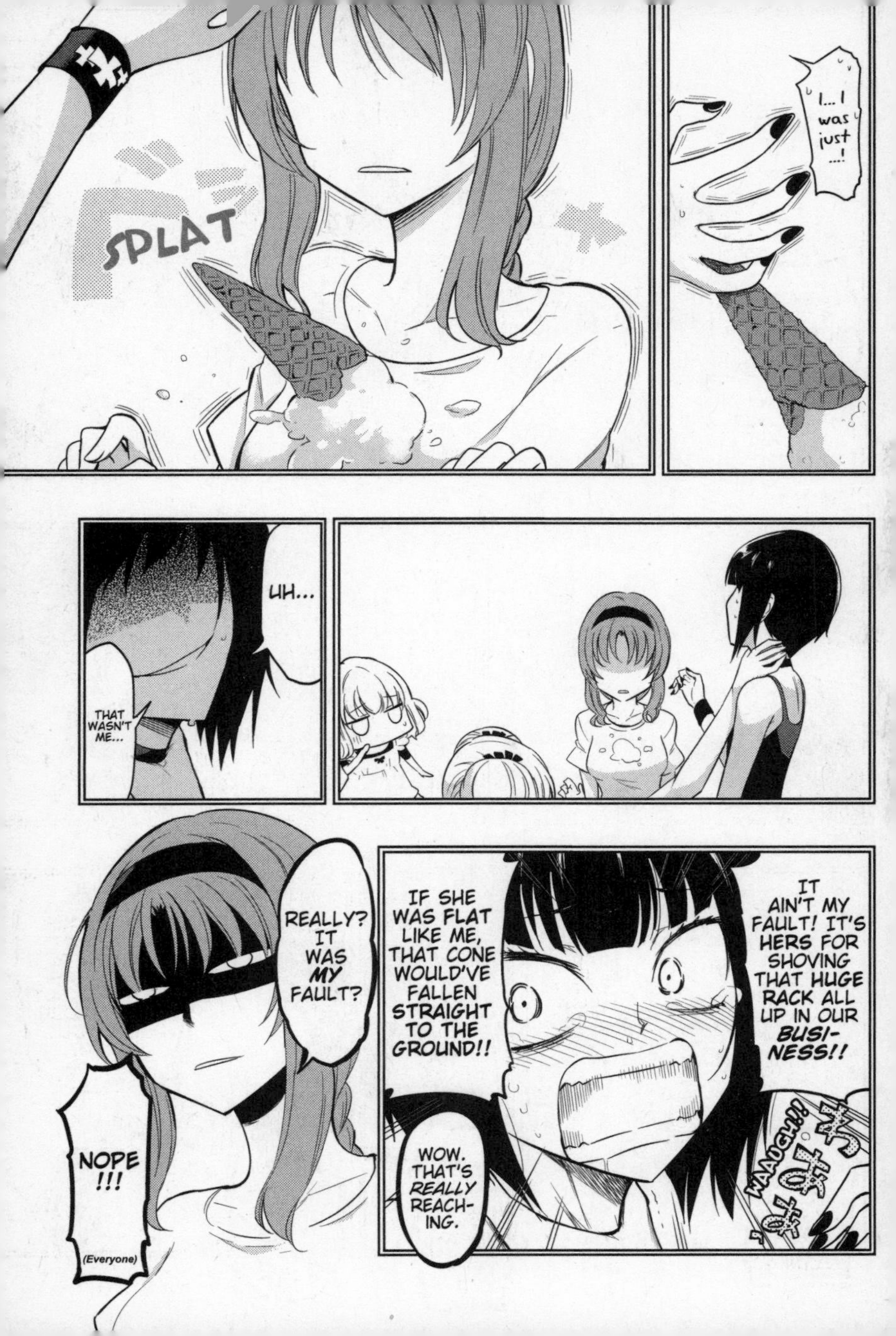
I... I was just ...!
SPLAT
UH...
THAT WASN'T ME...
IT AIN'T MY FAULT! IT'S HERS FOR SHOVING THAT HUGE RACK ALL UP IN OUR *BUSI-NESS!!*
IF SHE WAS FLAT LIKE ME, THAT CONE WOULD'VE FALLEN STRAIGHT TO THE GROUND!!
WAAUGH!!
WOW. THAT'S *REALLY* REACH-ING.
REALLY? IT WAS *MY* FAULT?
NOPE!!!
(Everyone)

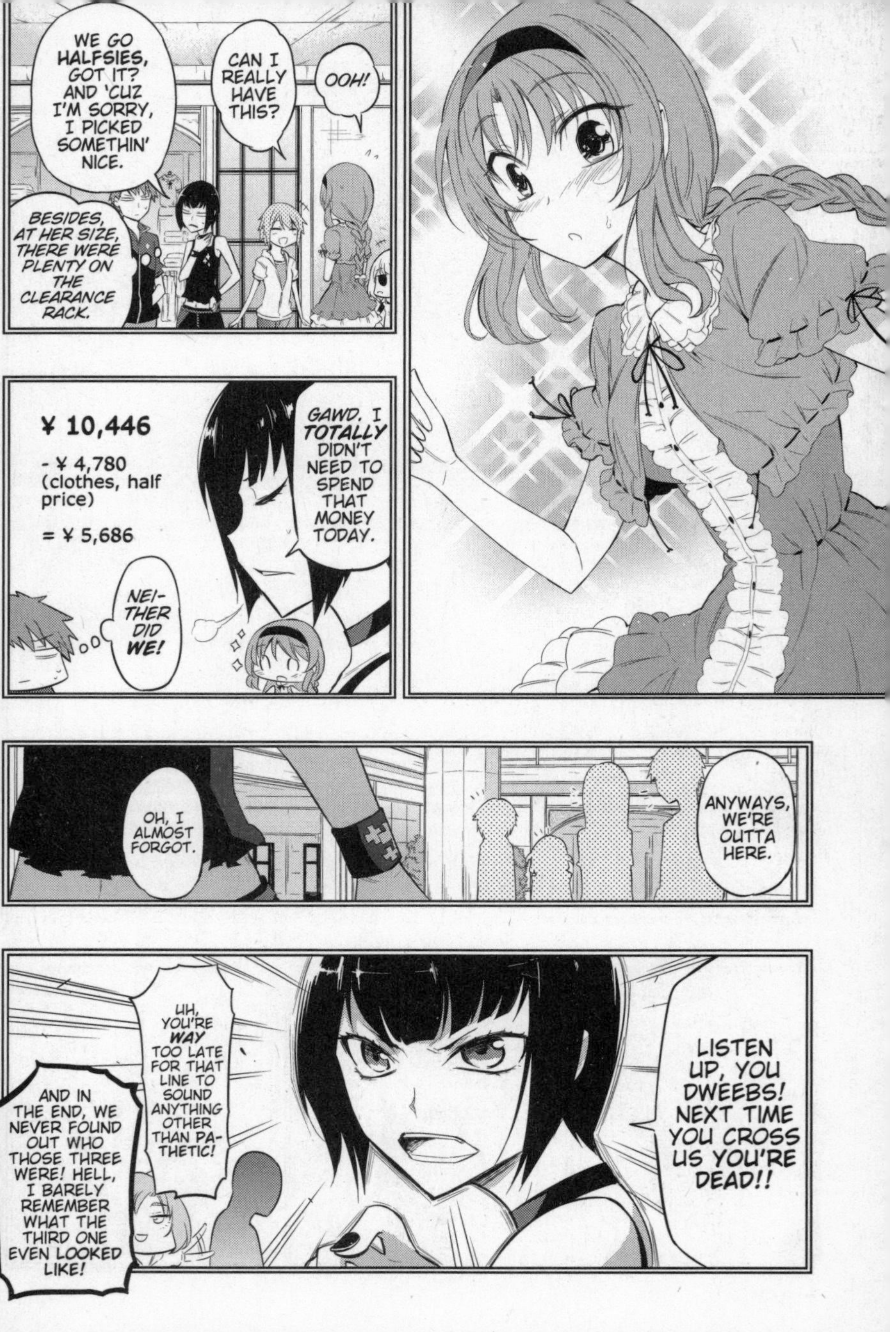
OOH!
CAN I REALLY HAVE THIS?
WE GO HALFSIES, GOT IT? AND 'CUZ I'M SORRY, I PICKED SOMETHIN' NICE.
BESIDES, AT HER SIZE, THERE WERE PLENTY ON THE CLEARANCE RACK.
GAWD. I TOTALLY DIDN'T NEED TO SPEND THAT MONEY TODAY.
¥ 10,446
- ¥ 4,780 (clothes, half price)
= ¥ 5,686
NEI-THER DID WE!
ANYWAYS, WE'RE OUTTA HERE.
OH, I ALMOST FORGOT.
LISTEN UP, YOU DWEEBS! NEXT TIME YOU CROSS US YOU'RE DEAD!!
UH, YOU'RE WAY TOO LATE FOR THAT LINE TO SOUND ANYTHING OTHER THAN PA-THETIC!
AND IN THE END, WE NEVER FOUND OUT WHO THOSE THREE WERE! HELL, I BARELY REMEMBER WHAT THE THIRD ONE EVEN LOOKED LIKE!

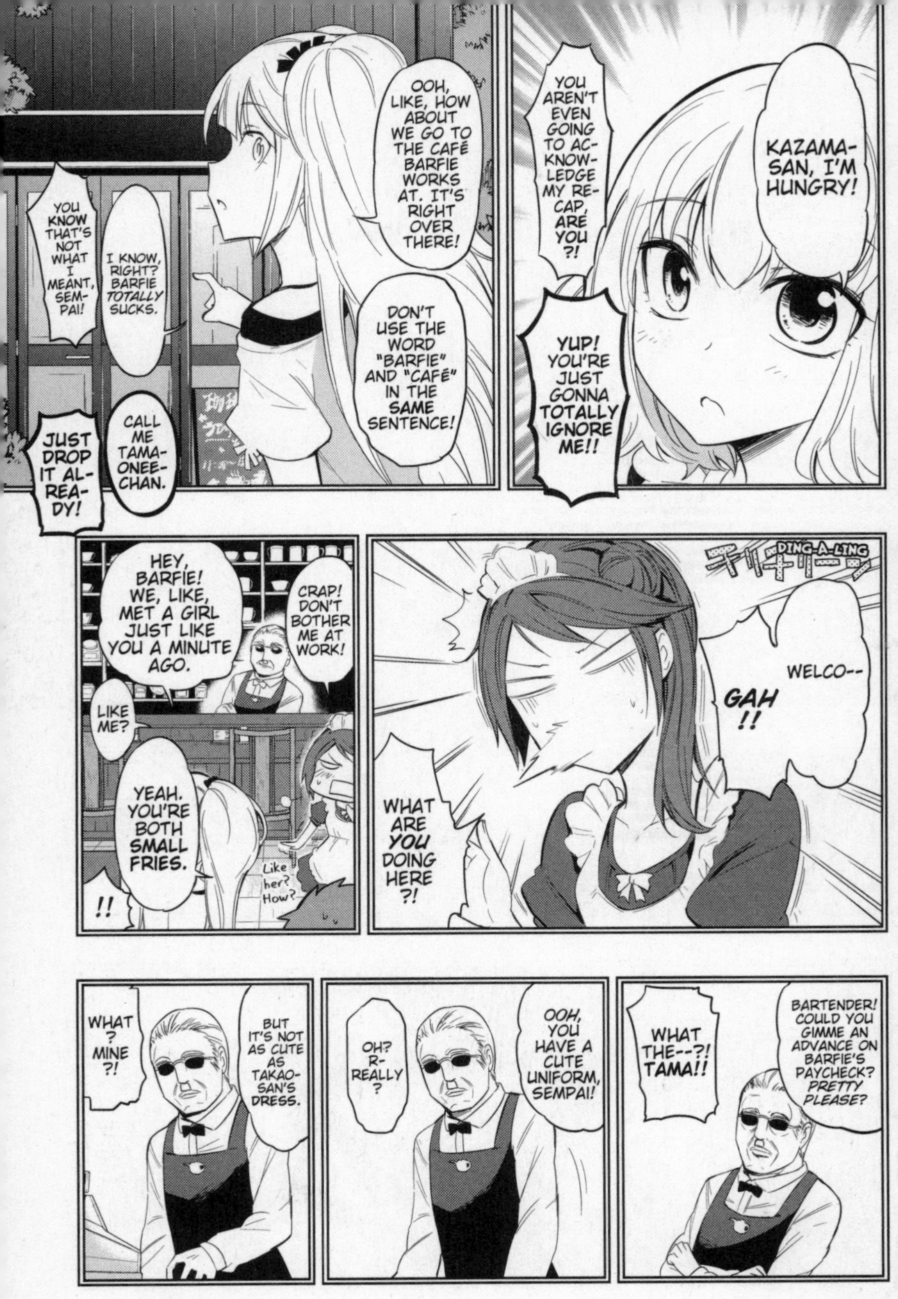
KAZAMA-SAN, I'M HUNGRY!
YOU AREN'T EVEN GOING TO ACKNOWLEDGE MY RECAP, ARE YOU?!
YUP! YOU'RE JUST GONNA TOTALLY IGNORE ME!!
OOH, LIKE, HOW ABOUT WE GO TO THE CAFÉ BARFIE WORKS AT. IT'S RIGHT OVER THERE!
DON'T USE THE WORD "BARFIE" AND "CAFÉ" IN THE SAME SENTENCE!
I KNOW, RIGHT? BARFIE *TOTALLY* SUCKS.
YOU KNOW THAT'S NOT WHAT I MEANT, SEMPAI!
CALL ME TAMA-ONEE-CHAN.
JUST DROP IT ALREADY!
DING-A-LING
WELCO--
GAH!!
WHAT ARE *YOU* DOING HERE?!
CRAP! DON'T BOTHER ME AT WORK!
HEY, BARFIE! WE, LIKE, MET A GIRL JUST LIKE YOU A MINUTE AGO.
LIKE ME?
Like her? How?
YEAH. YOU'RE BOTH SMALL FRIES.
!!
BARTENDER! COULD YOU GIMME AN ADVANCE ON BARFIE'S PAYCHECK? *PRETTY PLEASE?*
WHAT THE--?! TAMA!!
OOH, YOU HAVE A CUTE UNIFORM, SEMPAI!
OH? R-REALLY?
BUT IT'S NOT AS CUTE AS TAKAO-SAN'S DRESS.
WHAT? MINE?!

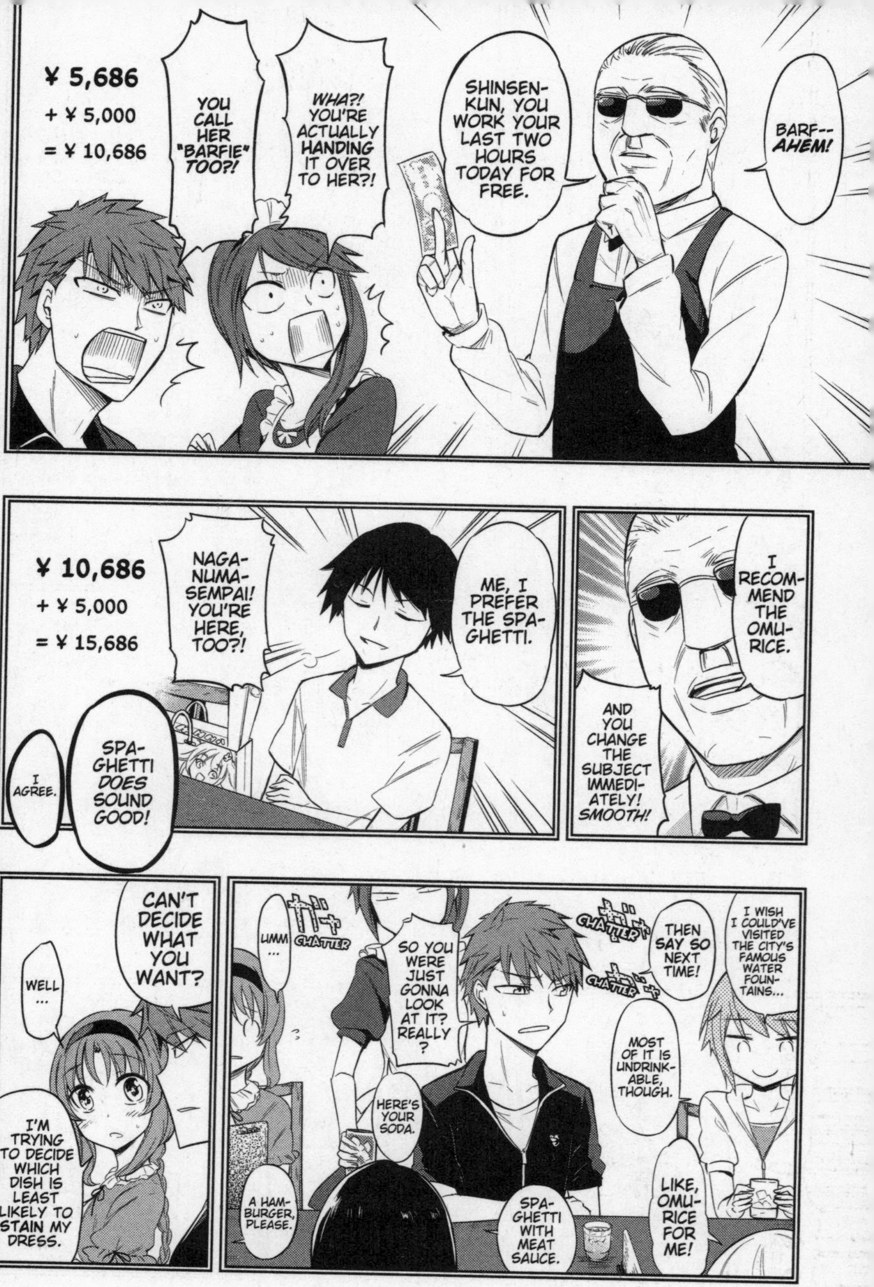
BARF-- AHEM!
SHINSEN-KUN, YOU WORK YOUR LAST TWO HOURS TODAY FOR FREE.
WHA?! YOU'RE ACTUALLY HANDING IT OVER TO HER?!
YOU CALL HER "BARFIE" TOO?!
¥ 5,686 + ¥ 5,000 = ¥ 10,686
I RECOMMEND THE OMURICE.
AND YOU CHANGE THE SUBJECT IMMEDIATELY! SMOOTH!
ME, I PREFER THE SPAGHETTI.
NAGANUMA-SEMPAI! YOU'RE HERE, TOO?!
¥ 10,686 + ¥ 5,000 = ¥ 15,686
SPAGHETTI DOES SOUND GOOD!
I AGREE.
I WISH I COULD'VE VISITED THE CITY'S FAMOUS WATER FOUNTAINS...
THEN SAY SO NEXT TIME!
CHATTER
CHATTER
MOST OF IT IS UNDRINKABLE, THOUGH.
SO YOU WERE JUST GONNA LOOK AT IT? REALLY?
CHATTER
UMM...
LIKE, OMURICE FOR ME!
HERE'S YOUR SODA.
SPAGHETTI WITH MEAT SAUCE.
A HAMBURGER, PLEASE.
CAN'T DECIDE WHAT YOU WANT?
WELL...
I'M TRYING TO DECIDE WHICH DISH IS LEAST LIKELY TO STAIN MY DRESS.

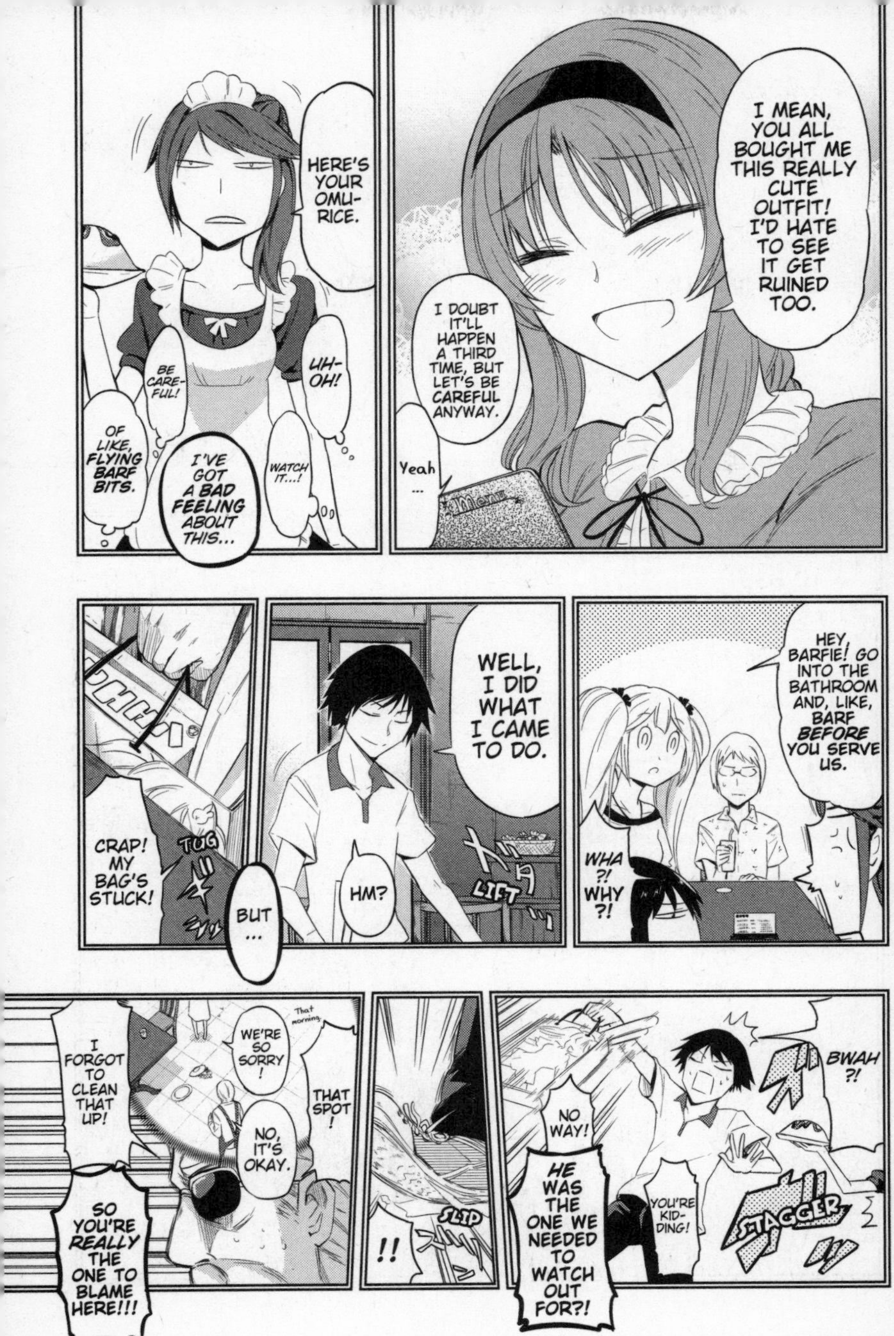
I MEAN, YOU ALL BOUGHT ME THIS REALLY CUTE OUTFIT! I'D HATE TO SEE IT GET RUINED TOO.
I DOUBT IT'LL HAPPEN A THIRD TIME, BUT LET'S BE CAREFUL ANYWAY.
Yeah ...
HERE'S YOUR OMU-RICE.
UH-OH!
BE CARE-FUL!
WATCH IT...!
I'VE GOT A BAD FEELING ABOUT THIS...
OF LIKE, FLYING BARF BITS.
HEY, BARFIE! GO INTO THE BATHROOM AND, LIKE, BARF BEFORE YOU SERVE US.
WHA?! WHY?!
WELL, I DID WHAT I CAME TO DO.
LIFT
HM?
BUT ...
CRAP! MY BAG'S STUCK!
TUG
BWAH?!
NO WAY!
STAGGER
YOU'RE KID-DING!
HE WAS THE ONE WE NEEDED TO WATCH OUT FOR?!
SLIP
!!
That morning
WE'RE SO SORRY!
THAT SPOT!
I FORGOT TO CLEAN THAT UP!
NO, IT'S OKAY.
SO YOU'RE REALLY THE ONE TO BLAME HERE!!!

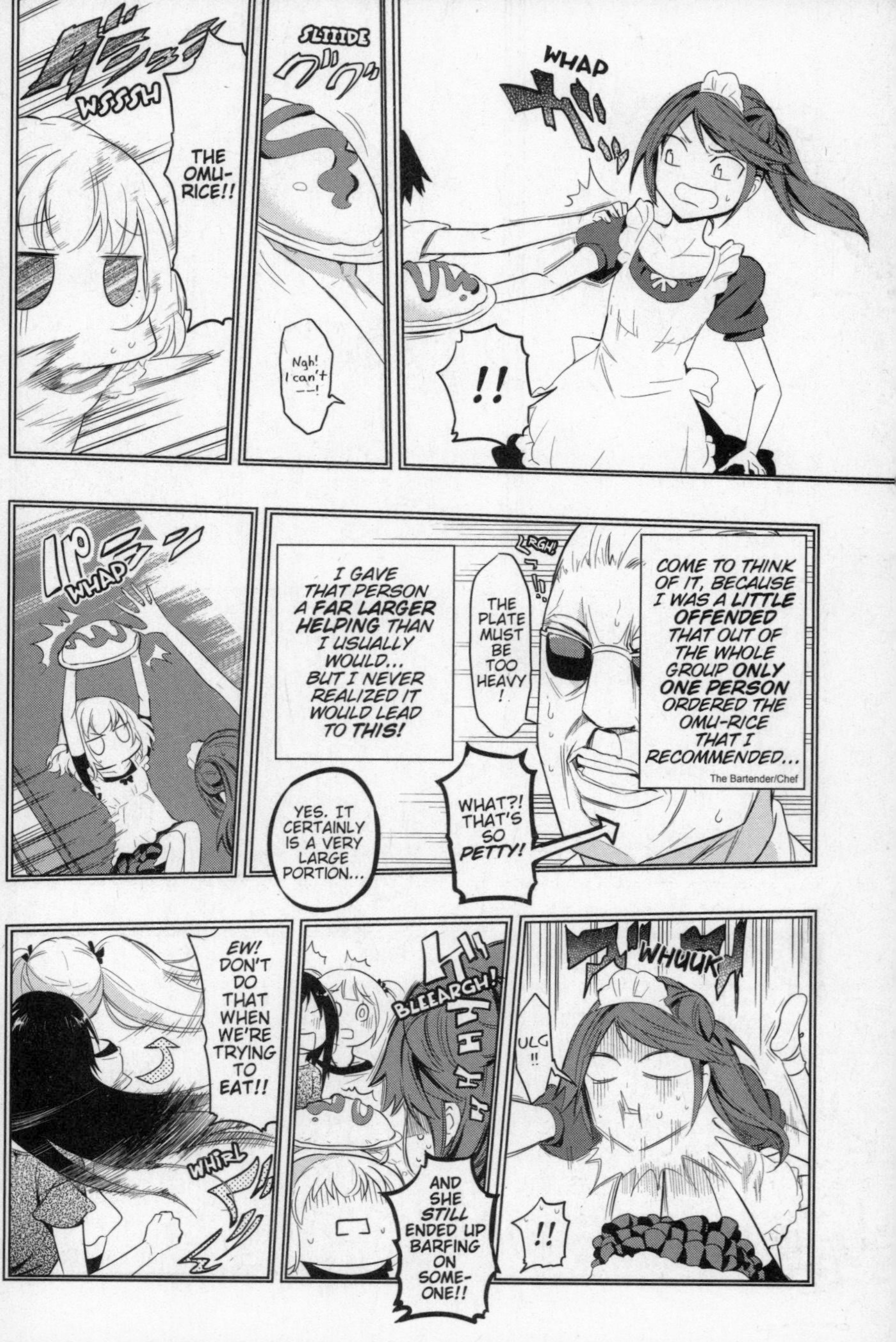
WHAP
!!
SLIIIDE
Ngh! I can't —!
WSSSH
THE OMU-RICE!!
COME TO THINK OF IT, BECAUSE I WAS A LITTLE OFFENDED THAT OUT OF THE WHOLE GROUP ONLY ONE PERSON ORDERED THE OMU-RICE THAT I RECOMMENDED...
The Bartender/Chef
LRGH!
THE PLATE MUST BE TOO HEAVY!
I GAVE THAT PERSON A FAR LARGER HELPING THAN I USUALLY WOULD... BUT I NEVER REALIZED IT WOULD LEAD TO THIS!
WHAT?! THAT'S SO PETTY!
YES. IT CERTAINLY IS A VERY LARGE PORTION...
WHAP
WHUUK
ULG!!
!!
BLEEARGH!
AND SHE STILL ENDED UP BARFING ON SOME-ONE!!
EW! DON'T DO THAT WHEN WE'RE TRYING TO EAT!!
WHIRL

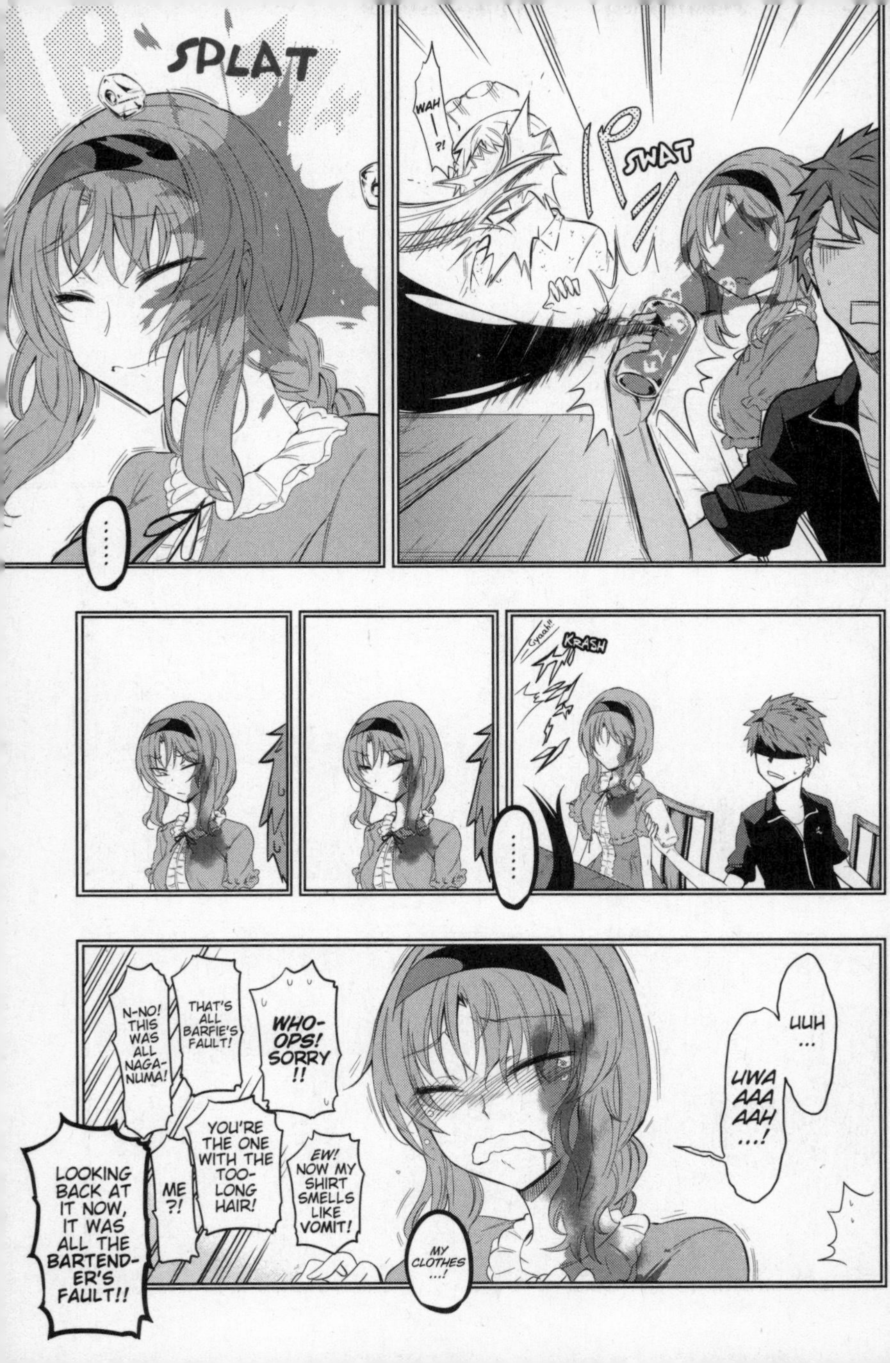

WAH—?!
SWAT
SPLAT
……
Gyaah!!
KRASH
……
UUH… UWAAAAAAH…!
MY CLOTHES…!
WHOOPS! SORRY!!
EW! NOW MY SHIRT SMELLS LIKE VOMIT!
THAT'S ALL BARFIE'S FAULT!
YOU'RE THE ONE WITH THE TOO-LONG HAIR!
N-NO! THIS WAS ALL NAGANUMA!
ME?!
LOOKING BACK AT IT NOW, IT WAS ALL THE BARTENDER'S FAULT!!

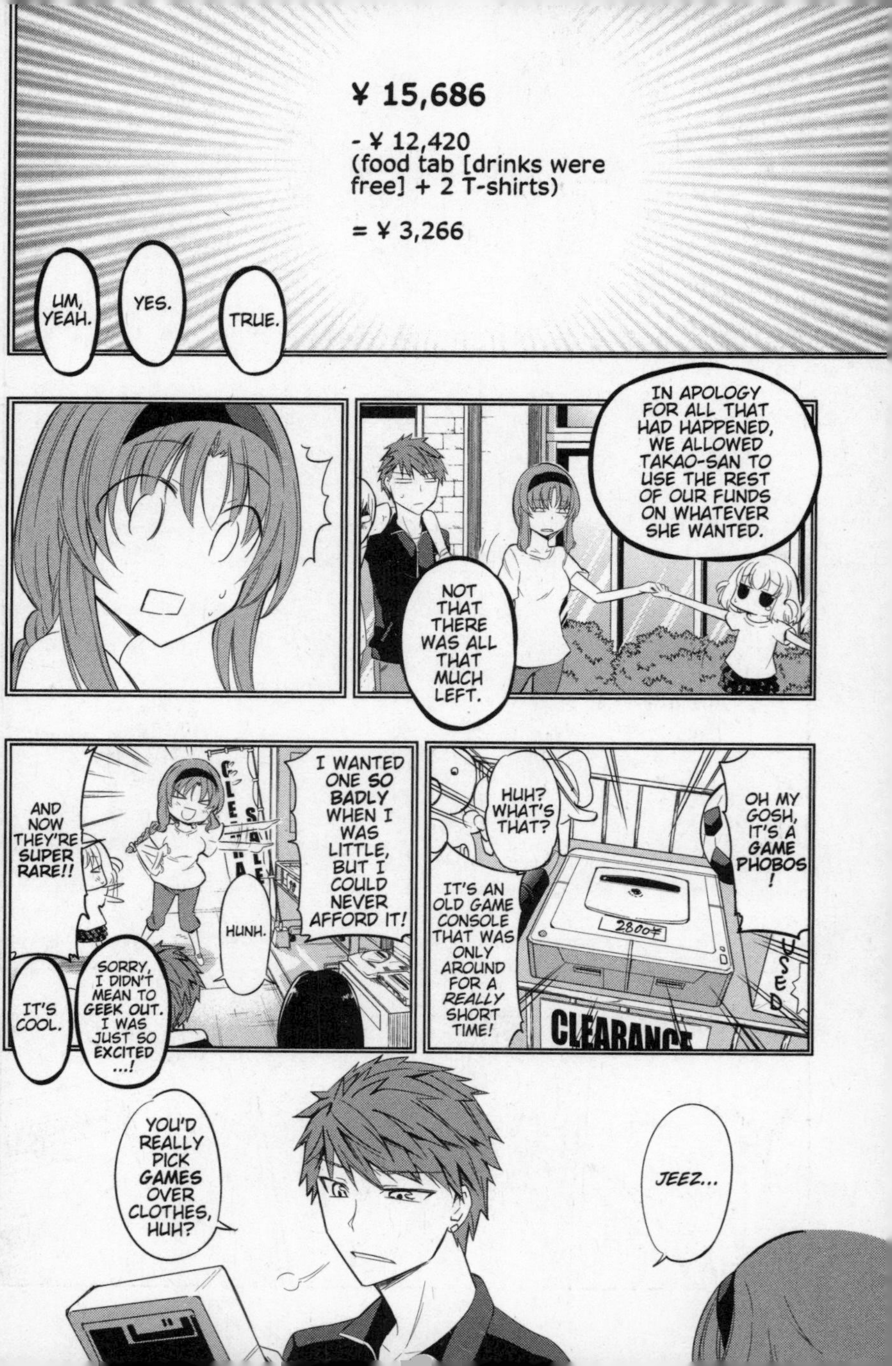
¥ 15,686
- ¥ 12,420
(food tab [drinks were free] + 2 T-shirts)
= ¥ 3,266
TRUE.
YES.
UM, YEAH.
IN APOLOGY FOR ALL THAT HAD HAPPENED, WE ALLOWED TAKAO-SAN TO USE THE REST OF OUR FUNDS ON WHATEVER SHE WANTED.
NOT THAT THERE WAS ALL THAT MUCH LEFT.
OH MY GOSH, IT'S A GAME PHOBOS!
USED
HUH? WHAT'S THAT?
2800円
IT'S AN OLD GAME CONSOLE THAT WAS ONLY AROUND FOR A *REALLY* SHORT TIME!
CLEARANCE
I WANTED ONE SO BADLY WHEN I WAS LITTLE, BUT I COULD NEVER AFFORD IT!
AND NOW THEY'RE SUPER RARE!!
HUNH.
SORRY, I DIDN'T MEAN TO GEEK OUT. I WAS JUST SO EXCITED ...!
IT'S COOL.
JEEZ...
YOU'D REALLY PICK GAMES OVER CLOTHES, HUH?

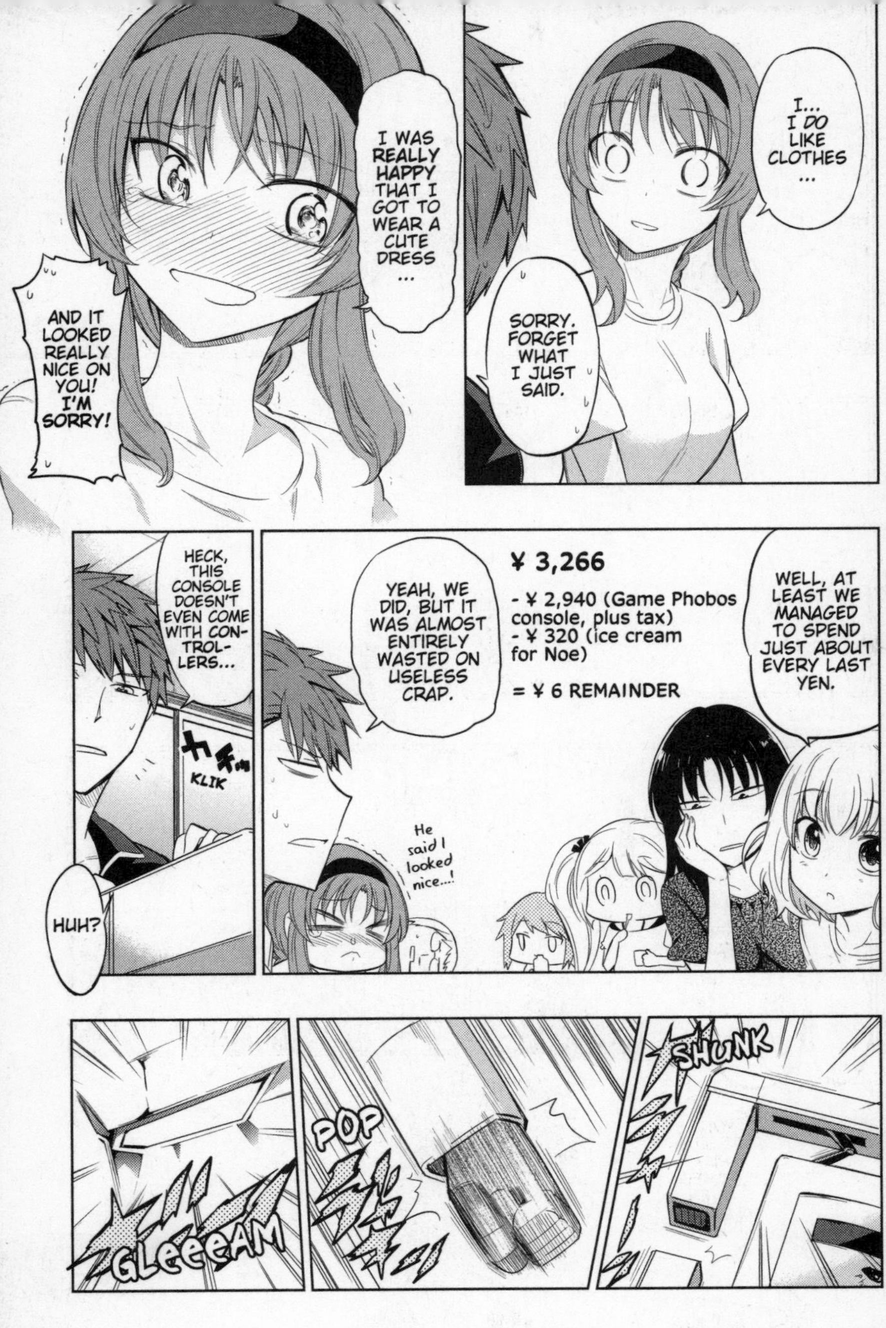
I... I DO LIKE CLOTHES...
SORRY. FORGET WHAT I JUST SAID.
I WAS REALLY HAPPY THAT I GOT TO WEAR A CUTE DRESS...
AND IT LOOKED REALLY NICE ON YOU! I'M SORRY!
WELL, AT LEAST WE MANAGED TO SPEND JUST ABOUT EVERY LAST YEN.
¥ 3,266
- ¥ 2,940 (Game Phobos console, plus tax)
- ¥ 320 (ice cream for Noe)
= ¥ 6 REMAINDER
YEAH, WE DID, BUT IT WAS ALMOST ENTIRELY WASTED ON USELESS CRAP.
He said I looked nice...!
HECK, THIS CONSOLE DOESN'T EVEN COME WITH CON-TROL-LERS...
KLIK
HUH?
SHUNK
POP
GLEEEAM

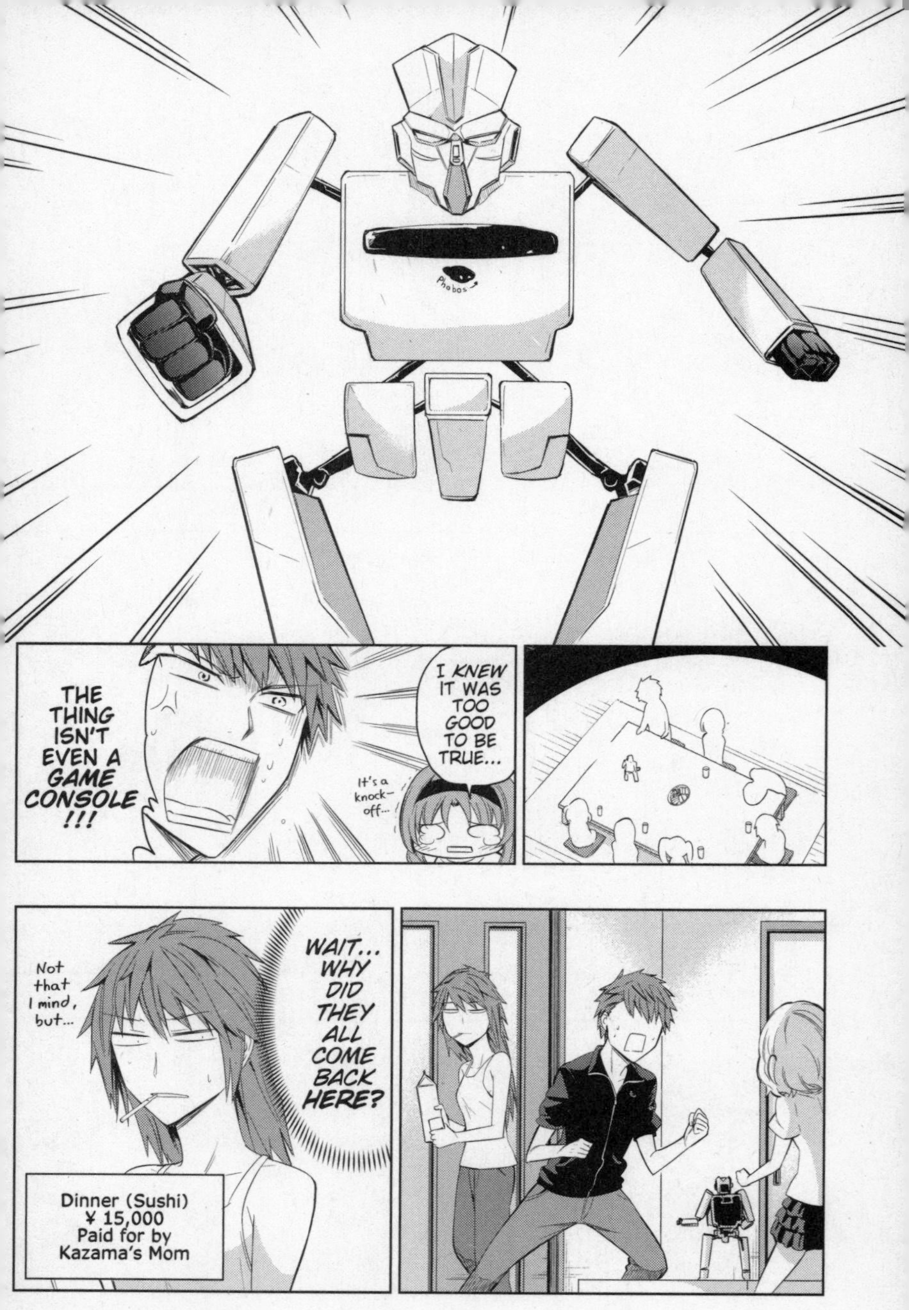
Phobos
I KNEW IT WAS TOO GOOD TO BE TRUE...
It's a knock-off...
THE THING ISN'T EVEN A GAME CONSOLE!!!
WAIT... WHY DID THEY ALL COME BACK HERE?
Not that I mind, but...
Dinner (Sushi) ¥ 15,000 Paid for by Kazama's Mom

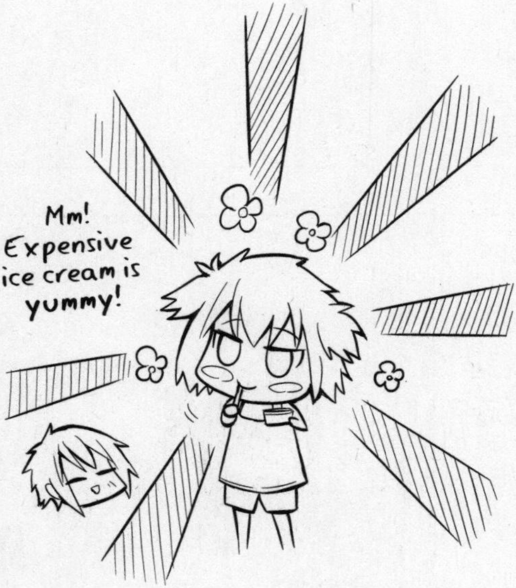
Mm! Expensive ice cream is yummy!

D-FRAGMENTS
ディーふらぐらぐ!

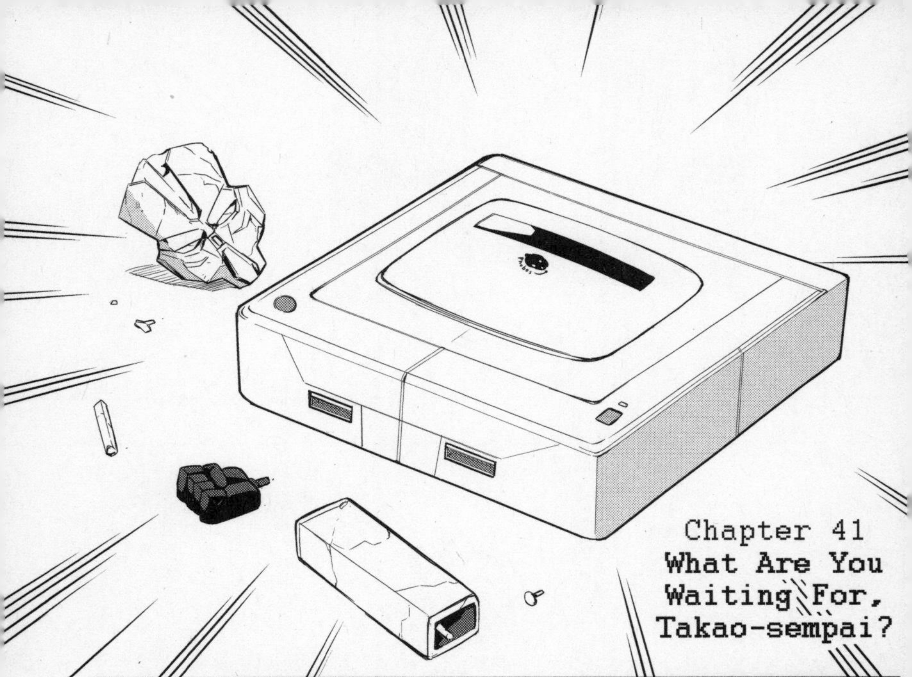

Chapter 41
What Are You Waiting For, Takao-sempai?

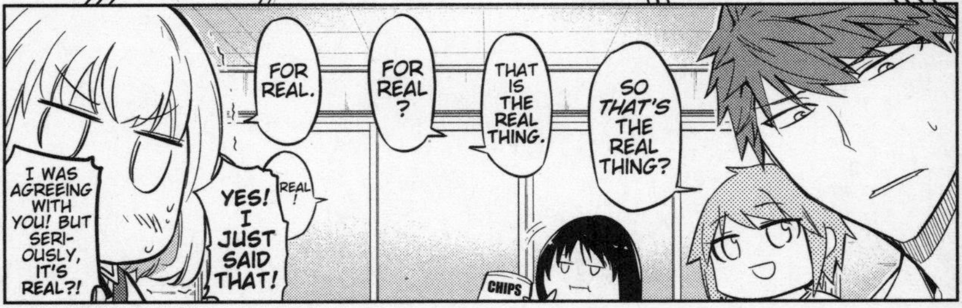
SO *THAT'S* THE REAL THING?
THAT IS THE REAL THING.
FOR REAL?
FOR REAL.
REAL!
YES! I JUST SAID THAT!
I WAS AGREEING WITH YOU! BUT SERIOUSLY, IT'S REAL?!
CHIPS

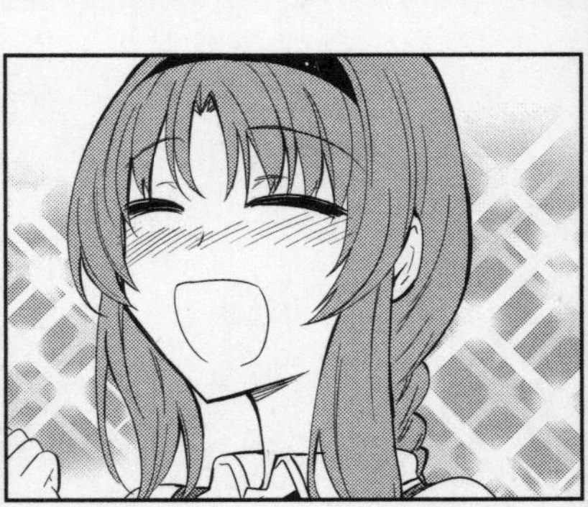

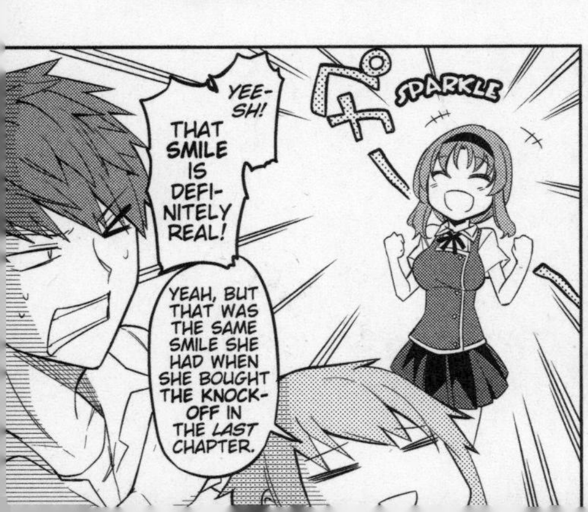
SPARKLE
YEESH! THAT SMILE IS DEFINITELY REAL!
YEAH, BUT THAT WAS THE SAME SMILE SHE HAD WHEN SHE BOUGHT THE KNOCK-OFF IN THE *LAST* CHAPTER.

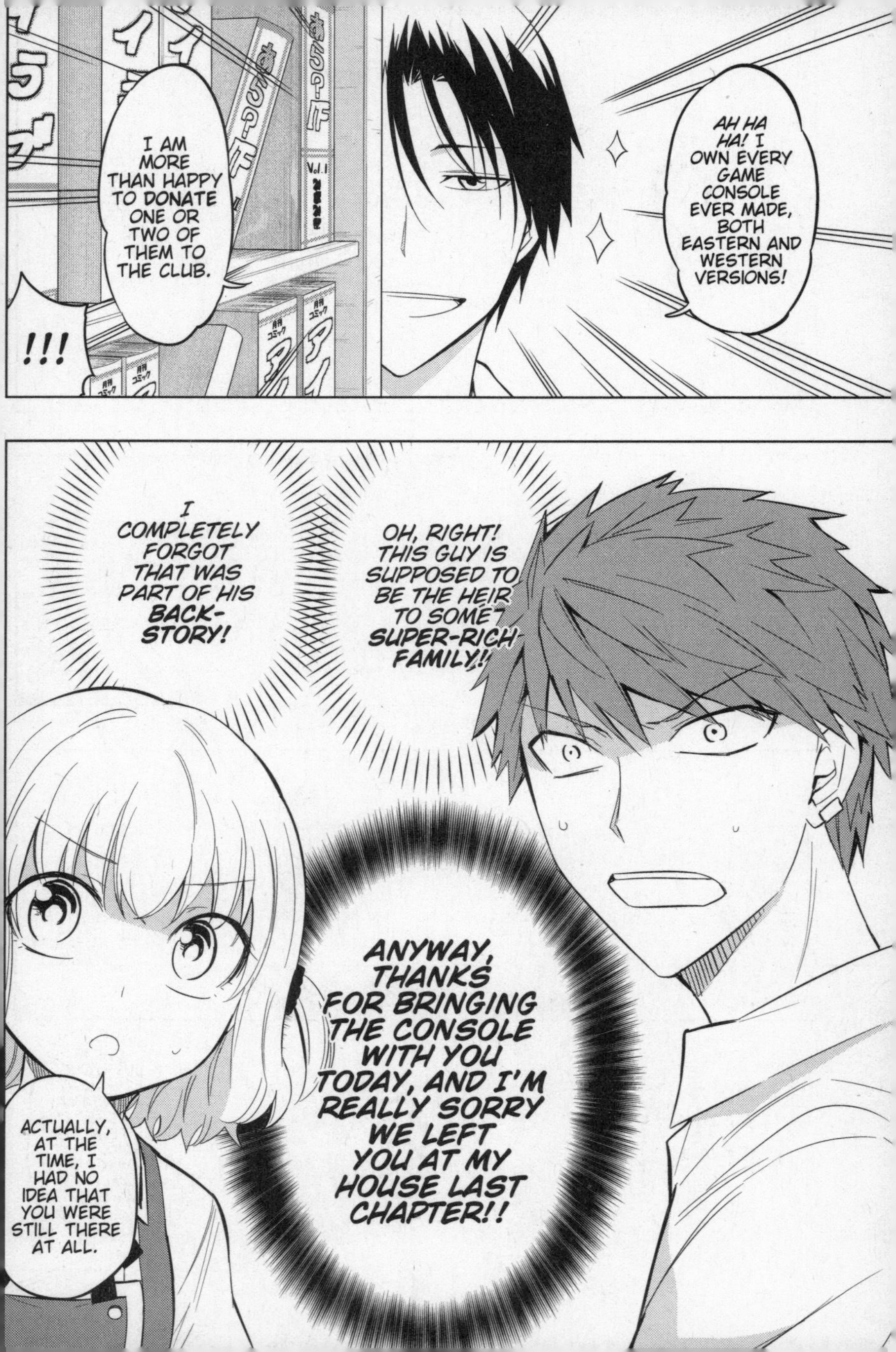
AH HA HA! I OWN EVERY GAME CONSOLE EVER MADE, BOTH EASTERN AND WESTERN VERSIONS!
I AM MORE THAN HAPPY TO DONATE ONE OR TWO OF THEM TO THE CLUB.
!!!
OH, RIGHT! THIS GUY IS SUPPOSED TO BE THE HEIR TO SOME SUPER-RICH FAMILY!!
I COMPLETELY FORGOT THAT WAS PART OF HIS BACK-STORY!
ANYWAY, THANKS FOR BRINGING THE CONSOLE WITH YOU TODAY, AND I'M REALLY SORRY WE LEFT YOU AT MY HOUSE LAST CHAPTER!!
ACTUALLY, AT THE TIME, I HAD NO IDEA THAT YOU WERE STILL THERE AT ALL.

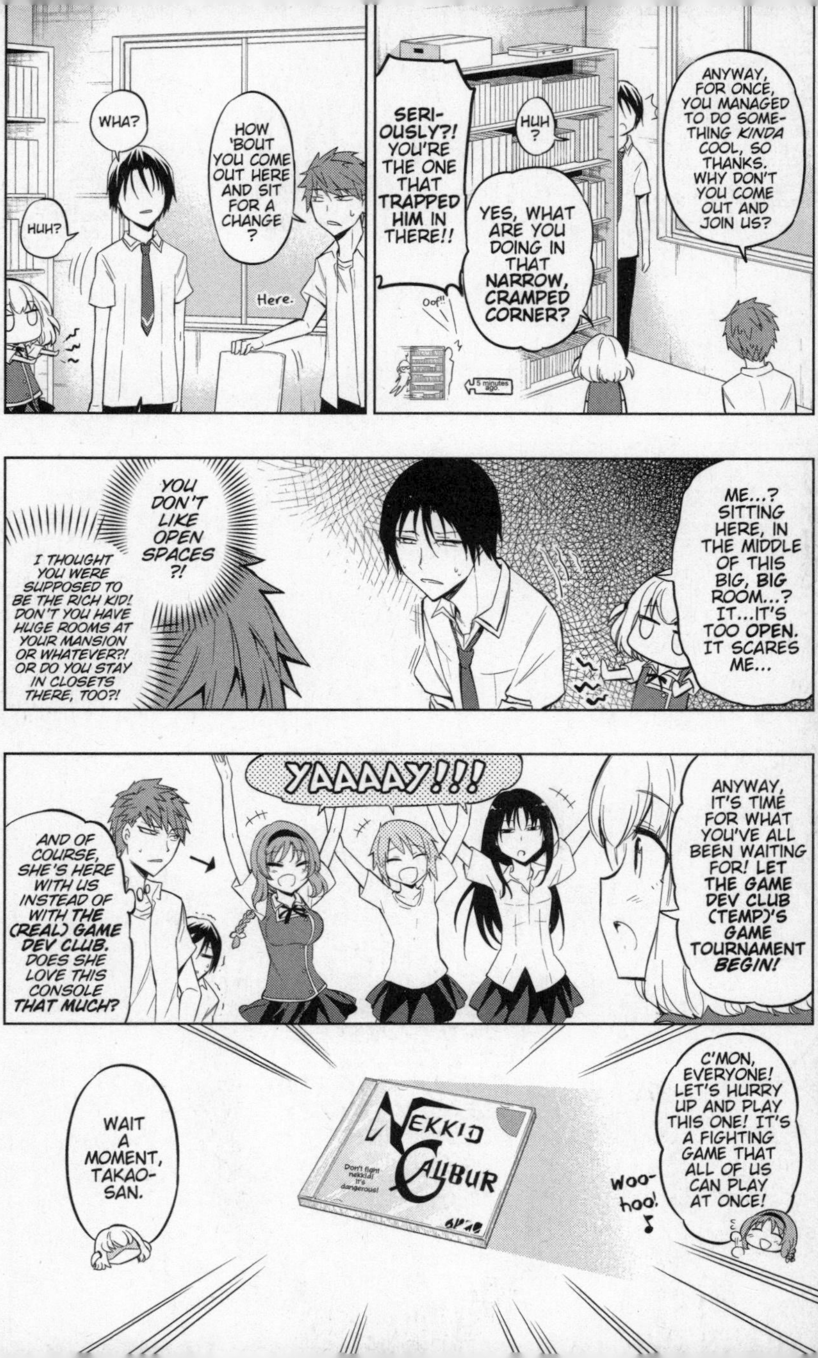

ANYWAY, FOR ONCE, YOU MANAGED TO DO SOMETHING KINDA COOL, SO THANKS. WHY DON'T YOU COME OUT AND JOIN US?
HUH?
SERIOUSLY?! YOU'RE THE ONE THAT TRAPPED HIM IN THERE!!
YES, WHAT ARE YOU DOING IN THAT NARROW, CRAMPED CORNER?
Oof!!
5 minutes ago.
HOW 'BOUT YOU COME OUT HERE AND SIT FOR A CHANGE?
WHA?
HUH?
Here.
ME...? SITTING HERE, IN THE MIDDLE OF THIS BIG, BIG ROOM...? IT...IT'S TOO OPEN. IT SCARES ME...
YOU DON'T LIKE OPEN SPACES?!
I THOUGHT YOU WERE SUPPOSED TO BE THE RICH KID! DON'T YOU HAVE HUGE ROOMS AT YOUR MANSION OR WHATEVER?! OR DO YOU STAY IN CLOSETS THERE, TOO?!
ANYWAY, IT'S TIME FOR WHAT YOU'VE ALL BEEN WAITING FOR! LET THE GAME DEV CLUB (TEMP)'S GAME TOURNAMENT BEGIN!
YAAAAY!!!
AND OF COURSE, SHE'S HERE WITH US INSTEAD OF WITH THE (REAL) GAME DEV CLUB. DOES SHE LOVE THIS CONSOLE THAT MUCH?
C'MON, EVERYONE! LET'S HURRY UP AND PLAY THIS ONE! IT'S A FIGHTING GAME THAT ALL OF US CAN PLAY AT ONCE!
Woo-hoo!
NEKKID CALIBUR
Don't fight nekkid! It's dangerous!
WAIT A MOMENT, TAKAO-SAN.

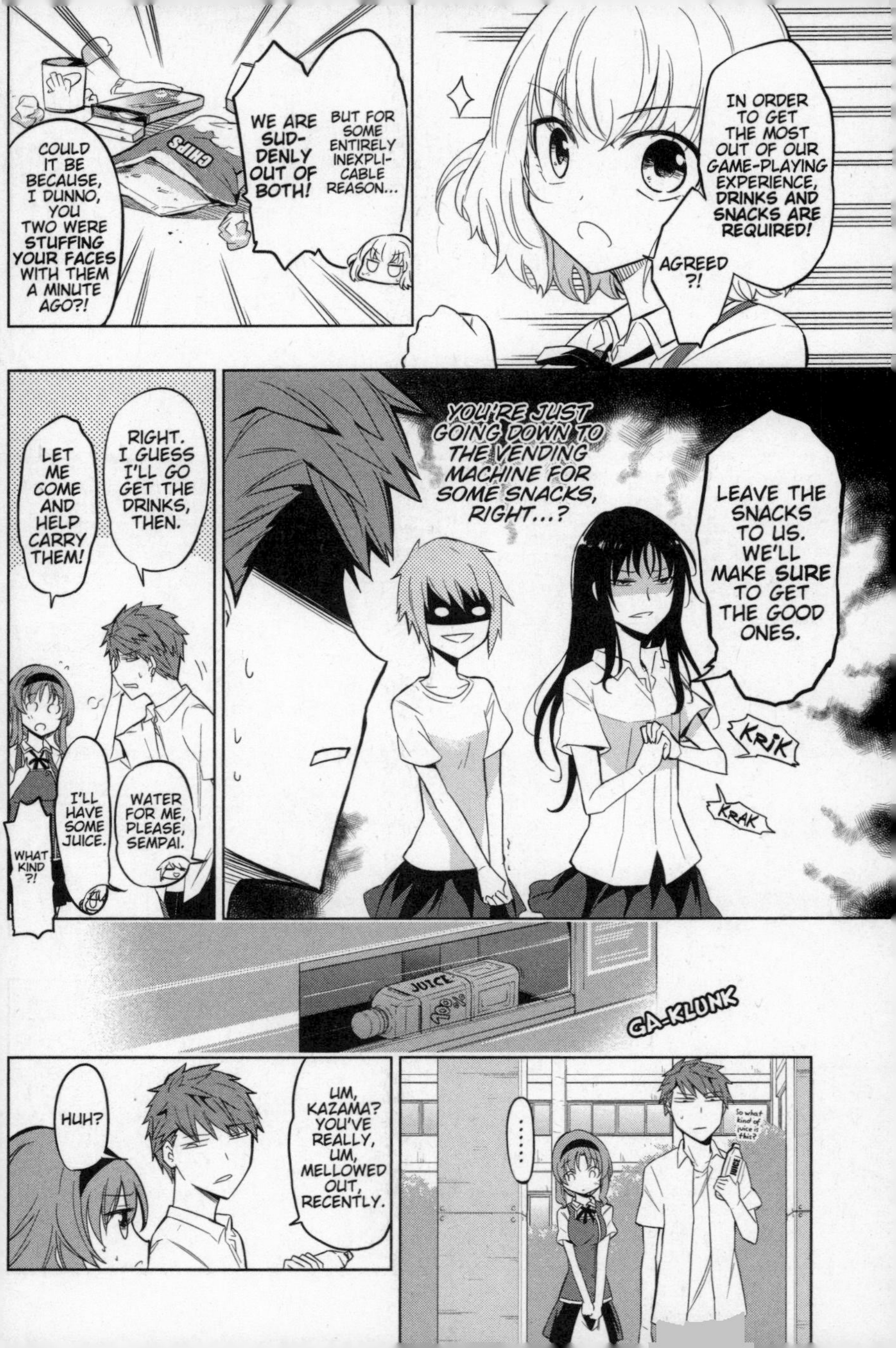
IN ORDER TO GET THE MOST OUT OF OUR GAME-PLAYING EXPERIENCE, DRINKS AND SNACKS ARE REQUIRED!
AGREED?!
BUT FOR SOME ENTIRELY INEXPLICABLE REASON...
WE ARE SUDDENLY OUT OF BOTH!
CHIPS
COULD IT BE BECAUSE, I DUNNO, YOU TWO WERE STUFFING YOUR FACES WITH THEM A MINUTE AGO?!
LEAVE THE SNACKS TO US. WE'LL MAKE SURE TO GET THE GOOD ONES.
YOU'RE JUST GOING DOWN TO THE VENDING MACHINE FOR SOME SNACKS, RIGHT...?
KRIK
KRAK
RIGHT. I GUESS I'LL GO GET THE DRINKS, THEN.
LET ME COME AND HELP CARRY THEM!
WATER FOR ME, PLEASE, SEMPAI.
I'LL HAVE SOME JUICE.
WHAT KIND?!
JUICE
GA-KLUNK
So what kind of juice is this?
......
UM, KAZAMA? YOU'VE REALLY, UM, MELLOWED OUT, RECENTLY.
HUH?

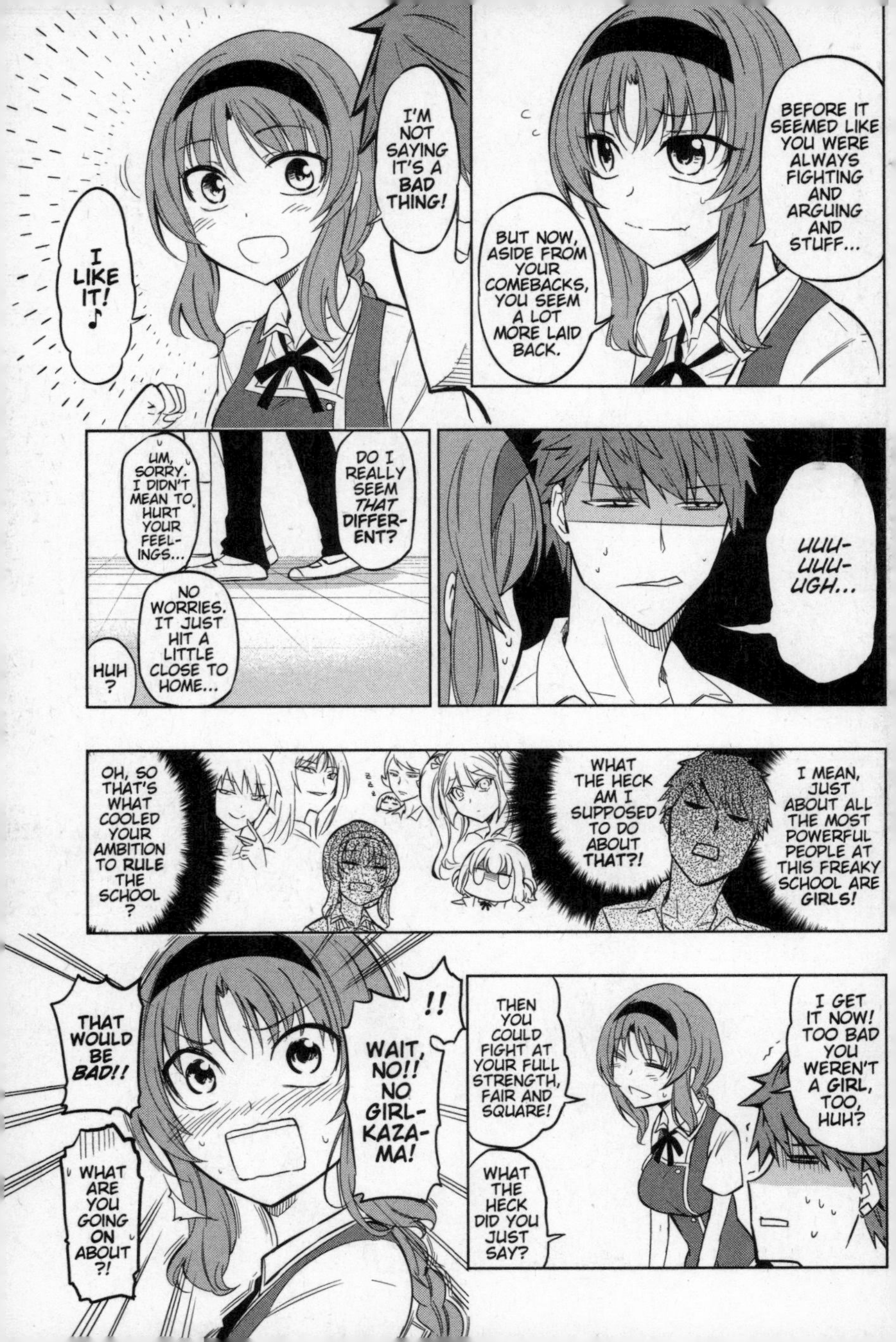
BEFORE IT SEEMED LIKE YOU WERE ALWAYS FIGHTING AND ARGUING AND STUFF...
BUT NOW, ASIDE FROM YOUR COMEBACKS, YOU SEEM A LOT MORE LAID BACK.
I'M NOT SAYING IT'S A BAD THING!
I LIKE IT! ♪
UUU-UUU-UGH...
DO I REALLY SEEM *THAT* DIFFERENT?
UM, SORRY. I DIDN'T MEAN TO HURT YOUR FEELINGS...
NO WORRIES. IT JUST HIT A LITTLE CLOSE TO HOME...
HUH?
I MEAN, JUST ABOUT ALL THE MOST POWERFUL PEOPLE AT THIS FREAKY SCHOOL ARE GIRLS!
WHAT THE HECK AM I SUPPOSED TO DO ABOUT THAT?!
OH, SO THAT'S WHAT COOLED YOUR AMBITION TO RULE THE SCHOOL?
I GET IT NOW! TOO BAD YOU WEREN'T A GIRL, TOO, HUH?
THEN YOU COULD FIGHT AT YOUR FULL STRENGTH, FAIR AND SQUARE!
WHAT THE HECK DID YOU JUST SAY?
!!
WAIT, NO!! NO GIRL-KAZAMA!
THAT WOULD BE *BAD*!!
WHAT ARE YOU GOING ON ABOUT?!

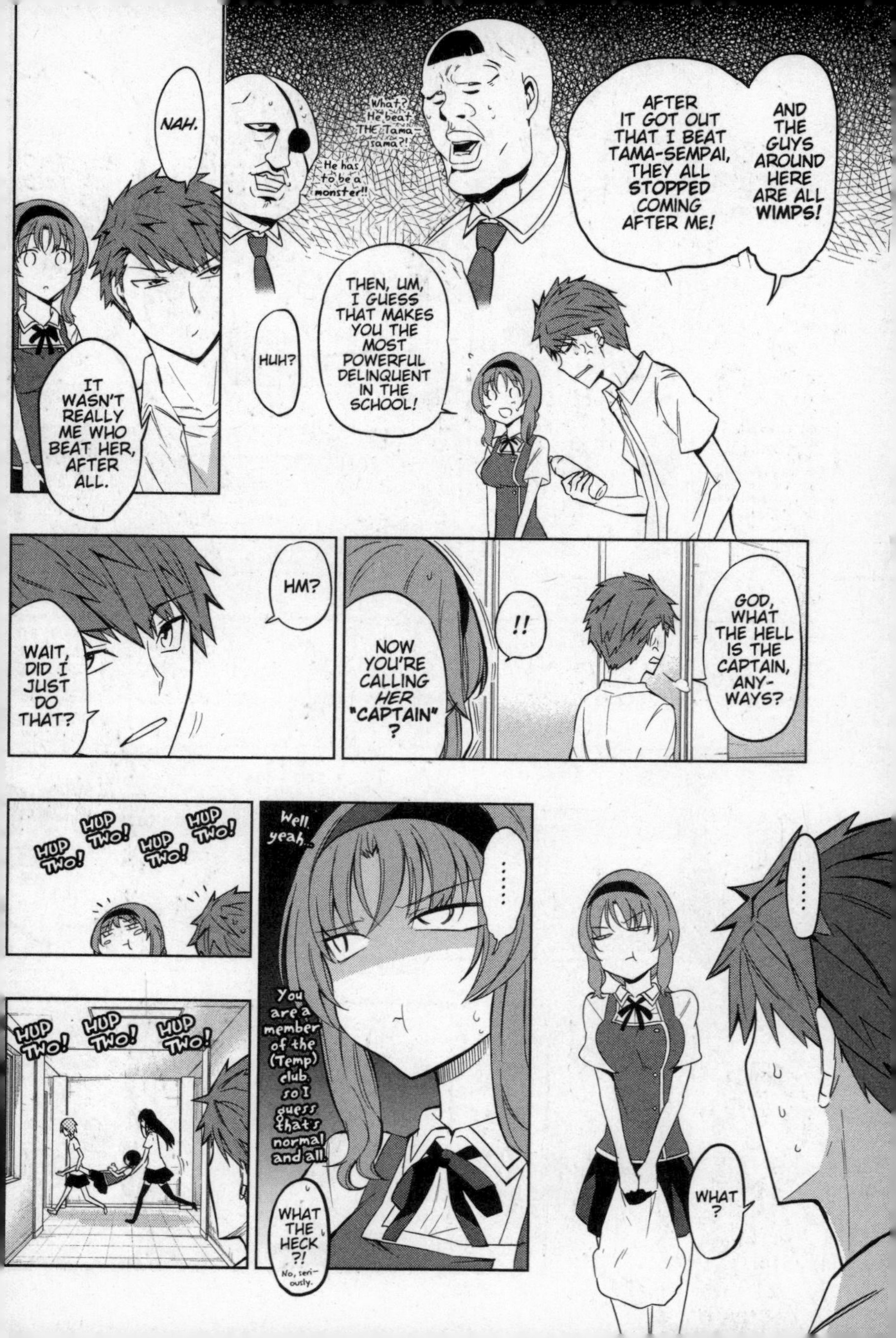
AND THE GUYS AROUND HERE ARE ALL WIMPS!
AFTER IT GOT OUT THAT I BEAT TAMA-SEMPAI, THEY ALL STOPPED COMING AFTER ME!
What? He beat THE Tama-sama?!
He has to be a monster!!
THEN, UM, I GUESS THAT MAKES YOU THE MOST POWERFUL DELINQUENT IN THE SCHOOL!
HUH?
NAH.
IT WASN'T REALLY ME WHO BEAT HER, AFTER ALL.
GOD, WHAT THE HELL IS THE CAPTAIN, ANY-WAYS?
!!
NOW YOU'RE CALLING *HER* "CAPTAIN"?
HM?
WAIT, DID I JUST DO THAT?
......
WHAT?
......
Well, yeah...
You are a member of the (Temp) club, so I guess that's normal and all.
WHAT THE HECK?!
No, seri-ously.
HUP TWO! HUP TWO! HUP TWO! HUP TWO!
HUP TWO! HUP TWO! HUP TWO!

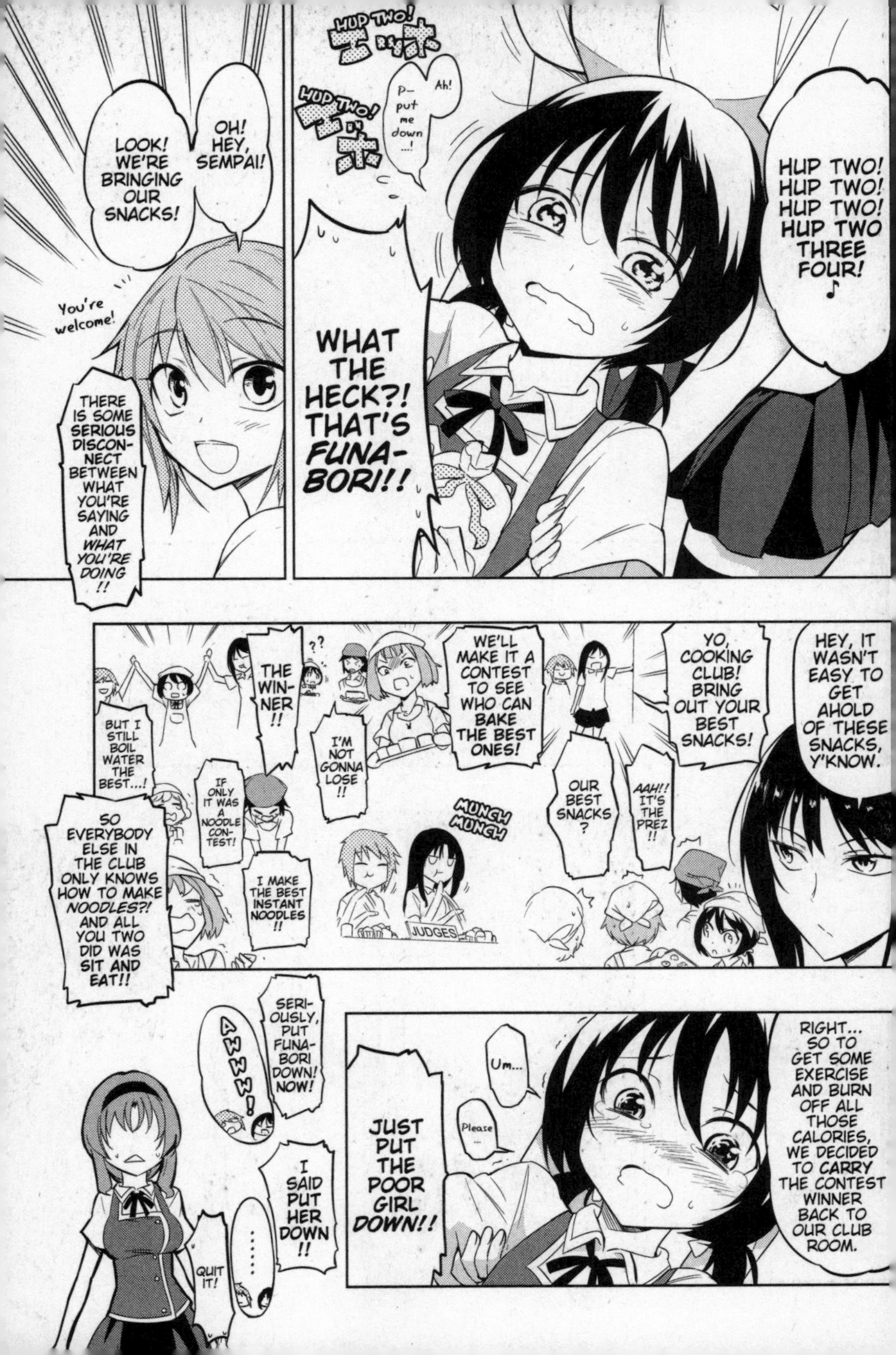
HUP TWO! HUP TWO! HUP TWO! HUP TWO THREE FOUR! ♪
HUP TWO!
HUP TWO!
Ah!
P-put me down...!
WHAT THE HECK?! THAT'S FUNABORI!!
OH! HEY, SEMPAI!
LOOK! WE'RE BRINGING OUR SNACKS!
You're welcome!
THERE IS SOME SERIOUS DISCONNECT BETWEEN WHAT YOU'RE SAYING AND WHAT YOU'RE DOING!!
HEY, IT WASN'T EASY TO GET AHOLD OF THESE SNACKS, Y'KNOW.
YO, COOKING CLUB! BRING OUT YOUR BEST SNACKS!
AAH!! IT'S THE PREZ!!
OUR BEST SNACKS?
WE'LL MAKE IT A CONTEST TO SEE WHO CAN BAKE THE BEST ONES!
I'M NOT GONNA LOSE!!
THE WINNER!!
BUT I STILL BOIL WATER THE BEST...!
IF ONLY IT WAS A NOODLE CONTEST!
I MAKE THE BEST INSTANT NOODLES!!
MUNCH MUNCH
JUDGES
SO EVERYBODY ELSE IN THE CLUB ONLY KNOWS HOW TO MAKE NOODLES?! AND ALL YOU TWO DID WAS SIT AND EAT!!
RIGHT... SO TO GET SOME EXERCISE AND BURN OFF ALL THOSE CALORIES, WE DECIDED TO CARRY THE CONTEST WINNER BACK TO OUR CLUB ROOM.
Um...
Please...
JUST PUT THE POOR GIRL DOWN!!
SERIOUSLY, PUT FUNABORI DOWN! NOW!
AWWW!
I SAID PUT HER DOWN!!
......
QUIT IT!

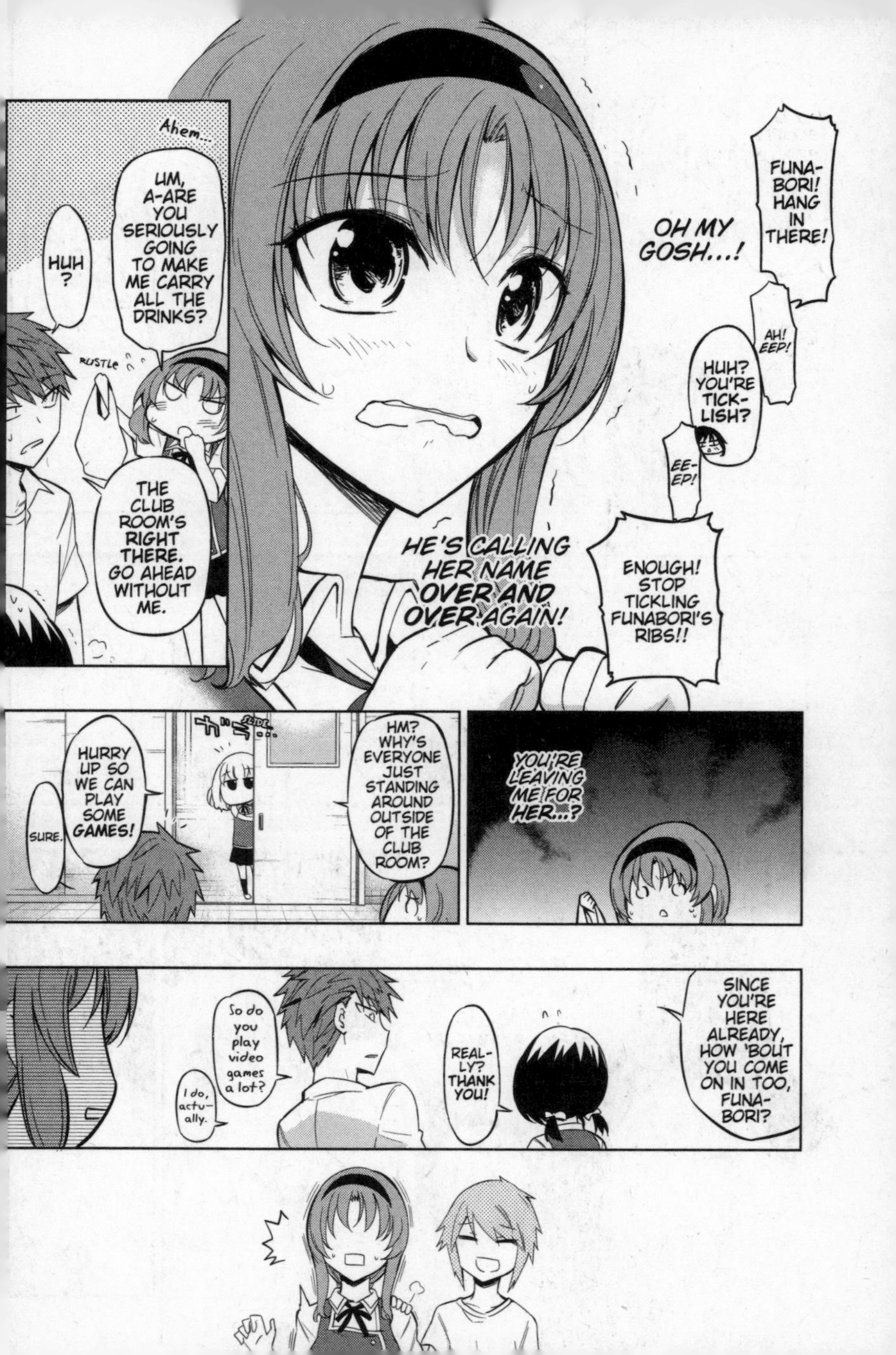
FUNA-BORI! HANG IN THERE!
OH MY GOSH...!
AH! EEP!
HUH? YOU'RE TICK-LISH?
EE-EP!
ENOUGH! STOP TICKLING FUNABORI'S RIBS!!
HE'S CALLING HER NAME OVER AND OVER AGAIN!
Ahem...
UM, A-ARE YOU SERIOUSLY GOING TO MAKE ME CARRY ALL THE DRINKS?
HUH?
RUSTLE
THE CLUB ROOM'S RIGHT THERE. GO AHEAD WITHOUT ME.
YOU'RE LEAVING ME FOR HER...?
HM? WHY'S EVERYONE JUST STANDING AROUND OUTSIDE OF THE CLUB ROOM?
SLIDE
HURRY UP SO WE CAN PLAY SOME GAMES!
SURE.
SINCE YOU'RE HERE ALREADY, HOW 'BOUT YOU COME ON IN TOO, FUNA-BORI?
REAL-LY? THANK YOU!
So do you play video games a lot?
I do, actu-ally.

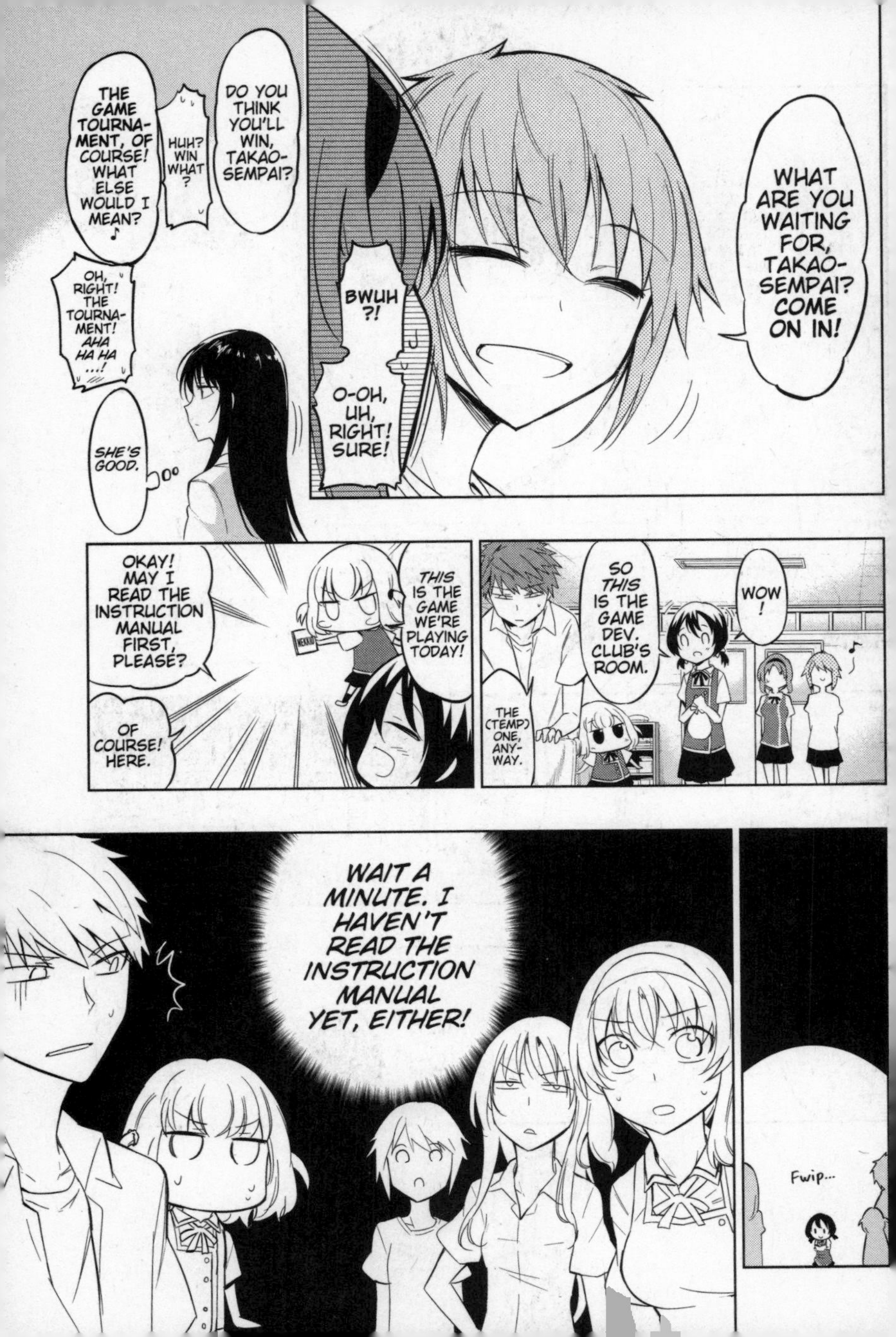
WHAT ARE YOU WAITING FOR, TAKAO-SEMPAI? COME ON IN!
BWUH?!
O-OH, UH, RIGHT! SURE!
DO YOU THINK YOU'LL WIN, TAKAO-SEMPAI?
HUH? WIN WHAT?
THE GAME TOURNAMENT, OF COURSE! WHAT ELSE WOULD I MEAN? ♪
OH, RIGHT! THE TOURNAMENT! AHA HA HA ...!
SHE'S GOOD.
WOW!
SO THIS IS THE GAME DEV. CLUB'S ROOM.
THE (TEMP) ONE, ANYWAY.
THIS IS THE GAME WE'RE PLAYING TODAY!
OKAY! MAY I READ THE INSTRUCTION MANUAL FIRST, PLEASE?
OF COURSE! HERE.
Fwip...
WAIT A MINUTE. I HAVEN'T READ THE INSTRUCTION MANUAL YET, EITHER!

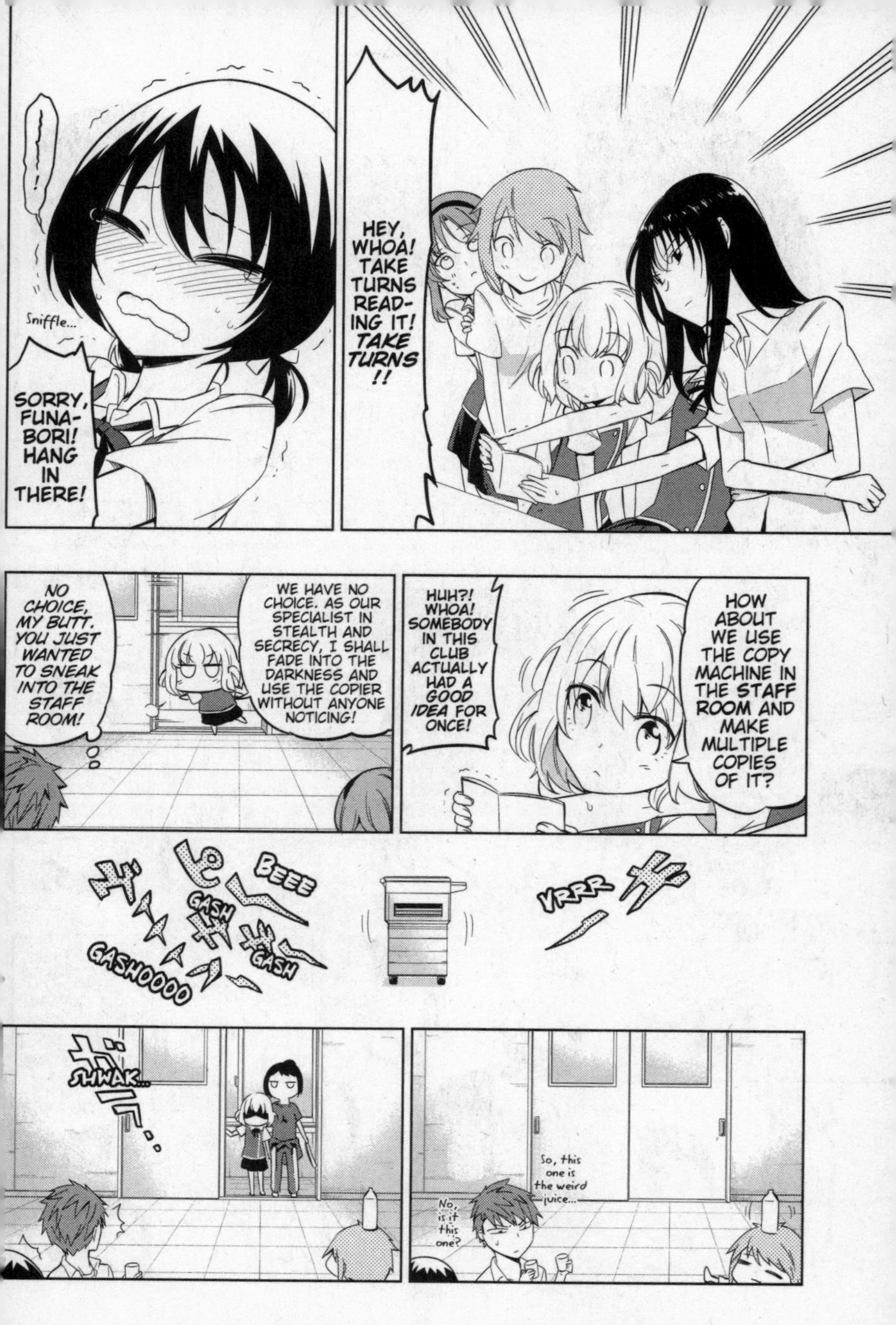
HEY, WHOA! TAKE TURNS READING IT! TAKE TURNS!!
Sniffle...
SORRY, FUNABORI! HANG IN THERE!
HOW ABOUT WE USE THE COPY MACHINE IN THE STAFF ROOM AND MAKE MULTIPLE COPIES OF IT?
HUH?! WHOA! SOMEBODY IN THIS CLUB ACTUALLY HAD A GOOD IDEA FOR ONCE!
WE HAVE NO CHOICE. AS OUR SPECIALIST IN STEALTH AND SECRECY, I SHALL FADE INTO THE DARKNESS AND USE THE COPIER WITHOUT ANYONE NOTICING!
NO CHOICE, MY BUTT. YOU JUST WANTED TO SNEAK INTO THE STAFF ROOM!
VRRR
BEEE
GASH
GASH
GASHOOOO
So, this one is the weird juice...
No, is it this one?
SHWAK...

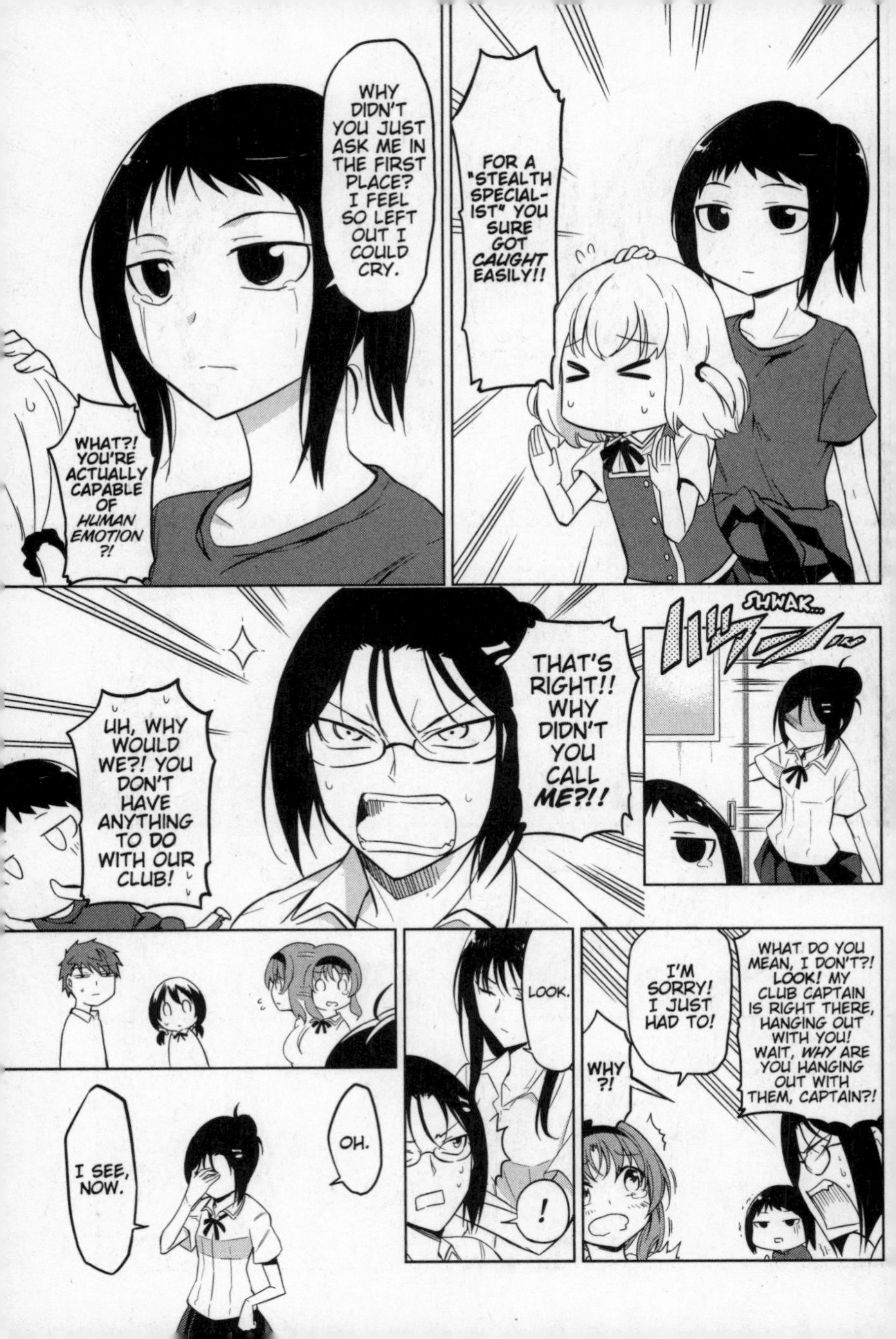
FOR A "STEALTH SPECIALIST" YOU SURE GOT *CAUGHT* EASILY!!
WHY DIDN'T YOU JUST ASK ME IN THE FIRST PLACE? I FEEL SO LEFT OUT I COULD CRY.
WHAT?! YOU'RE ACTUALLY CAPABLE OF *HUMAN EMOTION*?!
SHWAK...
THAT'S RIGHT!! WHY DIDN'T YOU CALL *ME*?!!
UH, WHY WOULD WE?! YOU DON'T HAVE ANYTHING TO DO WITH OUR CLUB!
WHAT DO YOU MEAN, I DON'T?! LOOK! MY CLUB CAPTAIN IS RIGHT THERE, HANGING OUT WITH YOU! WAIT, *WHY* ARE YOU HANGING OUT WITH THEM, CAPTAIN?!
I'M SORRY! I JUST HAD TO!
WHY?!
LOOK.
!
OH.
I SEE, NOW.

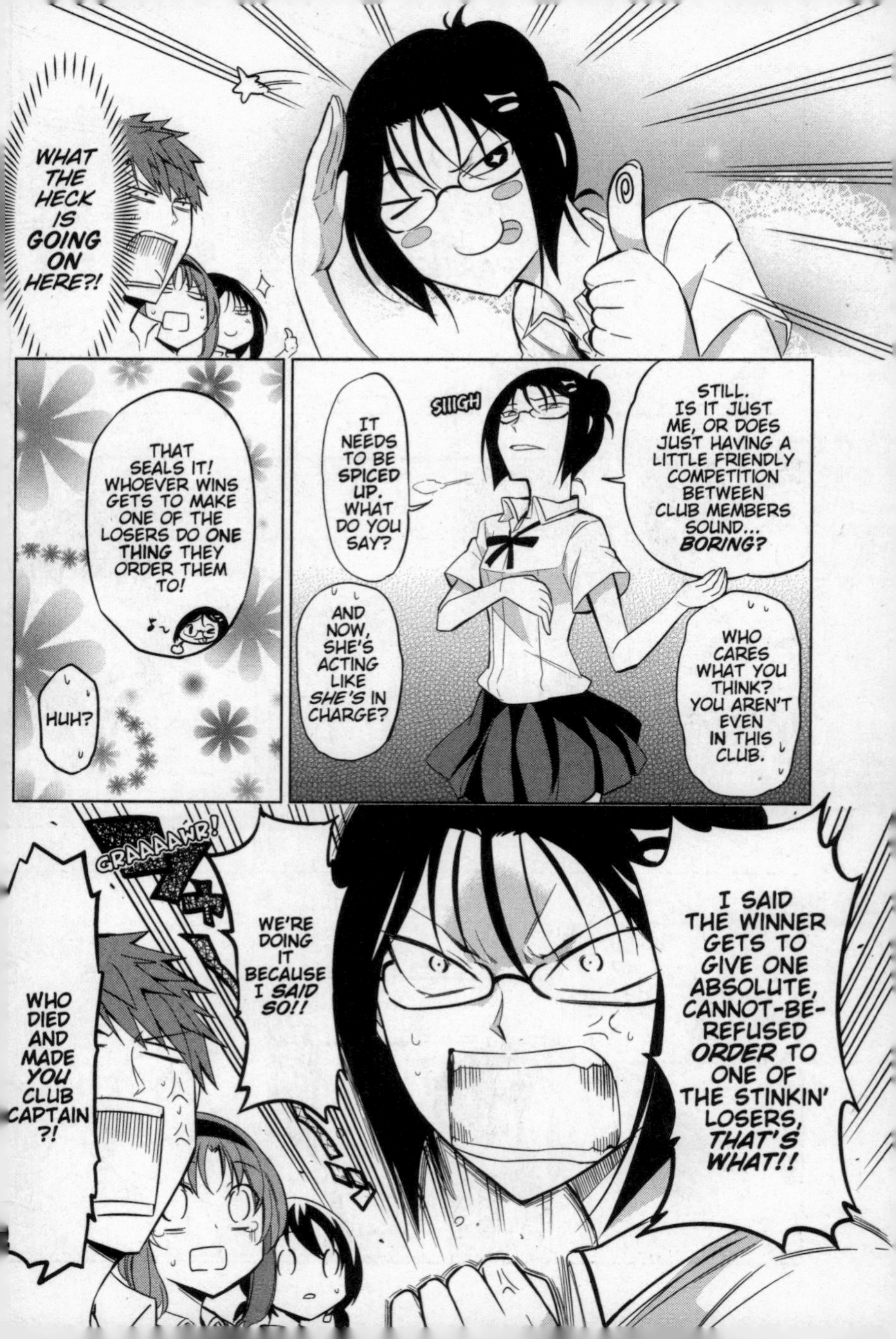

WHAT THE HECK IS GOING ON HERE?!
STILL. IS IT JUST ME, OR DOES JUST HAVING A LITTLE FRIENDLY COMPETITION BETWEEN CLUB MEMBERS SOUND... *BORING?*
SIIIGH
IT NEEDS TO BE SPICED UP. WHAT DO YOU SAY?
WHO CARES WHAT YOU THINK? YOU AREN'T EVEN IN THIS CLUB.
AND NOW, SHE'S ACTING LIKE *SHE'S* IN CHARGE?
THAT SEALS IT! WHOEVER WINS GETS TO MAKE ONE OF THE LOSERS DO ONE THING THEY ORDER THEM TO!
HUH?
I SAID THE WINNER GETS TO GIVE ONE ABSOLUTE, CANNOT-BE-REFUSED *ORDER* TO ONE OF THE STINKIN' LOSERS, *THAT'S WHAT!!*
WE'RE DOING IT BECAUSE I *SAID SO!!*
GRAAAAWR!
WHO DIED AND MADE *YOU* CLUB CAPTAIN?!

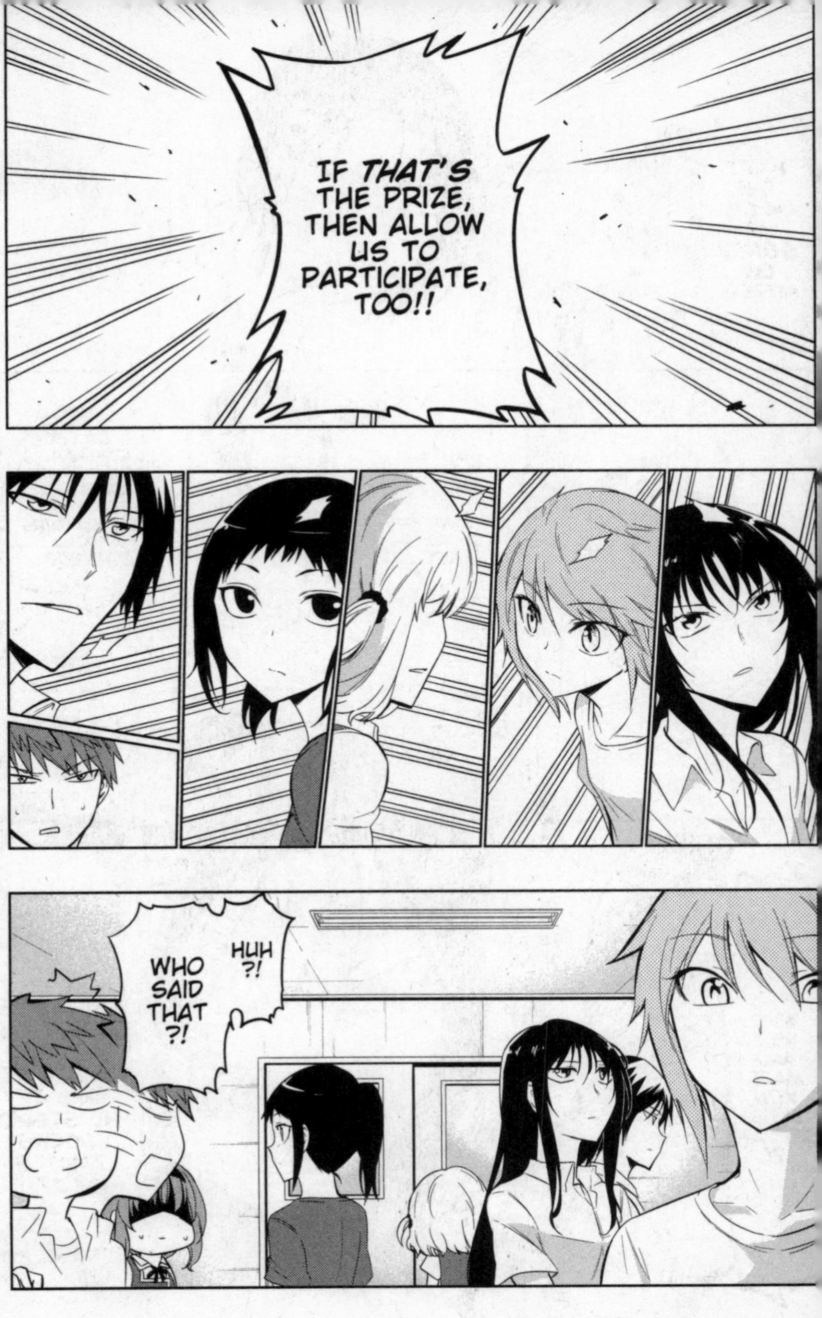
IF *THAT'S* THE PRIZE, THEN ALLOW US TO PARTICIPATE, TOO!!
HUH ?!
WHO SAID THAT ?!

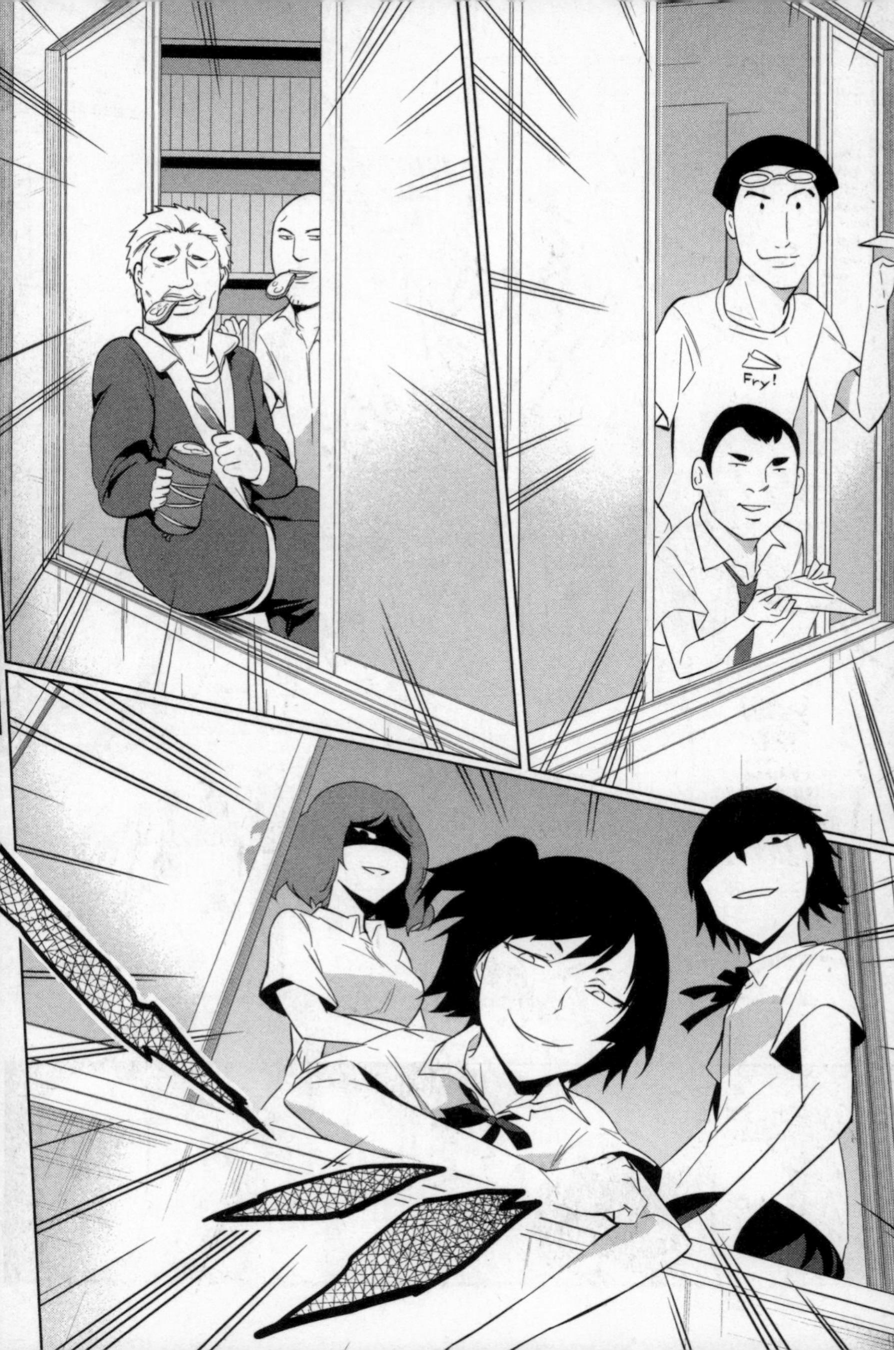
Fry!

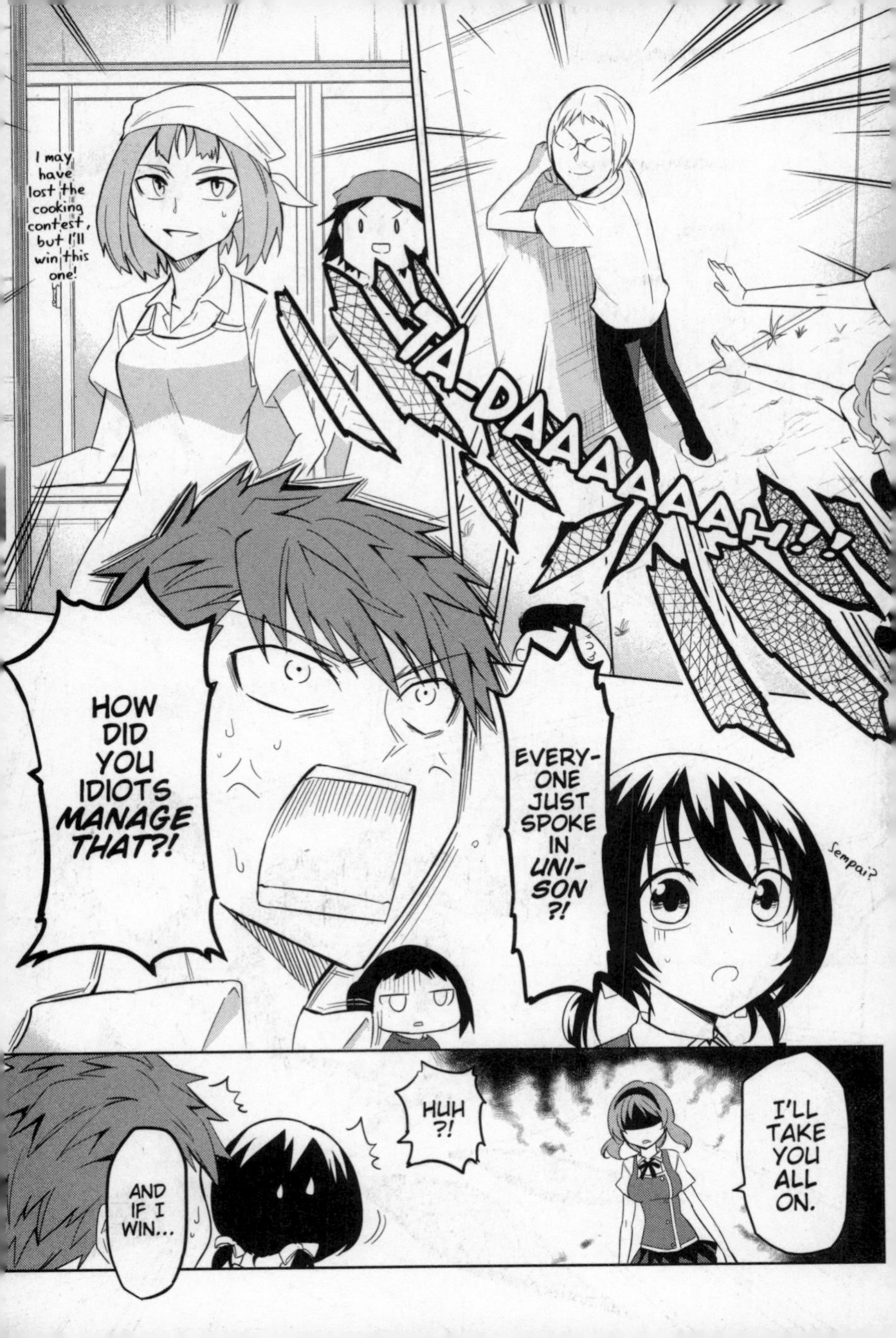
I may have lost the cooking contest, but I'll win this one!
TA-DAAAAAAAH!!
EVERY-ONE JUST SPOKE IN UNI-SON?!
Sempai?
HOW DID YOU IDIOTS MANAGE THAT?!
I'LL TAKE YOU ALL ON.
HUH?!
AND IF I WIN...

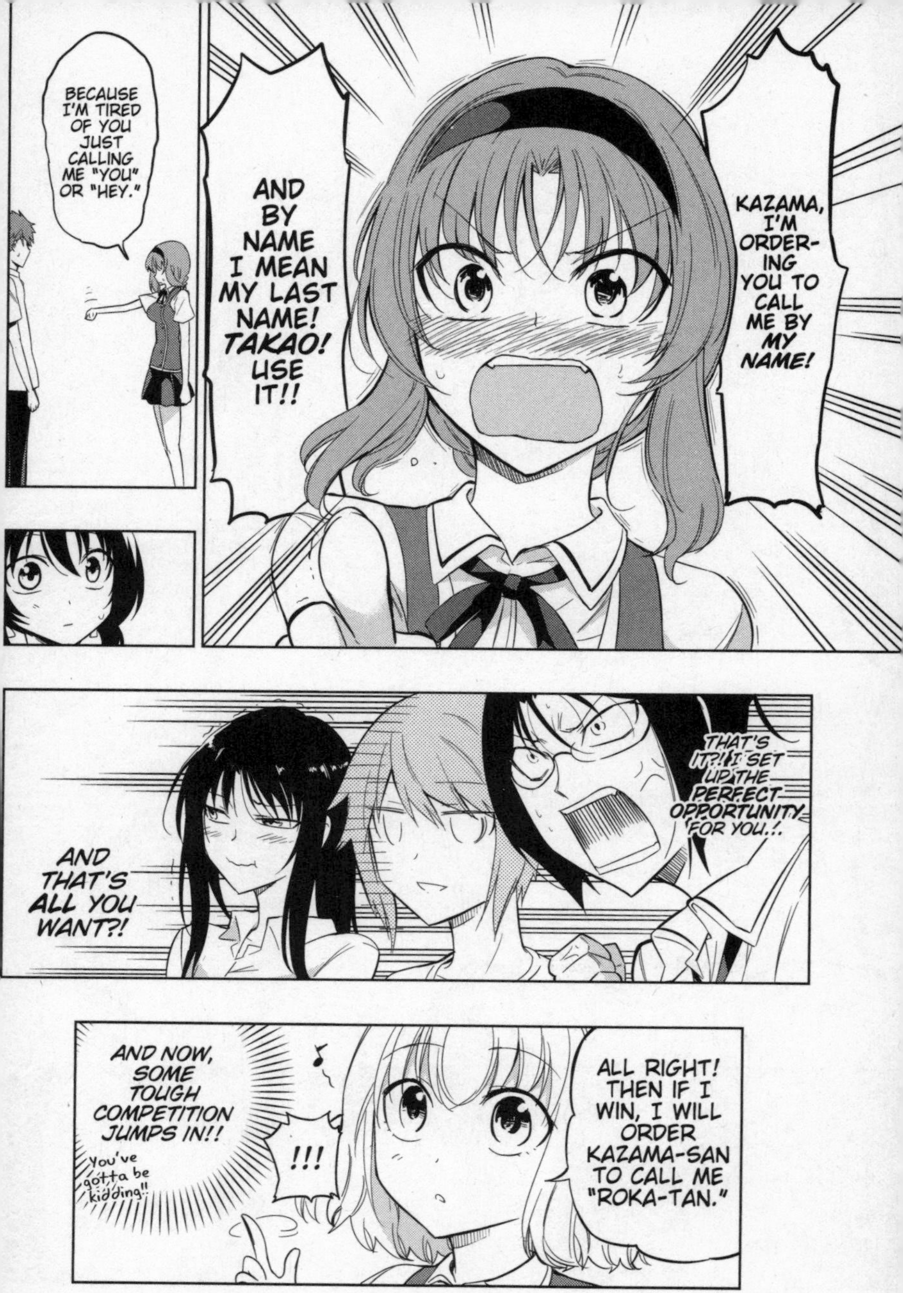
KAZAMA, I'M ORDERING YOU TO CALL ME BY MY NAME!
AND BY NAME I MEAN MY LAST NAME! TAKAO! USE IT!!
BECAUSE I'M TIRED OF YOU JUST CALLING ME "YOU" OR "HEY."
THAT'S IT?! I SET UP THE PERFECT OPPORTUNITY FOR YOU..!
AND THAT'S ALL YOU WANT?!
ALL RIGHT! THEN IF I WIN, I WILL ORDER KAZAMA-SAN TO CALL ME "ROKA-TAN."
!!!
AND NOW, SOME TOUGH COMPETITION JUMPS IN!!
You've gotta be kidding!!

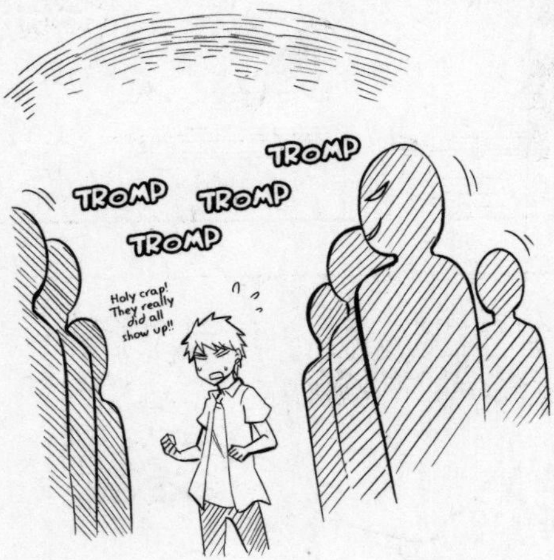
TROMP
TROMP
TROMP
TROMP
Holy crap! They really did all show up!!

D-FRAGMENTS
ディーふらぐ!

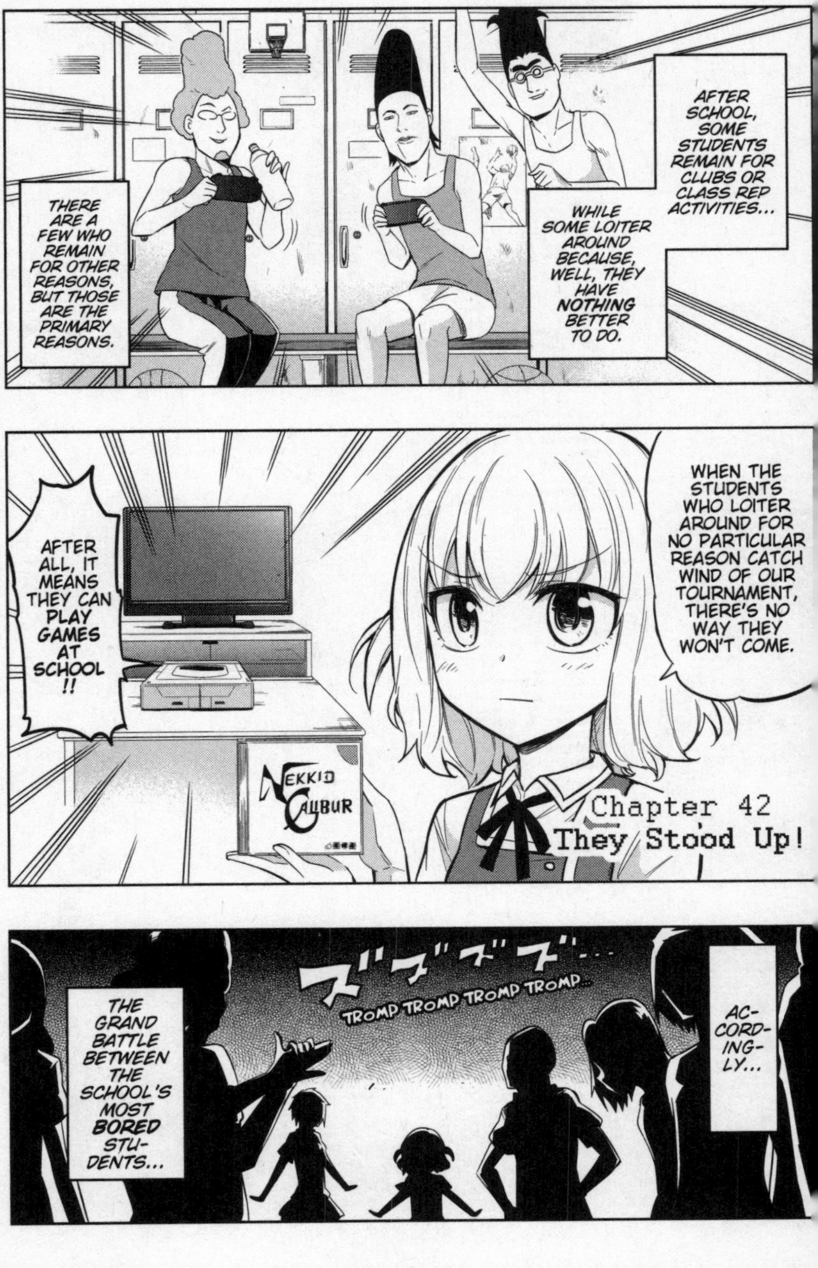
AFTER SCHOOL, SOME STUDENTS REMAIN FOR CLUBS OR CLASS REP ACTIVITIES...
WHILE SOME LOITER AROUND BECAUSE, WELL, THEY HAVE NOTHING BETTER TO DO.
THERE ARE A FEW WHO REMAIN FOR OTHER REASONS, BUT THOSE ARE THE PRIMARY REASONS.
WHEN THE STUDENTS WHO LOITER AROUND FOR NO PARTICULAR REASON CATCH WIND OF OUR TOURNAMENT, THERE'S NO WAY THEY WON'T COME.
AFTER ALL, IT MEANS THEY CAN PLAY GAMES AT SCHOOL !!
NEKKID CALIBUR
Chapter 42
They Stood Up!
AC-CORD-ING-LY...
TROMP TROMP TROMP TROMP...
THE GRAND BATTLE BETWEEN THE SCHOOL'S MOST BORED STU-DENTS...

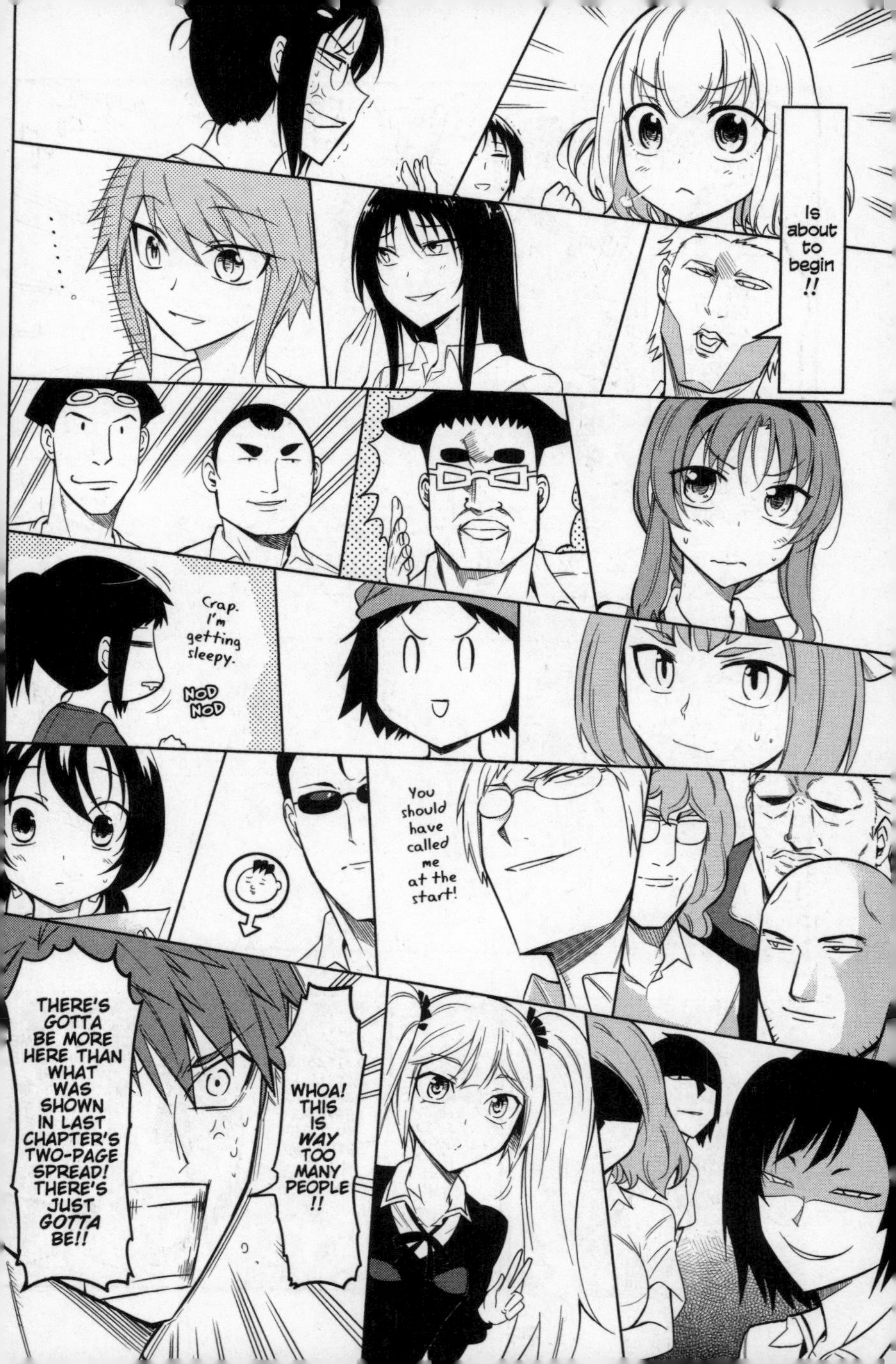
Is about to begin!!
Crap. I'm getting sleepy.
NOD NOD
You should have called me at the start!
WHOA! THIS IS WAY TOO MANY PEOPLE!!
THERE'S GOTTA BE MORE HERE THAN WHAT WAS SHOWN IN LAST CHAPTER'S TWO-PAGE SPREAD! THERE'S JUST GOTTA BE!!

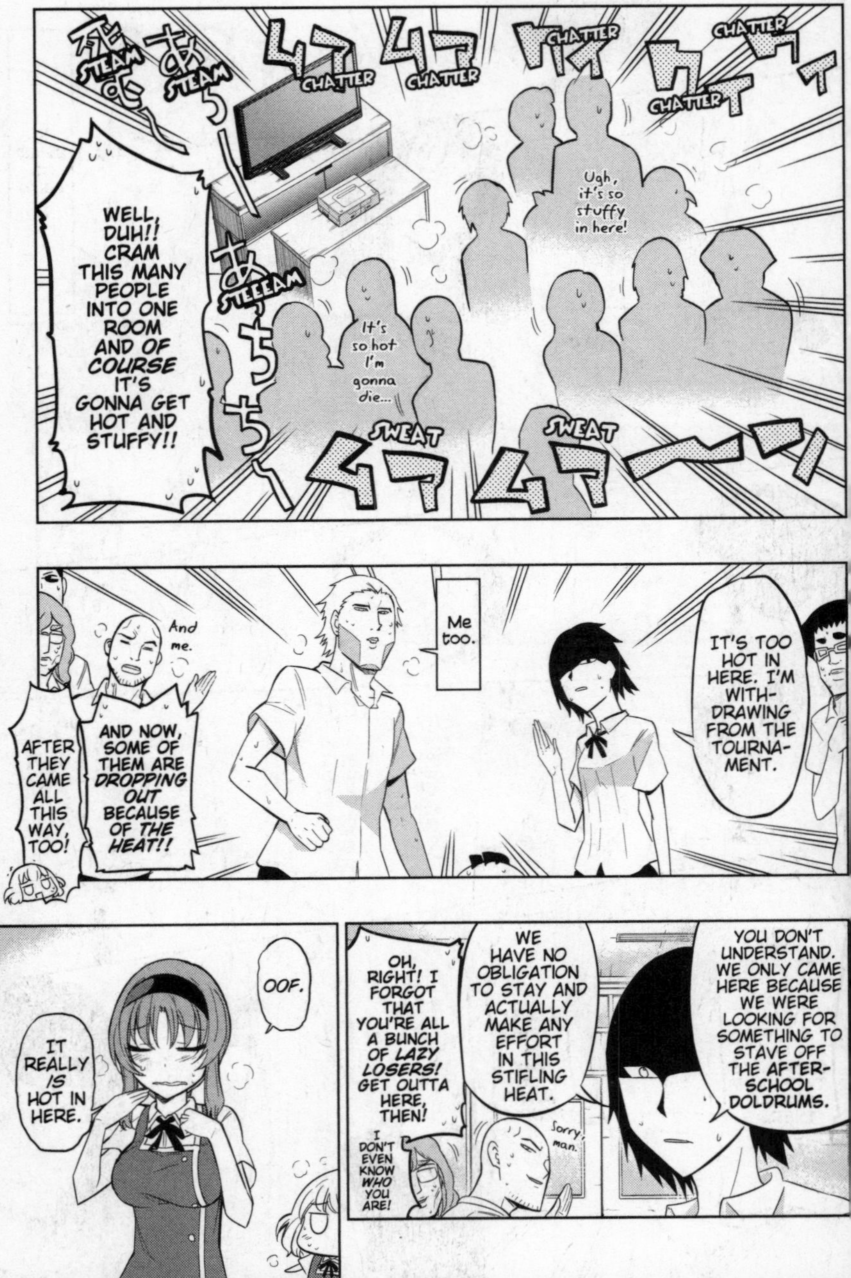

CHATTER
CHATTER
CHATTER
CHATTER
STEAM
STEAM
Ugh, it's so stuffy in here!
It's so hot I'm gonna die...
SWEAT
SWEAT
STEEEAM
WELL, DUH!! CRAM THIS MANY PEOPLE INTO ONE ROOM AND OF COURSE IT'S GONNA GET HOT AND STUFFY!!
IT'S TOO HOT IN HERE. I'M WITH-DRAWING FROM THE TOURNA-MENT.
Me too.
And me.
AND NOW, SOME OF THEM ARE DROPPING OUT BECAUSE OF THE HEAT!!
AFTER THEY CAME ALL THIS WAY, TOO!
YOU DON'T UNDERSTAND. WE ONLY CAME HERE BECAUSE WE WERE LOOKING FOR SOMETHING TO STAVE OFF THE AFTER-SCHOOL DOLDRUMS.
WE HAVE NO OBLIGATION TO STAY AND ACTUALLY MAKE ANY EFFORT IN THIS STIFLING HEAT.
OH, RIGHT! I FORGOT THAT YOU'RE ALL A BUNCH OF LAZY LOSERS! GET OUTTA HERE, THEN!
Sorry, man.
I DON'T EVEN KNOW WHO YOU ARE!
OOF.
IT REALLY IS HOT IN HERE.

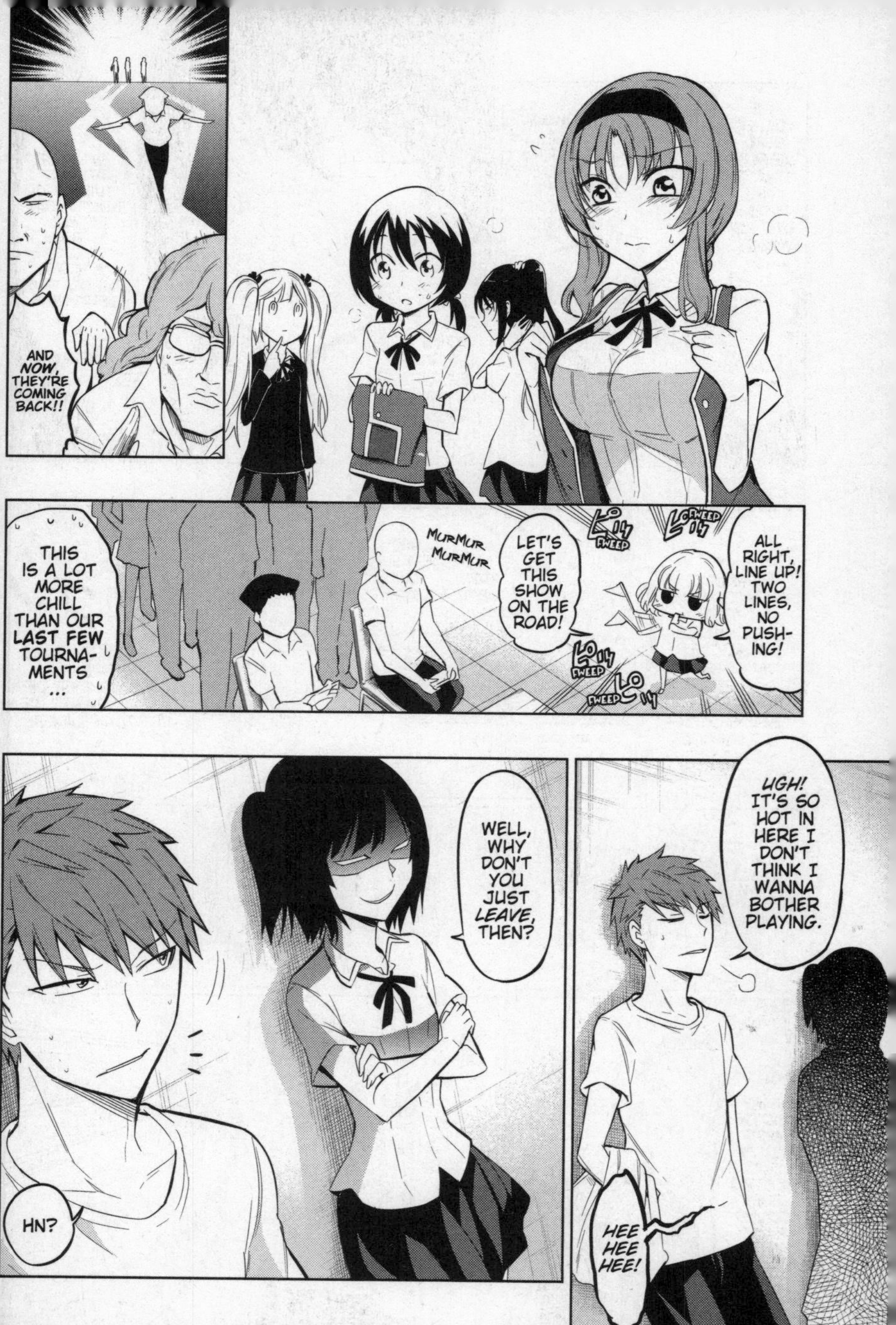
AND NOW, THEY'RE COMING BACK!!
ALL RIGHT, LINE UP! TWO LINES, NO PUSH-ING!
FWEEP
FWEEP
LET'S GET THIS SHOW ON THE ROAD!
FWEEP
FWEEP
MURMUR MURMUR
THIS IS A LOT MORE CHILL THAN OUR LAST FEW TOURNA-MENTS ...
UGH! IT'S SO HOT IN HERE I DON'T THINK I WANNA BOTHER PLAYING.
HEE HEE HEE!
WELL, WHY DON'T YOU JUST LEAVE, THEN?
HN?

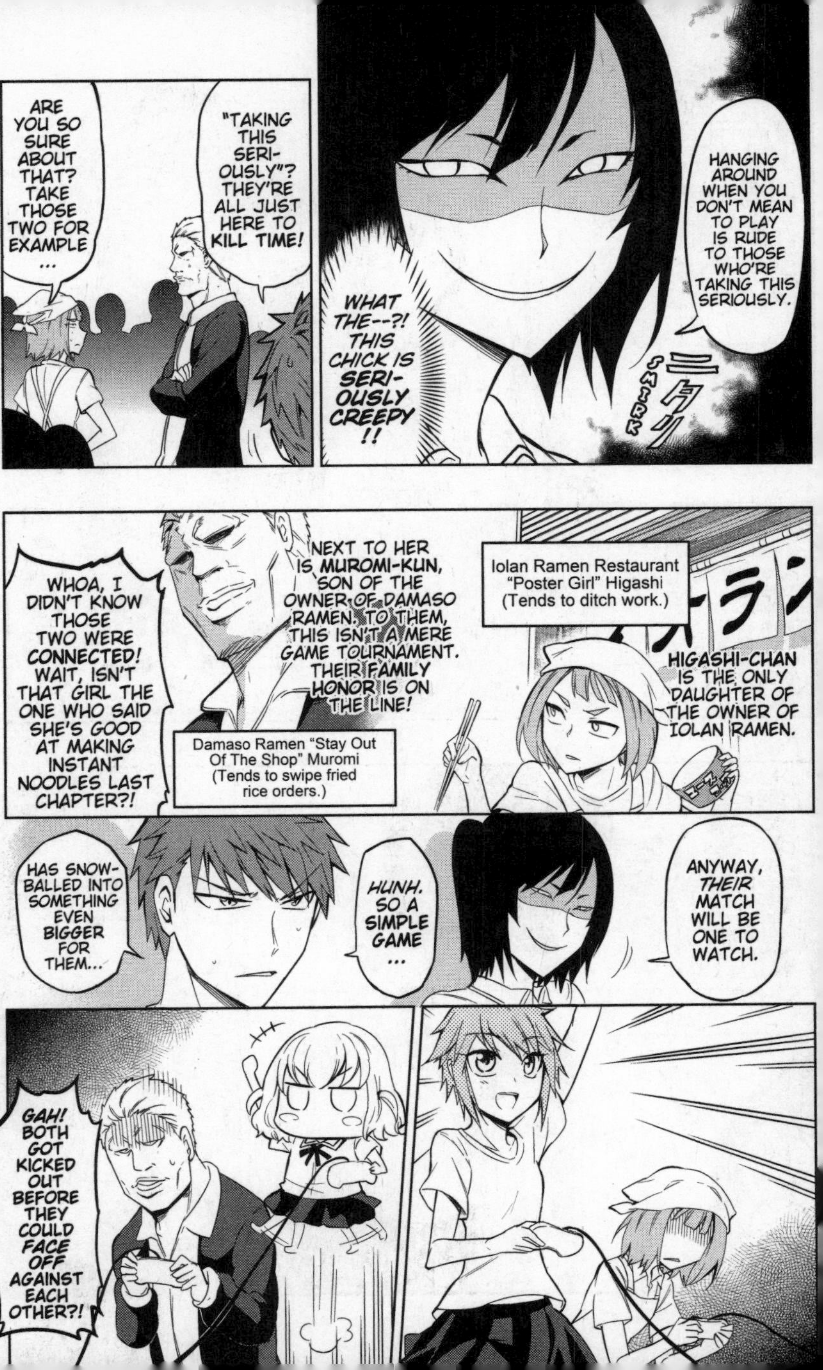
HANGING AROUND WHEN YOU DON'T MEAN TO PLAY IS RUDE TO THOSE WHO'RE TAKING THIS SERIOUSLY.
ニタリ SMIRK
WHAT THE--?! THIS CHICK IS SERI-OUSLY CREEPY!!
"TAKING THIS SERI-OUSLY"? THEY'RE ALL JUST HERE TO KILL TIME!
ARE YOU SO SURE ABOUT THAT? TAKE THOSE TWO FOR EXAMPLE ...
Iolan Ramen Restaurant "Poster Girl" Higashi (Tends to ditch work.)
HIGASHI-CHAN IS THE ONLY DAUGHTER OF THE OWNER OF IOLAN RAMEN.
NEXT TO HER IS MUROMI-KUN, SON OF THE OWNER OF DAMASO RAMEN. TO THEM, THIS ISN'T A MERE GAME TOURNAMENT. THEIR FAMILY HONOR IS ON THE LINE!
Damaso Ramen "Stay Out Of The Shop" Muromi (Tends to swipe fried rice orders.)
WHOA, I DIDN'T KNOW THOSE TWO WERE CONNECTED! WAIT, ISN'T THAT GIRL THE ONE WHO SAID SHE'S GOOD AT MAKING INSTANT NOODLES LAST CHAPTER?!
ANYWAY, THEIR MATCH WILL BE ONE TO WATCH.
HUNH. SO A SIMPLE GAME ...
HAS SNOW-BALLED INTO SOMETHING EVEN BIGGER FOR THEM...
GAH! BOTH GOT KICKED OUT BEFORE THEY COULD FACE OFF AGAINST EACH OTHER?!

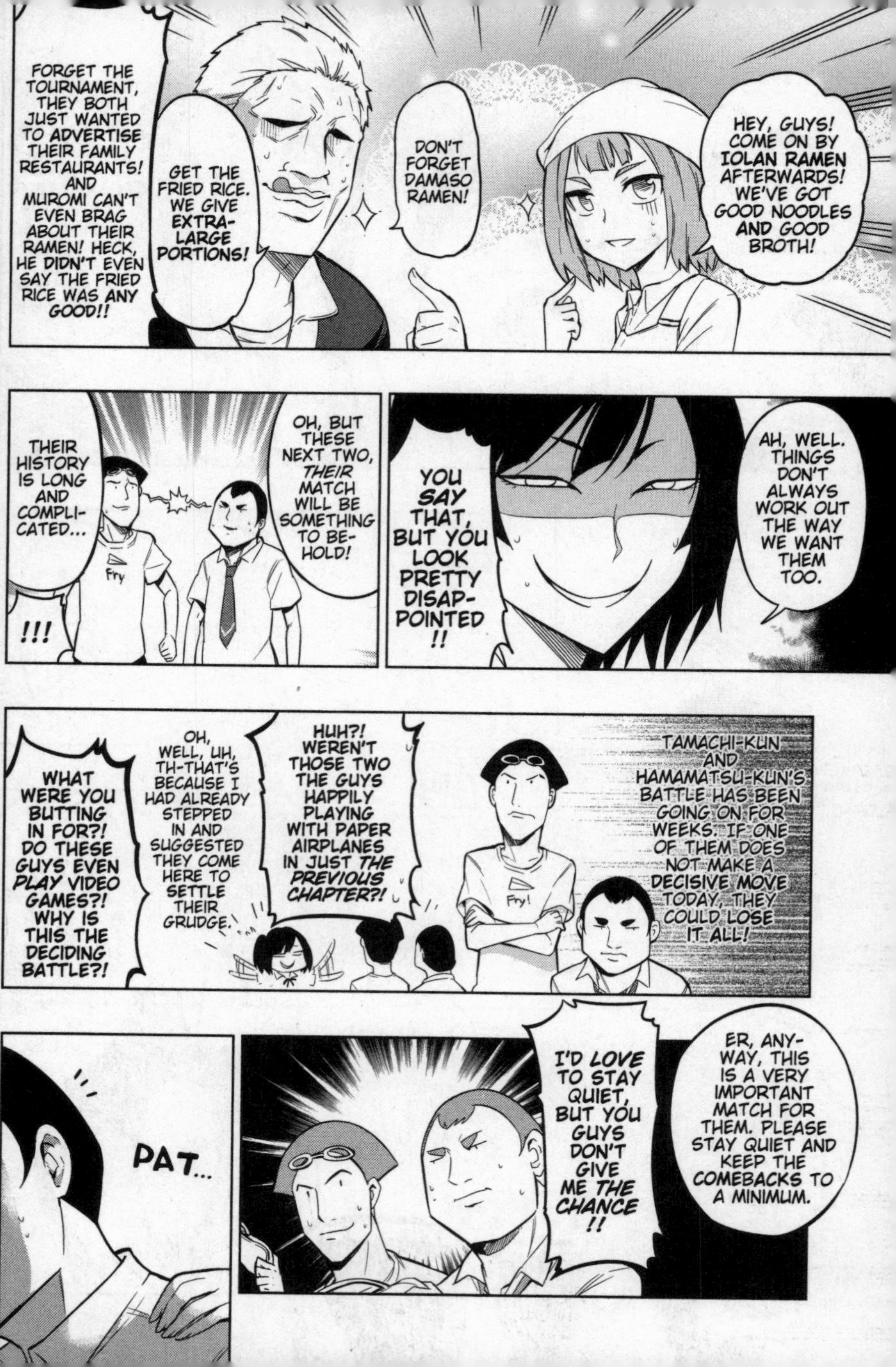
HEY, GUYS! COME ON BY IOLAN RAMEN AFTERWARDS! WE'VE GOT GOOD NOODLES AND GOOD BROTH!
DON'T FORGET DAMASO RAMEN!
GET THE FRIED RICE. WE GIVE EXTRA-LARGE PORTIONS!
FORGET THE TOURNAMENT, THEY BOTH JUST WANTED TO ADVERTISE THEIR FAMILY RESTAURANTS! AND MUROMI CAN'T EVEN BRAG ABOUT THEIR RAMEN! HECK, HE DIDN'T EVEN SAY THE FRIED RICE WAS ANY GOOD!!
AH, WELL. THINGS DON'T ALWAYS WORK OUT THE WAY WE WANT THEM TOO.
YOU SAY THAT, BUT YOU LOOK PRETTY DISAP-POINTED!!
OH, BUT THESE NEXT TWO, THEIR MATCH WILL BE SOMETHING TO BE-HOLD!
THEIR HISTORY IS LONG AND COMPLI-CATED...
!!!
TAMACHI-KUN AND HAMAMATSU-KUN'S BATTLE HAS BEEN GOING ON FOR WEEKS. IF ONE OF THEM DOES NOT MAKE A DECISIVE MOVE TODAY, THEY COULD LOSE IT ALL!
HUH?! WEREN'T THOSE TWO THE GUYS HAPPILY PLAYING WITH PAPER AIRPLANES IN JUST THE PREVIOUS CHAPTER?!
OH, WELL, UH, TH-THAT'S BECAUSE I HAD ALREADY STEPPED IN AND SUGGESTED THEY COME HERE TO SETTLE THEIR GRUDGE.
WHAT WERE YOU BUTTING IN FOR?! DO THESE GUYS EVEN PLAY VIDEO GAMES?! WHY IS THIS THE DECIDING BATTLE?!
ER, ANY-WAY, THIS IS A VERY IMPORTANT MATCH FOR THEM. PLEASE STAY QUIET AND KEEP THE COMEBACKS TO A MINIMUM.
I'D LOVE TO STAY QUIET, BUT YOU GUYS DON'T GIVE ME THE CHANCE!!
PAT...

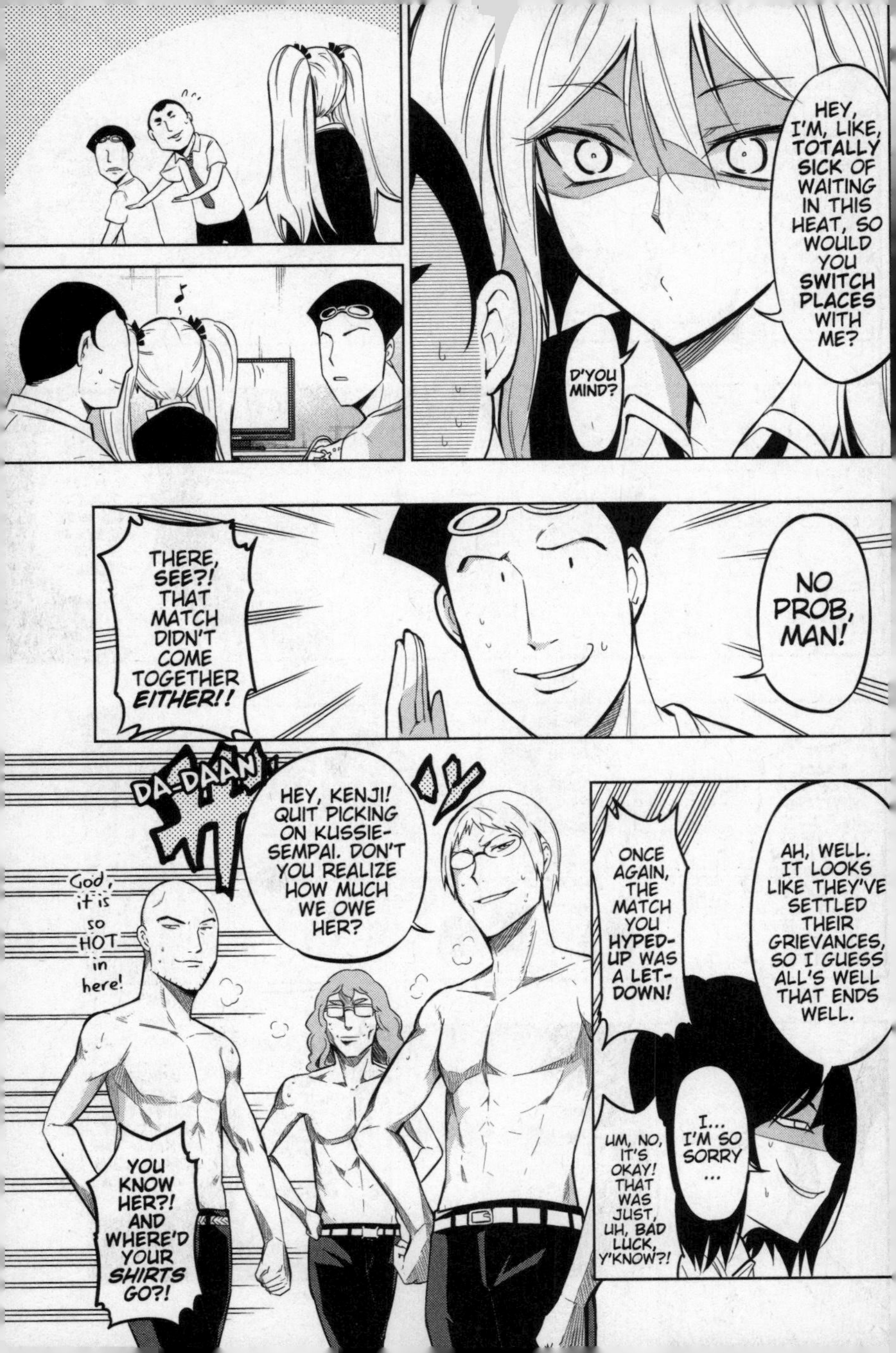
HEY, I'M, LIKE, TOTALLY SICK OF WAITING IN THIS HEAT, SO WOULD YOU SWITCH PLACES WITH ME?
D'YOU MIND?
NO PROB, MAN!
THERE, SEE?! THAT MATCH DIDN'T COME TOGETHER *EITHER!!*
AH, WELL. IT LOOKS LIKE THEY'VE SETTLED THEIR GRIEVANCES, SO I GUESS ALL'S WELL THAT ENDS WELL.
ONCE AGAIN, THE MATCH YOU HYPED-UP WAS A LET-DOWN!
I... I'M SO SORRY ...
UM, NO, IT'S OKAY! THAT WAS JUST, UH, BAD LUCK, Y'KNOW?!
OY
HEY, KENJI! QUIT PICKING ON KUSSIE-SEMPAI. DON'T YOU REALIZE HOW MUCH WE OWE HER?
DA-DAAN
God, it is so HOT in here!
YOU KNOW HER?! AND WHERE'D YOUR *SHIRTS* GO?!

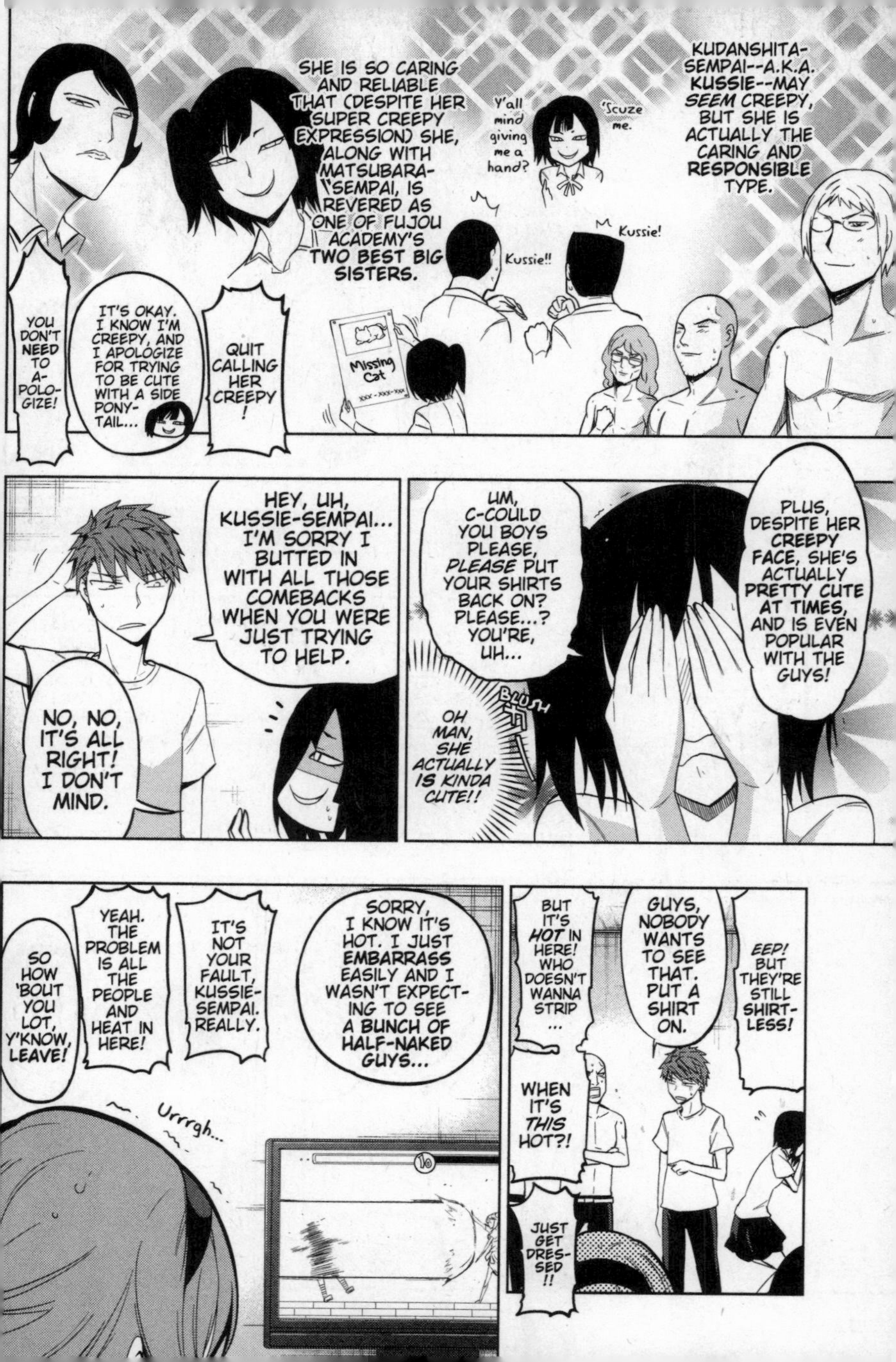
KUDANSHITA-SEMPAI--A.K.A. KUSSIE--MAY *SEEM* CREEPY, BUT SHE IS ACTUALLY THE CARING AND RESPONSIBLE TYPE.
'Scuze me.
Y'all mind giving me a hand?
Kussie!
Kussie!!
Missing Cat
XXX-XXX-XXX
SHE IS SO CARING AND RELIABLE THAT (DESPITE HER SUPER CREEPY EXPRESSION) SHE, ALONG WITH MATSUBARA-SEMPAI, IS REVERED AS ONE OF FUJOU ACADEMY'S TWO BEST BIG SISTERS.
QUIT CALLING HER CREEPY!
IT'S OKAY. I KNOW I'M CREEPY, AND I APOLOGIZE FOR TRYING TO BE CUTE WITH A SIDE PONY-TAIL...
YOU DON'T NEED TO A-POLO-GIZE!
PLUS, DESPITE HER CREEPY FACE, SHE'S ACTUALLY PRETTY CUTE AT TIMES, AND IS EVEN POPULAR WITH THE GUYS!
UM, C-COULD YOU BOYS PLEASE, *PLEASE* PUT YOUR SHIRTS BACK ON? PLEASE...? YOU'RE, UH...
BLUSH
OH MAN, SHE ACTUALLY IS KINDA CUTE!!
HEY, UH, KUSSIE-SEMPAI... I'M SORRY I BUTTED IN WITH ALL THOSE COMEBACKS WHEN YOU WERE JUST TRYING TO HELP.
NO, NO, IT'S ALL RIGHT! I DON'T MIND.
EEP! BUT THEY'RE STILL SHIRT-LESS!
GUYS, NOBODY WANTS TO SEE THAT. PUT A SHIRT ON.
BUT IT'S *HOT* IN HERE! WHO DOESN'T WANNA STRIP...
WHEN IT'S *THIS* HOT?!
JUST GET DRES-SED!!
SORRY, I KNOW IT'S HOT. I JUST **EMBARRASS** EASILY AND I WASN'T EXPECT-ING TO SEE **A BUNCH OF HALF-NAKED GUYS...**
IT'S NOT YOUR FAULT, KUSSIE-SEMPAI. REALLY.
YEAH. THE PROBLEM IS ALL THE PEOPLE AND HEAT IN HERE!
SO HOW 'BOUT YOU LOT, Y'KNOW, LEAVE!
Urrrgh...

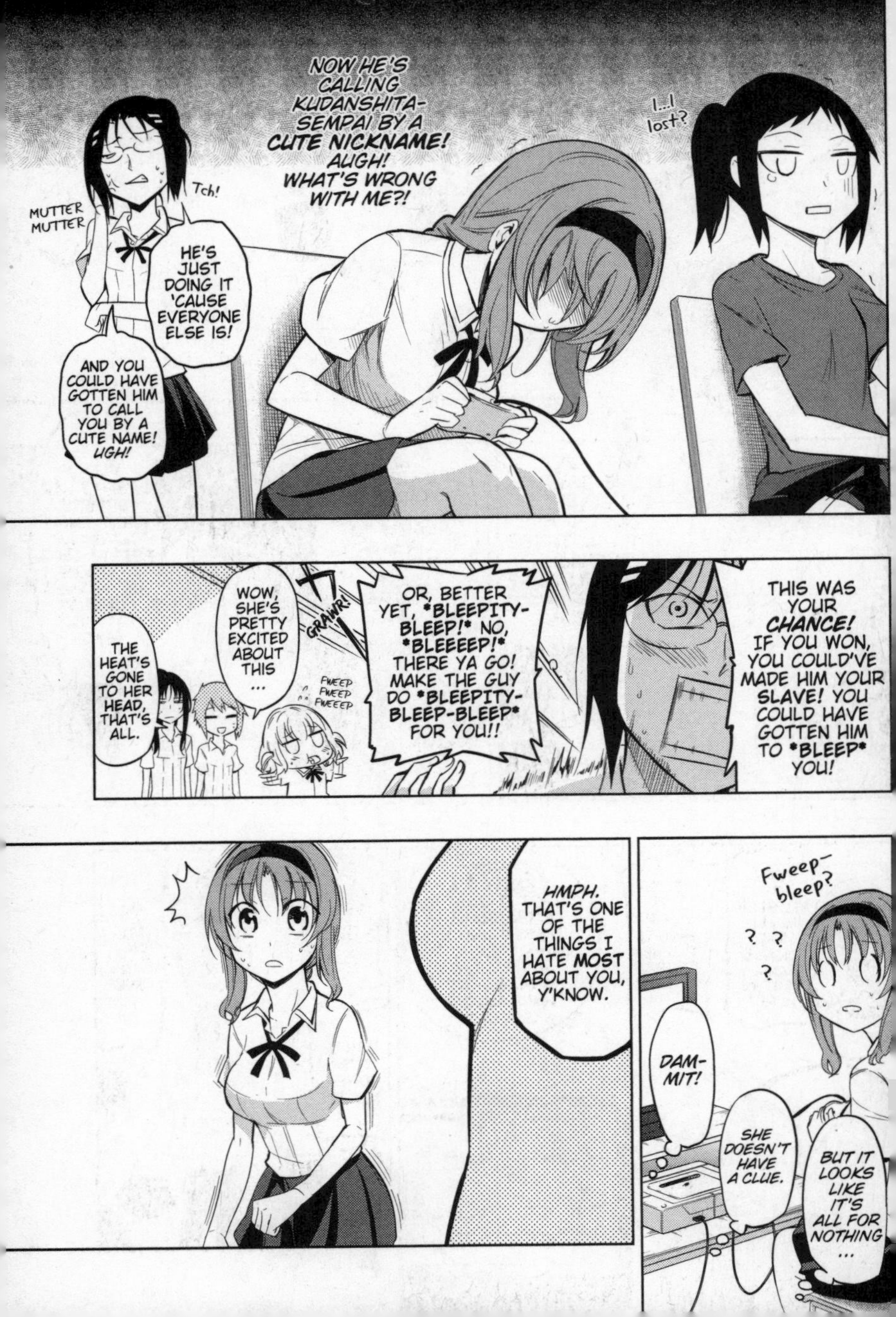
I...I lost?
NOW HE'S CALLING KUDANSHITA-SEMPAI BY A CUTE NICKNAME! AUGH! WHAT'S WRONG WITH ME?!
Tch!
MUTTER MUTTER
HE'S JUST DOING IT 'CAUSE EVERYONE ELSE IS!
AND YOU COULD HAVE GOTTEN HIM TO CALL YOU BY A CUTE NAME! UGH!
THIS WAS YOUR CHANCE! IF YOU WON, YOU COULD'VE MADE HIM YOUR SLAVE! YOU COULD HAVE GOTTEN HIM TO *BLEEP* YOU!
OR, BETTER YET, *BLEEPITY-BLEEP!* NO, *BLEEEEP!* THERE YA GO! MAKE THE GUY DO *BLEEPITY-BLEEP-BLEEP* FOR YOU!!
GRAWR!
FWEEP FWEEP FWEEEP
WOW, SHE'S PRETTY EXCITED ABOUT THIS ...
THE HEAT'S GONE TO HER HEAD, THAT'S ALL.
Fweep-bleep?
DAM-MIT!
BUT IT LOOKS LIKE IT'S ALL FOR NOTHING ...
SHE DOESN'T HAVE A CLUE.
HMPH. THAT'S ONE OF THE THINGS I HATE MOST ABOUT YOU, Y'KNOW.

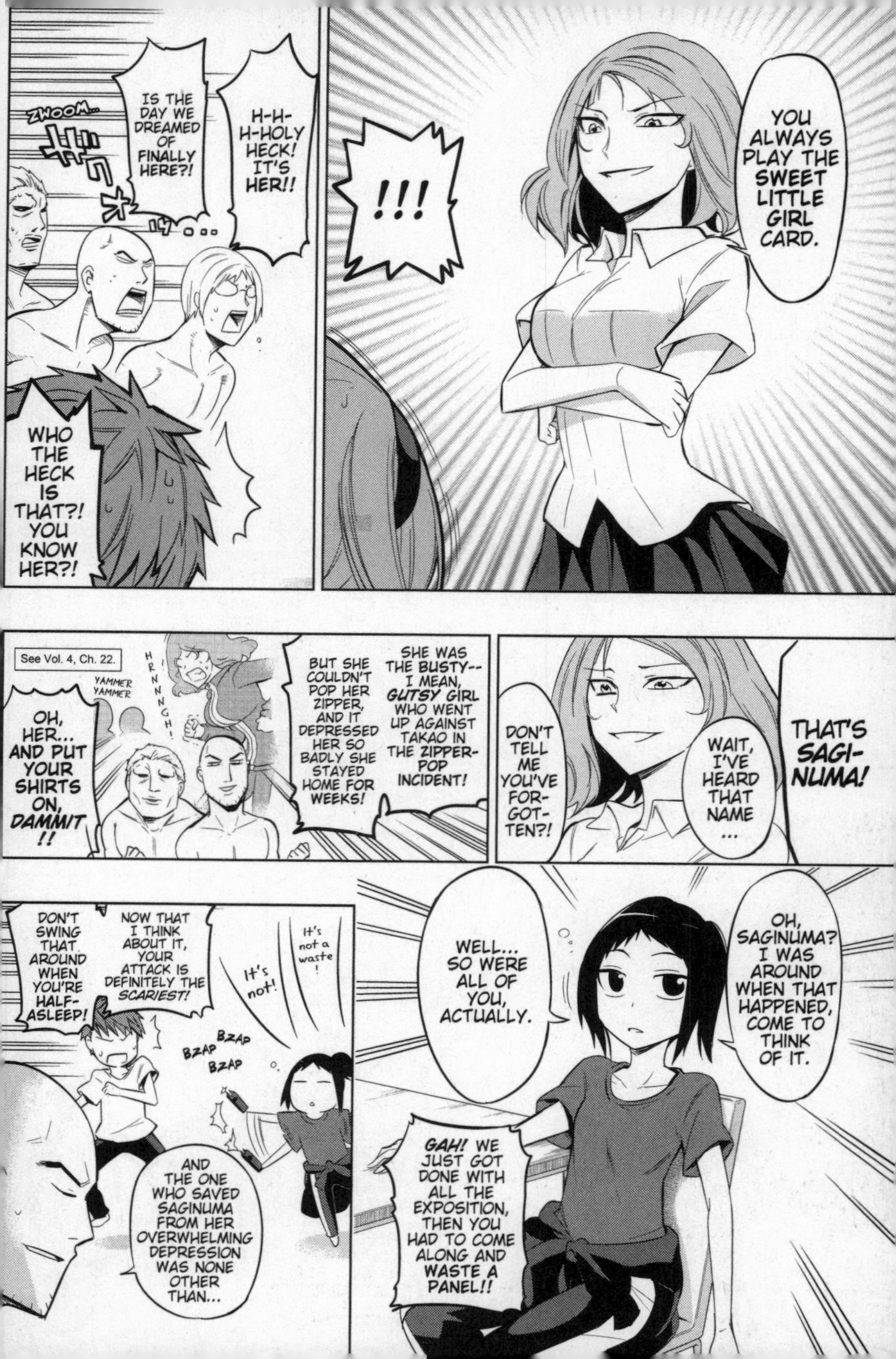
YOU ALWAYS PLAY THE SWEET LITTLE GIRL CARD.
!!!
H-H-H-HOLY HECK! IT'S HER!!
IS THE DAY WE DREAMED OF FINALLY HERE?!
ZWOOM...
WHO THE HECK IS THAT?! YOU KNOW HER?!
THAT'S SAGINUMA!
WAIT, I'VE HEARD THAT NAME...
DON'T TELL ME YOU'VE FORGOTTEN?!
SHE WAS THE BUSTY-- I MEAN, GUTSY GIRL WHO WENT UP AGAINST TAKAO IN THE ZIPPER-POP INCIDENT!
BUT SHE COULDN'T POP HER ZIPPER, AND IT DEPRESSED HER SO BADLY SHE STAYED HOME FOR WEEKS!
HRNNNGH!
See Vol. 4, Ch. 22.
YAMMER YAMMER
OH, HER... AND PUT YOUR SHIRTS ON, DAMMIT!!
OH, SAGINUMA? I WAS AROUND WHEN THAT HAPPENED, COME TO THINK OF IT.
WELL... SO WERE ALL OF YOU, ACTUALLY.
GAH! WE JUST GOT DONE WITH ALL THE EXPOSITION, THEN YOU HAD TO COME ALONG AND WASTE A PANEL!!
AND THE ONE WHO SAVED SAGINUMA FROM HER OVERWHELMING DEPRESSION WAS NONE OTHER THAN...
BZAP BZAP BZAP
It's not a waste!
It's not!
NOW THAT I THINK ABOUT IT, YOUR ATTACK IS DEFINITELY THE SCARIEST!
DON'T SWING THAT AROUND WHEN YOU'RE HALF-ASLEEP!

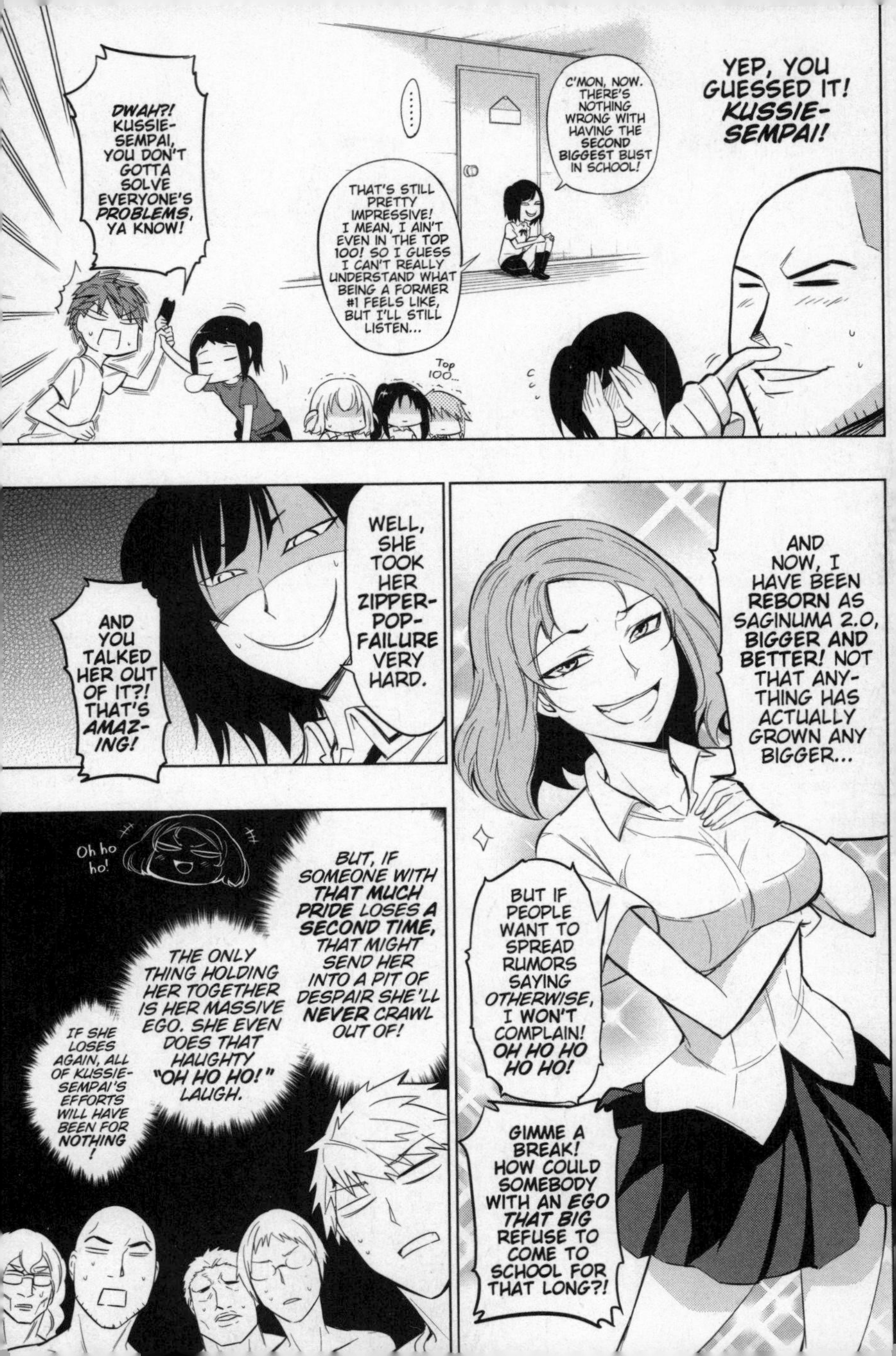

YEP, YOU GUESSED IT! KUSSIE-SEMPAI!
C'MON, NOW. THERE'S NOTHING WRONG WITH HAVING THE SECOND BIGGEST BUST IN SCHOOL!
......
THAT'S STILL PRETTY IMPRESSIVE! I MEAN, I AIN'T EVEN IN THE TOP 100! SO I GUESS I CAN'T REALLY UNDERSTAND WHAT BEING A FORMER #1 FEELS LIKE, BUT I'LL STILL LISTEN...
Top 100...
DWAH?! KUSSIE-SEMPAI, YOU DON'T GOTTA SOLVE EVERYONE'S PROBLEMS, YA KNOW!
AND NOW, I HAVE BEEN REBORN AS SAGINUMA 2.0, BIGGER AND BETTER! NOT THAT ANYTHING HAS ACTUALLY GROWN ANY BIGGER...
BUT IF PEOPLE WANT TO SPREAD RUMORS SAYING OTHERWISE, I WON'T COMPLAIN! OH HO HO HO HO!
GIMME A BREAK! HOW COULD SOMEBODY WITH AN EGO THAT BIG REFUSE TO COME TO SCHOOL FOR THAT LONG?!
WELL, SHE TOOK HER ZIPPER-POP-FAILURE VERY HARD.
AND YOU TALKED HER OUT OF IT?! THAT'S AMAZING!
THE ONLY THING HOLDING HER TOGETHER IS HER MASSIVE EGO. SHE EVEN DOES THAT HAUGHTY "OH HO HO!" LAUGH.
Oh ho ho!
BUT, IF SOMEONE WITH THAT MUCH PRIDE LOSES A SECOND TIME, THAT MIGHT SEND HER INTO A PIT OF DESPAIR SHE'LL NEVER CRAWL OUT OF!
IF SHE LOSES AGAIN, ALL OF KUSSIE-SEMPAI'S EFFORTS WILL HAVE BEEN FOR NOTHING!

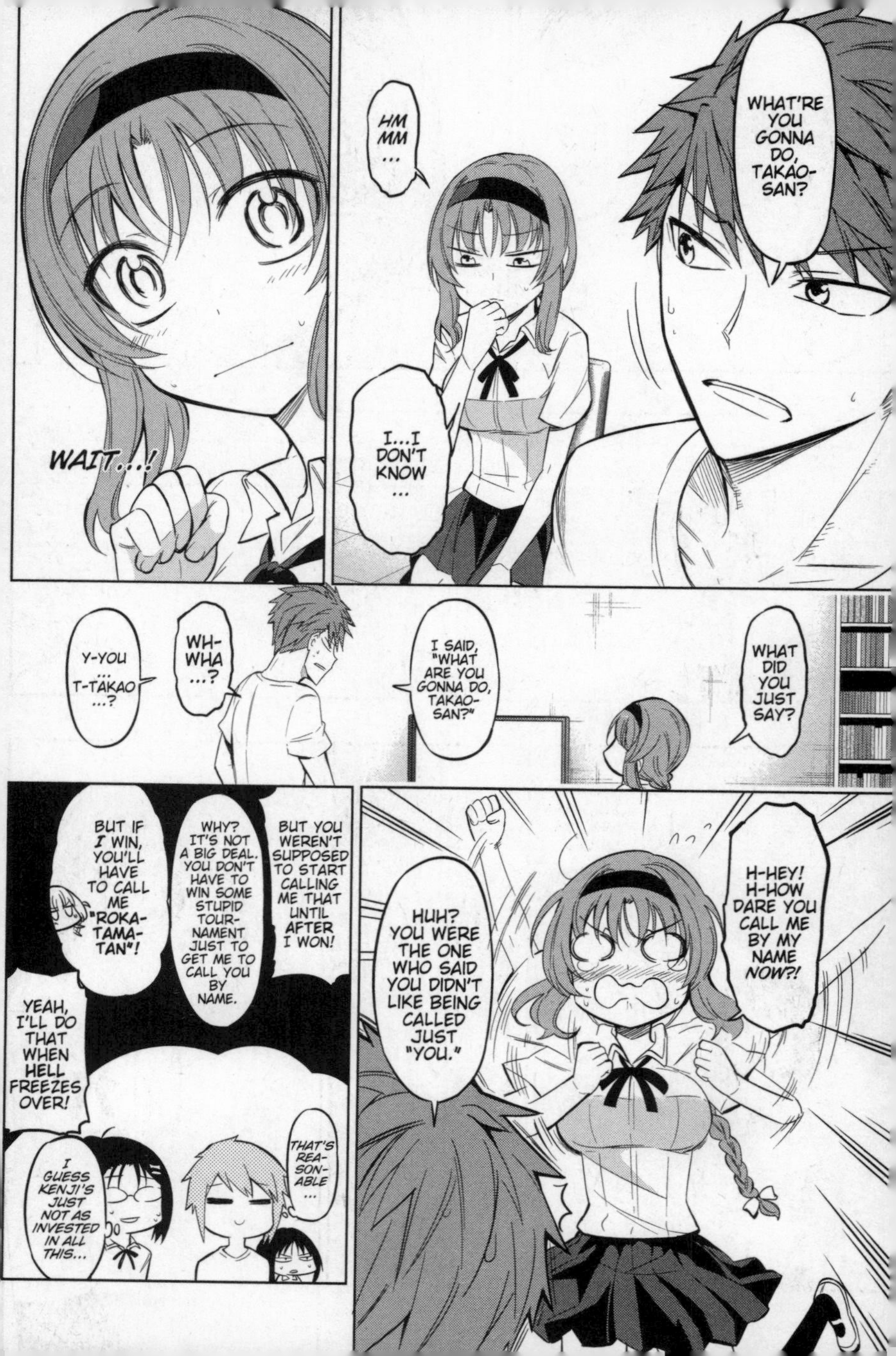
WHAT'RE YOU GONNA DO, TAKAO-SAN?
HMM MM ...
I...I DON'T KNOW ...
WAIT...!
WHAT DID YOU JUST SAY?
I SAID, "WHAT ARE YOU GONNA DO, TAKAO-SAN?"
WH-WHA ...?
Y-YOU ... T-TAKAO ...?
H-HEY! H-HOW DARE YOU CALL ME BY MY NAME NOW?!
HUH? YOU WERE THE ONE WHO SAID YOU DIDN'T LIKE BEING CALLED JUST "YOU."
BUT YOU WEREN'T SUPPOSED TO START CALLING ME THAT UNTIL AFTER I WON!
WHY? IT'S NOT A BIG DEAL. YOU DON'T HAVE TO WIN SOME STUPID TOURNAMENT JUST TO GET ME TO CALL YOU BY NAME.
BUT IF I WIN, YOU'LL HAVE TO CALL ME "ROKA-TAMA-TAN"!
YEAH, I'LL DO THAT WHEN HELL FREEZES OVER!
THAT'S REASONABLE ...
I GUESS KENJI'S JUST NOT AS INVESTED IN ALL THIS...

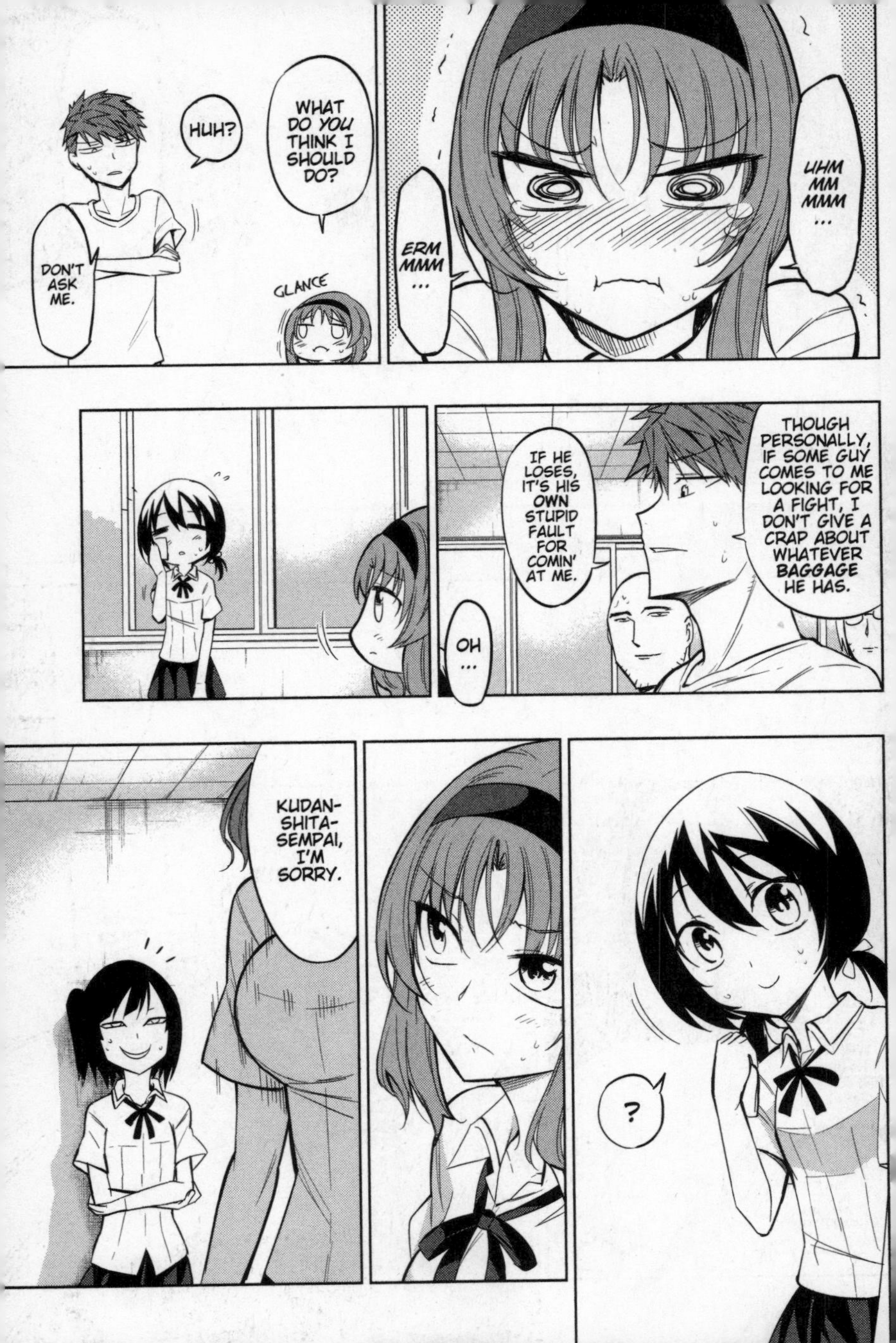
UHM MM MMM ...
ERM MMM ...
WHAT DO YOU THINK I SHOULD DO?
GLANCE
HUH?
DON'T ASK ME.
THOUGH PERSONALLY, IF SOME GUY COMES TO ME LOOKING FOR A FIGHT, I DON'T GIVE A CRAP ABOUT WHATEVER BAGGAGE HE HAS.
IF HE LOSES, IT'S HIS OWN STUPID FAULT FOR COMIN' AT ME.
OH ...
?
KUDAN-SHITA-SEMPAI, I'M SORRY.

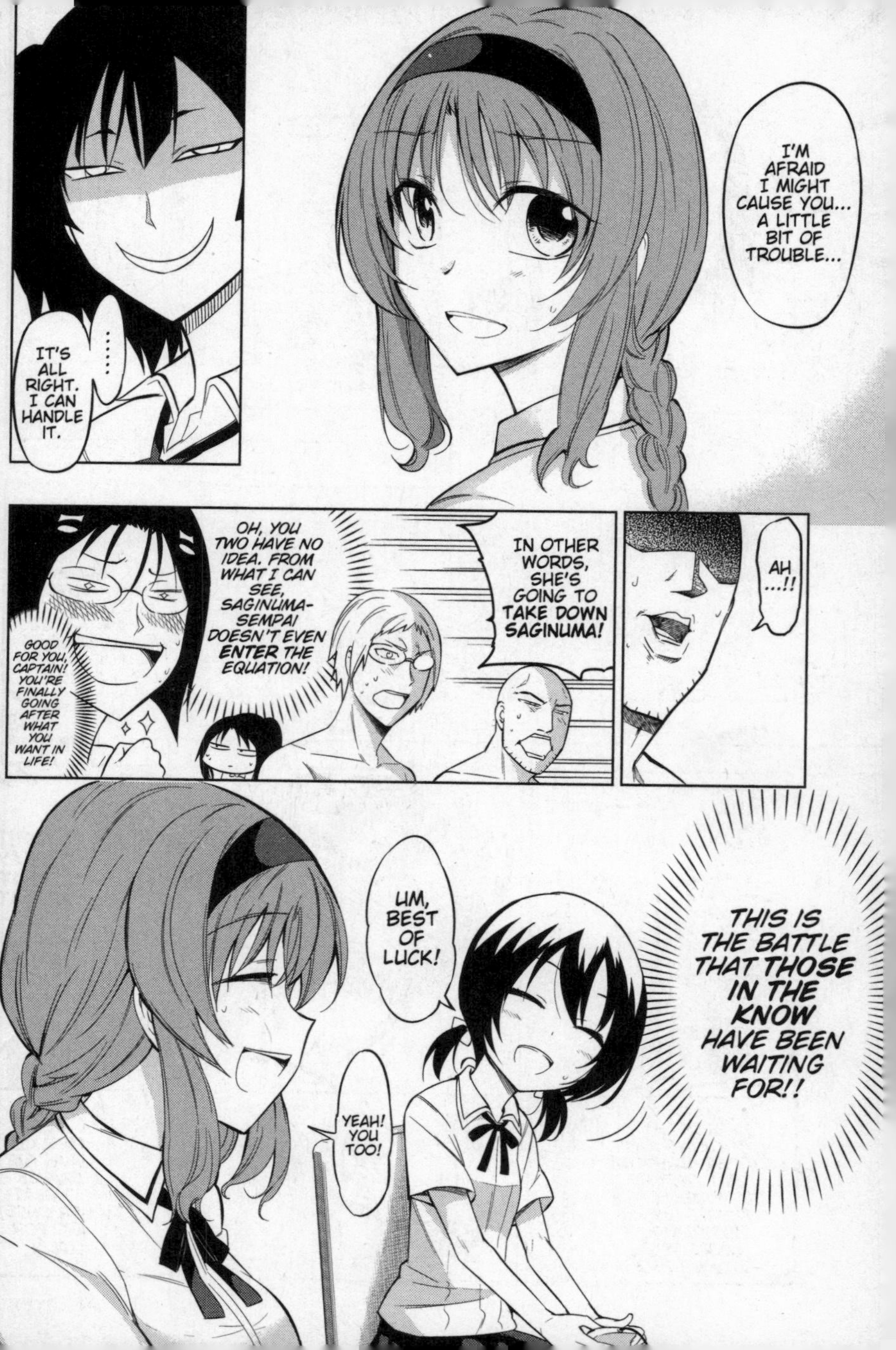
I'M AFRAID I MIGHT CAUSE YOU... A LITTLE BIT OF TROUBLE...
......
IT'S ALL RIGHT. I CAN HANDLE IT.
AH ...!!
IN OTHER WORDS, SHE'S GOING TO TAKE DOWN SAGINUMA!
OH, YOU TWO HAVE NO IDEA. FROM WHAT I CAN SEE, SAGINUMA-SEMPAI DOESN'T EVEN ENTER THE EQUATION!
GOOD FOR YOU, CAPTAIN! YOU'RE FINALLY GOING AFTER WHAT YOU WANT IN LIFE!
THIS IS THE BATTLE THAT THOSE IN THE KNOW HAVE BEEN WAITING FOR!!
UM, BEST OF LUCK!
YEAH! YOU TOO!

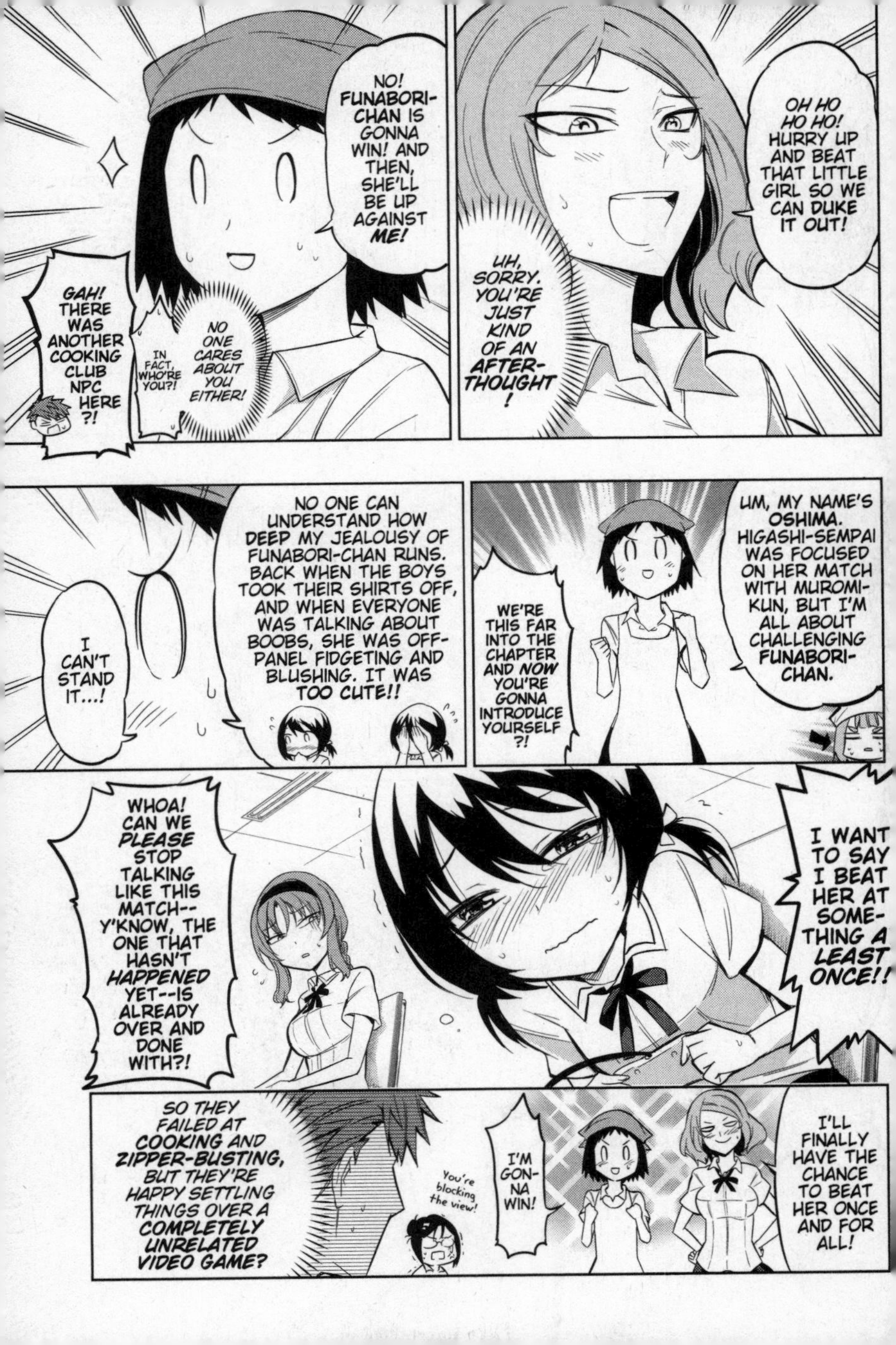
OH HO HO HO! HURRY UP AND BEAT THAT LITTLE GIRL SO WE CAN DUKE IT OUT!
UH, SORRY. YOU'RE JUST KIND OF AN AFTER-THOUGHT!
NO! FUNABORI-CHAN IS GONNA WIN! AND THEN, SHE'LL BE UP AGAINST ME!
NO ONE CARES ABOUT YOU EITHER!
IN FACT, WHO'RE YOU?!
GAH! THERE WAS ANOTHER COOKING CLUB NPC HERE?!
UM, MY NAME'S OSHIMA. HIGASHI-SEMPAI WAS FOCUSED ON HER MATCH WITH MUROMI-KUN, BUT I'M ALL ABOUT CHALLENGING FUNABORI-CHAN.
WE'RE THIS FAR INTO THE CHAPTER AND NOW YOU'RE GONNA INTRODUCE YOURSELF?!
NO ONE CAN UNDERSTAND HOW DEEP MY JEALOUSY OF FUNABORI-CHAN RUNS. BACK WHEN THE BOYS TOOK THEIR SHIRTS OFF, AND WHEN EVERYONE WAS TALKING ABOUT BOOBS, SHE WAS OFF-PANEL FIDGETING AND BLUSHING. IT WAS TOO CUTE!!
I CAN'T STAND IT...!
I WANT TO SAY I BEAT HER AT SOME-THING A LEAST ONCE!!
WHOA! CAN WE PLEASE STOP TALKING LIKE THIS MATCH--Y'KNOW, THE ONE THAT HASN'T HAPPENED YET--IS ALREADY OVER AND DONE WITH?!
I'LL FINALLY HAVE THE CHANCE TO BEAT HER ONCE AND FOR ALL!
I'M GON-NA WIN!
You're blocking the view!
SO THEY FAILED AT COOKING AND ZIPPER-BUSTING, BUT THEY'RE HAPPY SETTLING THINGS OVER A COMPLETELY UNRELATED VIDEO GAME?

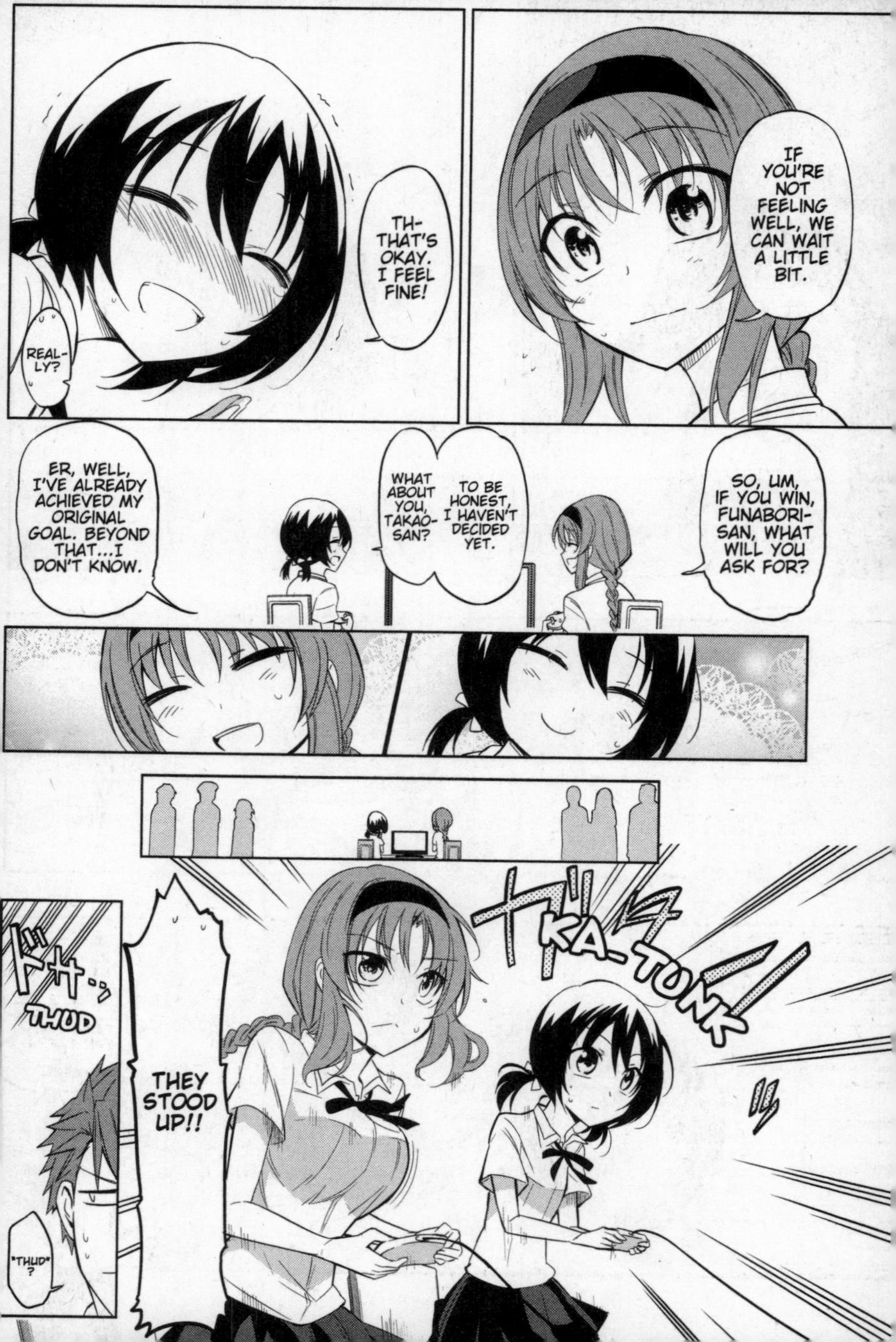
IF YOU'RE NOT FEELING WELL, WE CAN WAIT A LITTLE BIT.
TH-THAT'S OKAY. I FEEL FINE!
REAL-LY?
SO, UM, IF YOU WIN, FUNABORI-SAN, WHAT WILL YOU ASK FOR?
TO BE HONEST, I HAVEN'T DECIDED YET.
WHAT ABOUT YOU, TAKAO-SAN?
ER, WELL, I'VE ALREADY ACHIEVED MY ORIGINAL GOAL. BEYOND THAT...I DON'T KNOW.
KA-TONK!!
THUD
THEY STOOD UP!!
"THUD"?

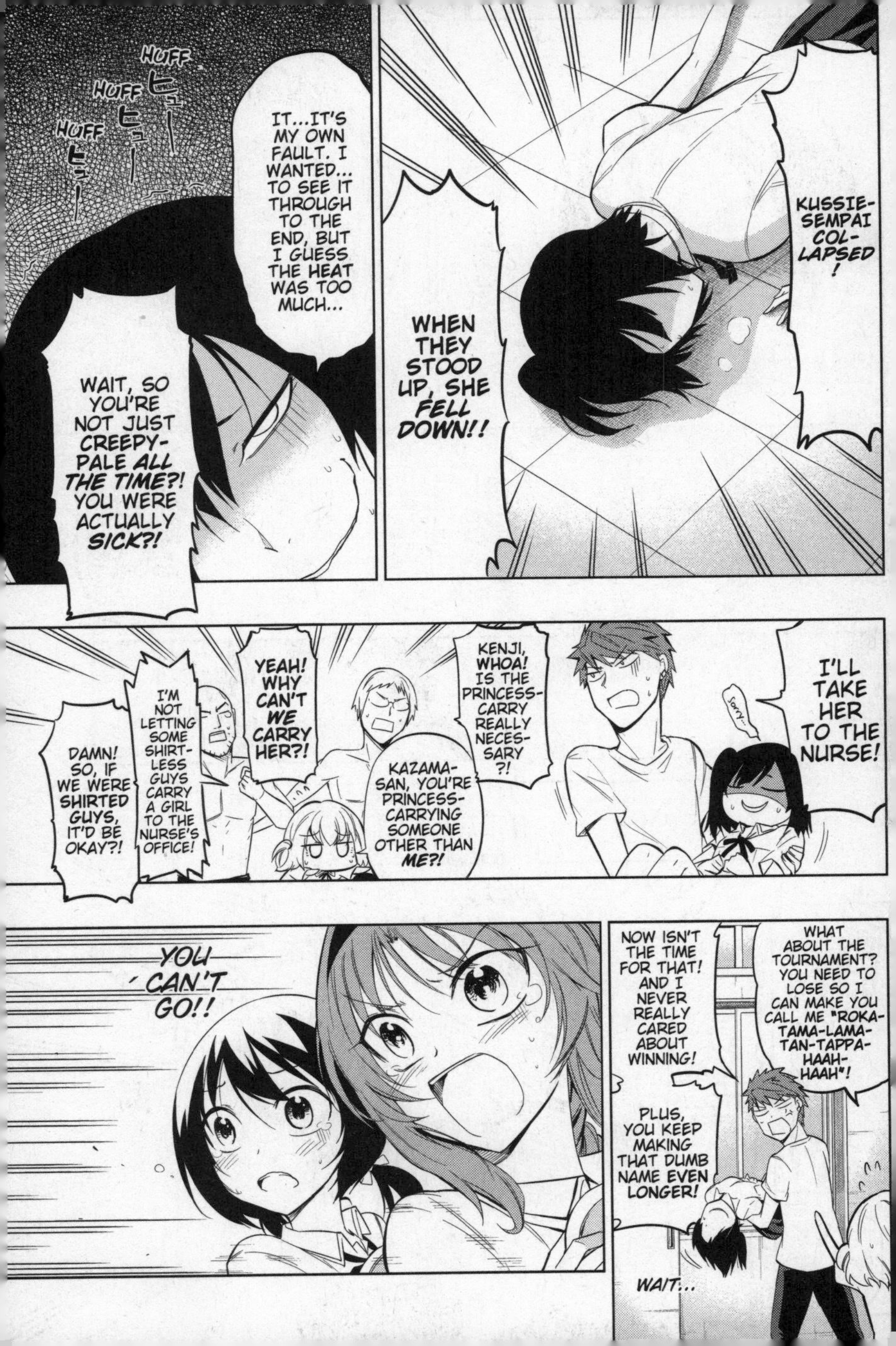
KUSSIE-SEMPAI COL-LAPSED!
WHEN THEY STOOD UP, SHE FELL DOWN!!
HUFF ヒュー
HUFF ヒュー
HUFF ヒュー
IT...IT'S MY OWN FAULT. I WANTED... TO SEE IT THROUGH TO THE END, BUT I GUESS THE HEAT WAS TOO MUCH...
WAIT, SO YOU'RE NOT JUST CREEPY-PALE ALL THE TIME?! YOU WERE ACTUALLY SICK?!
I'LL TAKE HER TO THE NURSE!
Sorry...
KENJI, WHOA! IS THE PRINCESS-CARRY REALLY NECES-SARY?!
KAZAMA-SAN, YOU'RE PRINCESS-CARRYING SOMEONE OTHER THAN ME?!
YEAH! WHY CAN'T WE CARRY HER?!
I'M NOT LETTING SOME SHIRT-LESS GUYS CARRY A GIRL TO THE NURSE'S OFFICE!
DAMN! SO, IF WE WERE SHIRTED GUYS, IT'D BE OKAY?!
WHAT ABOUT THE TOURNAMENT? YOU NEED TO LOSE SO I CAN MAKE YOU CALL ME "ROKA-TAMA-LAMA-TAN-TAPPA-HAAH-HAAH"!
NOW ISN'T THE TIME FOR THAT! AND I NEVER REALLY CARED ABOUT WINNING!
PLUS, YOU KEEP MAKING THAT DUMB NAME EVEN LONGER!
WAIT...
YOU CAN'T GO!!

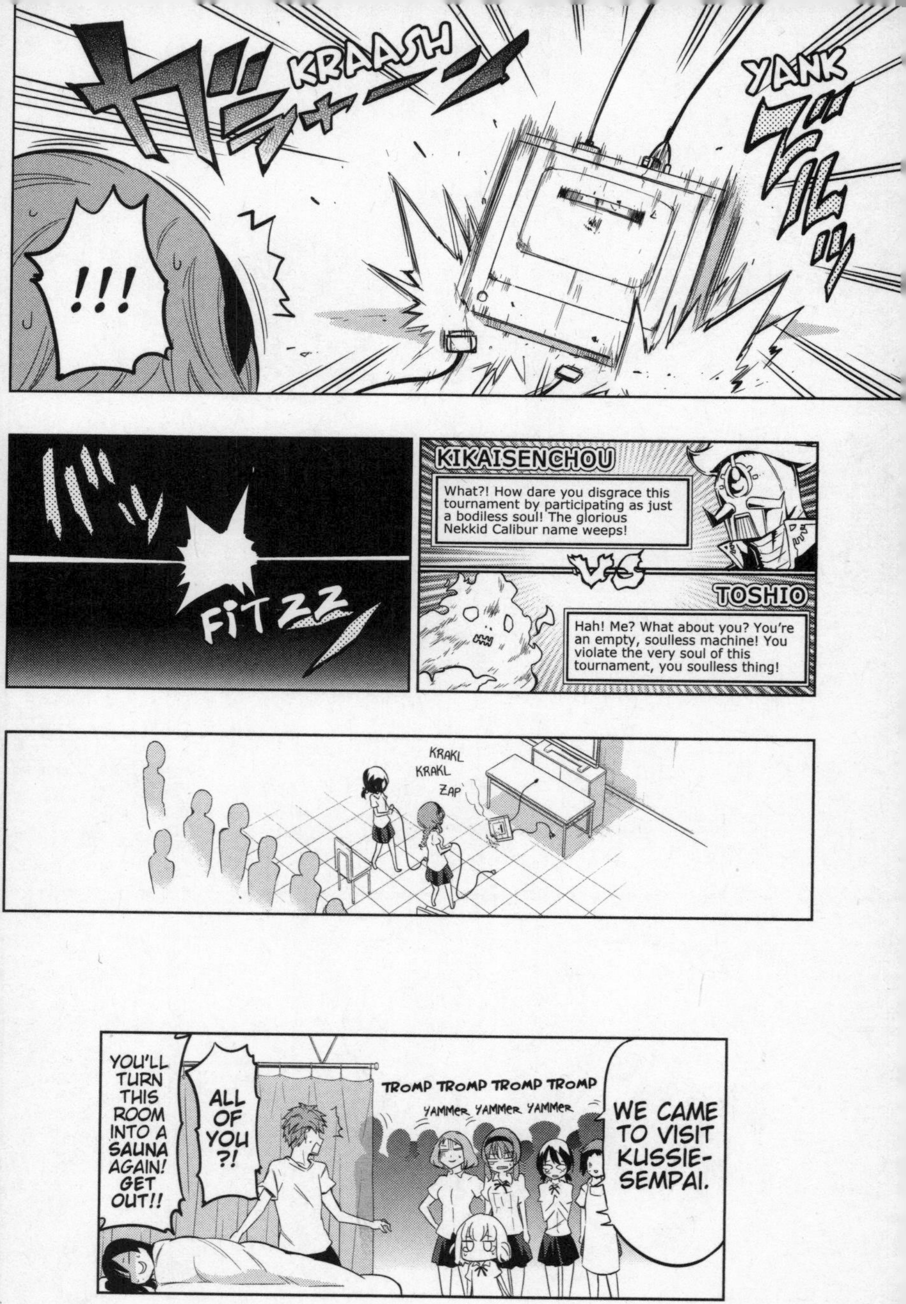
YANK
KRAASH
!!!
KIKAISENCHOU
What?! How dare you disgrace this tournament by participating as just a bodiless soul! The glorious Nekkid Calibur name weeps!
VS
TOSHIO
Hah! Me? What about you? You're an empty, soulless machine! You violate the very soul of this tournament, you soulless thing!
FITZZ
KRAKL
KRAKL
ZAP
WE CAME TO VISIT KUSSIE-SEMPAI.
TROMP TROMP TROMP TROMP
YAMMER YAMMER YAMMER
ALL OF YOU?!
YOU'LL TURN THIS ROOM INTO A SAUNA AGAIN! GET OUT!!

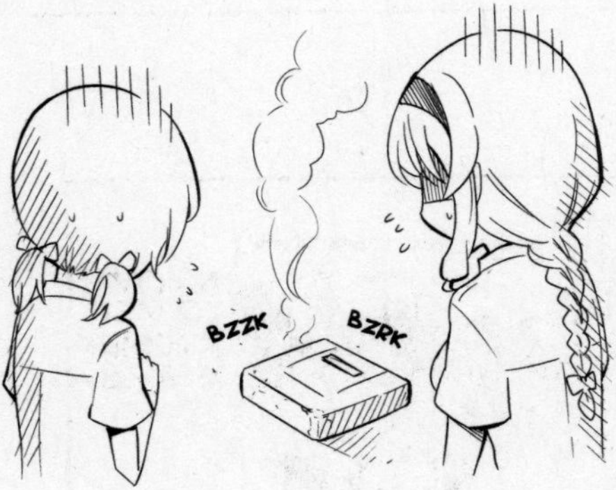
BZZK
BZRK

D-FRAGMENTS

ディーふらぐ!

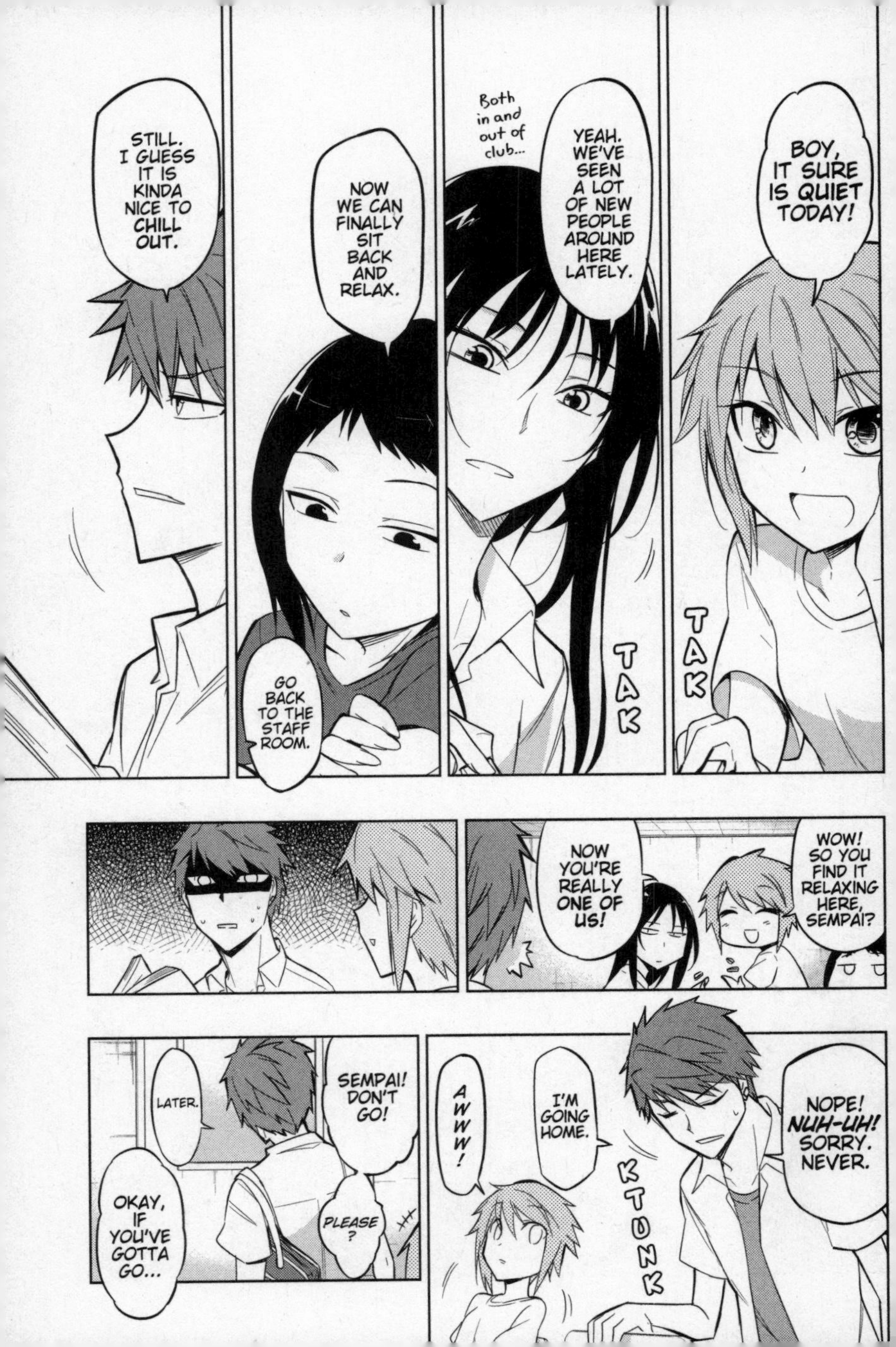
BOY, IT SURE IS QUIET TODAY!
TAK
Both in and out of club...
YEAH. WE'VE SEEN A LOT OF NEW PEOPLE AROUND HERE LATELY.
TAK
NOW WE CAN FINALLY SIT BACK AND RELAX.
GO BACK TO THE STAFF ROOM.
STILL. I GUESS IT IS KINDA NICE TO CHILL OUT.
WOW! SO YOU FIND IT RELAXING HERE, SEMPAI?
NOW YOU'RE REALLY ONE OF US!
NOPE! NUH-UH! SORRY. NEVER.
I'M GOING HOME.
KTONK
AWWW!
SEMPAI! DON'T GO!
LATER.
PLEASE?
OKAY, IF YOU'VE GOTTA GO...

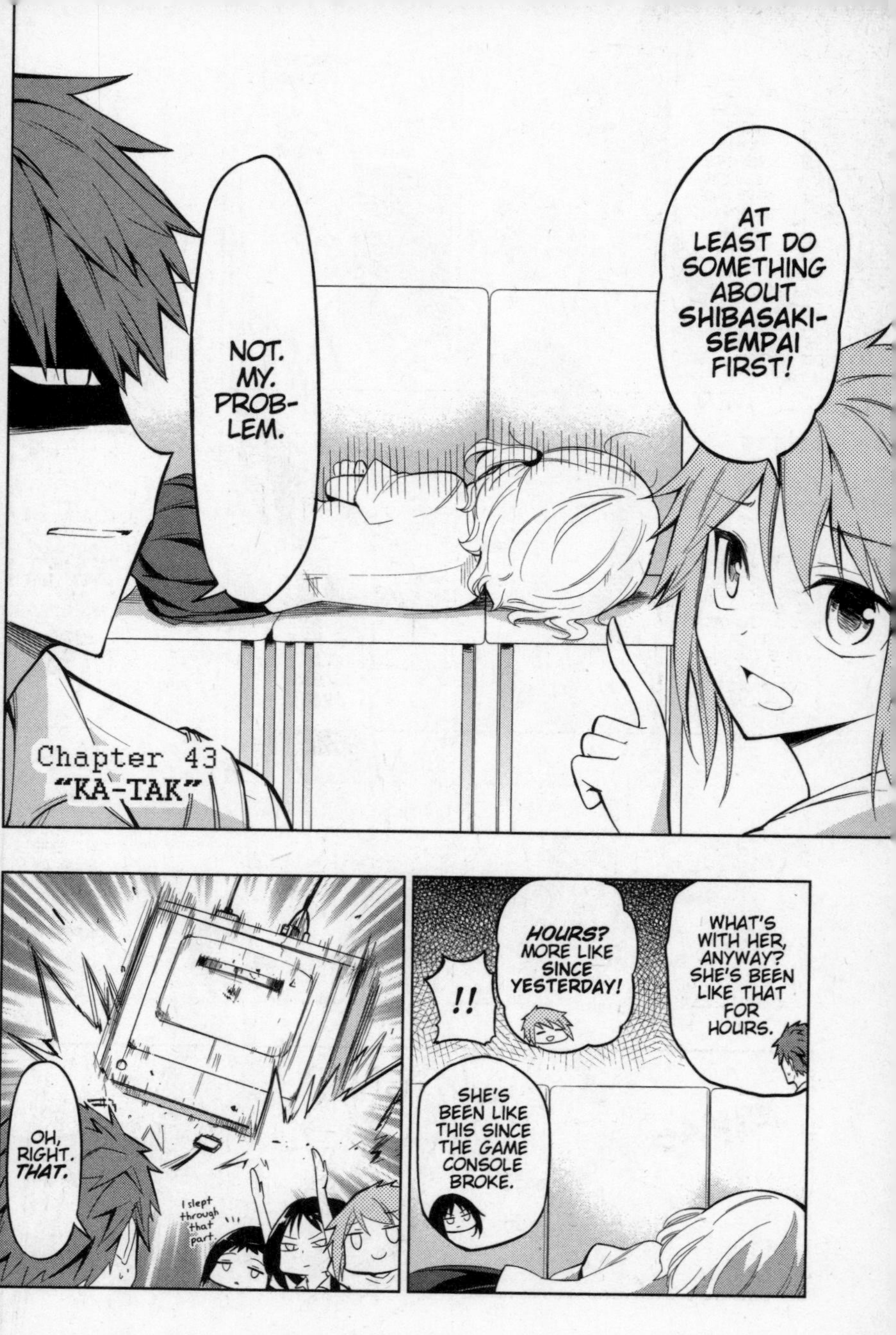
AT LEAST DO SOMETHING ABOUT SHIBASAKI-SEMPAI FIRST!
NOT. MY. PROB-LEM.
Chapter 43
"KA-TAK"
WHAT'S WITH HER, ANYWAY? SHE'S BEEN LIKE THAT FOR HOURS.
HOURS? MORE LIKE SINCE YESTERDAY!
!!
SHE'S BEEN LIKE THIS SINCE THE GAME CONSOLE BROKE.
OH, RIGHT. *THAT.*
I slept through that part.

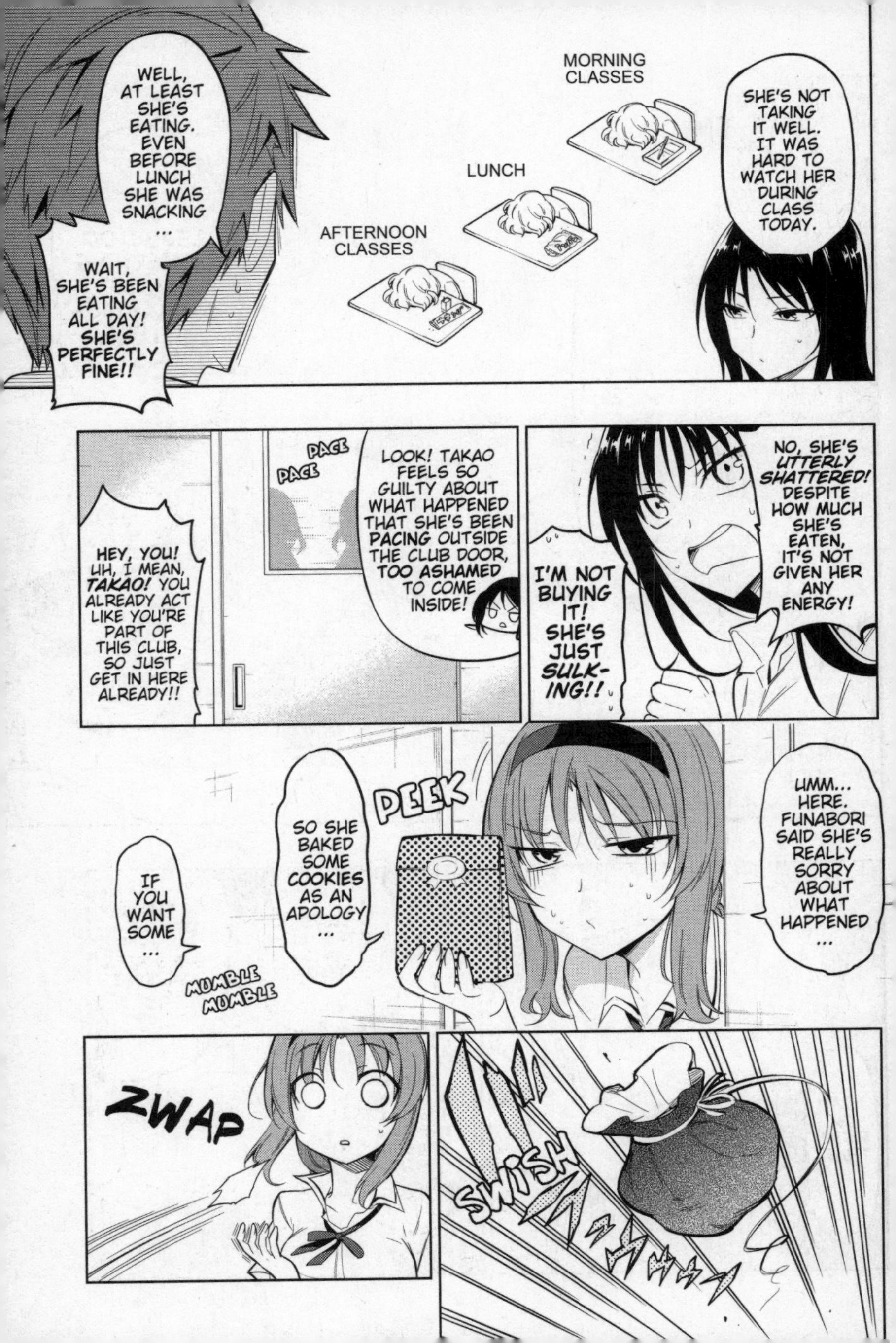
SHE'S NOT TAKING IT WELL. IT WAS HARD TO WATCH HER DURING CLASS TODAY.
MORNING CLASSES
LUNCH
AFTERNOON CLASSES
WELL, AT LEAST SHE'S EATING. EVEN BEFORE LUNCH SHE WAS SNACKING ...
WAIT, SHE'S BEEN EATING ALL DAY! SHE'S PERFECTLY FINE!!
NO, SHE'S UTTERLY SHATTERED! DESPITE HOW MUCH SHE'S EATEN, IT'S NOT GIVEN HER ANY ENERGY!
I'M NOT BUYING IT! SHE'S JUST SULKING!!
PACE
PACE
LOOK! TAKAO FEELS SO GUILTY ABOUT WHAT HAPPENED THAT SHE'S BEEN PACING OUTSIDE THE CLUB DOOR, TOO ASHAMED TO COME INSIDE!
HEY, YOU! UH, I MEAN, TAKAO! YOU ALREADY ACT LIKE YOU'RE PART OF THIS CLUB, SO JUST GET IN HERE ALREADY!!
UMM... HERE. FUNABORI SAID SHE'S REALLY SORRY ABOUT WHAT HAPPENED ...
PEEK
SO SHE BAKED SOME COOKIES AS AN APOLOGY ...
IF YOU WANT SOME ...
MUMBLE MUMBLE
SWISH
ZWAP

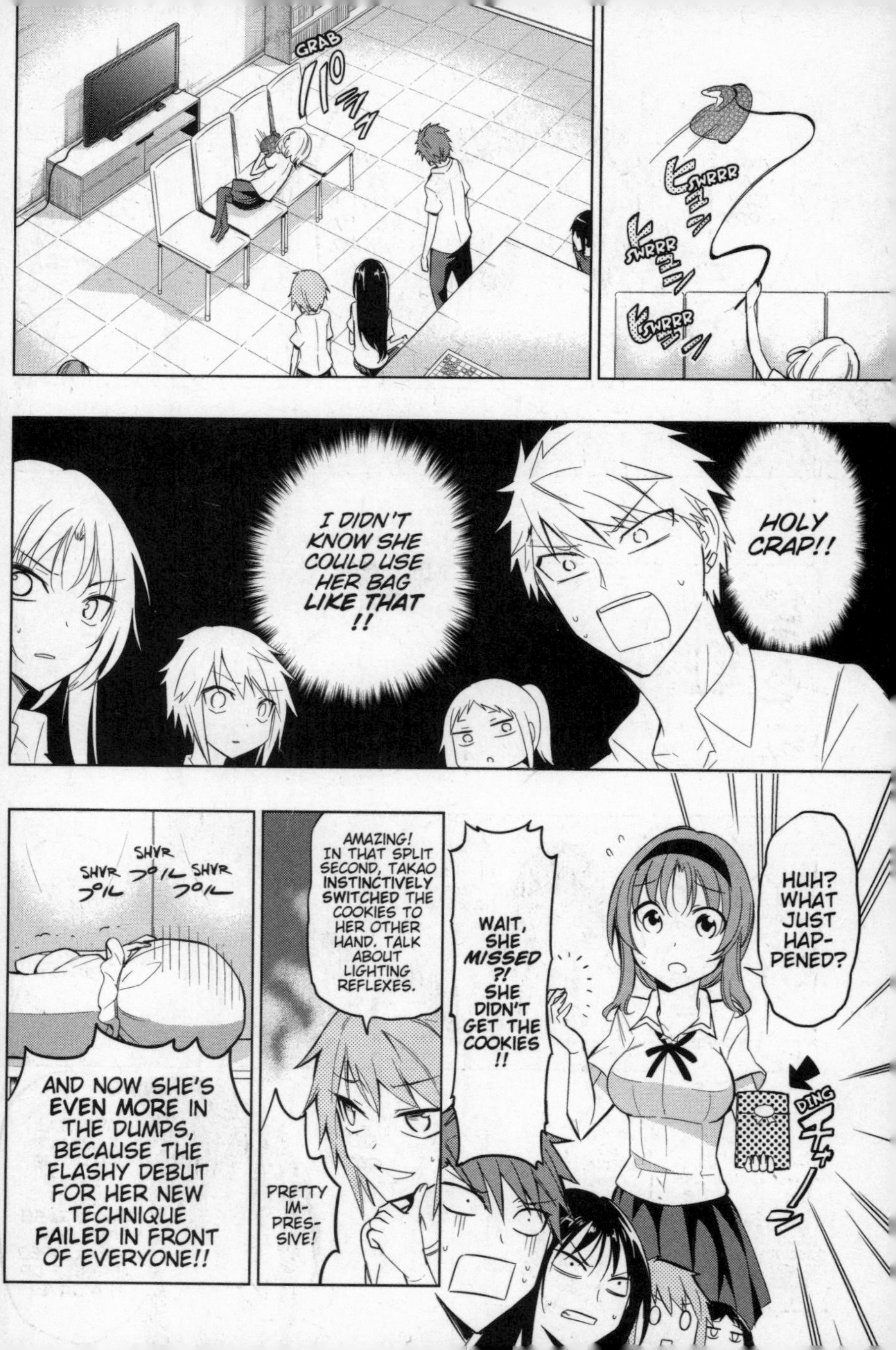
SWRRR
SWRRR
SWRRR
GRAB
HOLY CRAP!!
I DIDN'T KNOW SHE COULD USE HER BAG LIKE THAT!!
HUH? WHAT JUST HAP-PENED?
WAIT, SHE MISSED?! SHE DIDN'T GET THE COOKIES!!
DING
AMAZING! IN THAT SPLIT SECOND, TAKAO INSTINCTIVELY SWITCHED THE COOKIES TO HER OTHER HAND. TALK ABOUT LIGHTING REFLEXES.
PRETTY IM-PRES-SIVE!
SHVR
SHVR
SHVR
AND NOW SHE'S EVEN MORE IN THE DUMPS, BECAUSE THE FLASHY DEBUT FOR HER NEW TECHNIQUE FAILED IN FRONT OF EVERYONE!!

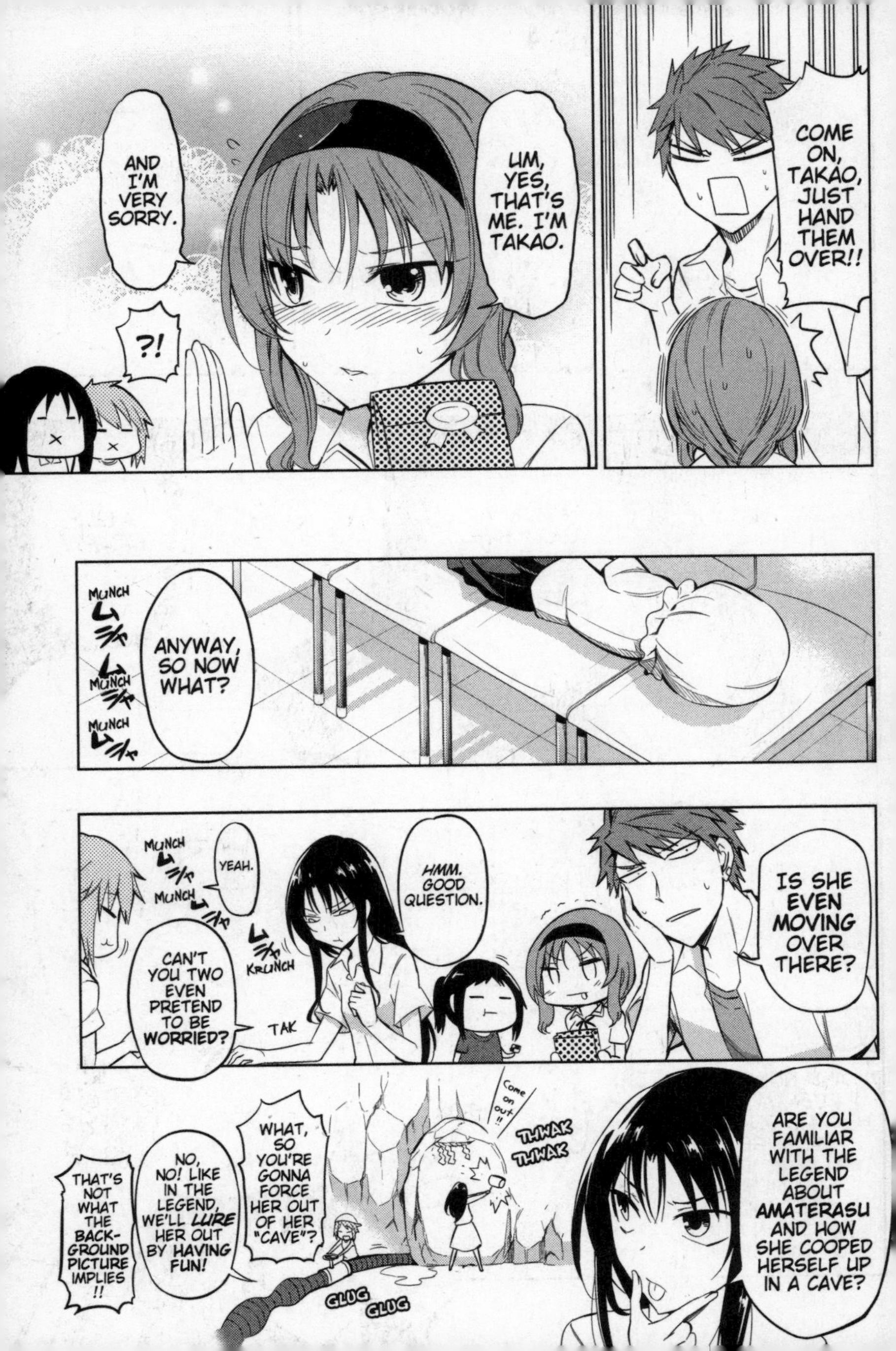
COME ON, TAKAO, JUST HAND THEM OVER!!
UM, YES, THAT'S ME. I'M TAKAO.
AND I'M VERY SORRY.
?!
ANYWAY, SO NOW WHAT?
MUNCH
MUNCH
MUNCH
IS SHE EVEN MOVING OVER THERE?
HMM. GOOD QUESTION.
YEAH.
MUNCH
MUNCH
KRUNCH
CAN'T YOU TWO EVEN PRETEND TO BE WORRIED?
TAK
ARE YOU FAMILIAR WITH THE LEGEND ABOUT AMATERASU AND HOW SHE COOPED HERSELF UP IN A CAVE?
THWAK THWAK
Come on out!!
WHAT, SO YOU'RE GONNA FORCE HER OUT OF HER "CAVE"?
NO, NO! LIKE IN THE LEGEND, WE'LL LURE HER OUT BY HAVING FUN!
THAT'S NOT WHAT THE BACKGROUND PICTURE IMPLIES!!
GLUG GLUG

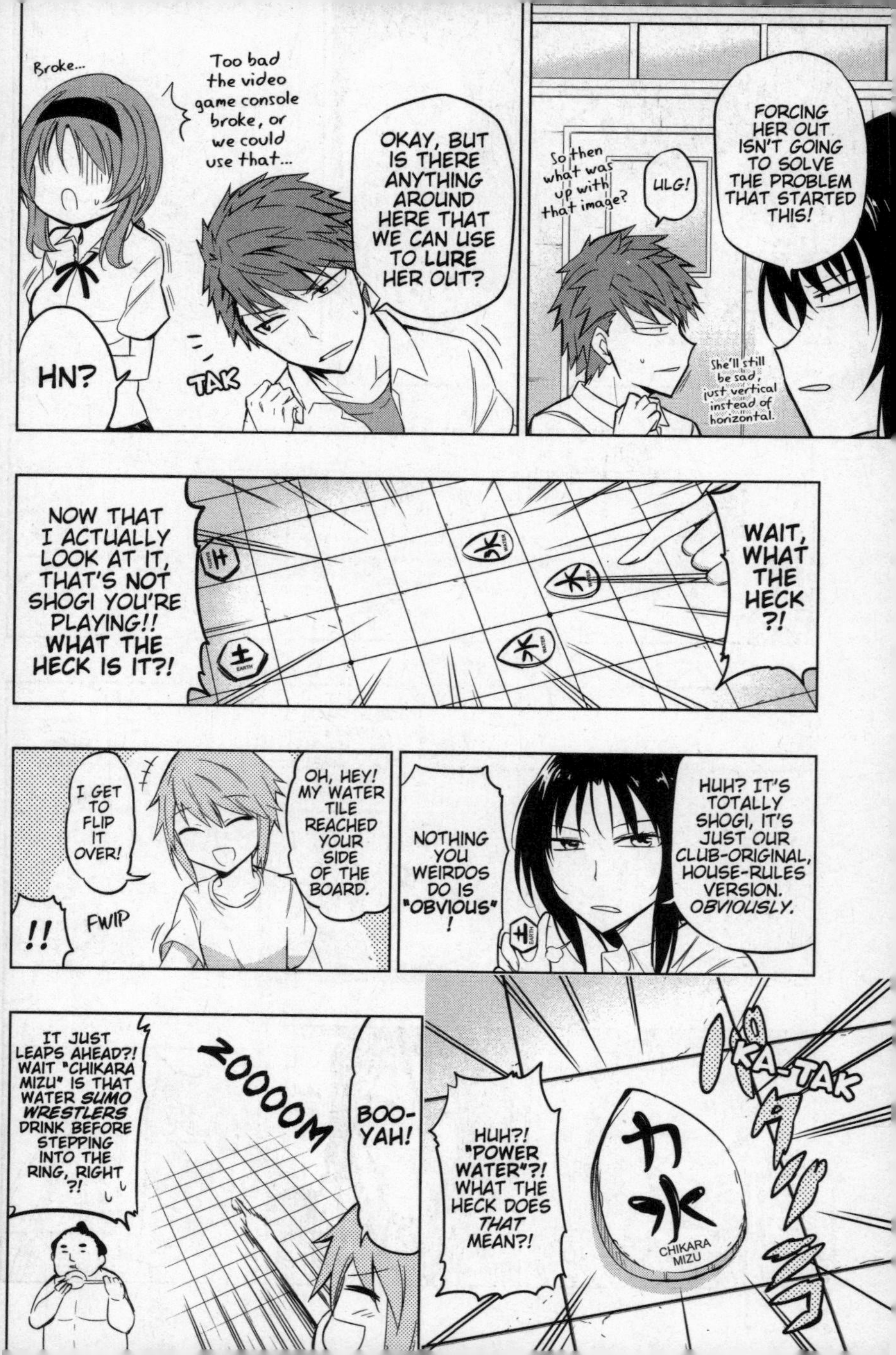
FORCING HER OUT ISN'T GOING TO SOLVE THE PROBLEM THAT STARTED THIS!
ULG!
So then what was up with that image?
She'll still be sad, just vertical instead of horizontal.
OKAY, BUT IS THERE ANYTHING AROUND HERE THAT WE CAN USE TO LURE HER OUT?
Too bad the video game console broke, or we could use that...
Broke...
TAK
HN?
WAIT, WHAT THE HECK ?!
NOW THAT I ACTUALLY LOOK AT IT, THAT'S NOT SHOGI YOU'RE PLAYING!! WHAT THE HECK IS IT?!
WATER
EARTH
HUH? IT'S TOTALLY SHOGI, IT'S JUST OUR CLUB-ORIGINAL, HOUSE-RULES VERSION. OBVIOUSLY.
NOTHING YOU WEIRDOS DO IS "OBVIOUS"!
OH, HEY! MY WATER TILE REACHED YOUR SIDE OF THE BOARD.
I GET TO FLIP IT OVER!
FWIP
!!
KA-TAK
HUH?! "POWER WATER"?! WHAT THE HECK DOES THAT MEAN?!
CHIKARA MIZU
BOO-YAH!
ZOOOOM
IT JUST LEAPS AHEAD?! WAIT "CHIKARA MIZU" IS THAT WATER SUMO WRESTLERS DRINK BEFORE STEPPING INTO THE RING, RIGHT ?!

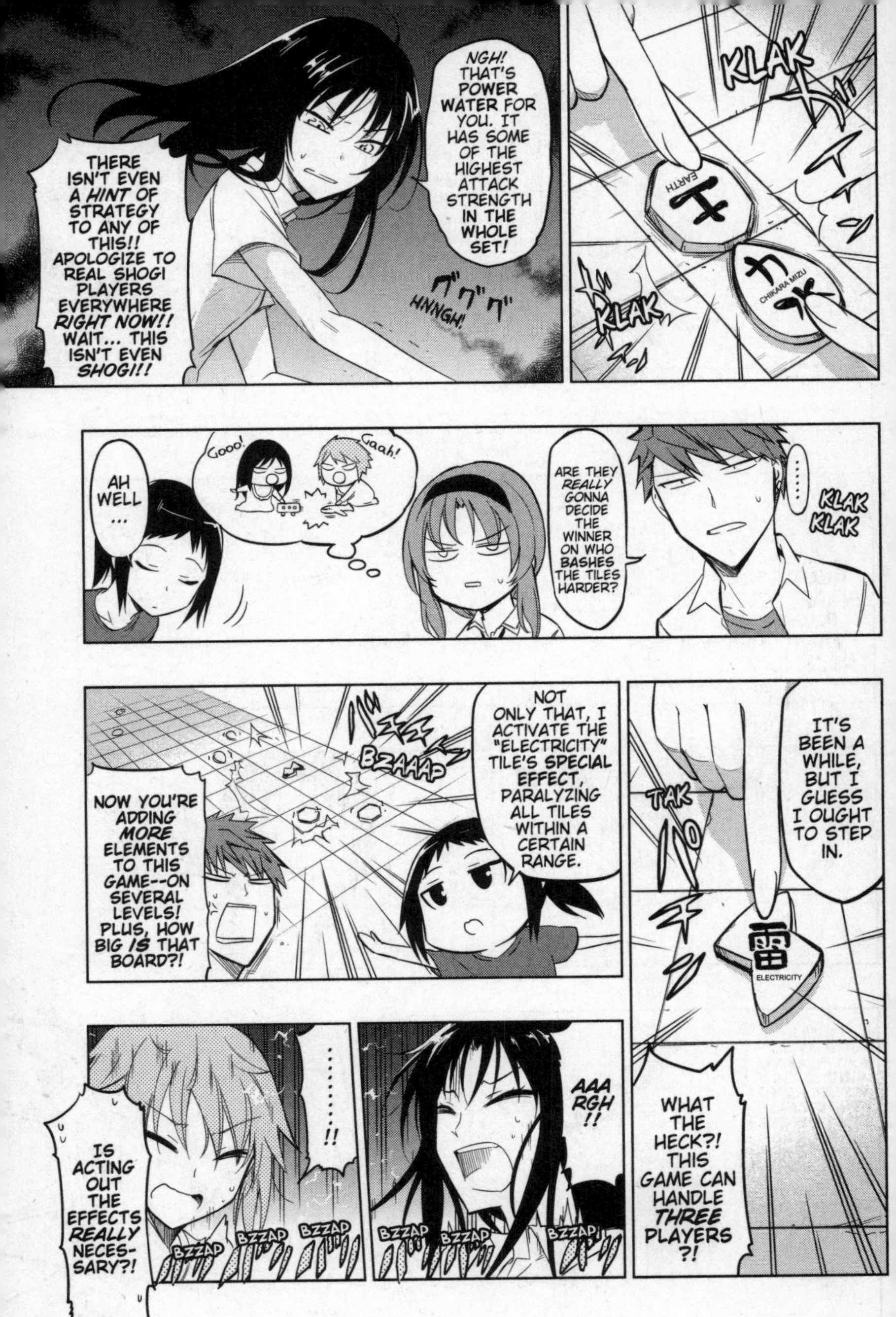
KLAK
EARTH
CHIKARA MIZU
KLAK
NGH! THAT'S POWER WATER FOR YOU. IT HAS SOME OF THE HIGHEST ATTACK STRENGTH IN THE WHOLE SET!
THERE ISN'T EVEN A *HINT* OF STRATEGY TO ANY OF THIS!! APOLOGIZE TO REAL SHOGI PLAYERS EVERYWHERE *RIGHT NOW!!* WAIT... THIS ISN'T EVEN *SHOGI!!*
HNNGH!
KLAK KLAK
......
ARE THEY *REALLY* GONNA DECIDE THE WINNER ON WHO BASHES THE TILES HARDER?
Gaah!
Gooo!
AH WELL ...
IT'S BEEN A WHILE, BUT I GUESS I OUGHT TO STEP IN.
TAK
ELECTRICITY
WHAT THE HECK?! THIS GAME CAN HANDLE *THREE* PLAYERS ?!
NOT ONLY THAT, I ACTIVATE THE "ELECTRICITY" TILE'S SPECIAL EFFECT, PARALYZING ALL TILES WITHIN A CERTAIN RANGE.
BZAAAP
NOW YOU'RE ADDING *MORE* ELEMENTS TO THIS GAME--ON SEVERAL LEVELS! PLUS, HOW BIG *IS* THAT BOARD?!
AAARGH!!
BZZAP
BZZAP
BZZAP
......!!
IS ACTING OUT THE EFFECTS *REALLY* NECES-SARY?!
BZZAP
BZZAP
BZZAP

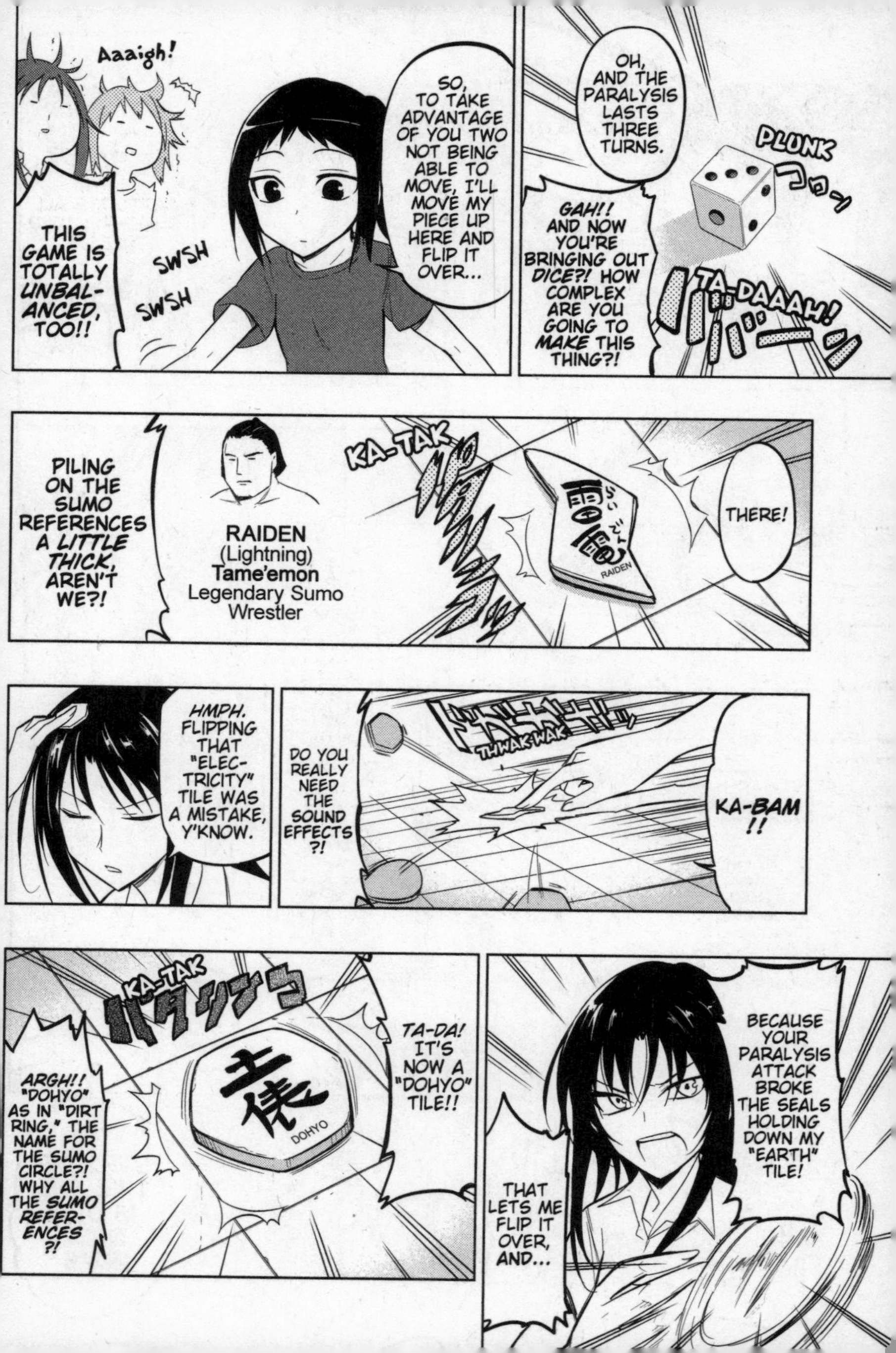
PLUNK
OH, AND THE PARALYSIS LASTS THREE TURNS.
GAH!! AND NOW YOU'RE BRINGING OUT DICE?! HOW COMPLEX ARE YOU GOING TO MAKE THIS THING?!
TA-DAAAH!
SO, TO TAKE ADVANTAGE OF YOU TWO NOT BEING ABLE TO MOVE, I'LL MOVE MY PIECE UP HERE AND FLIP IT OVER...
Aaaigh!
SWSH
SWSH
THIS GAME IS TOTALLY UNBALANCED, TOO!!
THERE!
RAIDEN
KA-TAK
RAIDEN (Lightning) Tame'emon Legendary Sumo Wrestler
PILING ON THE SUMO REFERENCES A LITTLE THICK, AREN'T WE?!
KA-BAM!!
THWAK WAK
DO YOU REALLY NEED THE SOUND EFFECTS?!
HMPH. FLIPPING THAT "ELECTRICITY" TILE WAS A MISTAKE, Y'KNOW.
BECAUSE YOUR PARALYSIS ATTACK BROKE THE SEALS HOLDING DOWN MY "EARTH" TILE!
THAT LETS ME FLIP IT OVER, AND...
TA-DA! IT'S NOW A "DOHYO" TILE!!
KA-TAK
DOHYO
ARGH!! "DOHYO" AS IN "DIRT RING," THE NAME FOR THE SUMO CIRCLE?! WHY ALL THE SUMO REFERENCES?!

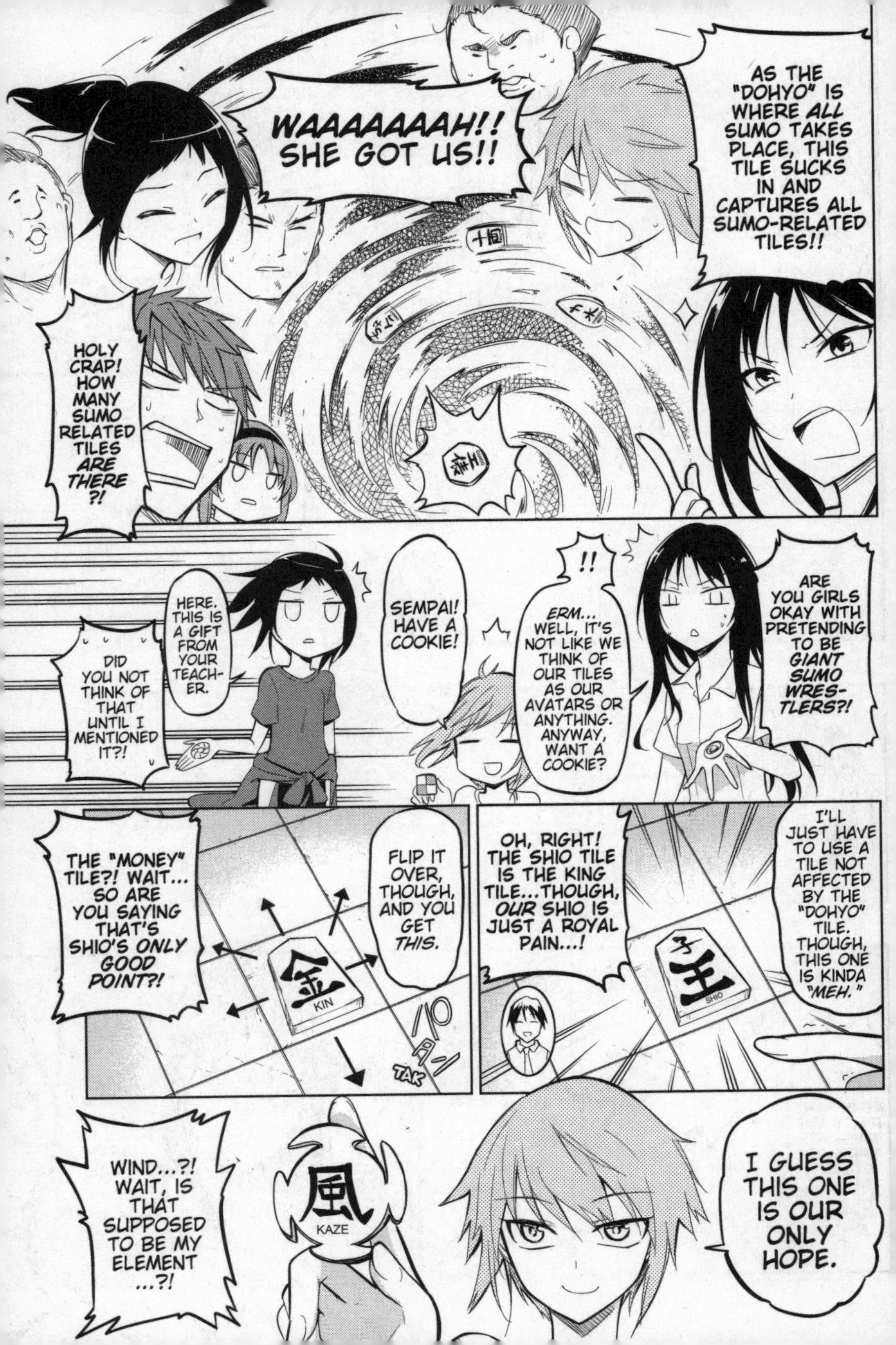
AS THE "DOHYO" IS WHERE ALL SUMO TAKES PLACE, THIS TILE SUCKS IN AND CAPTURES ALL SUMO-RELATED TILES!!
WAAAAAAAH!! SHE GOT US!!
HOLY CRAP! HOW MANY SUMO RELATED TILES ARE THERE?!
ARE YOU GIRLS OKAY WITH PRETENDING TO BE GIANT SUMO WRESTLERS?!
!!
ERM... WELL, IT'S NOT LIKE WE THINK OF OUR TILES AS OUR AVATARS OR ANYTHING. ANYWAY, WANT A COOKIE?
SEMPAI! HAVE A COOKIE!
HERE. THIS IS A GIFT FROM YOUR TEACHER.
DID YOU NOT THINK OF THAT UNTIL I MENTIONED IT?!
I'LL JUST HAVE TO USE A TILE NOT AFFECTED BY THE "DOHYO" TILE. THOUGH, THIS ONE IS KINDA "MEH."
王
SHIO
OH, RIGHT! THE SHIO TILE IS THE KING TILE...THOUGH, OUR SHIO IS JUST A ROYAL PAIN...!
FLIP IT OVER, THOUGH, AND YOU GET THIS.
TAK
金
KIN
THE "MONEY" TILE?! WAIT... SO ARE YOU SAYING THAT'S SHIO'S ONLY GOOD POINT?!
I GUESS THIS ONE IS OUR ONLY HOPE.
風
KAZE
WIND...?! WAIT, IS THAT SUPPOSED TO BE MY ELEMENT ...?!

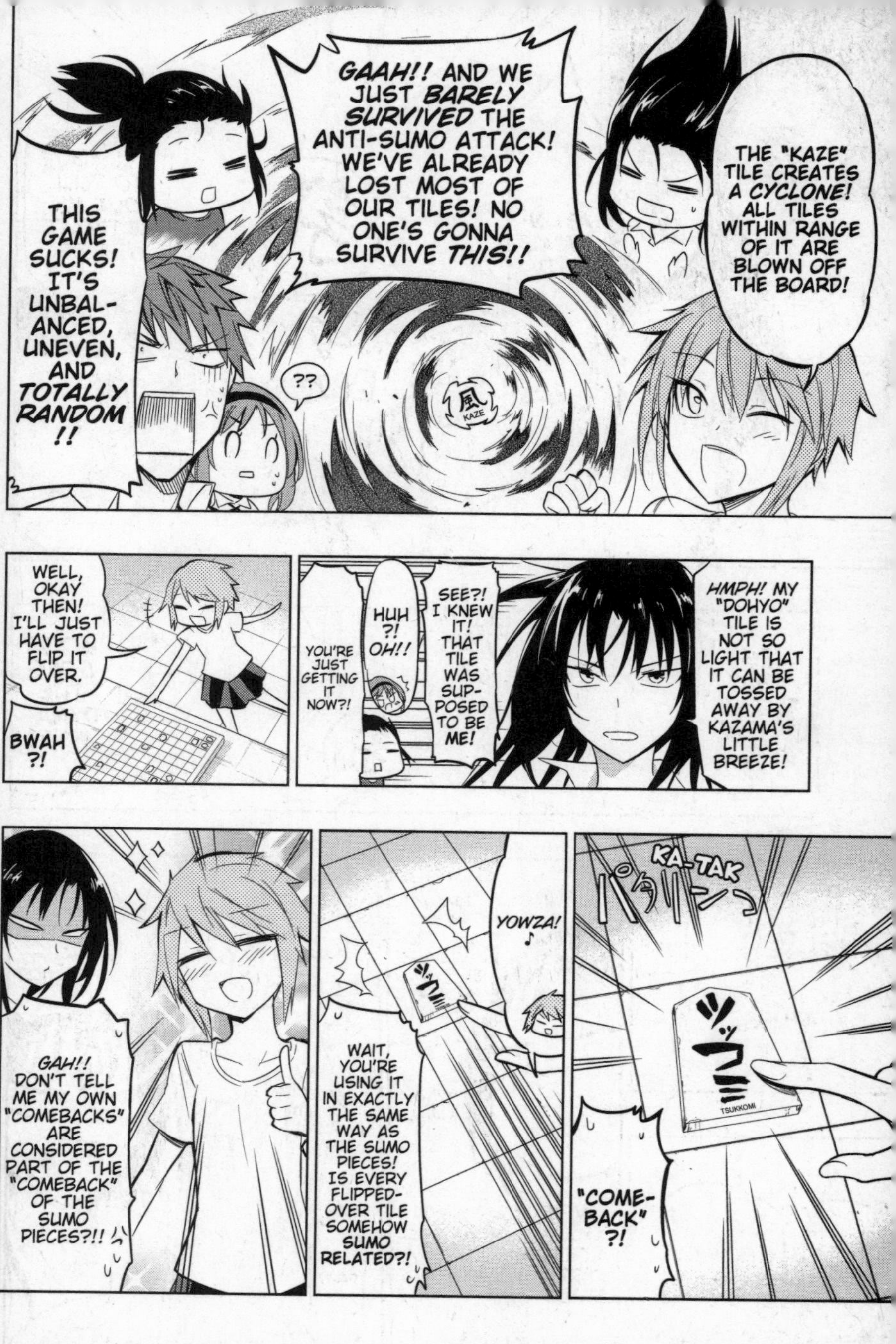
THE "KAZE" TILE CREATES A CYCLONE! ALL TILES WITHIN RANGE OF IT ARE BLOWN OFF THE BOARD!
GAAH!! AND WE JUST BARELY SURVIVED THE ANTI-SUMO ATTACK! WE'VE ALREADY LOST MOST OF OUR TILES! NO ONE'S GONNA SURVIVE THIS!!
THIS GAME SUCKS! IT'S UNBAL-ANCED, UNEVEN, AND TOTALLY RANDOM!!
??
風
KAZE
HMPH! MY "DOHYO" TILE IS NOT SO LIGHT THAT IT CAN BE TOSSED AWAY BY KAZAMA'S LITTLE BREEZE!
SEE?! I KNEW IT! THAT TILE WAS SUP-POSED TO BE ME!
HUH?! OH!!
YOU'RE JUST GETTING IT NOW?!
WELL, OKAY THEN! I'LL JUST HAVE TO FLIP IT OVER.
BWAH?!
KA-TAK
"COME-BACK"?!
TSUKKOMI
YOWZA! ♪
WAIT, YOU'RE USING IT IN EXACTLY THE SAME WAY AS THE SUMO PIECES! IS EVERY FLIPPED-OVER TILE SOMEHOW SUMO RELATED?!
GAH!! DON'T TELL ME MY OWN "COMEBACKS" ARE CONSIDERED PART OF THE "COMEBACK" OF THE SUMO PIECES?!!

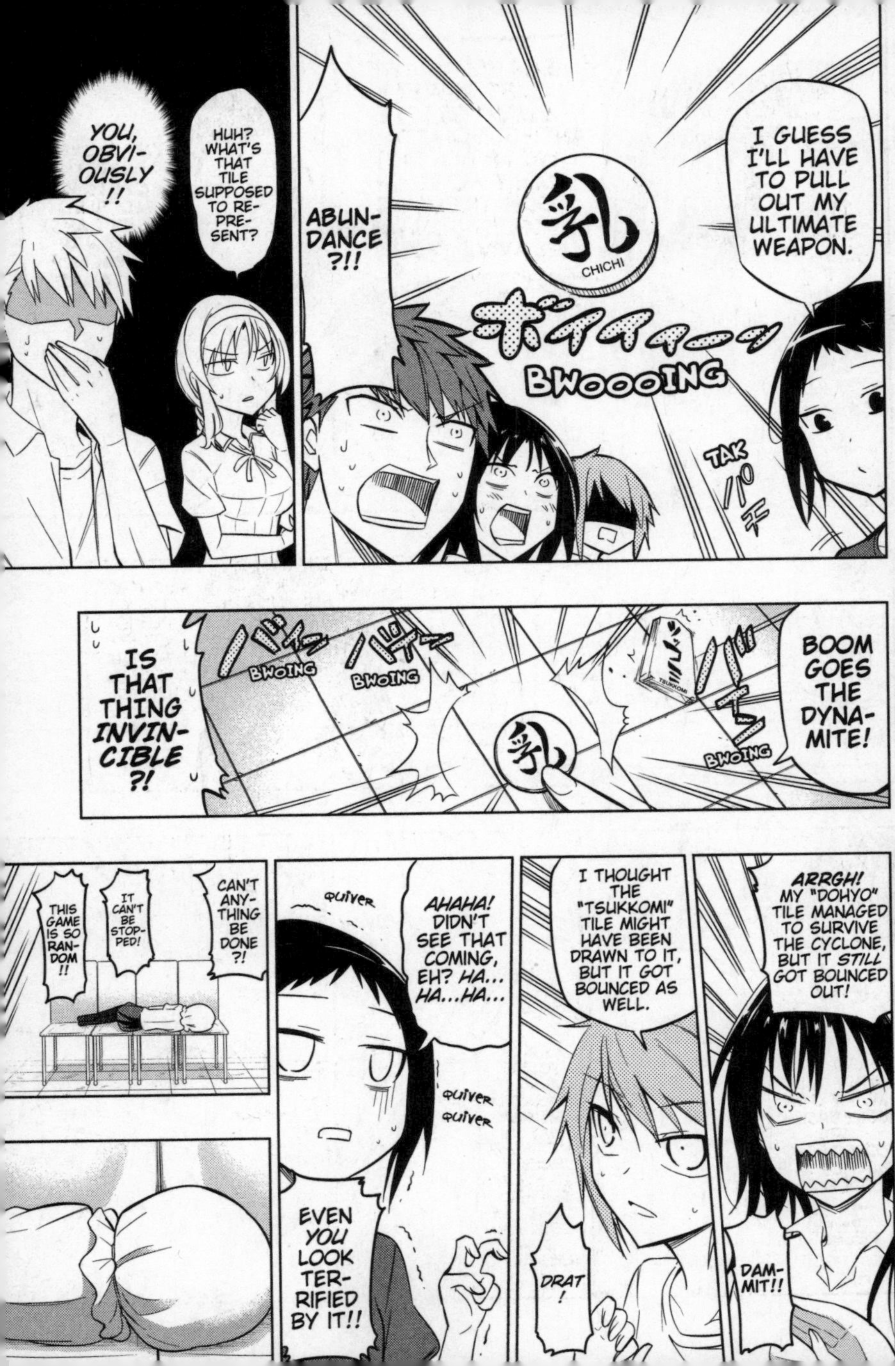
I GUESS I'LL HAVE TO PULL OUT MY ULTIMATE WEAPON.
乳
CHICHI
ボイイィーン
BWOOOOING
TAK
パチ
ABUN-DANCE?!!
HUH? WHAT'S THAT TILE SUPPOSED TO RE-PRE-SENT?
YOU, OBVI-OUSLY!!
BOOM GOES THE DYNA-MITE!
TSUKKOMI
BWOING
BWOING
BWOING
IS THAT THING INVIN-CIBLE?!
ARRGH! MY "DOHYO" TILE MANAGED TO SURVIVE THE CYCLONE, BUT IT STILL GOT BOUNCED OUT!
DAM-MIT!!
I THOUGHT THE "TSUKKOMI" TILE MIGHT HAVE BEEN DRAWN TO IT, BUT IT GOT BOUNCED AS WELL.
DRAT!
quiver
AHAHA! DIDN'T SEE THAT COMING, EH? HA... HA...HA...
quiver quiver
EVEN YOU LOOK TER-RIFIED BY IT!!
CAN'T ANY-THING BE DONE?!
IT CAN'T BE STOP-PED!
THIS GAME IS SO RAN-DOM!!

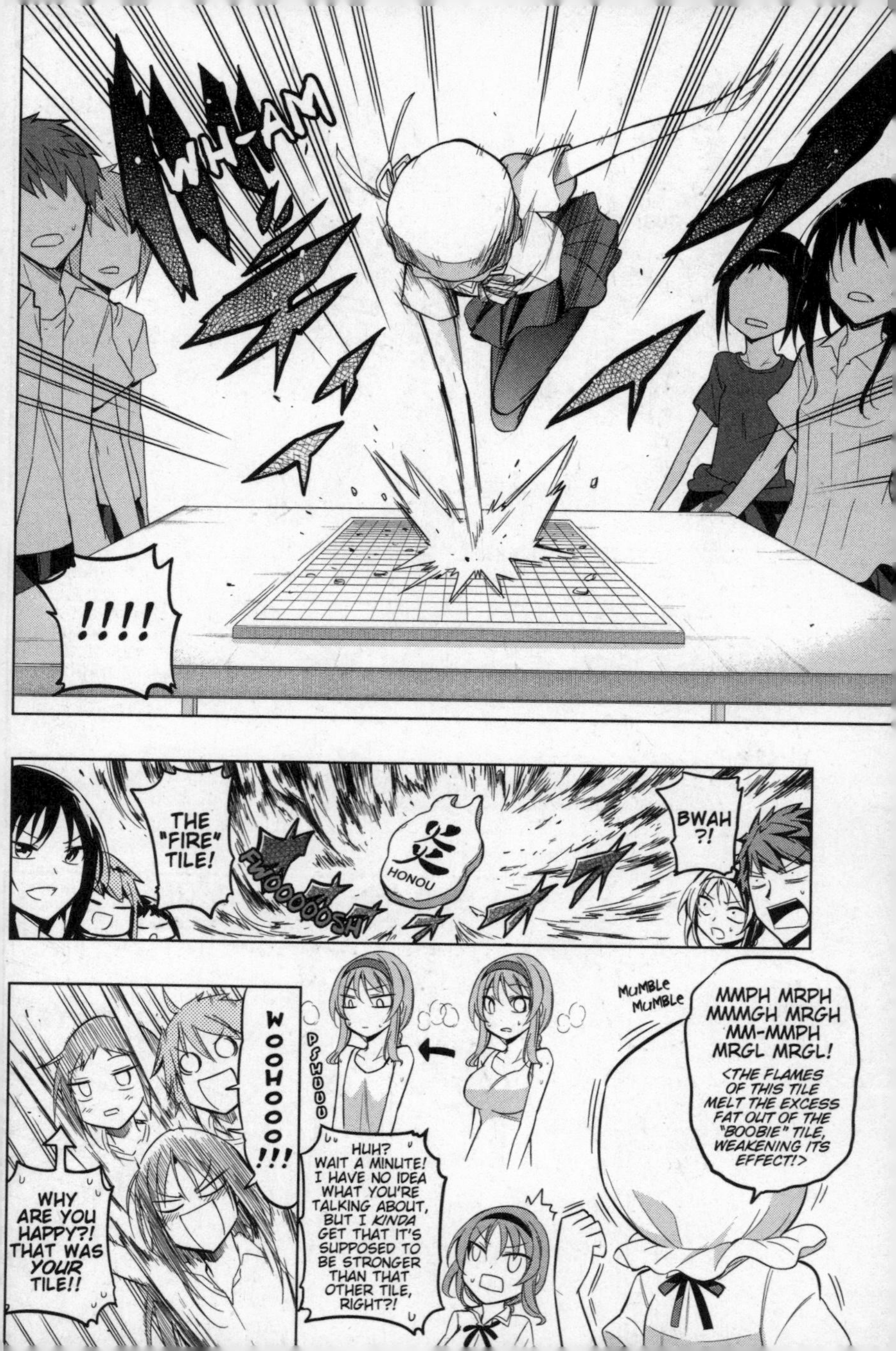
WH-AM
!!!!
BWAH ?!
炎
HONOU
FWOOOOOSH
THE "FIRE" TILE!
MUMBLE MUMBLE
MMPH MRPH MMMGH MRGH MM-MMPH MRGL MRGL!
<THE FLAMES OF THIS TILE MELT THE EXCESS FAT OUT OF THE "BOOBIE" TILE, WEAKENING ITS EFFECT!>
PSHUUU
HUH? WAIT A MINUTE! I HAVE NO IDEA WHAT YOU'RE TALKING ABOUT, BUT I *KINDA* GET THAT IT'S SUPPOSED TO BE STRONGER THAN THAT OTHER TILE, RIGHT?!
WOOHOOOO!!!
WHY ARE YOU HAPPY?! THAT WAS *YOUR* TILE!!

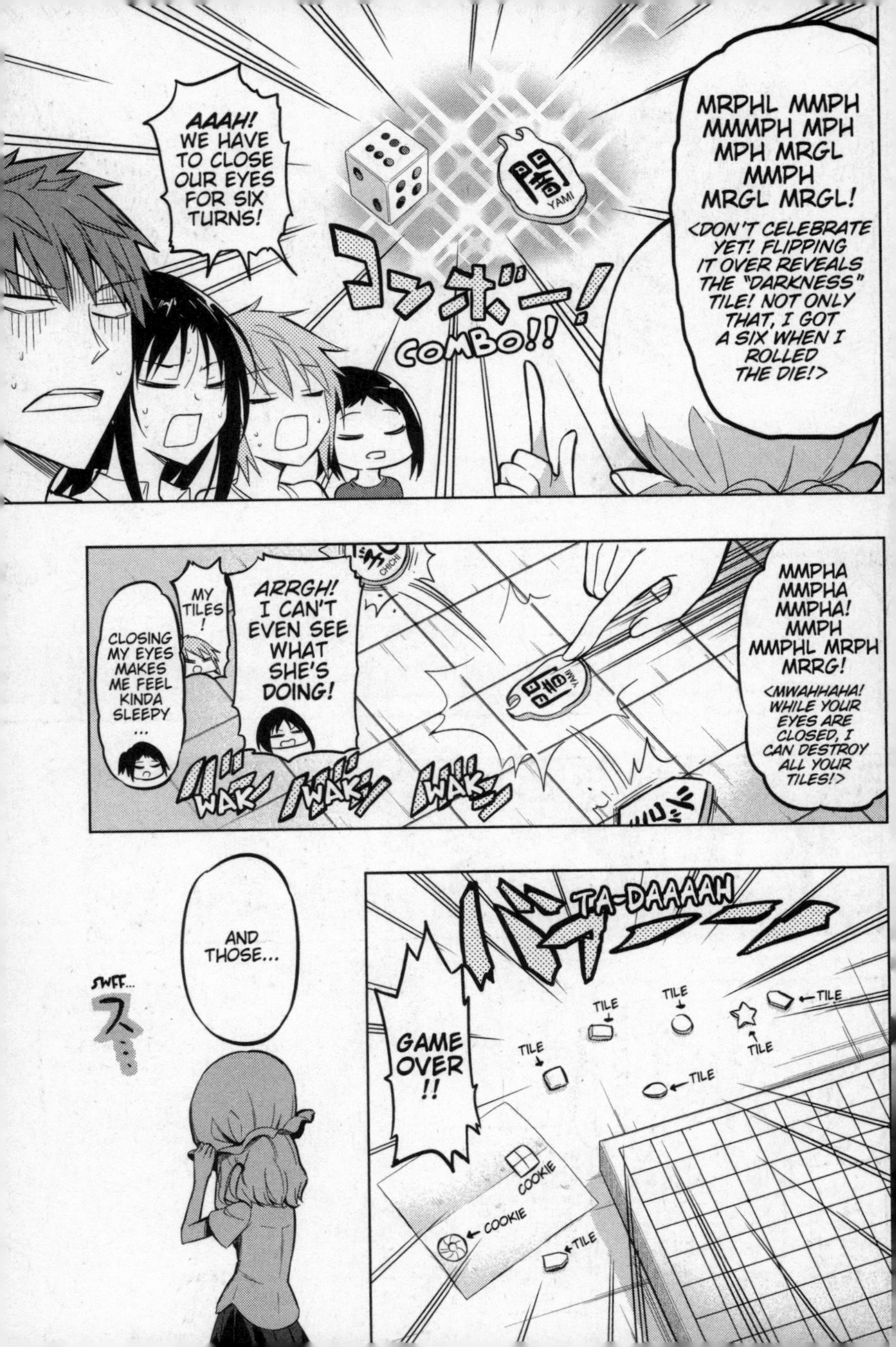
MRPHL MMPH MMMPH MPH MPH MRGL MMPH MRGL MRGL!
<DON'T CELEBRATE YET! FLIPPING IT OVER REVEALS THE "DARKNESS" TILE! NOT ONLY THAT, I GOT A SIX WHEN I ROLLED THE DIE!>
闇
YAMI
コンボー!
COMBO!!
AAAH! WE HAVE TO CLOSE OUR EYES FOR SIX TURNS!
MMPHA MMPHA MMPHA! MMPH MMPHL MRPH MRRG!
<MWAHHAHA! WHILE YOUR EYES ARE CLOSED, I CAN DESTROY ALL YOUR TILES!>
CHICHI
ARRGH! I CAN'T EVEN SEE WHAT SHE'S DOING!
MY TILES!
CLOSING MY EYES MAKES ME FEEL KINDA SLEEPY...
WAK WAK WAK
TA-DAAAAH
GAME OVER!!
TILE
TILE
TILE
TILE
TILE
TILE
COOKIE
COOKIE
TILE
AND THOSE...
SWFF...

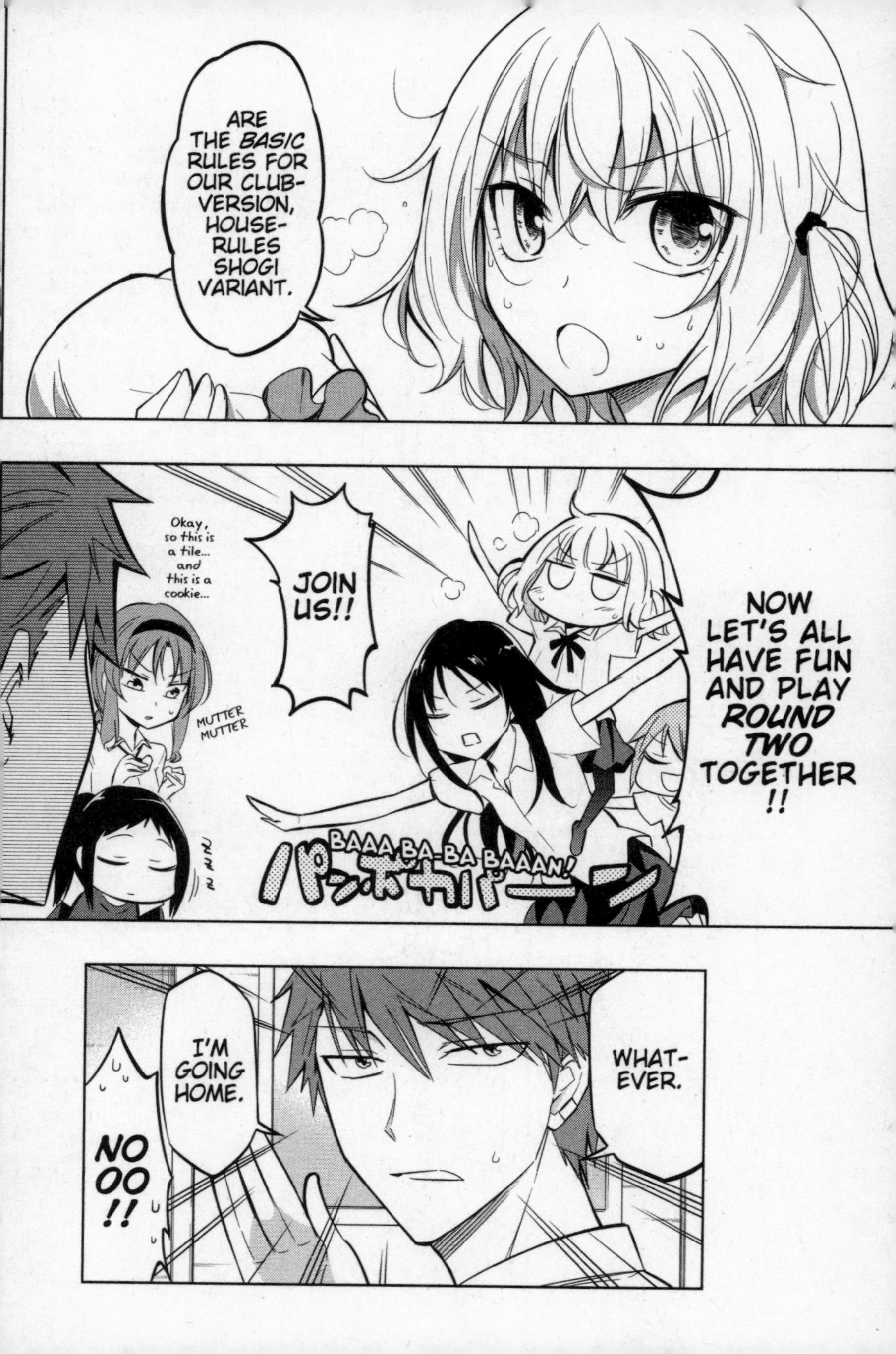
ARE THE BASIC RULES FOR OUR CLUB-VERSION, HOUSE-RULES SHOGI VARIANT.
NOW LET'S ALL HAVE FUN AND PLAY ROUND TWO TOGETHER!!
BAAA BA-BA BAAAN!
JOIN US!!
Okay, so this is a tile... and this is a cookie...
MUTTER MUTTER
WHAT-EVER.
I'M GOING HOME.
NOOO!!

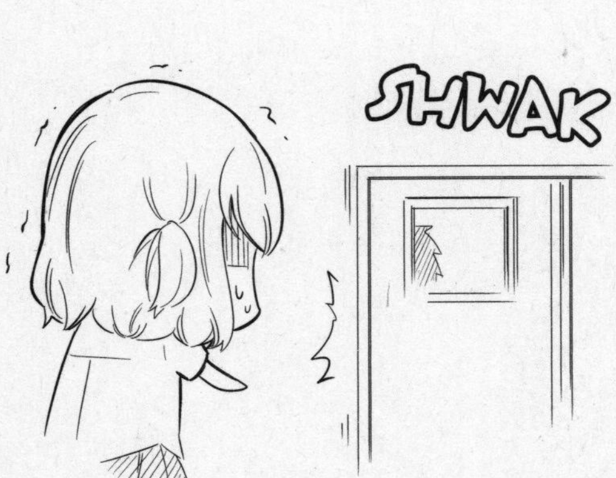
SHWAK

D-FRAGMENTS
ディーフラグメンツ！

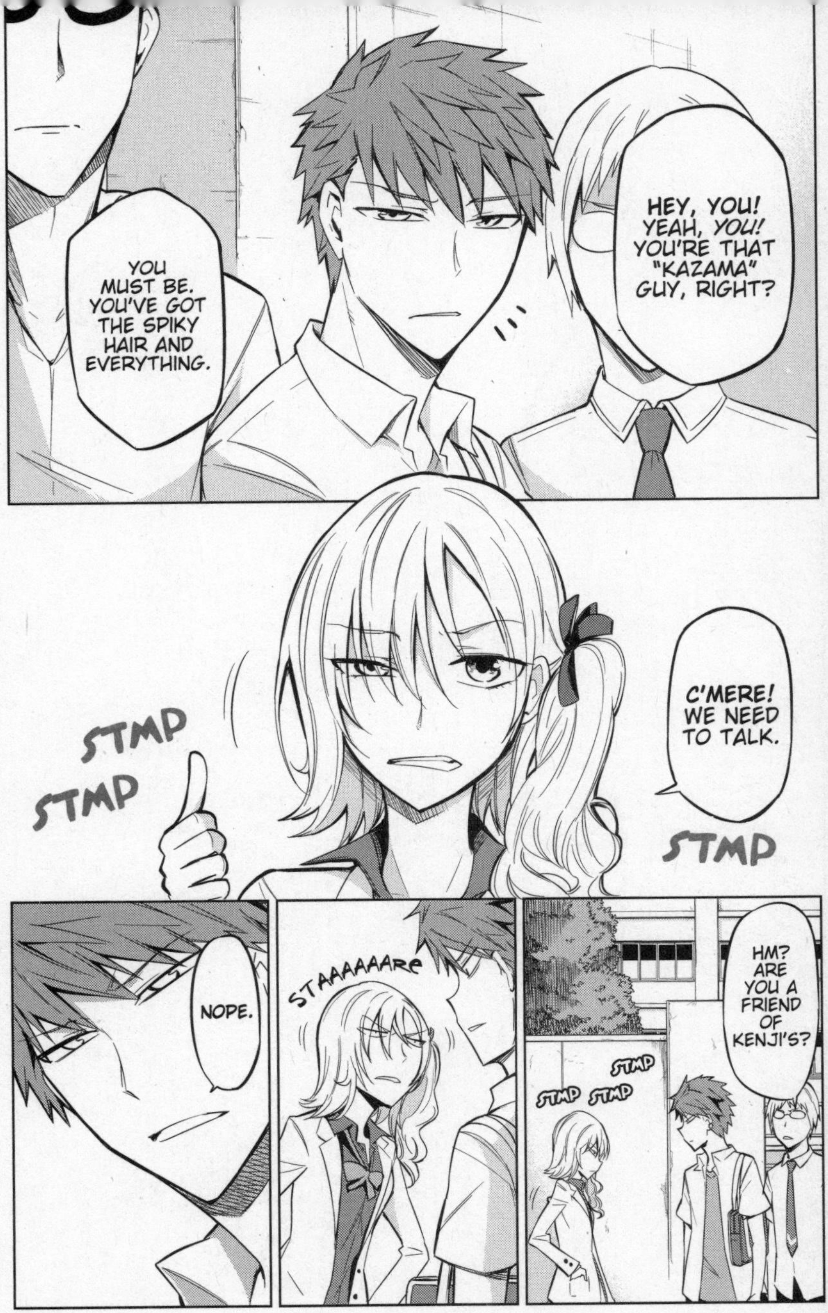
HEY, YOU! YEAH, YOU! YOU'RE THAT "KAZAMA" GUY, RIGHT?
YOU MUST BE. YOU'VE GOT THE SPIKY HAIR AND EVERYTHING.
C'MERE! WE NEED TO TALK.
STMP
STMP
STMP
HM? ARE YOU A FRIEND OF KENJI'S?
STMP
STMP STMP
STAAAAAARE
NOPE.

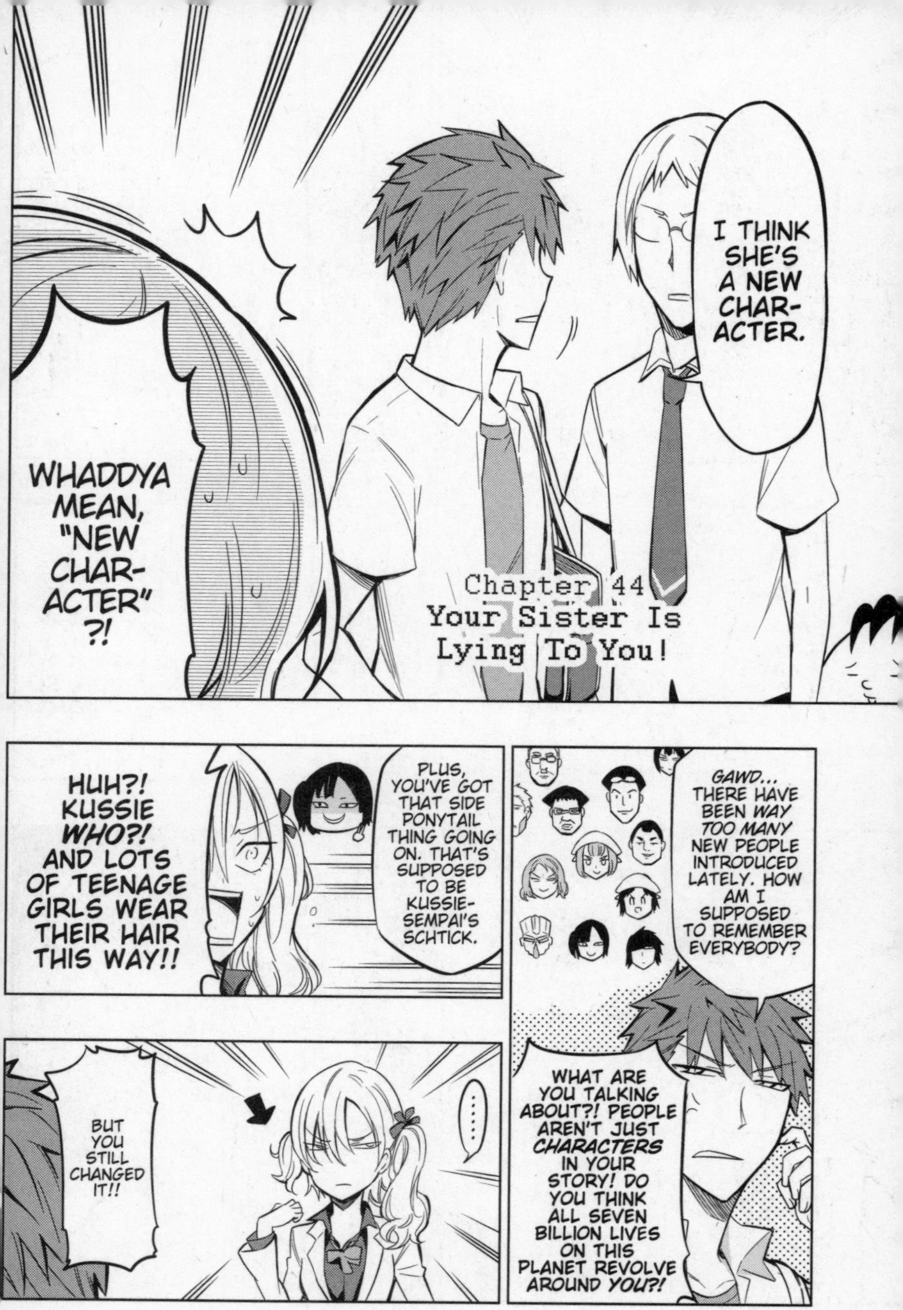
I THINK SHE'S A NEW CHARACTER.
WHADDYA MEAN, "NEW CHARACTER"?!
Chapter 44
Your Sister Is Lying To You!
GAWD... THERE HAVE BEEN WAY TOO MANY NEW PEOPLE INTRODUCED LATELY. HOW AM I SUPPOSED TO REMEMBER EVERYBODY?
WHAT ARE YOU TALKING ABOUT?! PEOPLE AREN'T JUST CHARACTERS IN YOUR STORY! DO YOU THINK ALL SEVEN BILLION LIVES ON THIS PLANET REVOLVE AROUND YOU?!
PLUS, YOU'VE GOT THAT SIDE PONYTAIL THING GOING ON. THAT'S SUPPOSED TO BE KUSSIE-SEMPAI'S SCHTICK.
HUH?! KUSSIE WHO?! AND LOTS OF TEENAGE GIRLS WEAR THEIR HAIR THIS WAY!!
......
BUT YOU STILL CHANGED IT!!

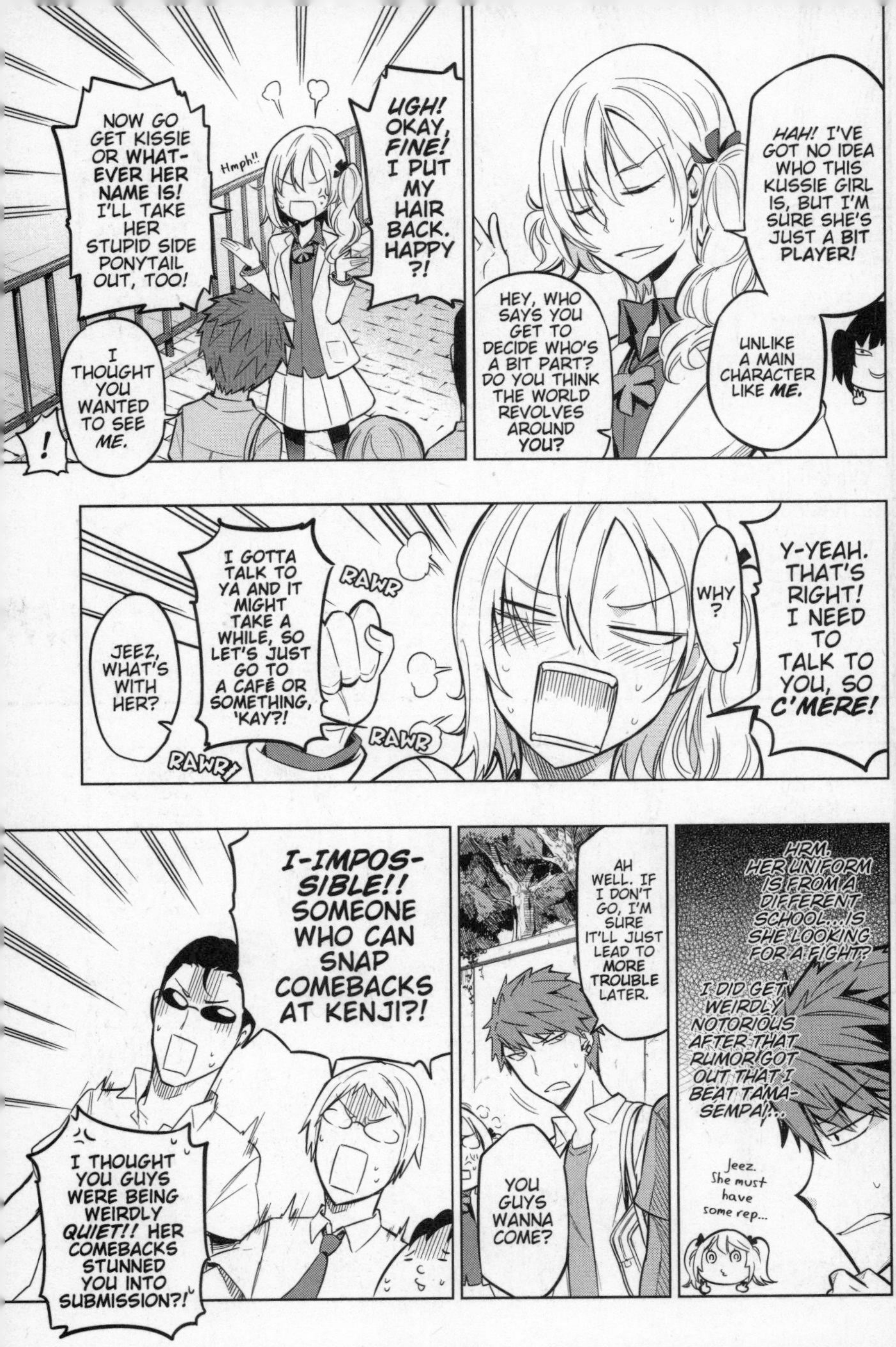
HAH! I'VE GOT NO IDEA WHO THIS KUSSIE GIRL IS, BUT I'M SURE SHE'S JUST A BIT PLAYER!
UNLIKE A MAIN CHARACTER LIKE ME.
HEY, WHO SAYS YOU GET TO DECIDE WHO'S A BIT PART? DO YOU THINK THE WORLD REVOLVES AROUND YOU?
UGH! OKAY, FINE! I PUT MY HAIR BACK. HAPPY?!
Hmph!!
NOW GO GET KISSIE OR WHAT-EVER HER NAME IS! I'LL TAKE HER STUPID SIDE PONYTAIL OUT, TOO!
I THOUGHT YOU WANTED TO SEE ME.
!
Y-YEAH. THAT'S RIGHT! I NEED TO TALK TO YOU, SO C'MERE!
WHY?
RAWR
RAWR
I GOTTA TALK TO YA AND IT MIGHT TAKE A WHILE, SO LET'S JUST GO TO A CAFÉ OR SOMETHING, 'KAY?!
JEEZ, WHAT'S WITH HER?
RAWR!
HRM. HER UNIFORM IS FROM A DIFFERENT SCHOOL... IS SHE LOOKING FOR A FIGHT?
I DID GET WEIRDLY NOTORIOUS AFTER THAT RUMOR GOT OUT THAT I BEAT TAMA-SEMPAI...
Jeez. She must have some rep...
AH WELL. IF I DON'T GO, I'M SURE IT'LL JUST LEAD TO MORE TROUBLE LATER.
YOU GUYS WANNA COME?
I-IMPOS-SIBLE!! SOMEONE WHO CAN SNAP COMEBACKS AT KENJI?!
I THOUGHT YOU GUYS WERE BEING WEIRDLY QUIET!! HER COMEBACKS STUNNED YOU INTO SUBMISSION?!

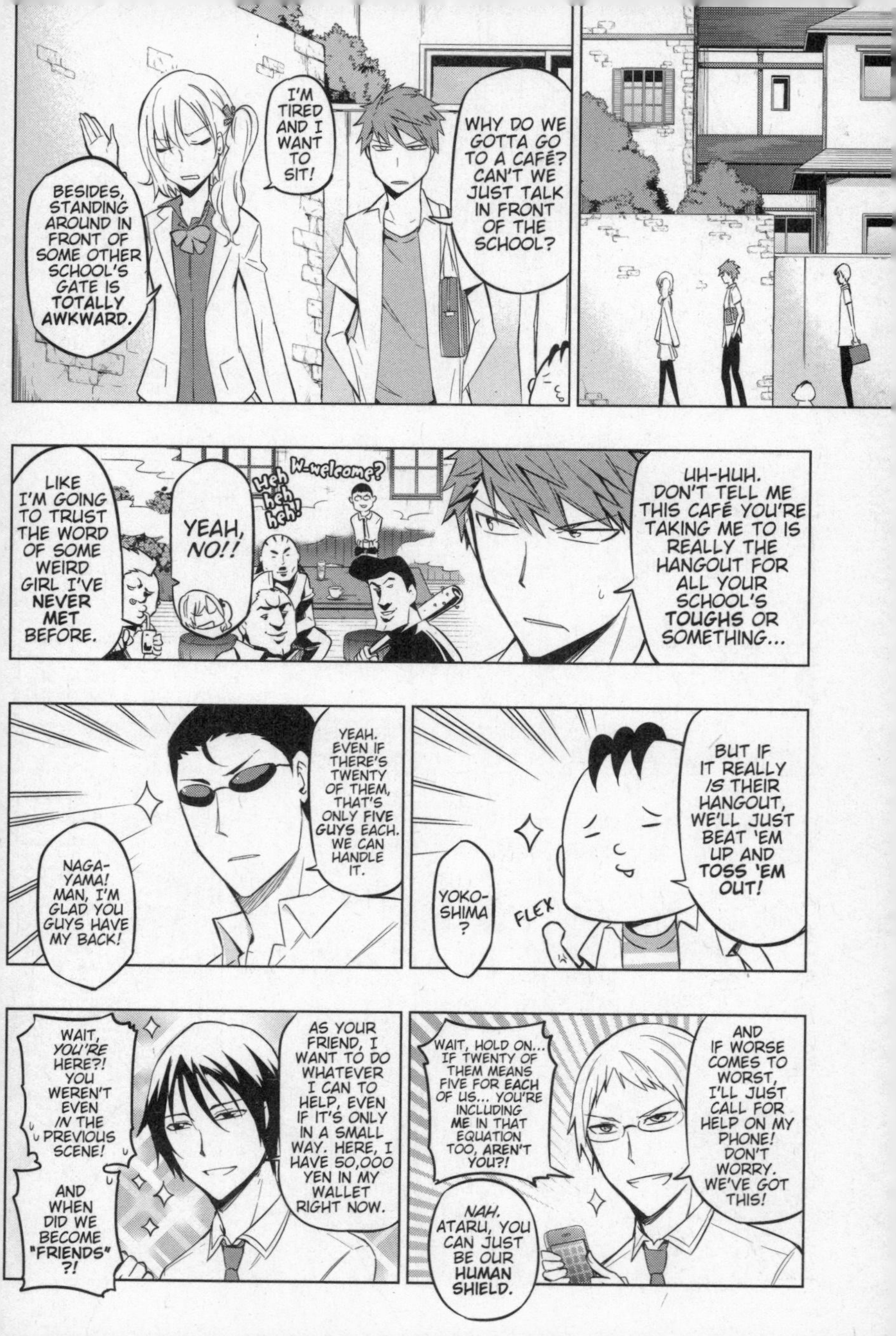
WHY DO WE GOTTA GO TO A CAFÉ? CAN'T WE JUST TALK IN FRONT OF THE SCHOOL?
I'M TIRED AND I WANT TO SIT!
BESIDES, STANDING AROUND IN FRONT OF SOME OTHER SCHOOL'S GATE IS **TOTALLY AWKWARD.**
UH-HUH. DON'T TELL ME THIS CAFÉ YOU'RE TAKING ME TO IS REALLY THE HANGOUT FOR ALL YOUR SCHOOL'S **TOUGHS** OR SOMETHING...
W-welcome?
Heh heh heh!
YEAH, *NO!!*
LIKE I'M GOING TO TRUST THE WORD OF SOME WEIRD GIRL I'VE **NEVER** MET BEFORE.
BUT IF IT REALLY *IS* THEIR HANGOUT, WE'LL JUST BEAT 'EM UP AND **TOSS 'EM OUT!**
FLEX
YOKO-SHIMA?
YEAH. EVEN IF THERE'S TWENTY OF THEM, THAT'S ONLY FIVE **GUYS** EACH. WE CAN HANDLE IT.
NAGA-YAMA! MAN, I'M GLAD YOU GUYS HAVE MY BACK!
AND IF WORSE COMES TO WORST, I'LL JUST CALL FOR HELP ON MY PHONE! DON'T WORRY. WE'VE GOT THIS!
WAIT, HOLD ON... IF TWENTY OF THEM MEANS FIVE FOR EACH OF US... YOU'RE INCLUDING **ME** IN THAT EQUATION TOO, AREN'T YOU?!
NAH. ATARU, YOU CAN JUST BE OUR **HUMAN SHIELD.**
AS YOUR FRIEND, I WANT TO DO WHATEVER I CAN TO HELP, EVEN IF IT'S ONLY IN A SMALL WAY. HERE, I HAVE 50,000 YEN IN MY WALLET RIGHT NOW.
WAIT, *YOU'RE* HERE?! YOU WEREN'T EVEN *IN* THE PREVIOUS SCENE!
AND WHEN DID WE BECOME **"FRIENDS"**?!

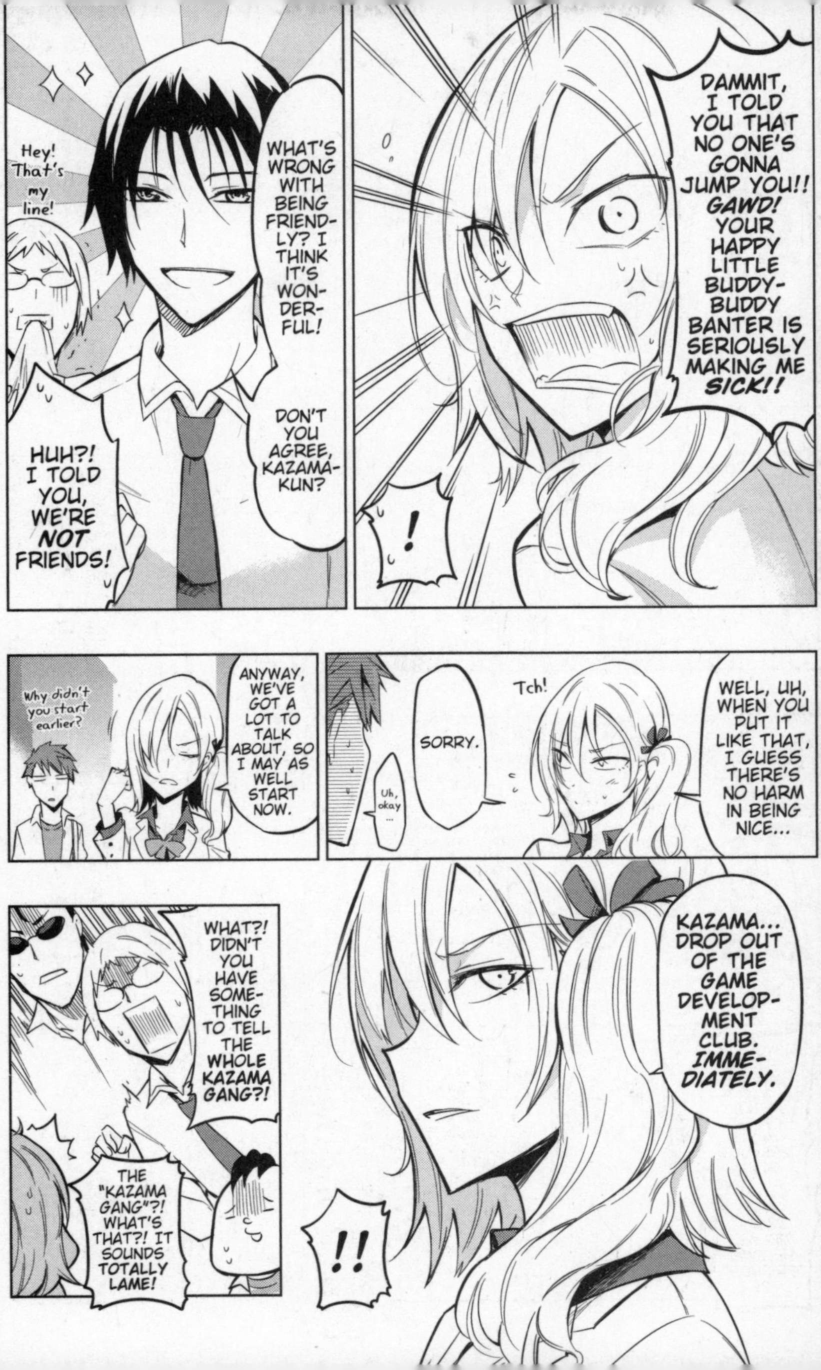
DAMMIT, I TOLD YOU THAT NO ONE'S GONNA JUMP YOU!! GAWD! YOUR HAPPY LITTLE BUDDY-BUDDY BANTER IS SERIOUSLY MAKING ME SICK!!
!
WHAT'S WRONG WITH BEING FRIENDLY? I THINK IT'S WONDERFUL!
DON'T YOU AGREE, KAZAMA-KUN?
Hey! That's my line!
HUH?! I TOLD YOU, WE'RE NOT FRIENDS!
WELL, UH, WHEN YOU PUT IT LIKE THAT, I GUESS THERE'S NO HARM IN BEING NICE...
Tch!
SORRY.
Uh, okay ...
ANYWAY, WE'VE GOT A LOT TO TALK ABOUT, SO I MAY AS WELL START NOW.
Why didn't you start earlier?
KAZAMA... DROP OUT OF THE GAME DEVELOPMENT CLUB. IMMEDIATELY.
!!
WHAT?! DIDN'T YOU HAVE SOMETHING TO TELL THE WHOLE KAZAMA GANG?!
THE "KAZAMA GANG"?! WHAT'S THAT?! IT SOUNDS TOTALLY LAME!

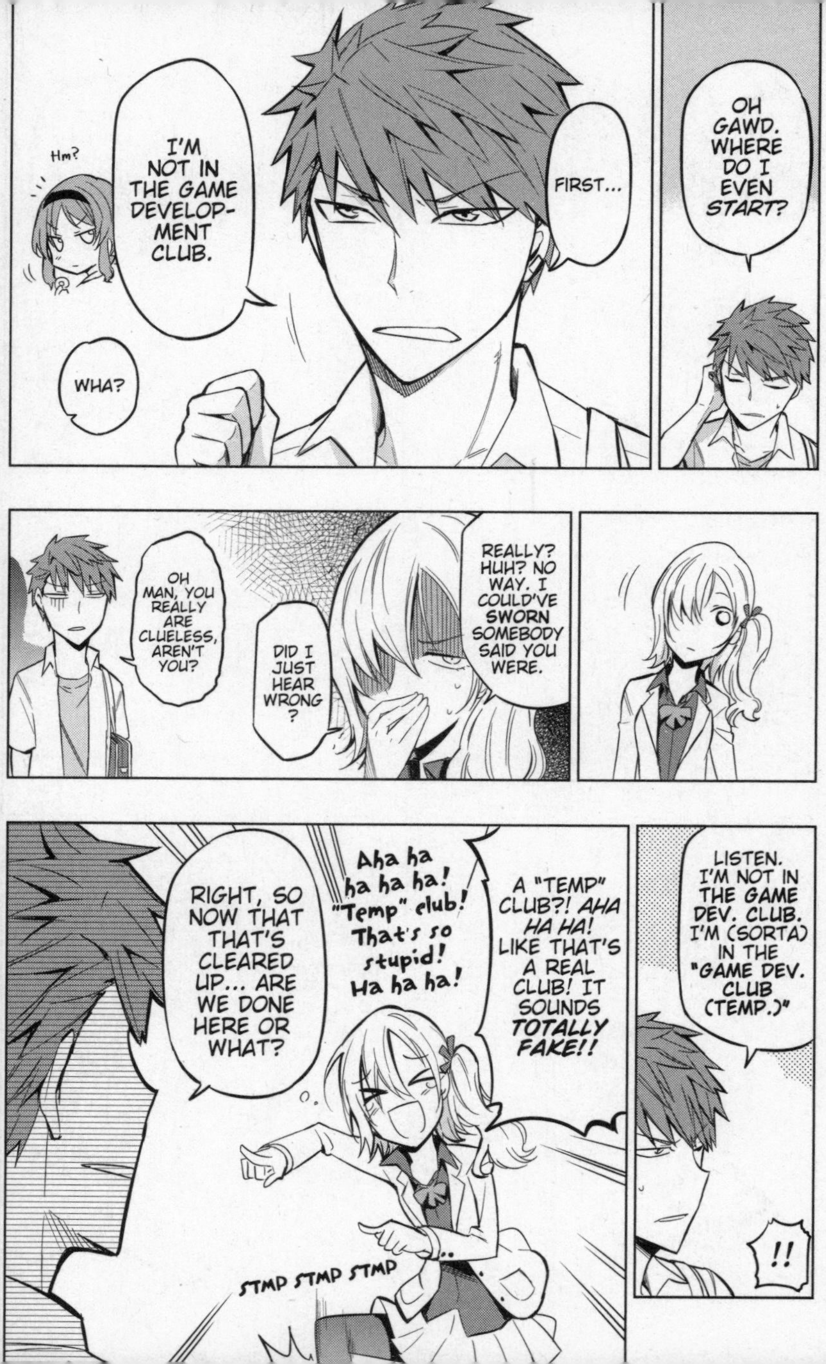
OH GAWD. WHERE DO I EVEN *START?*
FIRST...
I'M NOT IN THE GAME DEVELOPMENT CLUB.
Hm?
WHA?
REALLY? HUH? NO WAY. I COULD'VE SWORN SOMEBODY SAID YOU WERE.
DID I JUST HEAR WRONG?
OH MAN, YOU REALLY ARE CLUELESS, AREN'T YOU?
LISTEN. I'M NOT IN THE GAME DEV. CLUB. I'M (SORTA) IN THE "GAME DEV. CLUB (TEMP.)"
!!
A "TEMP" CLUB?! *AHA HA HA!* LIKE THAT'S A REAL CLUB! IT SOUNDS *TOTALLY FAKE!!*
Aha ha ha ha ha! "Temp" club! That's so stupid! Ha ha ha!
RIGHT, SO NOW THAT THAT'S CLEARED UP... ARE WE DONE HERE OR WHAT?
STMP STMP STMP

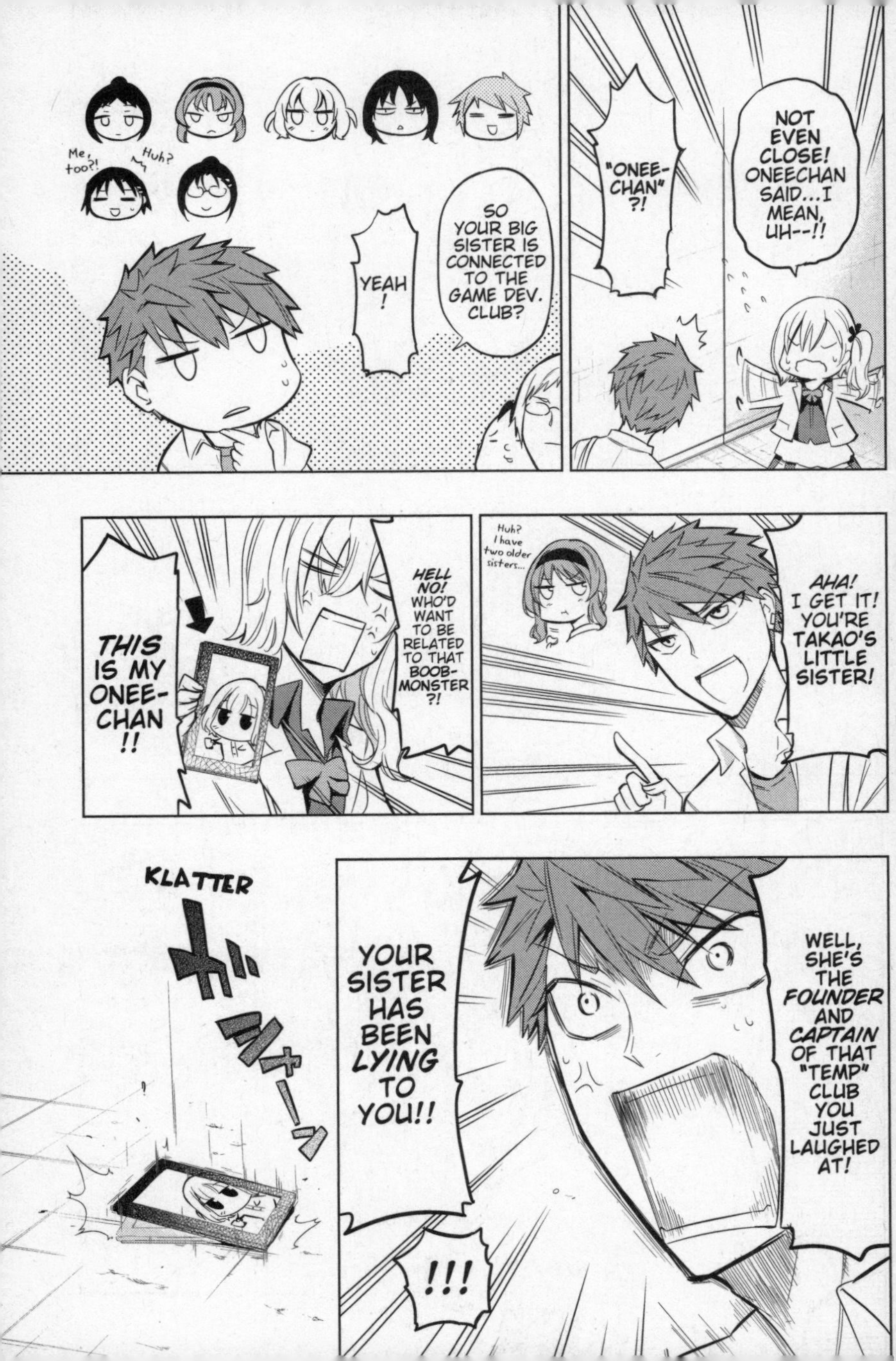
NOT EVEN CLOSE! ONEECHAN SAID...I MEAN, UH--!!
"ONEE-CHAN" ?!
SO YOUR BIG SISTER IS CONNECTED TO THE GAME DEV. CLUB?
YEAH!
Huh?
Me, too?!
AHA! I GET IT! YOU'RE TAKAO'S LITTLE SISTER!
Huh? I have two older sisters...
HELL NO! WHO'D WANT TO BE RELATED TO THAT BOOB-MONSTER?!
THIS IS MY ONEE-CHAN!!
WELL, SHE'S THE FOUNDER AND CAPTAIN OF THAT "TEMP" CLUB YOU JUST LAUGHED AT!
YOUR SISTER HAS BEEN LYING TO YOU!!
!!!
KLATTER

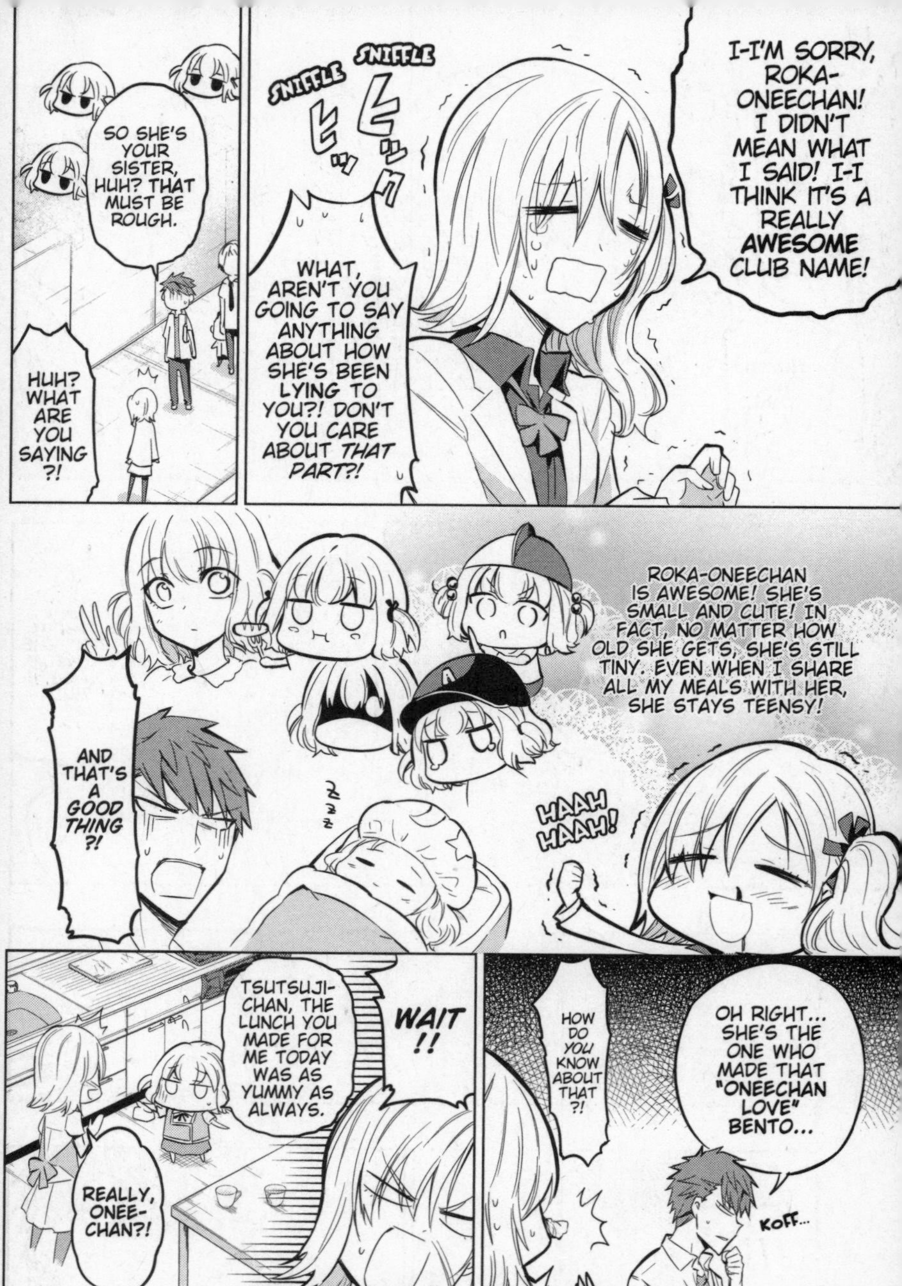
I-I'M SORRY, ROKA-ONEECHAN! I DIDN'T MEAN WHAT I SAID! I-I THINK IT'S A REALLY AWESOME CLUB NAME!
SNIFFLE
SNIFFLE
WHAT, AREN'T YOU GOING TO SAY ANYTHING ABOUT HOW SHE'S BEEN LYING TO YOU?! DON'T YOU CARE ABOUT THAT PART?!
SO SHE'S YOUR SISTER, HUH? THAT MUST BE ROUGH.
HUH? WHAT ARE YOU SAYING?!
ROKA-ONEECHAN IS AWESOME! SHE'S SMALL AND CUTE! IN FACT, NO MATTER HOW OLD SHE GETS, SHE'S STILL TINY. EVEN WHEN I SHARE ALL MY MEALS WITH HER, SHE STAYS TEENSY!
HAAH HAAH!
AND THAT'S A GOOD THING?!
OH RIGHT... SHE'S THE ONE WHO MADE THAT "ONEECHAN LOVE" BENTO...
HOW DO YOU KNOW ABOUT THAT?!
KOFF...
WAIT!!
TSUTSUJI-CHAN, THE LUNCH YOU MADE FOR ME TODAY WAS AS YUMMY AS ALWAYS.
REALLY, ONEE-CHAN?!

※See Vol. 5, Ch. 29.

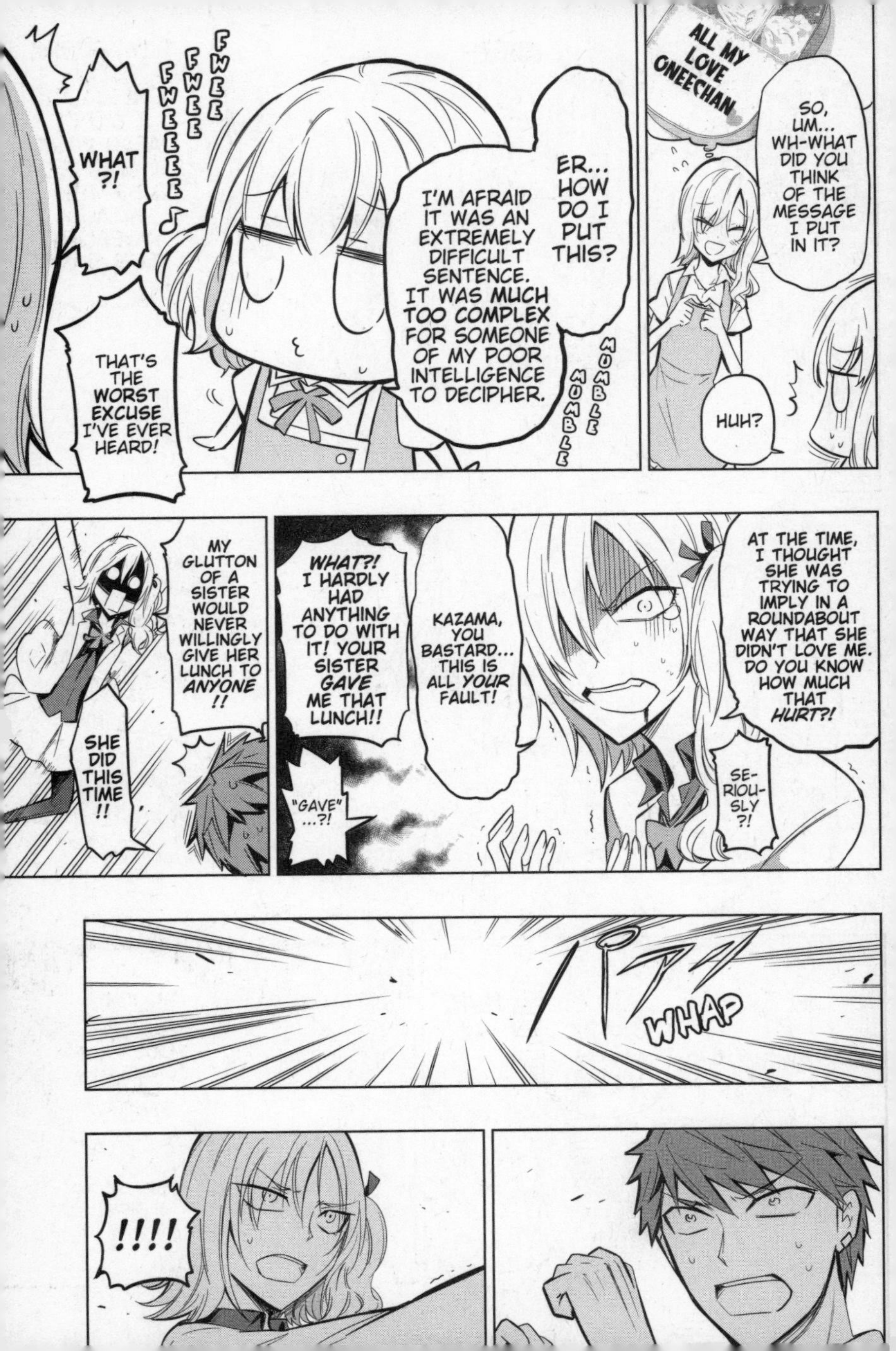
ALL MY LOVE ONEECHAN
SO, UM... WH-WHAT DID YOU THINK OF THE MESSAGE I PUT IN IT?
HUH?
ER... HOW DO I PUT THIS?
I'M AFRAID IT WAS AN EXTREMELY DIFFICULT SENTENCE. IT WAS MUCH TOO COMPLEX FOR SOMEONE OF MY POOR INTELLIGENCE TO DECIPHER.
MUMBLE MUMBLE
FWEE FWEE FWEEEE
WHAT ?!
THAT'S THE WORST EXCUSE I'VE EVER HEARD!
AT THE TIME, I THOUGHT SHE WAS TRYING TO IMPLY IN A ROUNDABOUT WAY THAT SHE DIDN'T LOVE ME. DO YOU KNOW HOW MUCH THAT HURT?!
SE-RIOUS-LY ?!
KAZAMA, YOU BASTARD... THIS IS ALL YOUR FAULT!
WHAT?! I HARDLY HAD ANYTHING TO DO WITH IT! YOUR SISTER GAVE ME THAT LUNCH!!
"GAVE" ...?!
MY GLUTTON OF A SISTER WOULD NEVER WILLINGLY GIVE HER LUNCH TO ANYONE !!
SHE DID THIS TIME !!
WHAP
!!!!

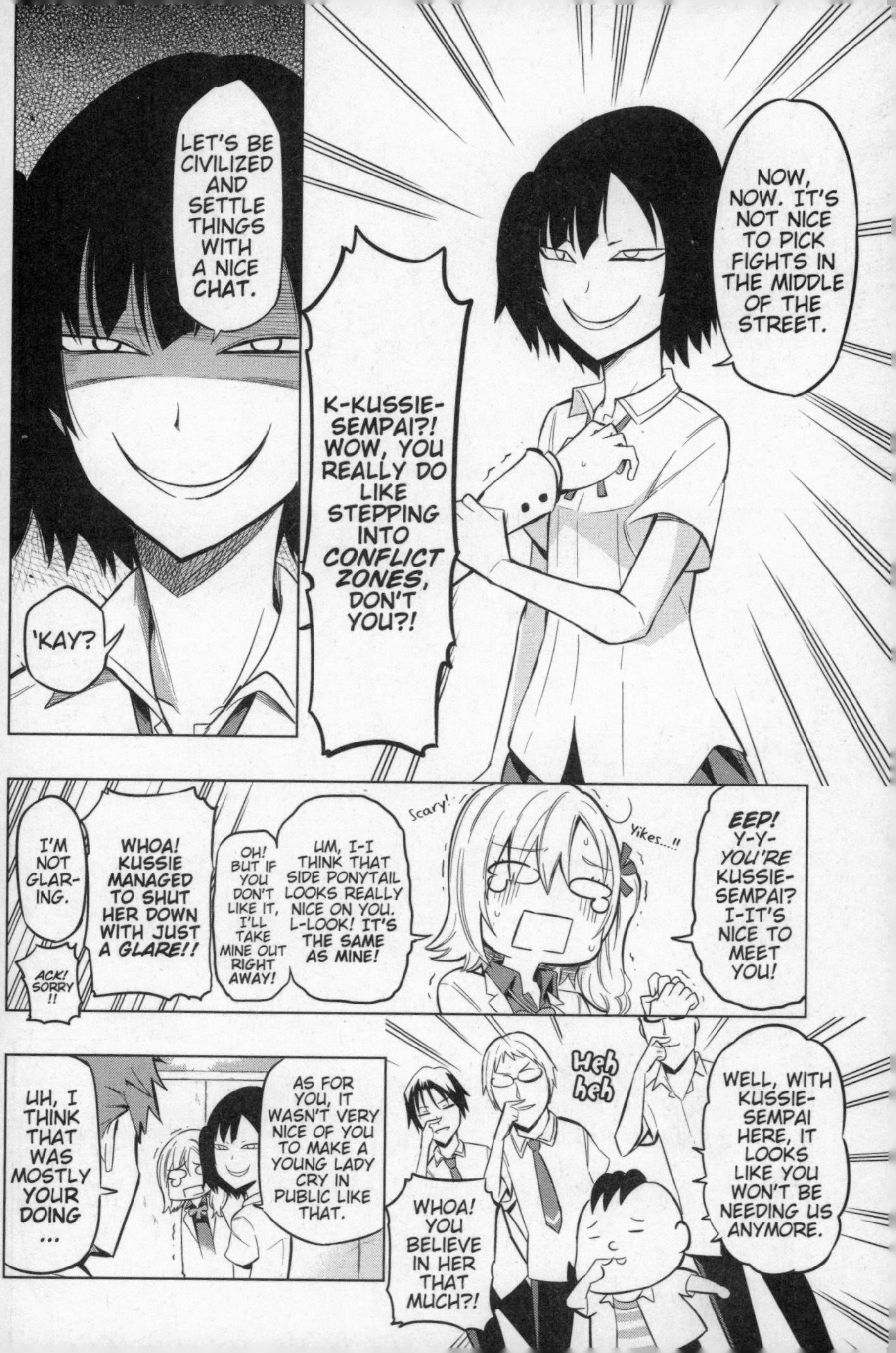
NOW, NOW. IT'S NOT NICE TO PICK FIGHTS IN THE MIDDLE OF THE STREET.
K-KUSSIE-SEMPAI?! WOW, YOU REALLY DO LIKE STEPPING INTO *CONFLICT ZONES*, DON'T YOU?!
LET'S BE CIVILIZED AND SETTLE THINGS WITH A NICE CHAT.
'KAY?
EEP! Y-Y-*YOU'RE* KUSSIE-SEMPAI? I-IT'S NICE TO MEET YOU!
Yikes...!!
Scary!
UM, I-I THINK THAT SIDE PONYTAIL LOOKS REALLY NICE ON YOU. L-LOOK! IT'S THE SAME AS MINE!
OH! BUT IF YOU DON'T LIKE IT, I'LL TAKE MINE OUT RIGHT AWAY!
WHOA! KUSSIE MANAGED TO SHUT HER DOWN WITH JUST A *GLARE!!*
I'M NOT GLARING.
ACK! SORRY!!
WELL, WITH KUSSIE-SEMPAI HERE, IT LOOKS LIKE YOU WON'T BE NEEDING US ANYMORE.
Heh heh
WHOA! YOU BELIEVE IN HER THAT MUCH?!
AS FOR YOU, IT WASN'T VERY NICE OF YOU TO MAKE A YOUNG LADY CRY IN PUBLIC LIKE THAT.
UH, I THINK THAT WAS MOSTLY YOUR DOING...

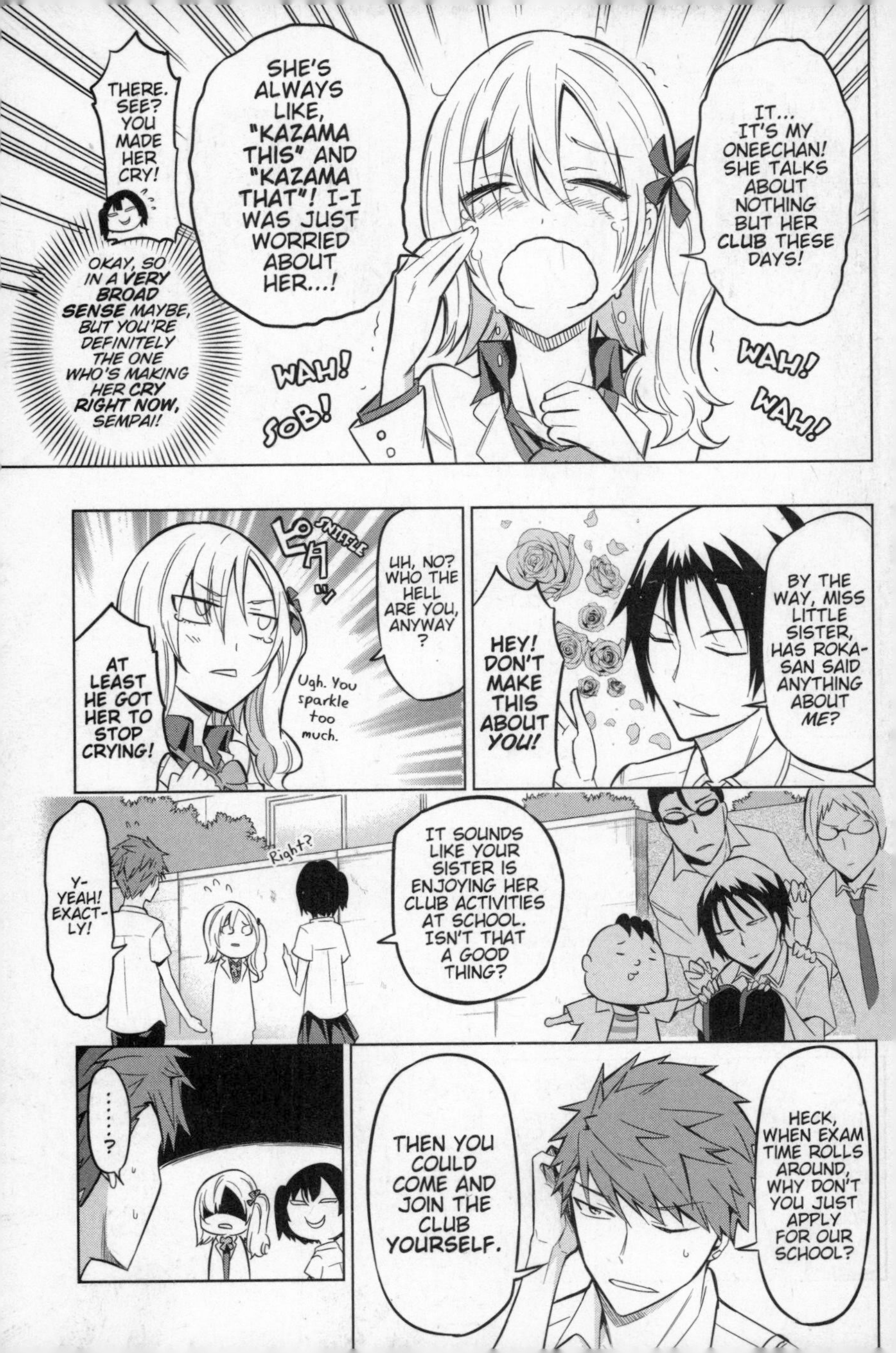
IT... IT'S MY ONEECHAN! SHE TALKS ABOUT NOTHING BUT HER CLUB THESE DAYS!
WAH!
WAH!
SHE'S ALWAYS LIKE, "KAZAMA THIS" AND "KAZAMA THAT"! I-I WAS JUST WORRIED ABOUT HER...!
WAH!
SOB!
THERE. SEE? YOU MADE HER CRY!
OKAY, SO IN A VERY BROAD SENSE MAYBE, BUT YOU'RE DEFINITELY THE ONE WHO'S MAKING HER CRY RIGHT NOW, SEMPAI!
BY THE WAY, MISS LITTLE SISTER, HAS ROKA-SAN SAID ANYTHING ABOUT ME?
HEY! DON'T MAKE THIS ABOUT YOU!
SNIFFLE
UH, NO? WHO THE HELL ARE YOU, ANYWAY?
Ugh. You sparkle too much.
AT LEAST HE GOT HER TO STOP CRYING!
IT SOUNDS LIKE YOUR SISTER IS ENJOYING HER CLUB ACTIVITIES AT SCHOOL. ISN'T THAT A GOOD THING?
Right?
Y-YEAH! EXACTLY!
HECK, WHEN EXAM TIME ROLLS AROUND, WHY DON'T YOU JUST APPLY FOR OUR SCHOOL?
THEN YOU COULD COME AND JOIN THE CLUB YOURSELF.
......?

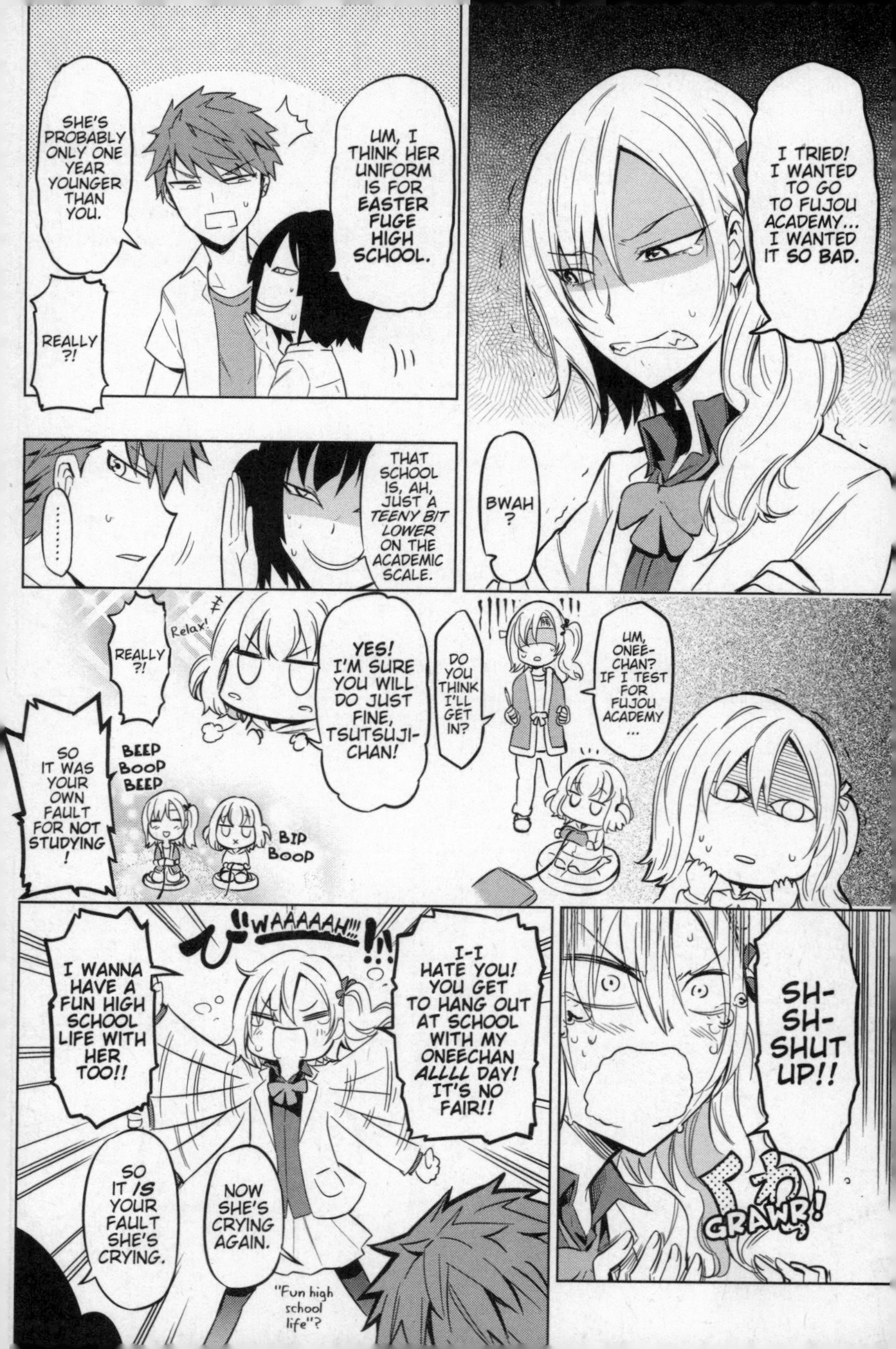
I TRIED! I WANTED TO GO TO FUJOU ACADEMY... I WANTED IT SO BAD.
BWAH?
UM, I THINK HER UNIFORM IS FOR EASTER FUGE HIGH SCHOOL.
SHE'S PROBABLY ONLY ONE YEAR YOUNGER THAN YOU.
REALLY?!
THAT SCHOOL IS, AH, JUST A *TEENY BIT LOWER* ON THE ACADEMIC SCALE.
......
UM, ONEE-CHAN? IF I TEST FOR FUJOU ACADEMY...
DO YOU THINK I'LL GET IN?
YES! I'M SURE YOU WILL DO JUST FINE, TSUTSUJI-CHAN!
Relax!
REALLY?!
BIP BOOP
BEEP BOOP BEEP
SO IT WAS YOUR OWN FAULT FOR NOT STUDYING!
SH-SH-SHUT UP!!
GRAWR!
WAAAAAH!!!
I-I HATE YOU! YOU GET TO HANG OUT AT SCHOOL WITH MY ONEECHAN *ALLLL* DAY! IT'S NO FAIR!!
I WANNA HAVE A FUN HIGH SCHOOL LIFE WITH HER TOO!!
NOW SHE'S CRYING AGAIN.
SO IT *IS* YOUR FAULT SHE'S CRYING.
"Fun high school life"?

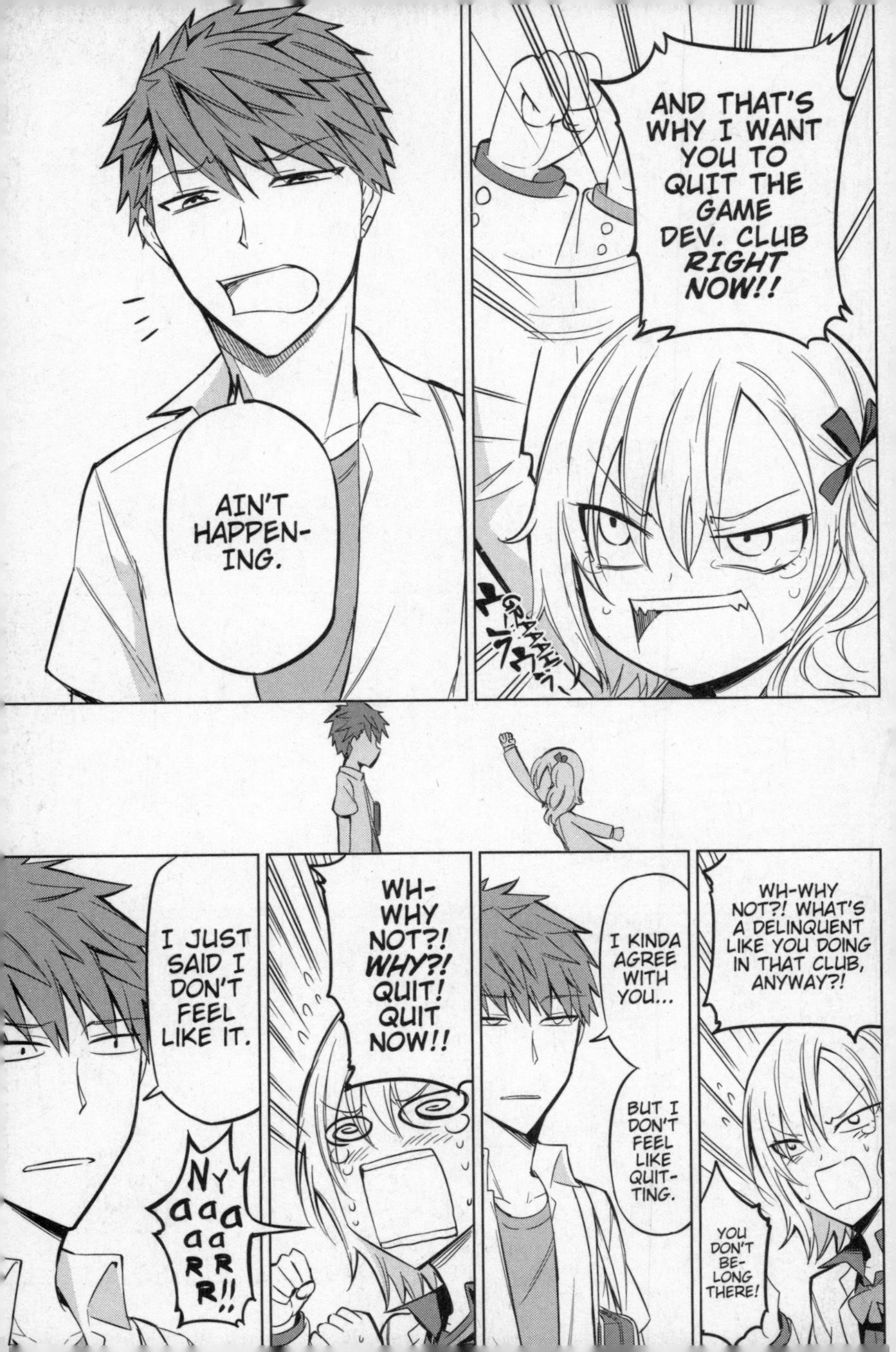
AND THAT'S WHY I WANT YOU TO QUIT THE GAME DEV. CLUB RIGHT NOW!!
GRAAAH!!
AIN'T HAPPEN-ING.
WH-WHY NOT?! WHAT'S A DELINQUENT LIKE YOU DOING IN THAT CLUB, ANYWAY?!
YOU DON'T BE-LONG THERE!
I KINDA AGREE WITH YOU...
BUT I DON'T FEEL LIKE QUIT-TING.
WH-WHY NOT?! WHY?! QUIT! QUIT NOW!!
I JUST SAID I DON'T FEEL LIKE IT.
NYAAAAARRR!!

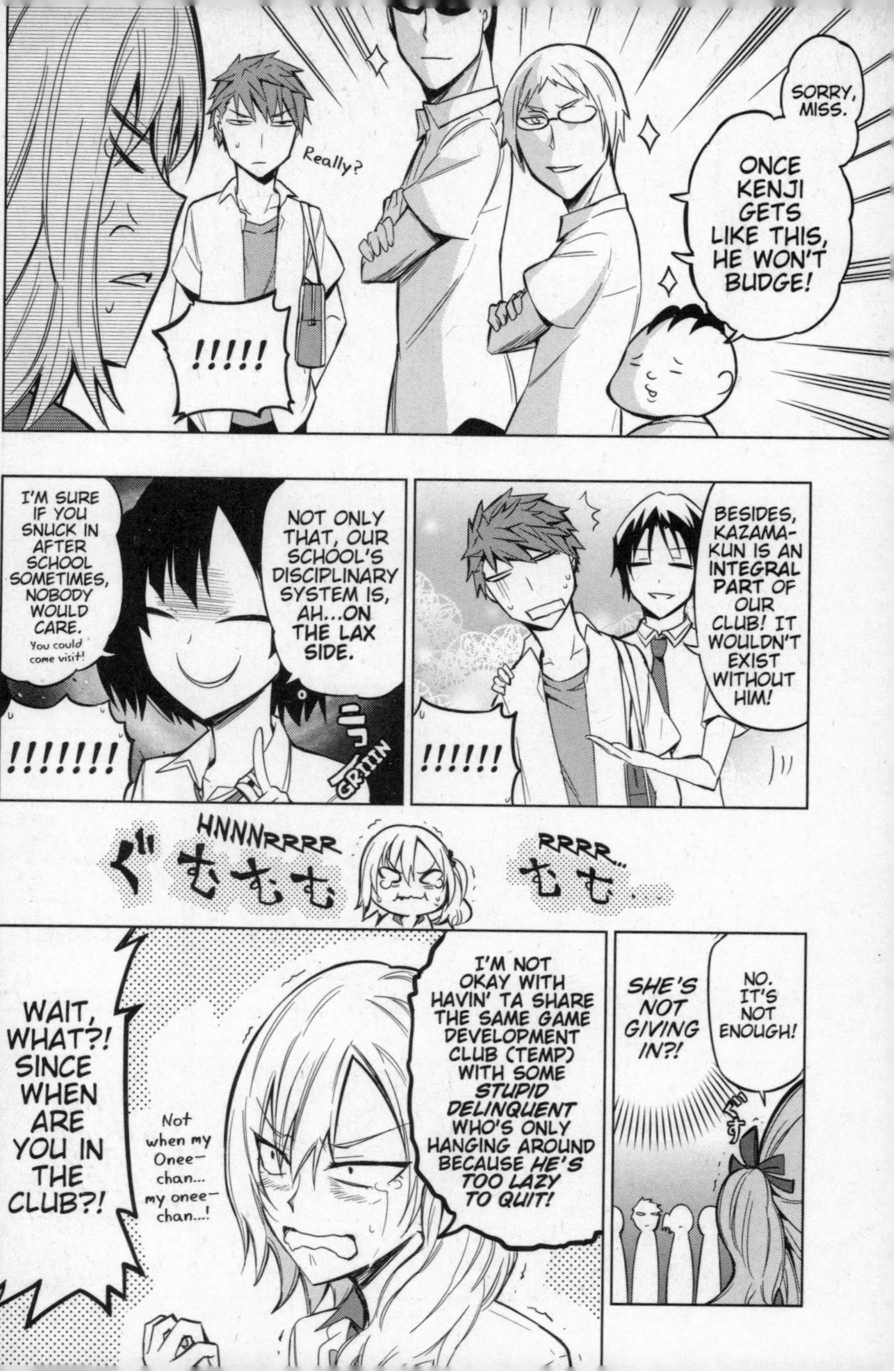
SORRY, MISS.
ONCE KENJI GETS LIKE THIS, HE WON'T BUDGE!
Really?
!!!!!
BESIDES, KAZAMA-KUN IS AN INTEGRAL PART OF OUR CLUB! IT WOULDN'T EXIST WITHOUT HIM!
!!!!!!
NOT ONLY THAT, OUR SCHOOL'S DISCIPLINARY SYSTEM IS, AH...ON THE LAX SIDE.
I'M SURE IF YOU SNUCK IN AFTER SCHOOL SOMETIMES, NOBODY WOULD CARE.
You could come visit!
GRIIIN
!!!!!!!
ぐむむむ
HNNNRRRR
むむ...
RRRR...
NO. IT'S NOT ENOUGH!
SHE'S NOT GIVING IN?!
I'M NOT OKAY WITH HAVIN' TA SHARE THE SAME GAME DEVELOPMENT CLUB (TEMP) WITH SOME STUPID DELINQUENT WHO'S ONLY HANGING AROUND BECAUSE HE'S TOO LAZY TO QUIT!
WAIT, WHAT?! SINCE WHEN ARE YOU IN THE CLUB?!
Not when my Onee-chan... my onee-chan...!

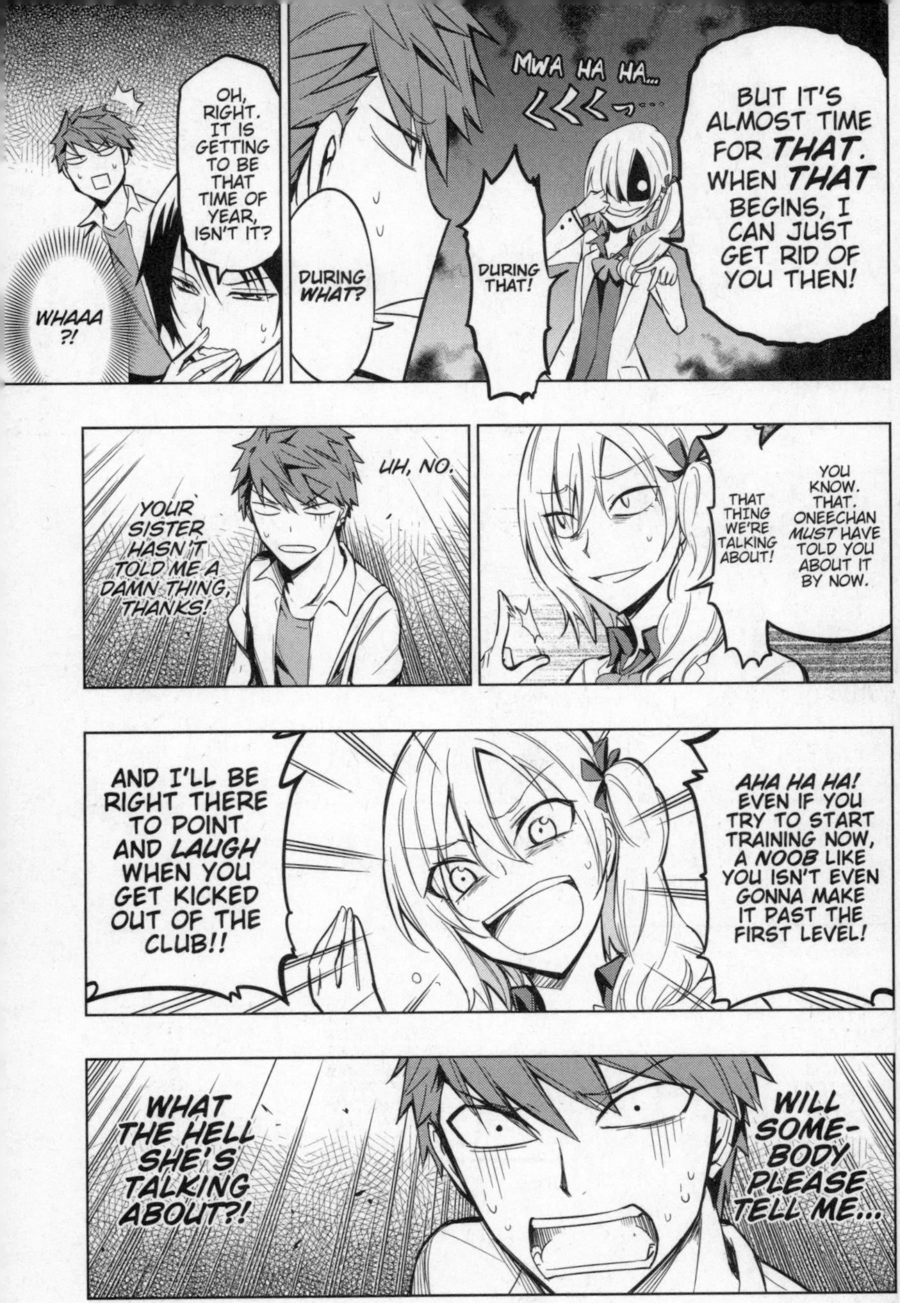
BUT IT'S ALMOST TIME FOR *THAT*. WHEN *THAT* BEGINS, I CAN JUST GET RID OF YOU THEN!
MWA HA HA...
くくくっ
DURING THAT!
DURING *WHAT*?
OH, RIGHT. IT IS GETTING TO BE THAT TIME OF YEAR, ISN'T IT?
WHAAA ?!
YOU KNOW. THAT. ONEECHAN *MUST* HAVE TOLD YOU ABOUT IT BY NOW.
THAT THING WE'RE TALKING ABOUT!
UH, NO.
YOUR SISTER HASN'T TOLD ME A DAMN THING, THANKS!
AHA HA HA! EVEN IF YOU TRY TO START TRAINING NOW, A *NOOB* LIKE YOU ISN'T EVEN GONNA MAKE IT PAST THE FIRST LEVEL!
AND I'LL BE RIGHT THERE TO POINT AND *LAUGH* WHEN YOU GET KICKED OUT OF THE CLUB!!
WILL SOMEBODY PLEASE TELL ME...
WHAT THE HELL SHE'S TALKING ABOUT?!

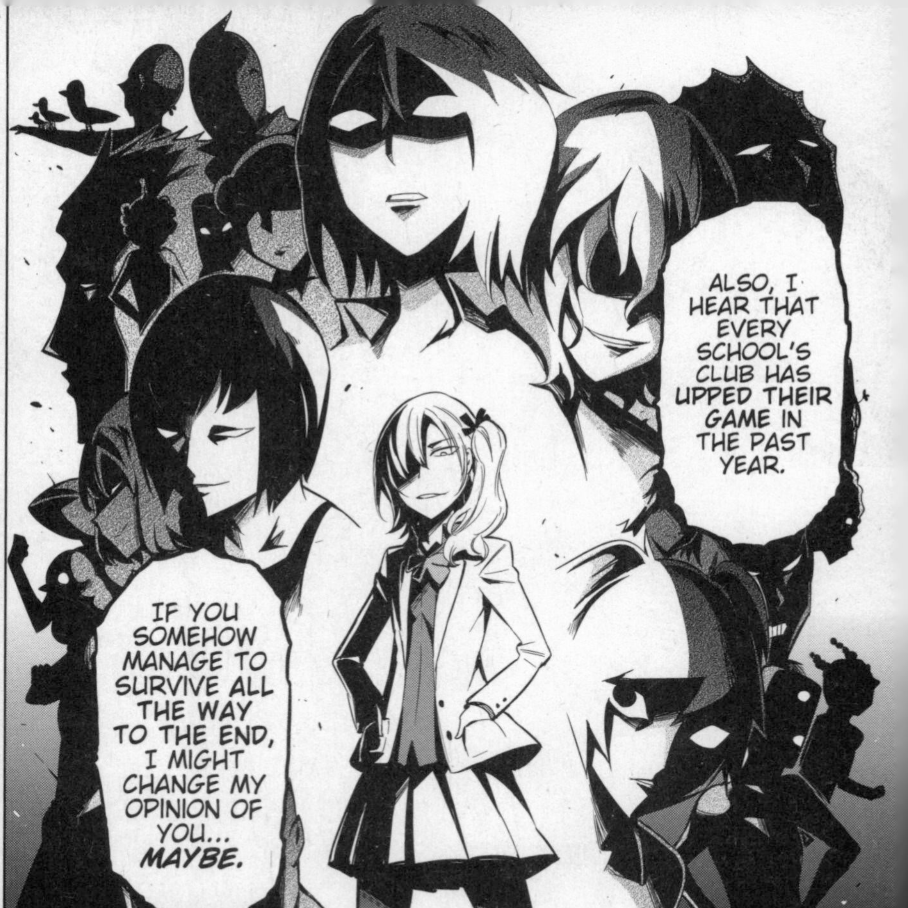
ALSO, I HEAR THAT EVERY SCHOOL'S CLUB HAS UPPED THEIR GAME IN THE PAST YEAR.
IF YOU SOMEHOW MANAGE TO SURVIVE ALL THE WAY TO THE END, I MIGHT CHANGE MY OPINION OF YOU... *MAYBE.*
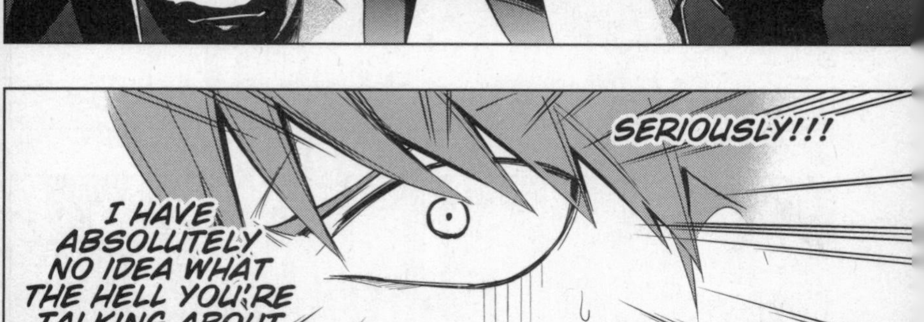
SERIOUSLY!!!
I HAVE ABSOLUTELY NO IDEA WHAT THE HELL YOU'RE TALKING ABOUT RIGHT NOW!!

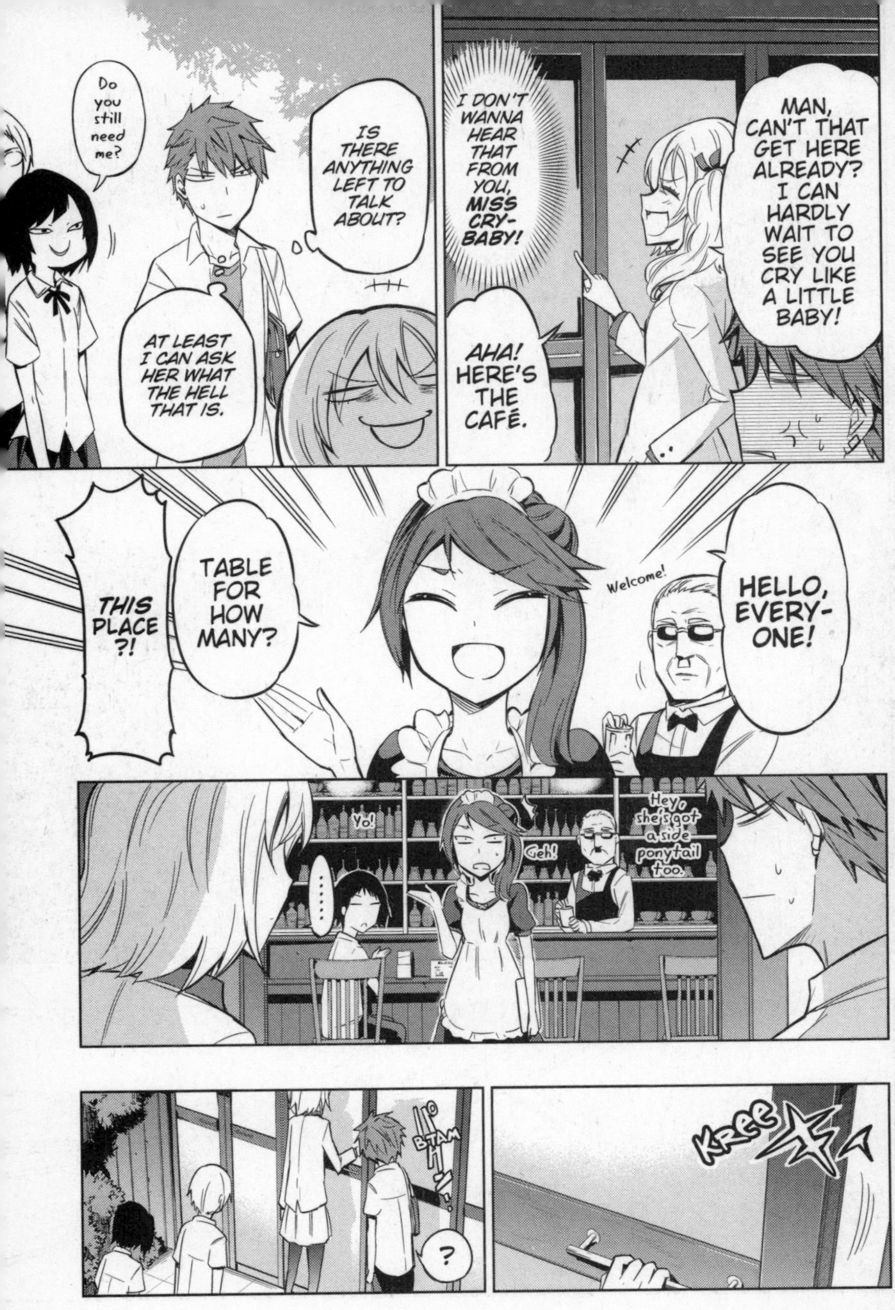

MAN, CAN'T THAT GET HERE ALREADY? I CAN HARDLY WAIT TO SEE YOU CRY LIKE A LITTLE BABY!
I DON'T WANNA HEAR THAT FROM YOU, MISS CRY-BABY!
AHA! HERE'S THE CAFÉ.
IS THERE ANYTHING LEFT TO TALK ABOUT?
Do you still need me?
AT LEAST I CAN ASK HER WHAT THE HELL THAT IS.
HELLO, EVERY-ONE!
Welcome!
TABLE FOR HOW MANY?
THIS PLACE?!
Hey, she's got a side ponytail too.
Geh!
Yo!
......
Kree
BTAM
?

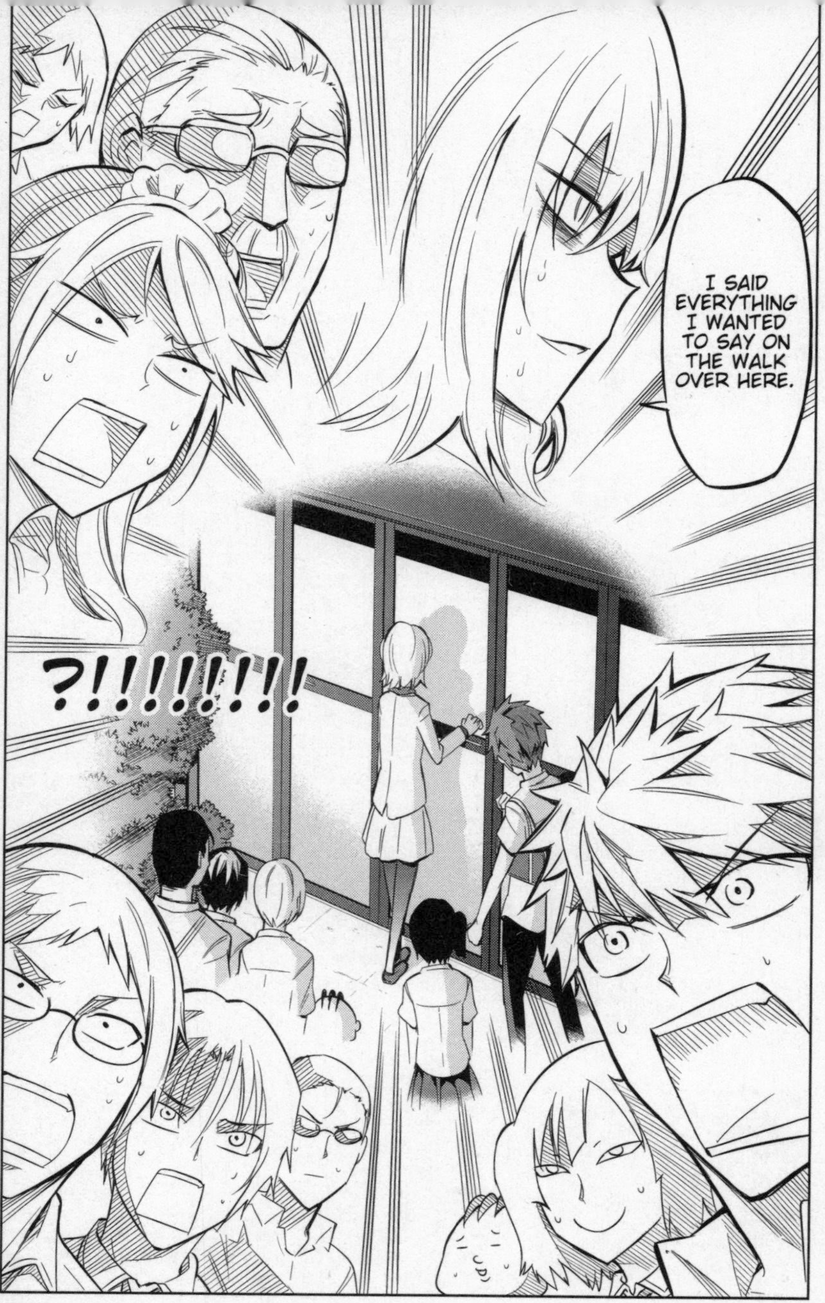
I SAID EVERYTHING I WANTED TO SAY ON THE WALK OVER HERE.
?!!!!!!!!

NEXT: Vol.07...

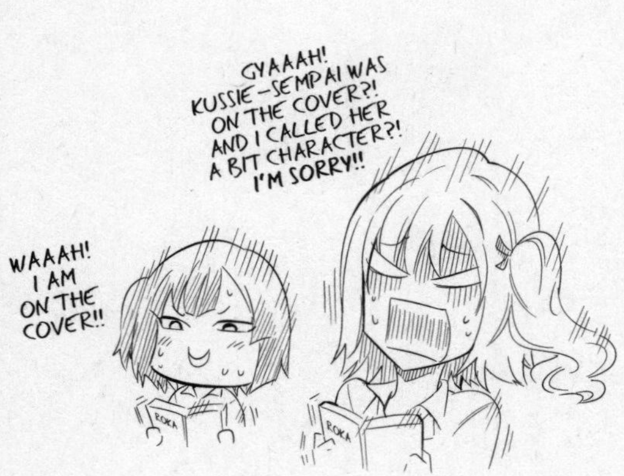
GYAAAH! KUSSIE-SEMPAI WAS ON THE COVER?! AND I CALLED HER A BIT CHARACTER?! I'M SORRY!!
ROKA
WAAAH! I AM ON THE COVER!!
ROKA

D-FRAGMENTS

ディーふらぐ!

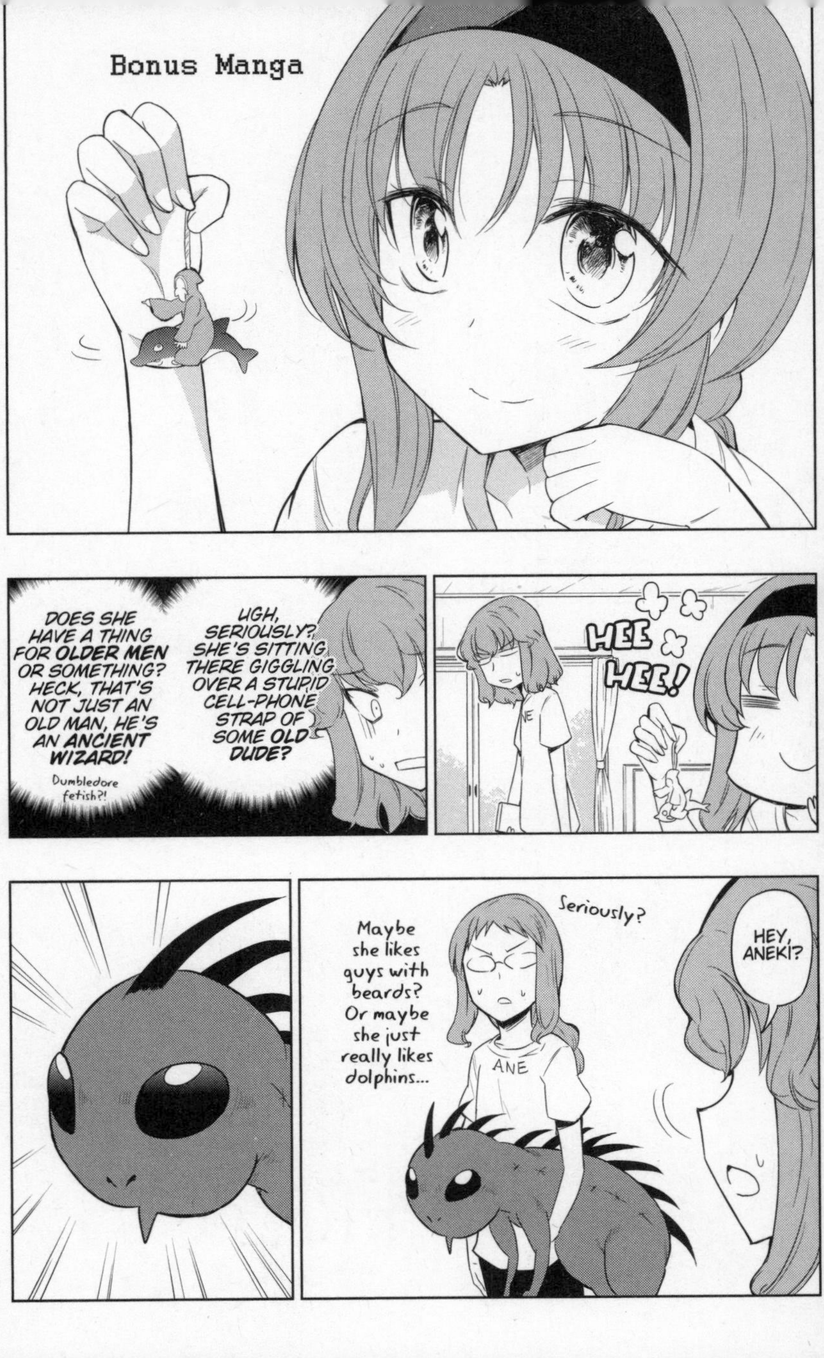
Bonus Manga
HEE HEE!
UGH, SERIOUSLY? SHE'S SITTING THERE GIGGLING OVER A STUPID CELL-PHONE STRAP OF SOME OLD DUDE?
DOES SHE HAVE A THING FOR OLDER MEN OR SOMETHING? HECK, THAT'S NOT JUST AN OLD MAN, HE'S AN ANCIENT WIZARD!
Dumbledore fetish?!
ANE
HEY, ANEKI?
Seriously?
Maybe she likes guys with beards? Or maybe she just really likes dolphins...
ANE

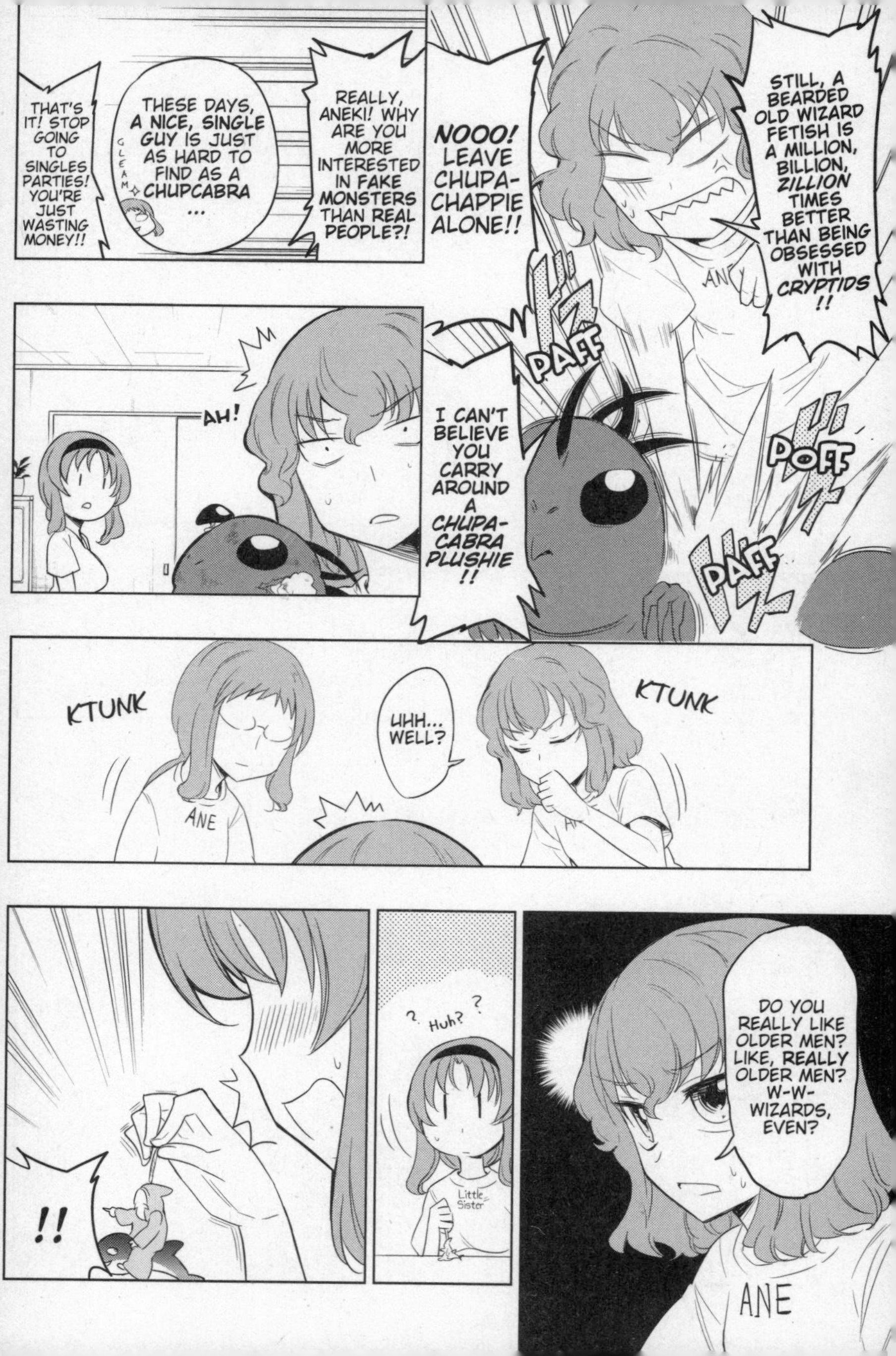

STILL, A BEARDED OLD WIZARD FETISH IS A MILLION, BILLION, *ZILLION* TIMES BETTER THAN BEING OBSESSED WITH *CRYPTIDS* !!
NOOO! LEAVE CHUPA-CHAPPIE ALONE!!
PAFF
POFF
PAFF
I CAN'T BELIEVE YOU CARRY AROUND A CHUPA-CABRA *PLUSHIE* !!
REALLY, ANEKI! WHY ARE YOU MORE INTERESTED IN FAKE MONSTERS THAN REAL PEOPLE?!
THESE DAYS, A NICE, SINGLE GUY IS JUST AS HARD TO FIND AS A CHUPCABRA ...
GLEAM
THAT'S IT! STOP GOING TO SINGLES PARTIES! YOU'RE JUST WASTING MONEY!!
AH!
KTUNK
UHH... WELL?
KTUNK
ANE
DO YOU REALLY LIKE OLDER MEN? LIKE, REALLY OLDER MEN? W-W-WIZARDS, EVEN?
ANE
Huh?
Little Sister
!!

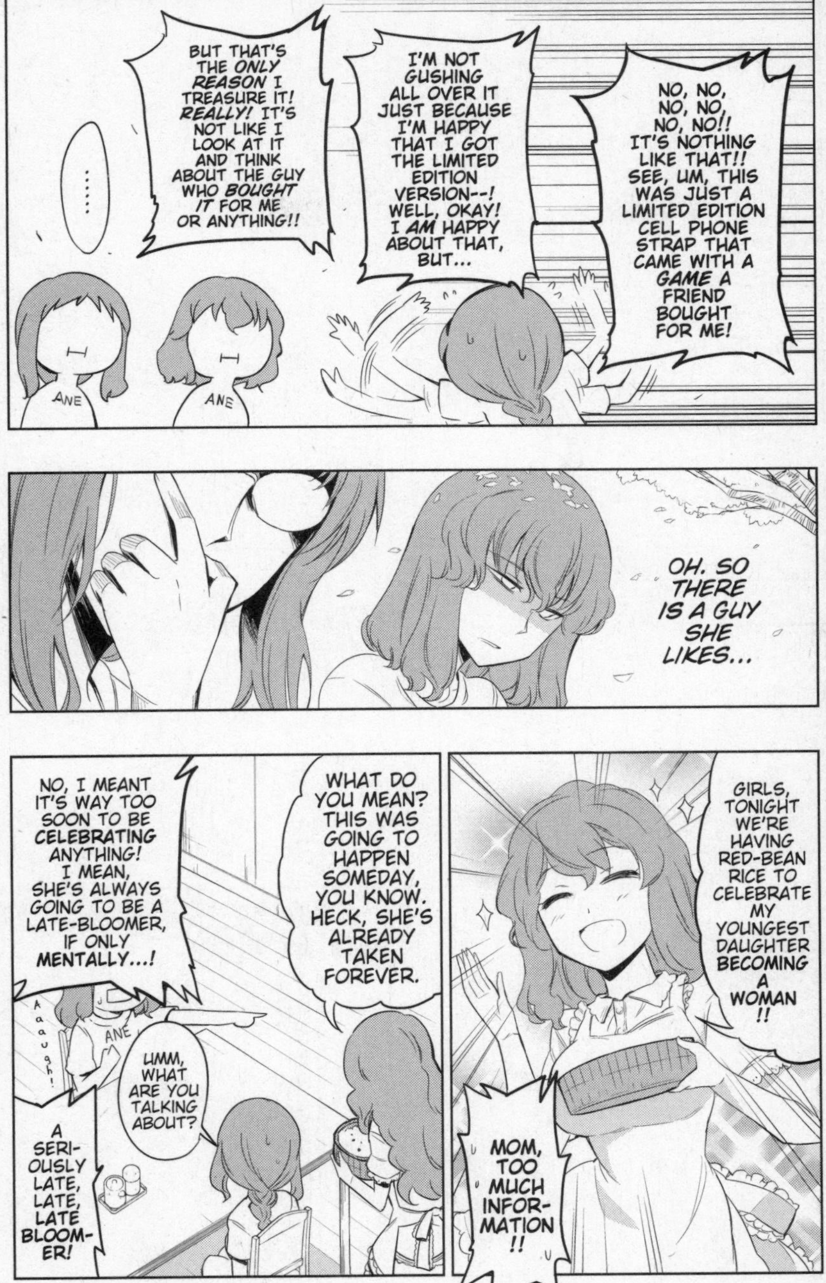
NO, NO, NO, NO, NO, NO!! IT'S NOTHING LIKE THAT!! SEE, UM, THIS WAS JUST A LIMITED EDITION CELL PHONE STRAP THAT CAME WITH A *GAME* A FRIEND BOUGHT FOR ME!
I'M NOT GUSHING ALL OVER IT JUST BECAUSE I'M HAPPY THAT I GOT THE LIMITED EDITION VERSION--! WELL, OKAY! I *AM* HAPPY ABOUT THAT, BUT...
BUT THAT'S THE *ONLY REASON* I TREASURE IT! *REALLY!* IT'S NOT LIKE I LOOK AT IT AND THINK ABOUT THE GUY WHO *BOUGHT IT* FOR ME OR ANYTHING!!
......
ANE
ANE
OH. SO THERE IS A GUY SHE LIKES...
GIRLS, TONIGHT WE'RE HAVING RED-BEAN RICE TO CELEBRATE MY YOUNGEST DAUGHTER BECOMING A WOMAN!!
MOM, TOO MUCH INFORMATION!!
WHAT DO YOU MEAN? THIS WAS GOING TO HAPPEN SOMEDAY, YOU KNOW. HECK, SHE'S ALREADY TAKEN FOREVER.
NO, I MEANT IT'S WAY TOO SOON TO BE CELEBRATING ANYTHING! I MEAN, SHE'S ALWAYS GOING TO BE A LATE-BLOOMER, IF ONLY MENTALLY...!
ANE
UMM, WHAT ARE YOU TALKING ABOUT?
Aaaugh!
A SERIOUSLY LATE, LATE, LATE BLOOMER!

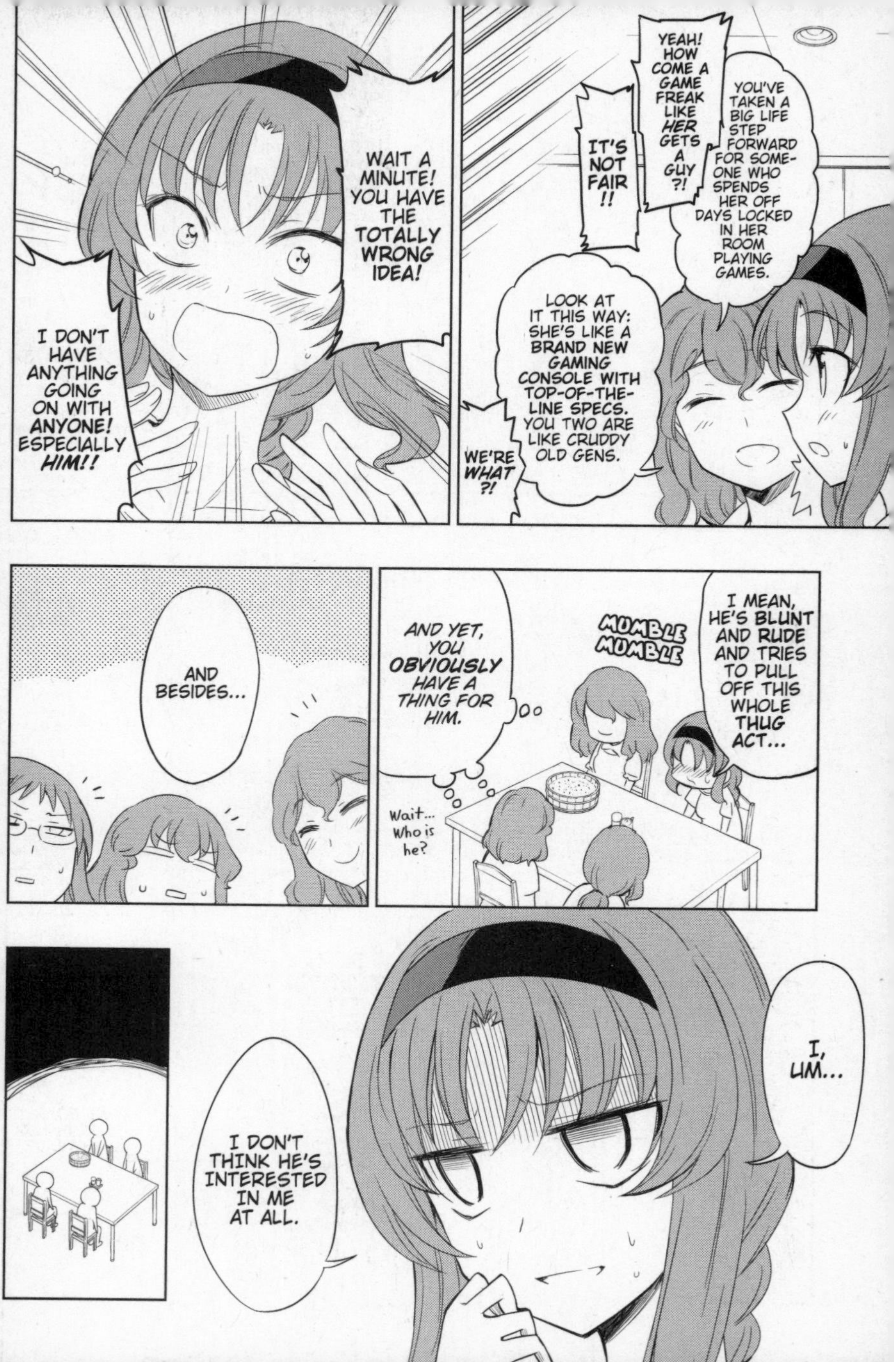

YOU'VE TAKEN A BIG LIFE STEP FORWARD FOR SOME-ONE WHO SPENDS HER OFF DAYS LOCKED IN HER ROOM PLAYING GAMES.
YEAH! HOW COME A GAME FREAK LIKE HER GETS A GUY ?!
IT'S NOT FAIR !!
LOOK AT IT THIS WAY: SHE'S LIKE A BRAND NEW GAMING CONSOLE WITH TOP-OF-THE-LINE SPECS. YOU TWO ARE LIKE CRUDDY OLD GENS.
WE'RE WHAT ?!
WAIT A MINUTE! YOU HAVE THE TOTALLY WRONG IDEA!
I DON'T HAVE ANYTHING GOING ON WITH ANYONE! ESPECIALLY HIM!!
I MEAN, HE'S BLUNT AND RUDE AND TRIES TO PULL OFF THIS WHOLE THUG ACT...
MUMBLE MUMBLE
AND YET, YOU OBVIOUSLY HAVE A THING FOR HIM.
Wait... Who is he?
AND BESIDES...
I, UM...
I DON'T THINK HE'S INTERESTED IN ME AT ALL.

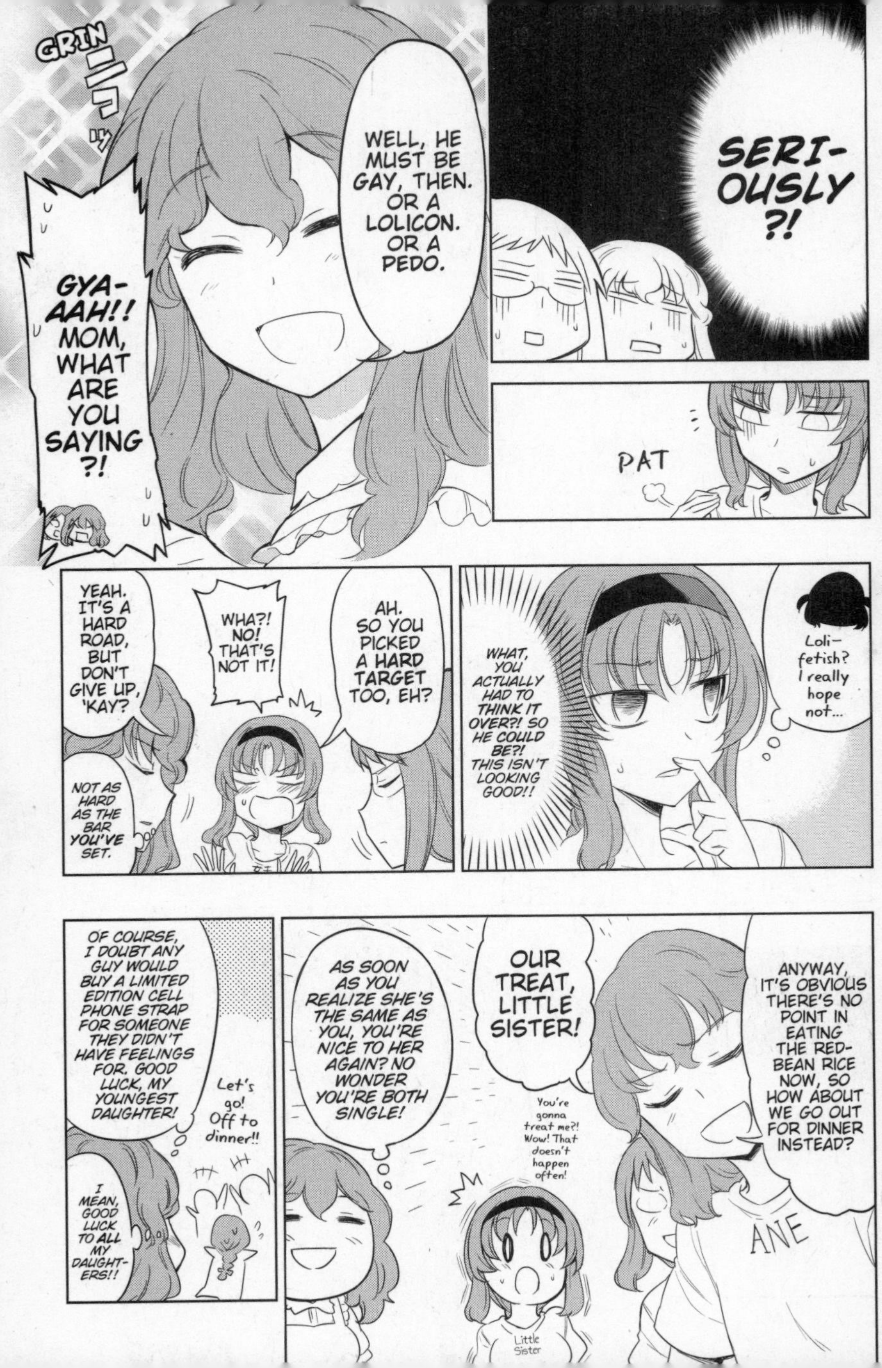
SERI-OUSLY?!
PAT
WELL, HE MUST BE GAY, THEN. OR A LOLICON. OR A PEDO.
GRIN
GYA-AAH!! MOM, WHAT ARE YOU SAYING?!
Loli-fetish? I really hope not...
WHAT, YOU ACTUALLY HAD TO THINK IT OVER?! SO HE COULD BE?! THIS ISN'T LOOKING GOOD!!
AH. SO YOU PICKED A HARD TARGET TOO, EH?
WHA?! NO! THAT'S NOT IT!
YEAH. IT'S A HARD ROAD, BUT DON'T GIVE UP, 'KAY?
NOT AS HARD AS THE BAR YOU'VE SET.
ANYWAY, IT'S OBVIOUS THERE'S NO POINT IN EATING THE RED-BEAN RICE NOW, SO HOW ABOUT WE GO OUT FOR DINNER INSTEAD?
ANE
OUR TREAT, LITTLE SISTER!
You're gonna treat me?! Wow! That doesn't happen often!
AS SOON AS YOU REALIZE SHE'S THE SAME AS YOU, YOU'RE NICE TO HER AGAIN? NO WONDER YOU'RE BOTH SINGLE!
Little Sister
OF COURSE, I DOUBT ANY GUY WOULD BUY A LIMITED EDITION CELL PHONE STRAP FOR SOMEONE THEY DIDN'T HAVE FEELINGS FOR. GOOD LUCK, MY YOUNGEST DAUGHTER!
Let's go! Off to dinner!!
I MEAN, GOOD LUCK TO ALL MY DAUGHTERS!!

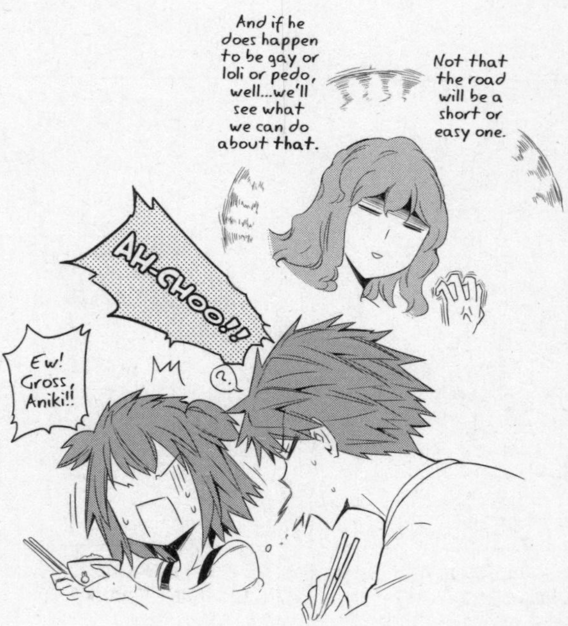
Not that the road will be a short or easy one.
And if he does happen to be gay or loli or pedo, well...we'll see what we can do about that.
AH-CHOO!!
Ew! Gross, Aniki!!

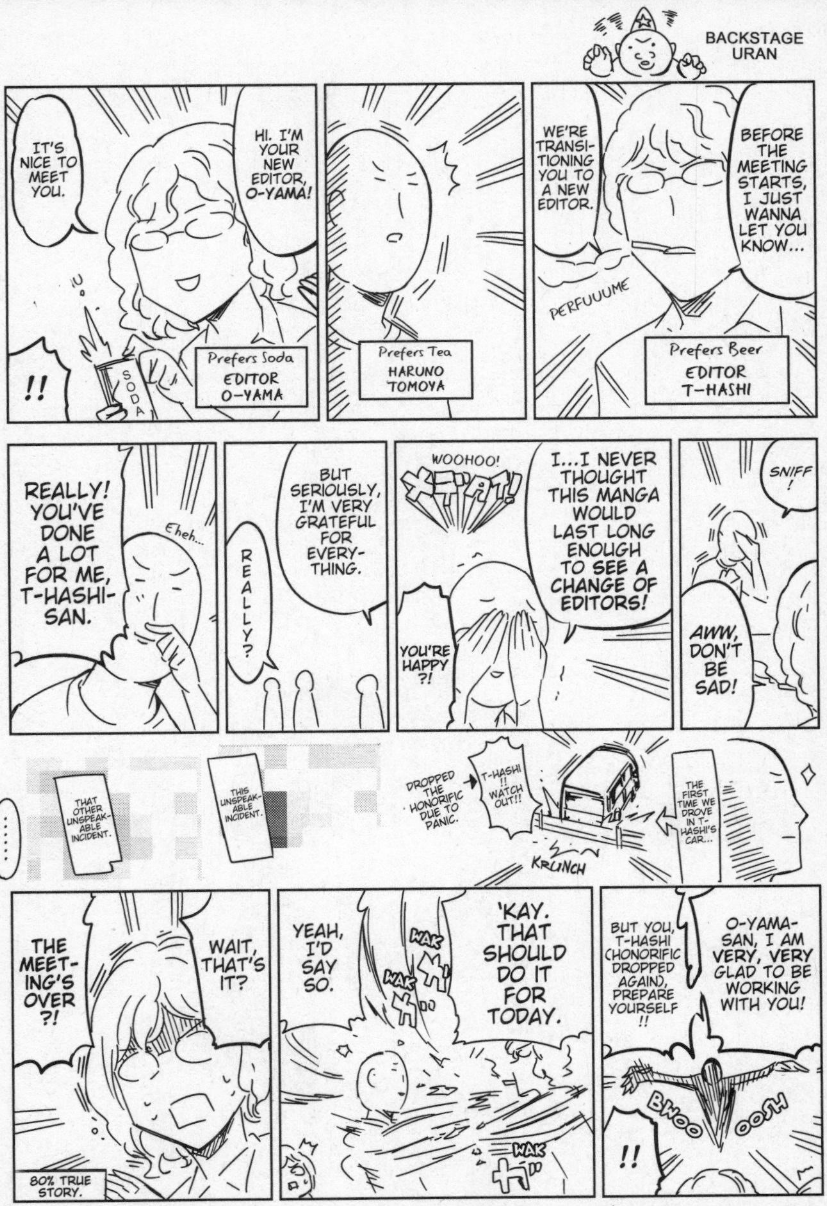
BACKSTAGE URAN
BEFORE THE MEETING STARTS, I JUST WANNA LET YOU KNOW...
WE'RE TRANSITIONING YOU TO A NEW EDITOR.
PERFUUUME
Prefers Beer
EDITOR T-HASHI
Prefers Tea
HARUNO TOMOYA
HI. I'M YOUR NEW EDITOR, O-YAMA!
IT'S NICE TO MEET YOU.
!!
SODA
Prefers Soda
EDITOR O-YAMA
SNIFF!
AWW, DON'T BE SAD!
I...I NEVER THOUGHT THIS MANGA WOULD LAST LONG ENOUGH TO SEE A CHANGE OF EDITORS!
WOOHOO!
YOU'RE HAPPY?!
BUT SERIOUSLY, I'M VERY GRATEFUL FOR EVERYTHING.
REALLY?
REALLY! YOU'VE DONE A LOT FOR ME, T-HASHI-SAN.
Eheh...
THE FIRST TIME WE DROVE IN T-HASHI'S CAR...
T-HASHI!! WATCH OUT!!
DROPPED THE HONORIFIC DUE TO PANIC.
KRUNCH
THIS UNSPEAKABLE INCIDENT.
THAT OTHER UNSPEAKABLE INCIDENT.
......
O-YAMA-SAN, I AM VERY, VERY GLAD TO BE WORKING WITH YOU!
BUT YOU, T-HASHI (HONORIFIC DROPPED AGAIN), PREPARE YOURSELF!!
BWOOOOSH
!!
'KAY. THAT SHOULD DO IT FOR TODAY.
YEAH, I'D SAY SO.
WAK
WAK
WAK
WAIT, THAT'S IT?
THE MEETING'S OVER?!
80% TRUE STORY.

SPECIAL THANKS!! BAKU MIKAGE-SAN, MAKOTO KADZUKI-SAN, YUKINOJOU-SAN
EDITORS: OHYAMA-SAN, TAKAHASHI-SAN (THANKS FOR EVERYTHING!)
DESIGN: LIGHTNING (TOMIYAMA-SAN)
OBI: SHIROU MIWA-SAN

AND THANKS TO MY WONDERFUL READERS!!

READ THIS AFTER THE MAIN STORY! A Day in the Life of Kussie-sempai.

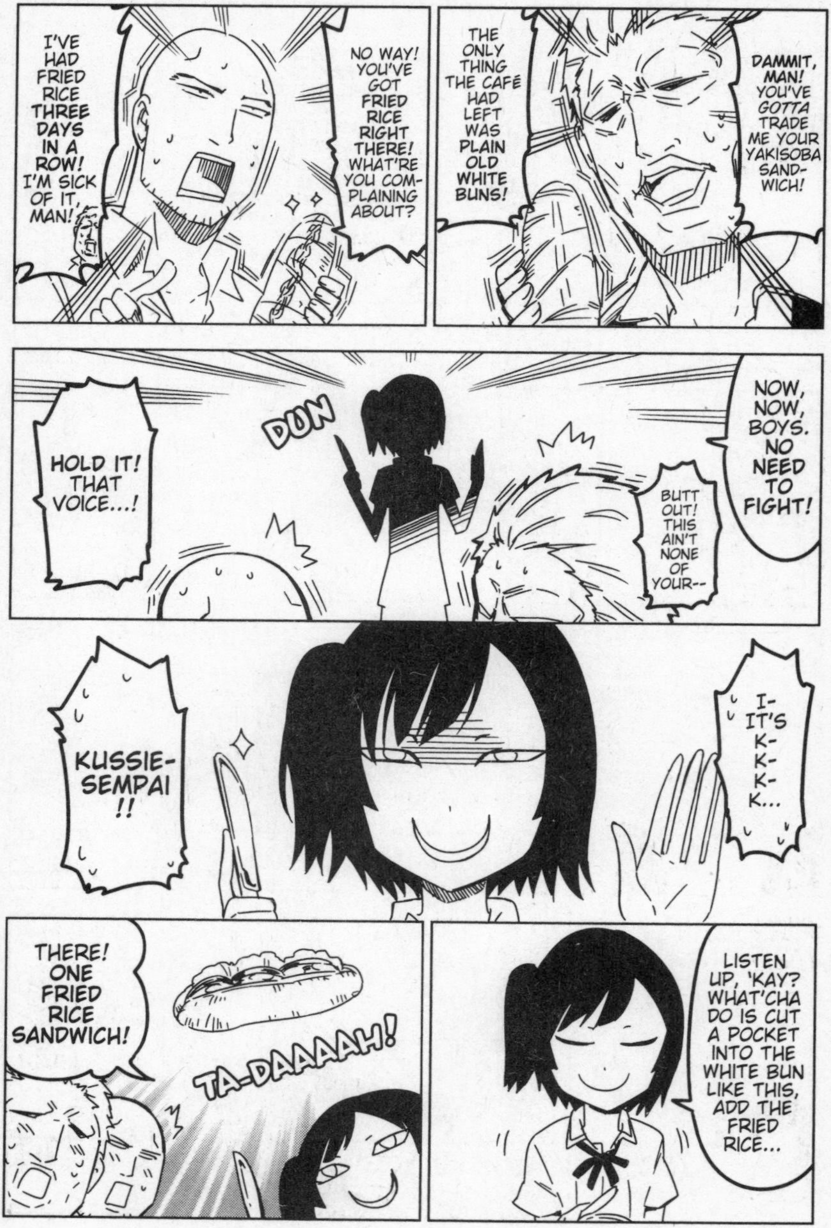
DAMMIT, MAN! YOU'VE GOTTA TRADE ME YOUR YAKISOBA SANDWICH!
THE ONLY THING THE CAFÉ HAD LEFT WAS PLAIN OLD WHITE BUNS!
NO WAY! YOU'VE GOT FRIED RICE RIGHT THERE! WHAT'RE YOU COMPLAINING ABOUT?
I'VE HAD FRIED RICE THREE DAYS IN A ROW! I'M SICK OF IT, MAN!
NOW, NOW, BOYS. NO NEED TO FIGHT!
BUTT OUT! THIS AIN'T NONE OF YOUR--
DUN
HOLD IT! THAT VOICE...!
I- IT'S K-K-K-K...
KUSSIE-SEMPAI!!
LISTEN UP, 'KAY? WHAT'CHA DO IS CUT A POCKET INTO THE WHITE BUN LIKE THIS, ADD THE FRIED RICE...
THERE! ONE FRIED RICE SANDWICH!
TA-DAAAAH!

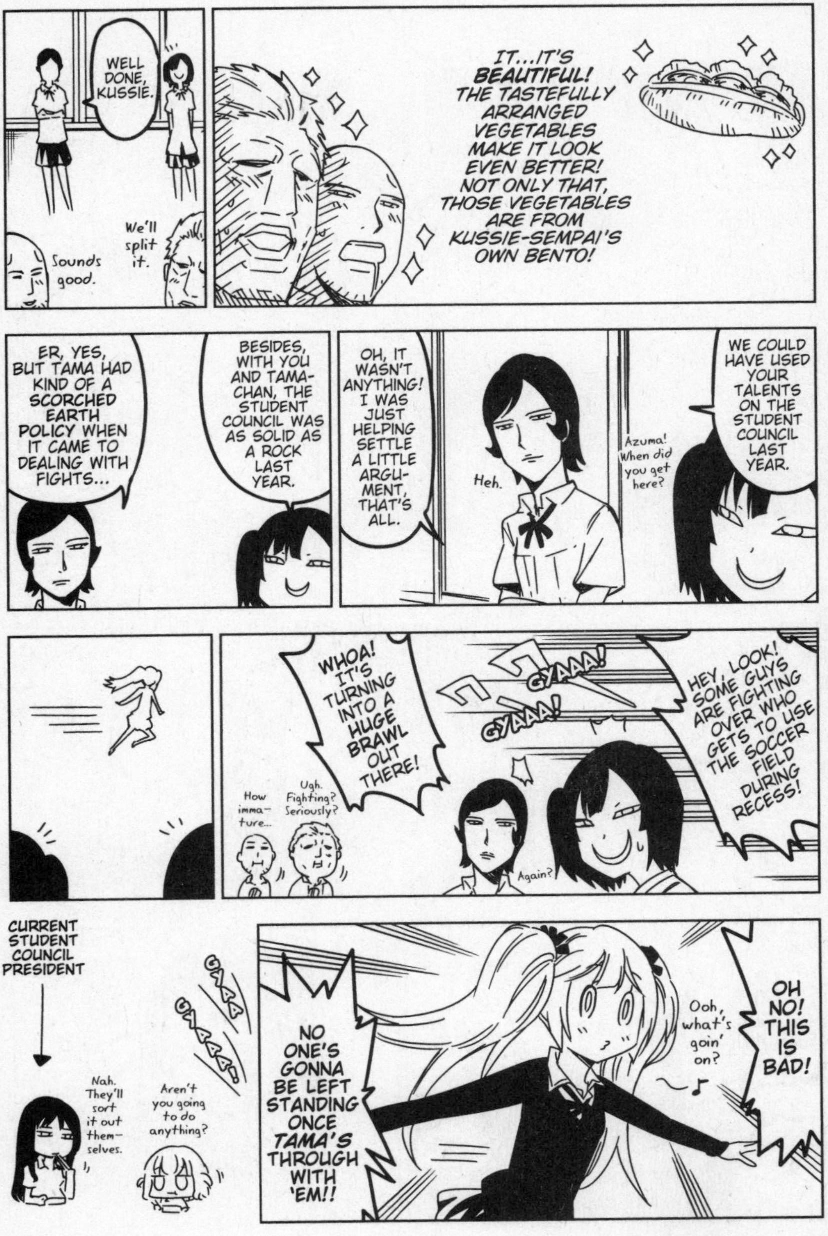
IT...IT'S BEAUTIFUL! THE TASTEFULLY ARRANGED VEGETABLES MAKE IT LOOK EVEN BETTER! NOT ONLY THAT, THOSE VEGETABLES ARE FROM KUSSIE-SEMPAI'S OWN BENTO!
WELL DONE, KUSSIE.
We'll split it.
Sounds good.
WE COULD HAVE USED YOUR TALENTS ON THE STUDENT COUNCIL LAST YEAR.
Azuma! When did you get here?
Heh.
OH, IT WASN'T ANYTHING! I WAS JUST HELPING SETTLE A LITTLE ARGUMENT, THAT'S ALL.
BESIDES, WITH YOU AND TAMA-CHAN, THE STUDENT COUNCIL WAS AS SOLID AS A ROCK LAST YEAR.
ER, YES, BUT TAMA HAD KIND OF A SCORCHED EARTH POLICY WHEN IT CAME TO DEALING WITH FIGHTS...
HEY, LOOK! SOME GUYS ARE FIGHTING OVER WHO GETS TO USE THE SOCCER FIELD DURING RECESS!
GYAAA!
GYAAA!
WHOA! IT'S TURNING INTO A HUGE BRAWL OUT THERE!
Again?
Ugh. Fighting? Seriously?
How immature...
OH NO! THIS IS BAD!
Ooh, what's goin' on?
NO ONE'S GONNA BE LEFT STANDING ONCE TAMA'S THROUGH WITH 'EM!!
GYAAA
GYAAAA!
CURRENT STUDENT COUNCIL PRESIDENT
Aren't you going to do anything?
Nah. They'll sort it out themselves.

D-FRAGMENTS

ディーふらぐ！

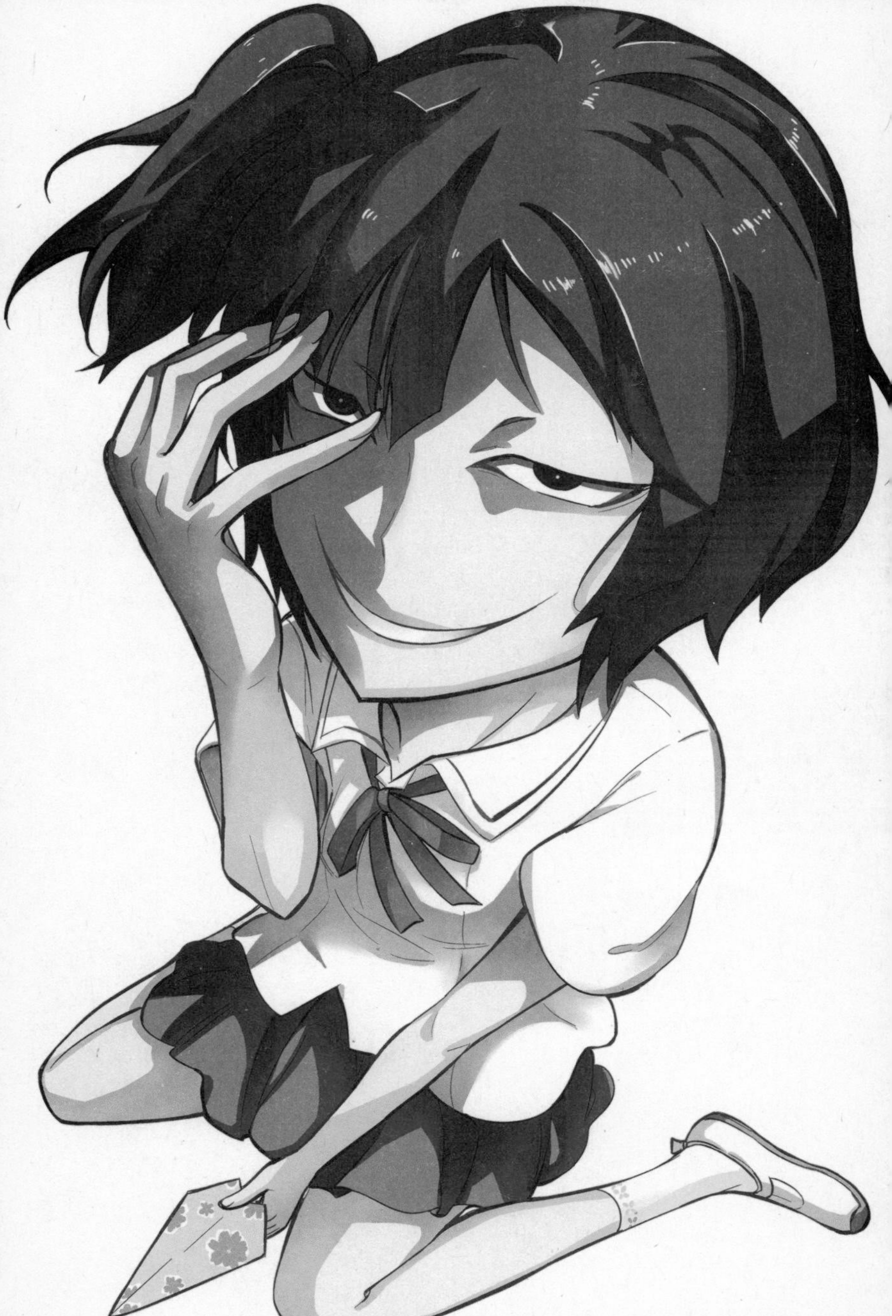

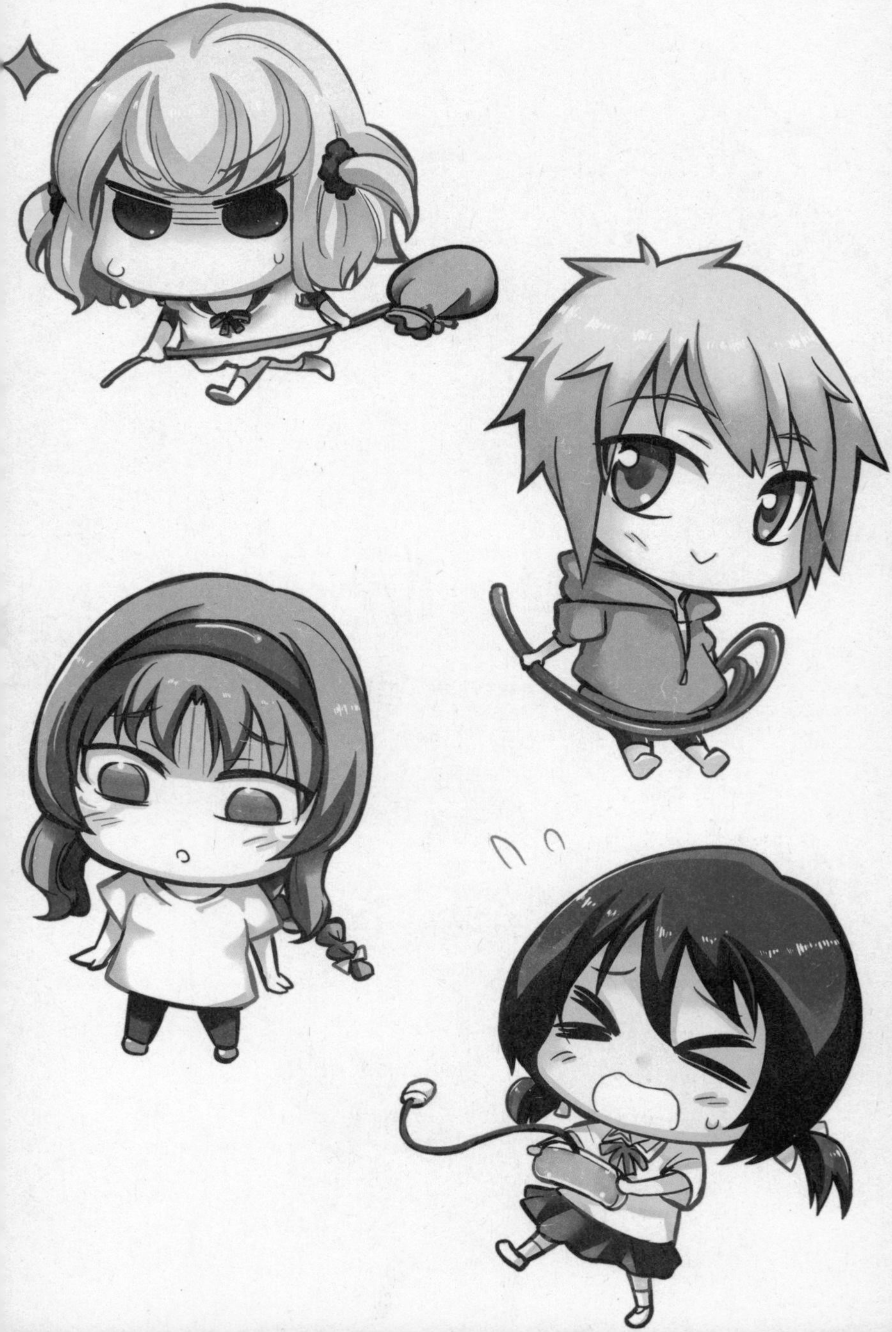

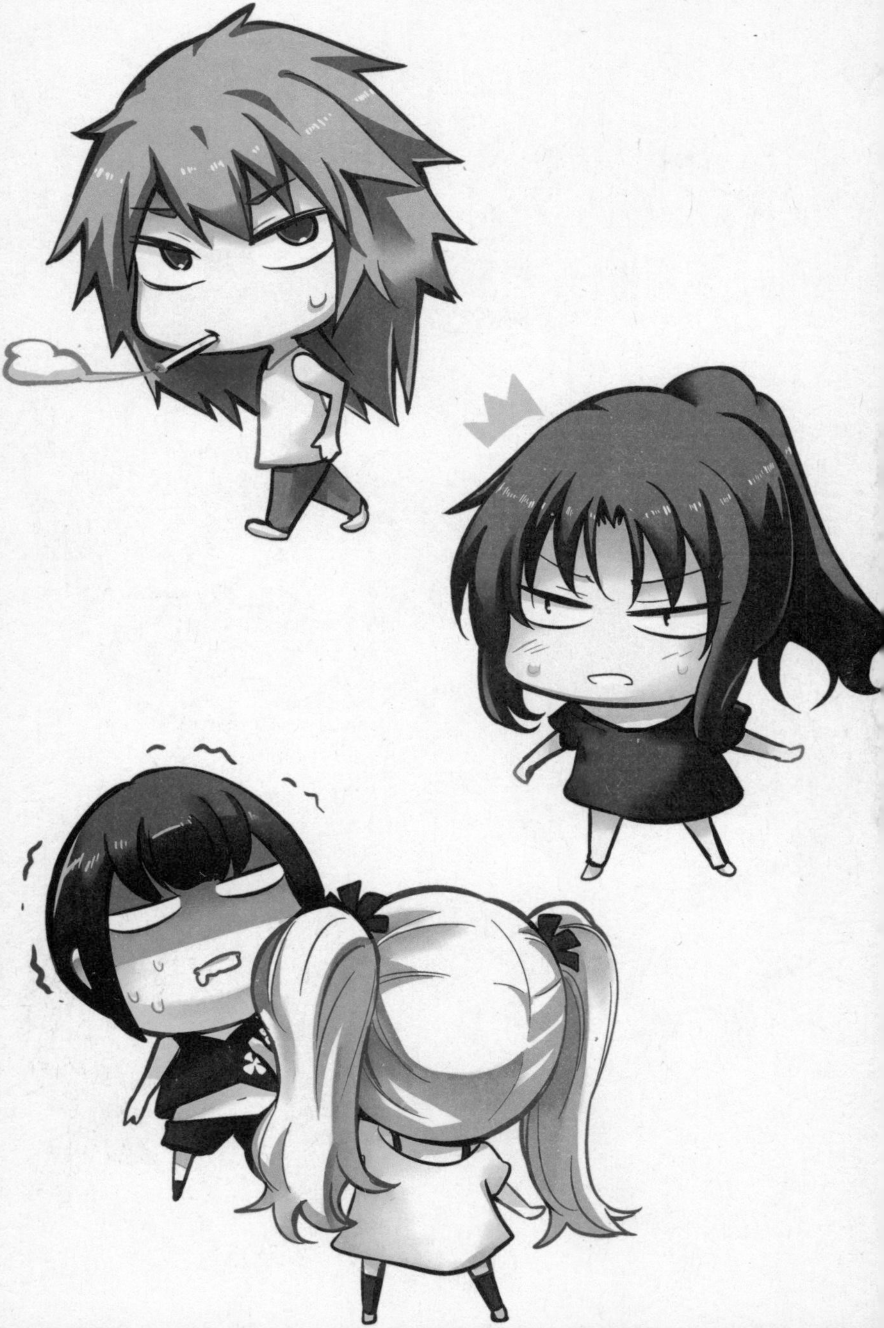

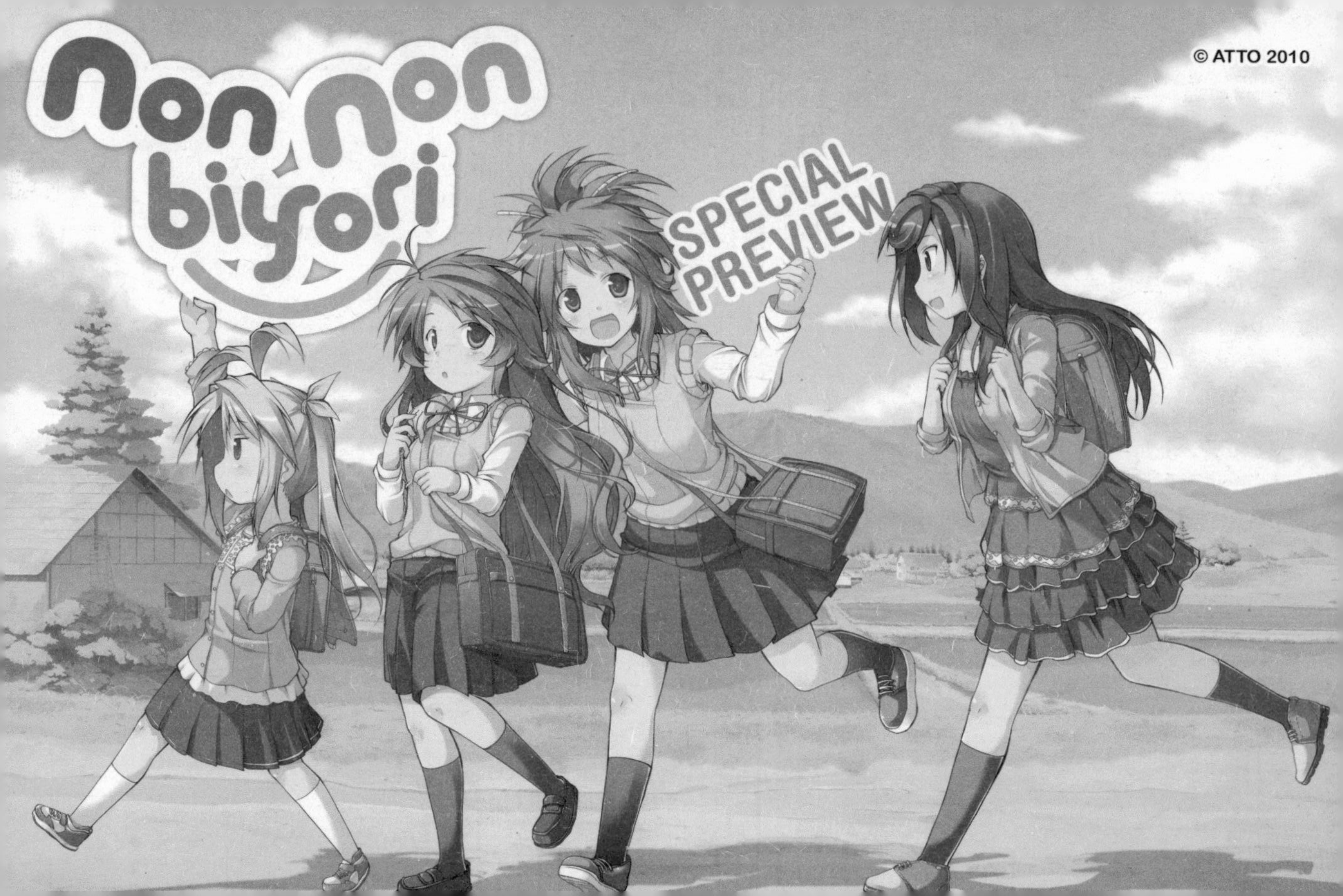
non non biyori
SPECIAL PREVIEW
© ATTO 2010

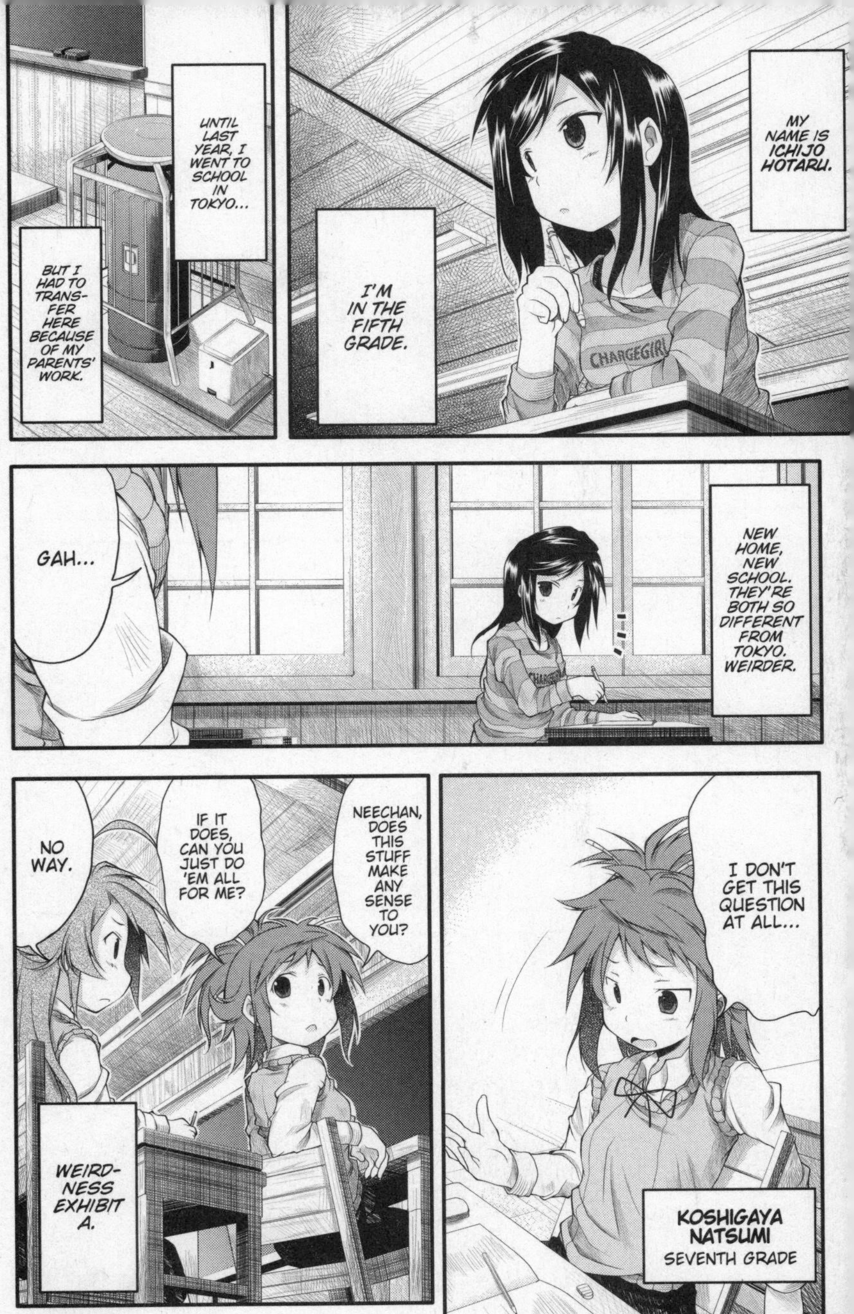
MY NAME IS ICHIJO HOTARU.
I'M IN THE FIFTH GRADE.
UNTIL LAST YEAR, I WENT TO SCHOOL IN TOKYO...
BUT I HAD TO TRANSFER HERE BECAUSE OF MY PARENTS' WORK.
NEW HOME, NEW SCHOOL. THEY'RE BOTH SO DIFFERENT FROM TOKYO. WEIRDER.
GAH...
I DON'T GET THIS QUESTION AT ALL...
KOSHIGAYA NATSUMI
SEVENTH GRADE
NEECHAN, DOES THIS STUFF MAKE ANY SENSE TO YOU?
IF IT DOES, CAN YOU JUST DO 'EM ALL FOR ME?
NO WAY.
WEIRDNESS EXHIBIT A.

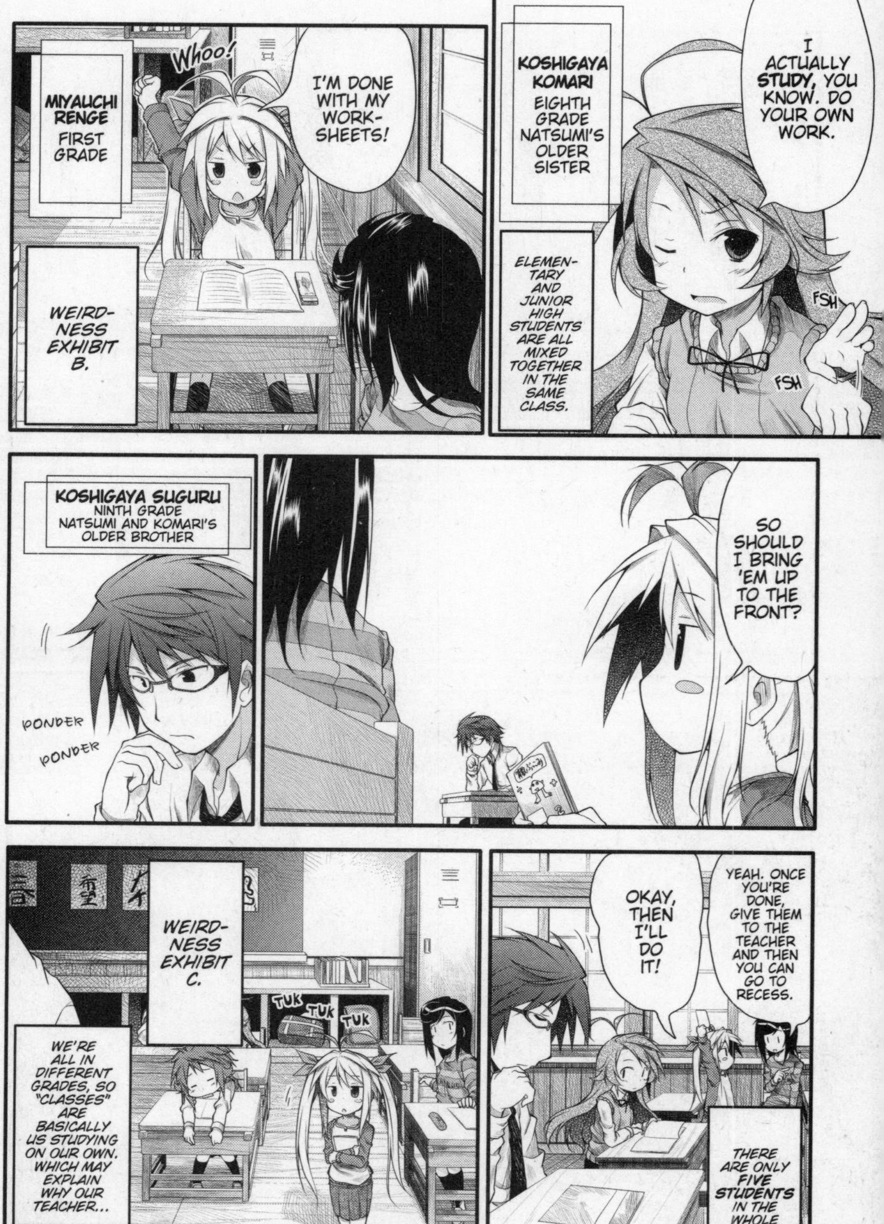
KOSHIGAYA KOMARI
EIGHTH GRADE
NATSUMI'S OLDER SISTER
I ACTUALLY STUDY, YOU KNOW. DO YOUR OWN WORK.
ELEMENTARY AND JUNIOR HIGH STUDENTS ARE ALL MIXED TOGETHER IN THE SAME CLASS.
FSH
FSH
MIYAUCHI RENGE
FIRST GRADE
Whoo!
I'M DONE WITH MY WORKSHEETS!
WEIRDNESS EXHIBIT B.
SO SHOULD I BRING 'EM UP TO THE FRONT?
KOSHIGAYA SUGURU
NINTH GRADE
NATSUMI AND KOMARI'S OLDER BROTHER
PONDER
PONDER
YEAH. ONCE YOU'RE DONE, GIVE THEM TO THE TEACHER AND THEN YOU CAN GO TO RECESS.
OKAY, THEN I'LL DO IT!
THERE ARE ONLY FIVE STUDENTS IN THE WHOLE SCHOOL.
WEIRDNESS EXHIBIT C.
TUK
TUK
TUK
WE'RE ALL IN DIFFERENT GRADES, SO "CLASSES" ARE BASICALLY US STUDYING ON OUR OWN. WHICH MAY EXPLAIN WHY OUR TEACHER...

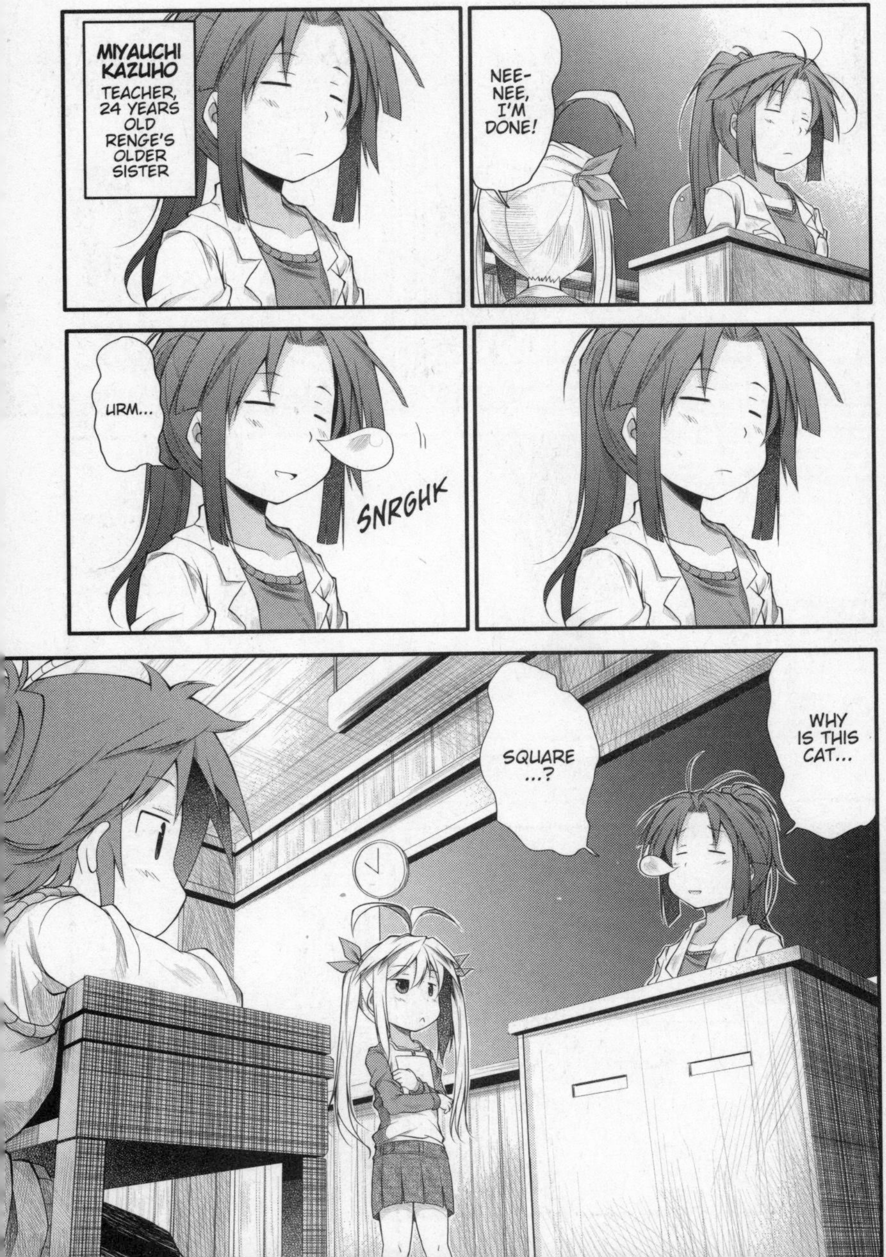
NEE-NEE, I'M DONE!
MIYAUCHI KAZUHO
TEACHER, 24 YEARS OLD
RENGE'S OLDER SISTER
URM...
SNRGHK
WHY IS THIS CAT...
SQUARE ...?

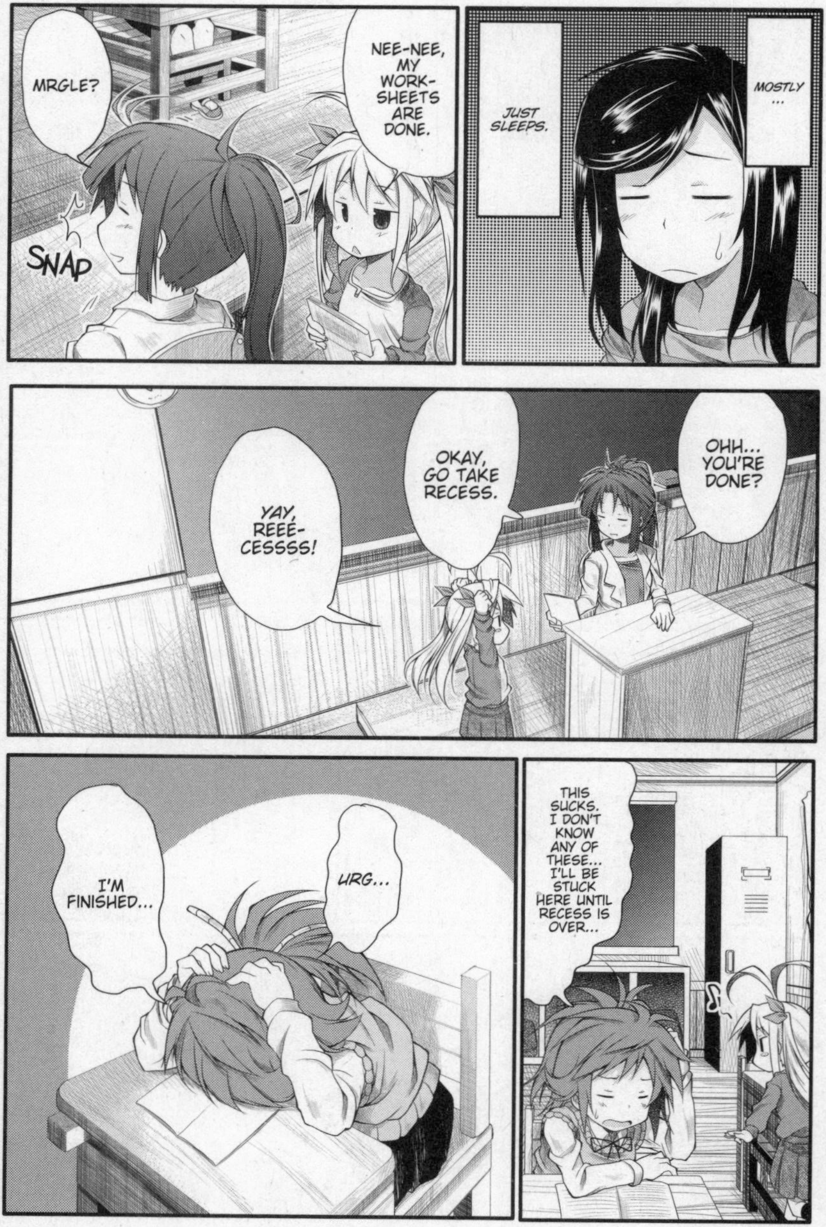
MOSTLY...
JUST SLEEPS.
NEE-NEE, MY WORK-SHEETS ARE DONE.
MRGLE?
SNAP
OHH... YOU'RE DONE?
OKAY, GO TAKE RECESS.
YAY, REEE-CESSSS!
THIS SUCKS. I DON'T KNOW ANY OF THESE... I'LL BE STUCK HERE UNTIL RECESS IS OVER...
URG...
I'M FINISHED...

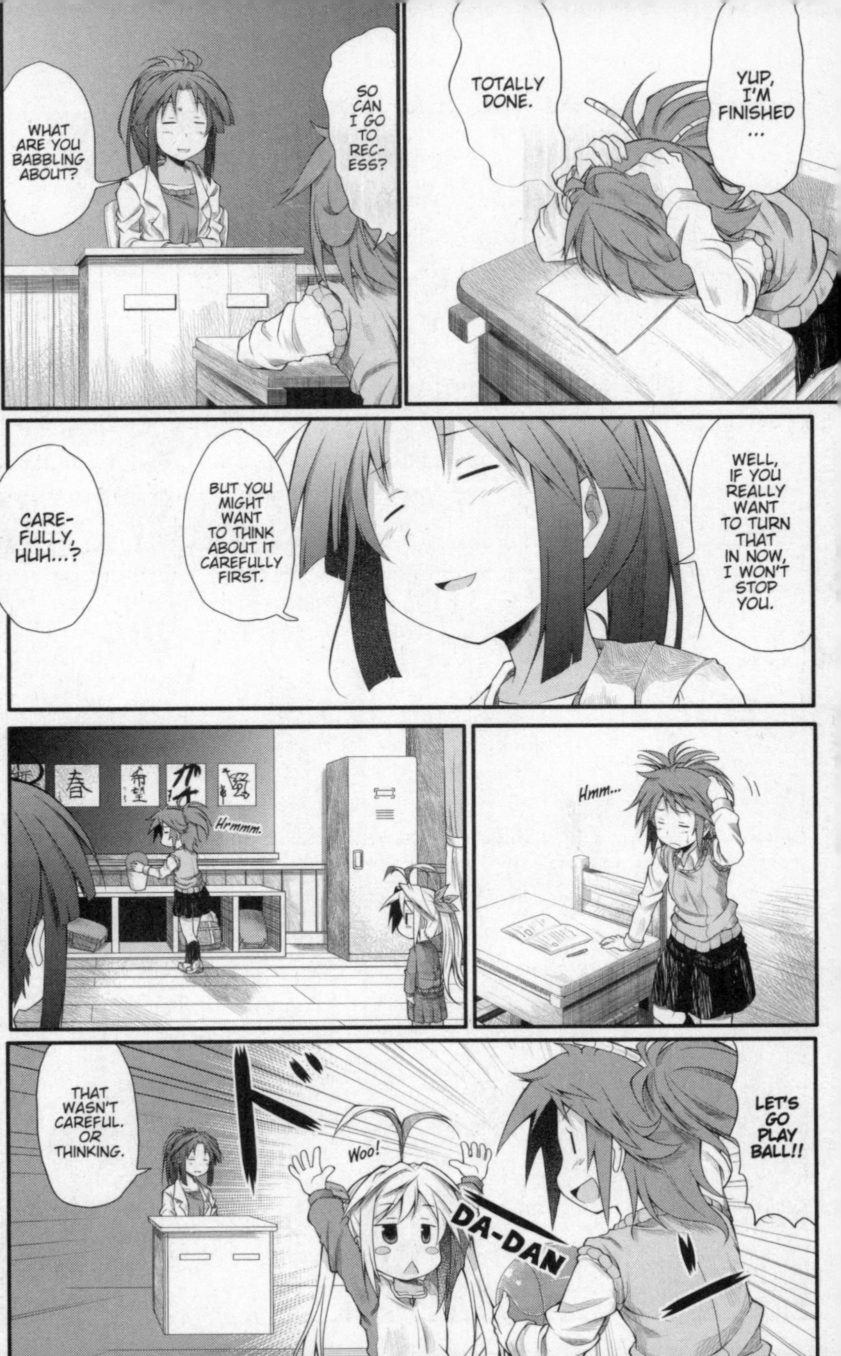
YUP, I'M FINISHED...
TOTALLY DONE.
SO CAN I GO TO RECESS?
WHAT ARE YOU BABBLING ABOUT?
WELL, IF YOU REALLY WANT TO TURN THAT IN NOW, I WON'T STOP YOU.
BUT YOU MIGHT WANT TO THINK ABOUT IT CAREFULLY FIRST.
CAREFULLY, HUH...?
Hmm...
春
希望
Hrmmm.
LET'S GO PLAY BALL!!
DA-DAN
Woo!
THAT WASN'T CAREFUL. OR THINKING.

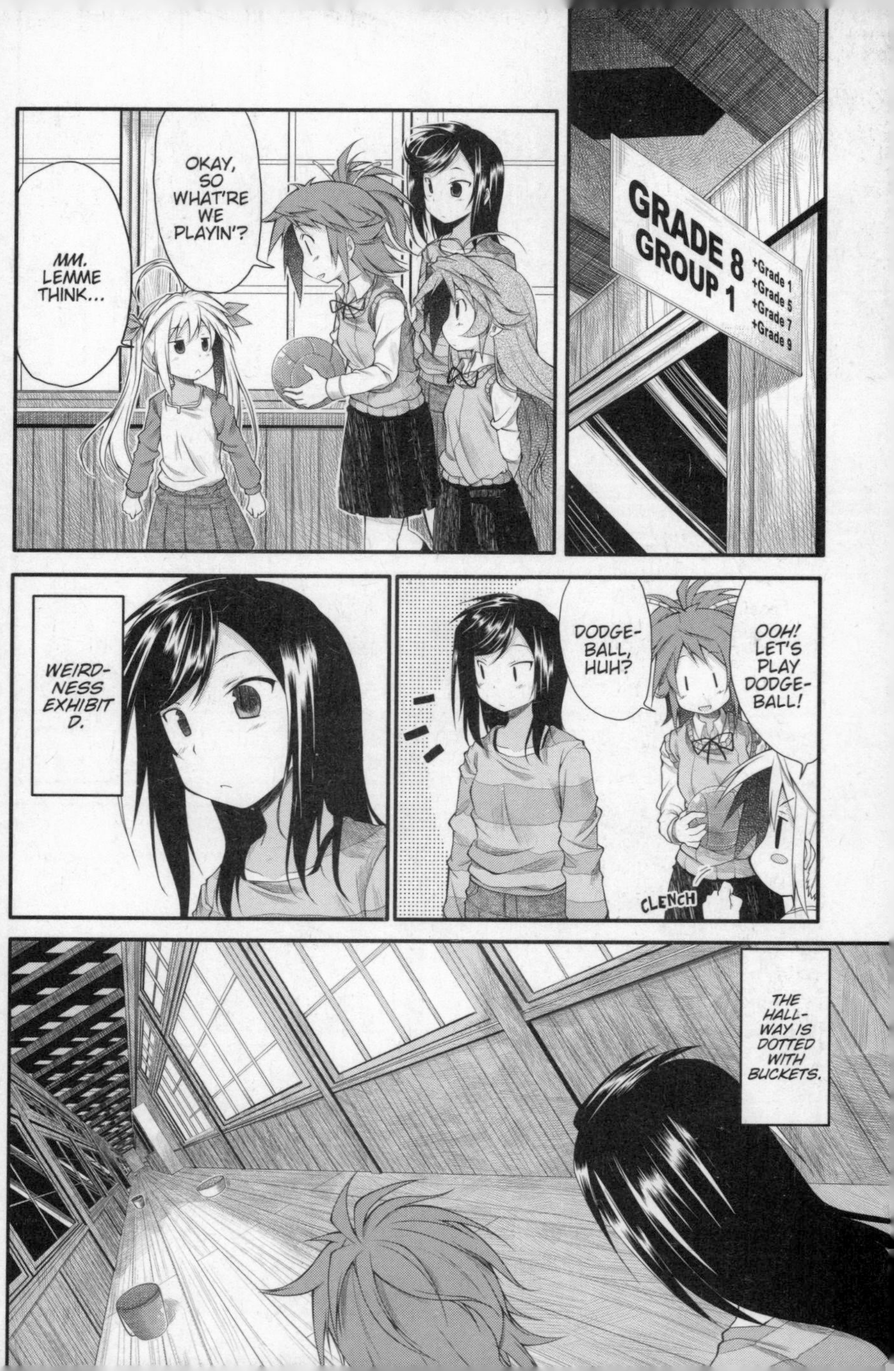
GRADE 8 GROUP 1
+Grade 1 +Grade 5 +Grade 7 +Grade 9
OKAY, SO WHAT'RE WE PLAYIN'?
MM. LEMME THINK...
OOH! LET'S PLAY DODGE-BALL!
DODGE-BALL, HUH?
CLENCH
WEIRD-NESS EXHIBIT D.
THE HALL-WAY IS DOTTED WITH BUCKETS.

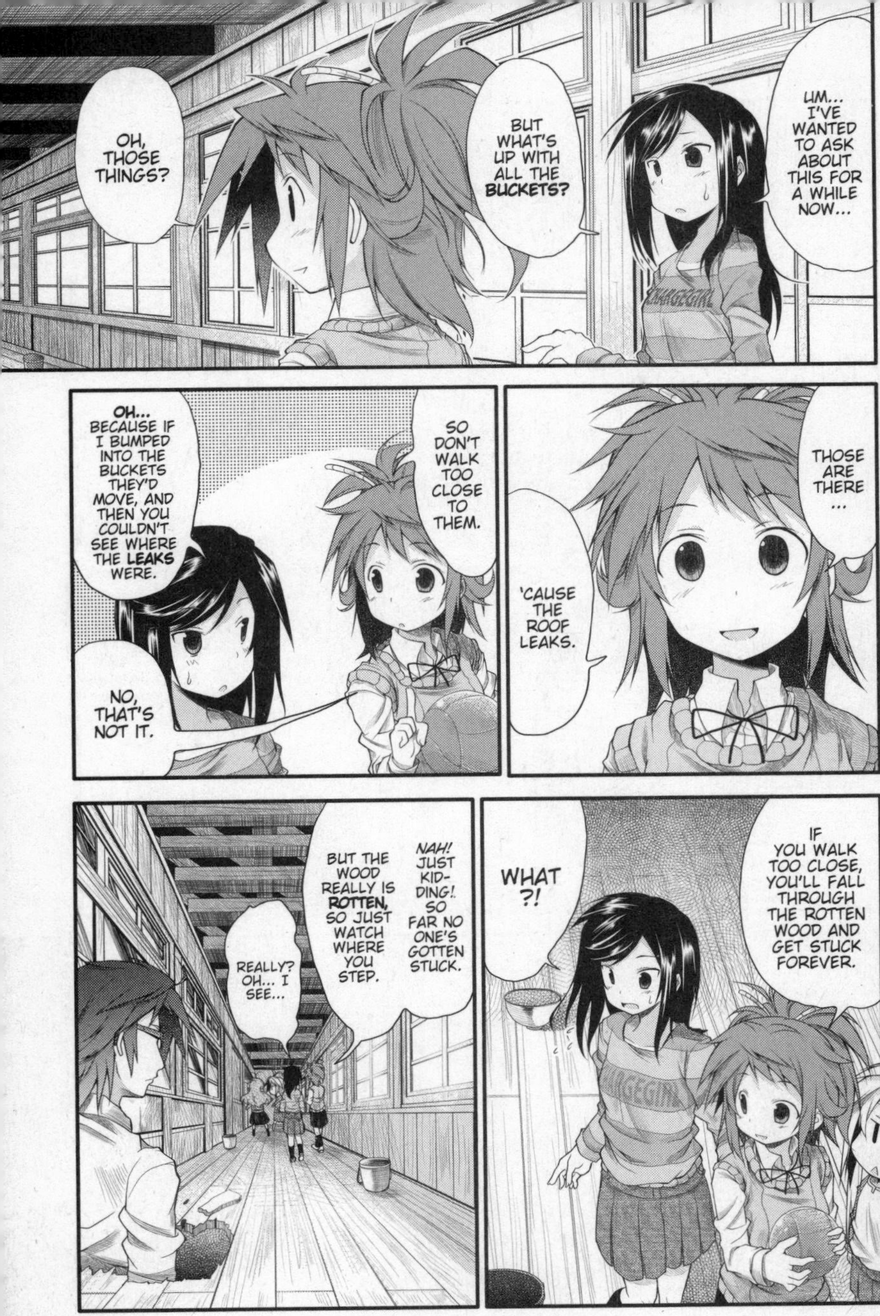
UM... I'VE WANTED TO ASK ABOUT THIS FOR A WHILE NOW...
BUT WHAT'S UP WITH ALL THE BUCKETS?
OH, THOSE THINGS?
THOSE ARE THERE ...
'CAUSE THE ROOF LEAKS.
SO DON'T WALK TOO CLOSE TO THEM.
OH... BECAUSE IF I BUMPED INTO THE BUCKETS THEY'D MOVE, AND THEN YOU COULDN'T SEE WHERE THE LEAKS WERE.
NO, THAT'S NOT IT.
IF YOU WALK TOO CLOSE, YOU'LL FALL THROUGH THE ROTTEN WOOD AND GET STUCK FOREVER.
WHAT ?!
NAH! JUST KID-DING! SO FAR NO ONE'S GOTTEN STUCK.
BUT THE WOOD REALLY IS ROTTEN, SO JUST WATCH WHERE YOU STEP.
REALLY? OH... I SEE...

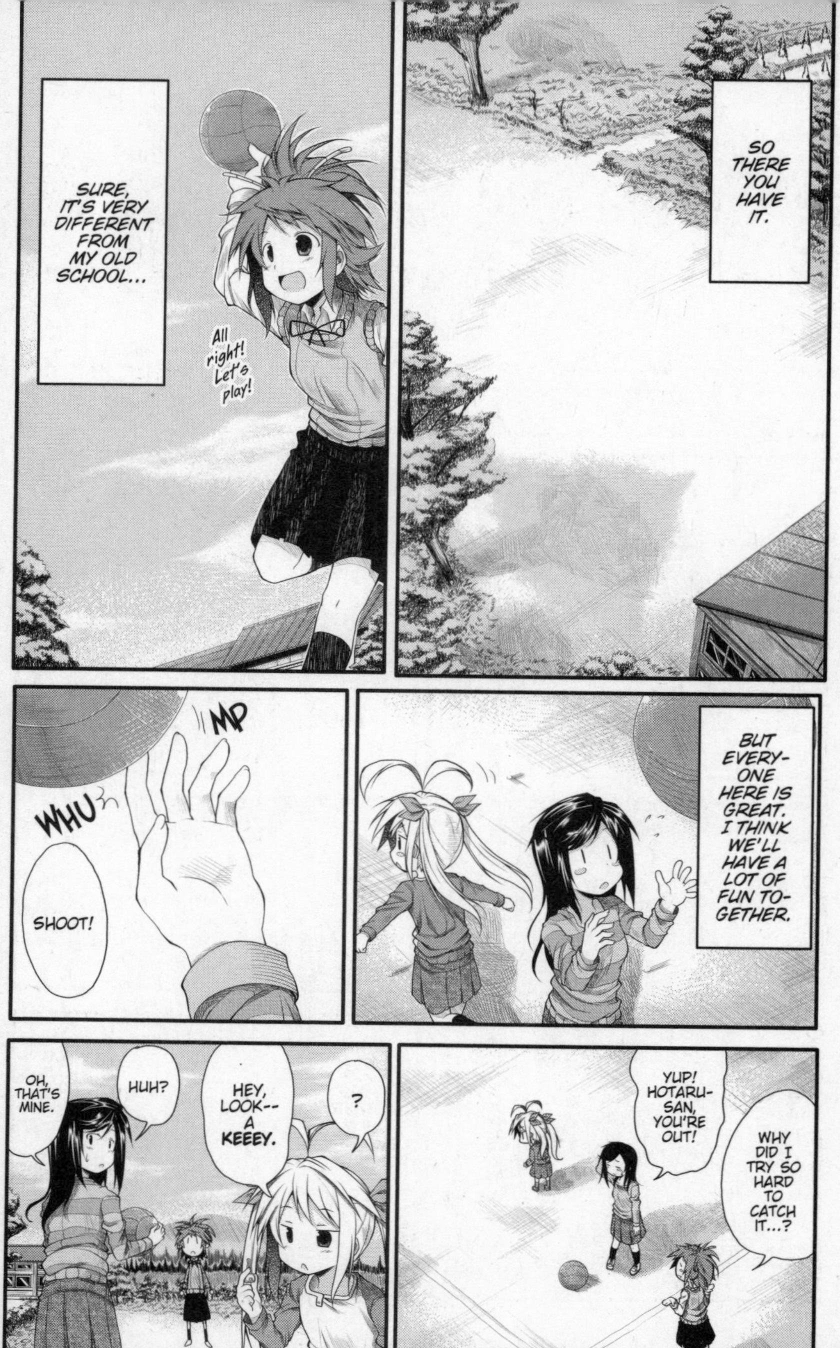
SO THERE YOU HAVE IT.
SURE, IT'S VERY DIFFERENT FROM MY OLD SCHOOL...
All right! Let's play!
BUT EVERY-ONE HERE IS GREAT. I THINK WE'LL HAVE A LOT OF FUN TO-GETHER.
MP
WHU
SHOOT!
YUP! HOTARU-SAN, YOU'RE OUT!
WHY DID I TRY SO HARD TO CATCH IT...?
?
HEY, LOOK--A KEEEY.
HUH?
OH, THAT'S MINE.

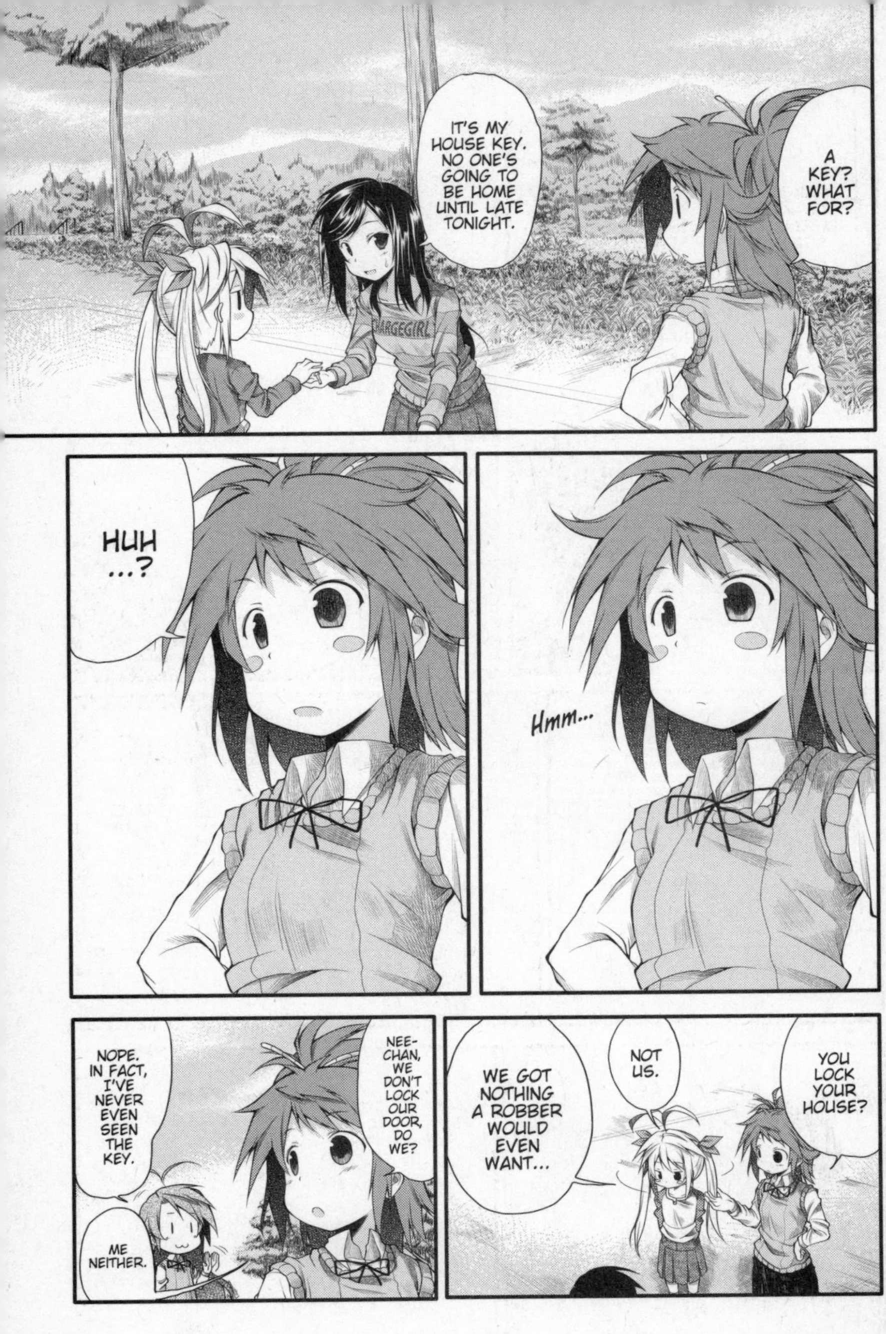
A KEY? WHAT FOR?
IT'S MY HOUSE KEY. NO ONE'S GOING TO BE HOME UNTIL LATE TONIGHT.
Hmm...
HUH ...?
YOU LOCK YOUR HOUSE?
NOT US.
WE GOT NOTHING A ROBBER WOULD EVEN WANT...
NEE-CHAN, WE DON'T LOCK OUR DOOR, DO WE?
NOPE. IN FACT, I'VE NEVER EVEN SEEN THE KEY.
ME NEITHER.

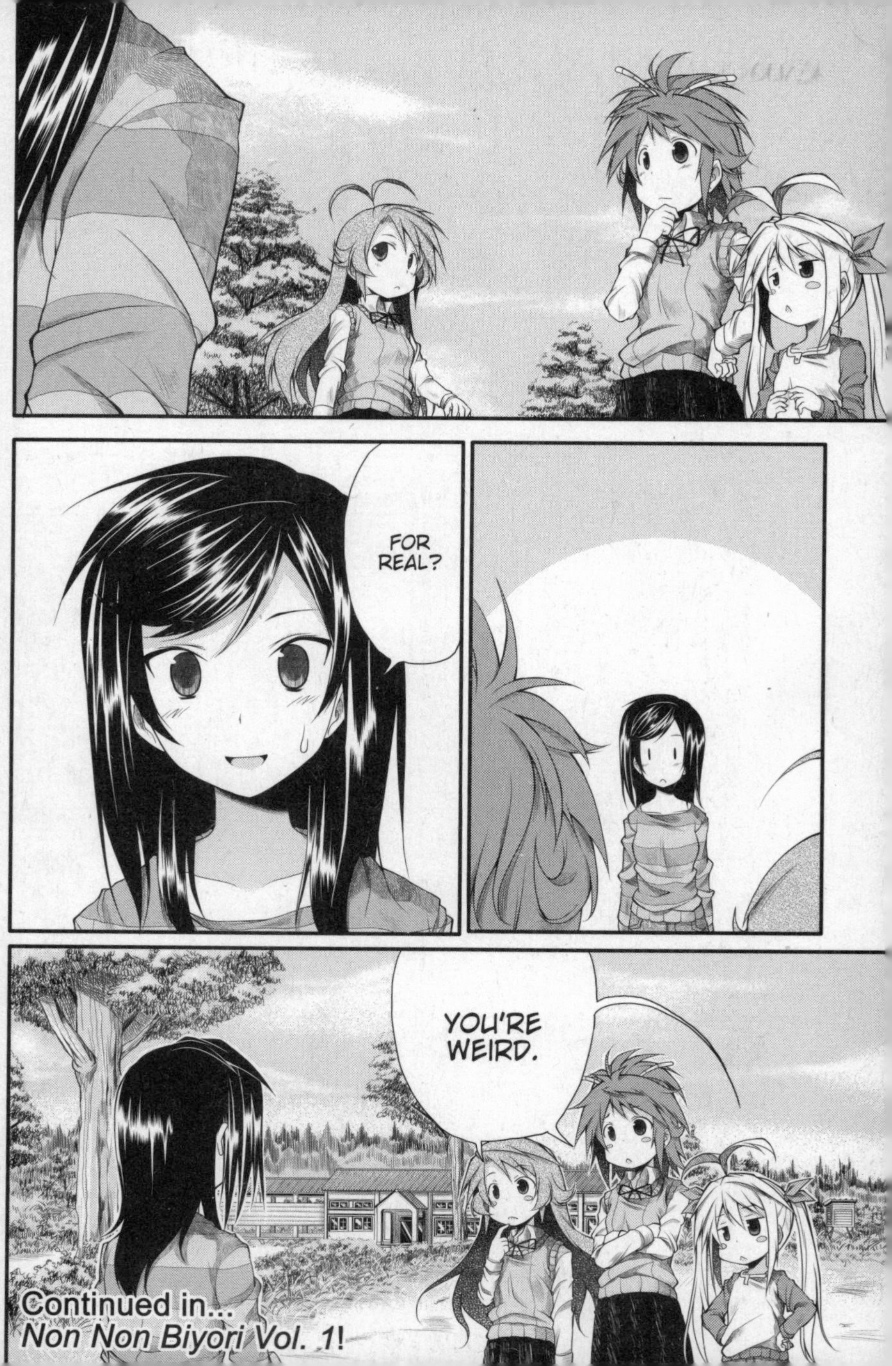
FOR REAL?
YOU'RE WEIRD.
Continued in...
Non Non Biyori Vol. 1!

SEVEN SEAS ENTERTAINMENT PRESENTS baya

D-FRAG!

story and art by TOMOYA HARUNO

VOLUME 6

TRANSLATION
Adrienne Beck

ADAPTATION
Shannon Fay

LETTERING AND LAYOUT
Ma. Victoria Robado

LOGO DESIGN
Courtney Williams

COVER DESIGN
Nicky Lim

PROOFREADER
Lee Otter
Janet Houck

ASSISTANT EDITOR
Lissa Pattillo

MANAGING EDITOR
Adam Arnold

PUBLISHER
Jason DeAngelis

D-FRAG! VOL. 6
© Tomoya Haruno 2012
Edited by MEDIA FACTORY.
First published in Japan in 2012 by KADOKAWA CORPORATION, Tokyo.
English translation rights reserved by Seven Seas Entertainment, LLC.
under the license from KADOKAWA CORPORATION, Tokyo.

Seven Seas books may be purchased in bulk for educational, business, or promotional use. For information on bulk purchases, please contact Macmillan Corporate & Premium Sales Department at 1-800-221-7945 (ext 5442) or write specialmarkets@macmillan.com.

Seven Seas and the Seven Seas logo are trademarks of Seven Seas Entertainment, LLC. All rights reserved.

ISBN: 978-1-626921-72-6

Printed in Canada

First Printing: September 2015

10 9 8 7 6 5 4 3 2 1

FOLLOW US ONLINE: *www.gomanga.com*

READING DIRECTIONS

This book reads from *right to left*, Japanese style. If this is your first time reading manga, you start reading from the top right panel on each page and take it from there. If you get lost, just follow the numbered diagram here. It may seem backwards at first, but you'll get the hang of it! Have fun!!

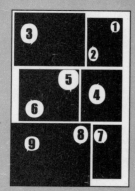